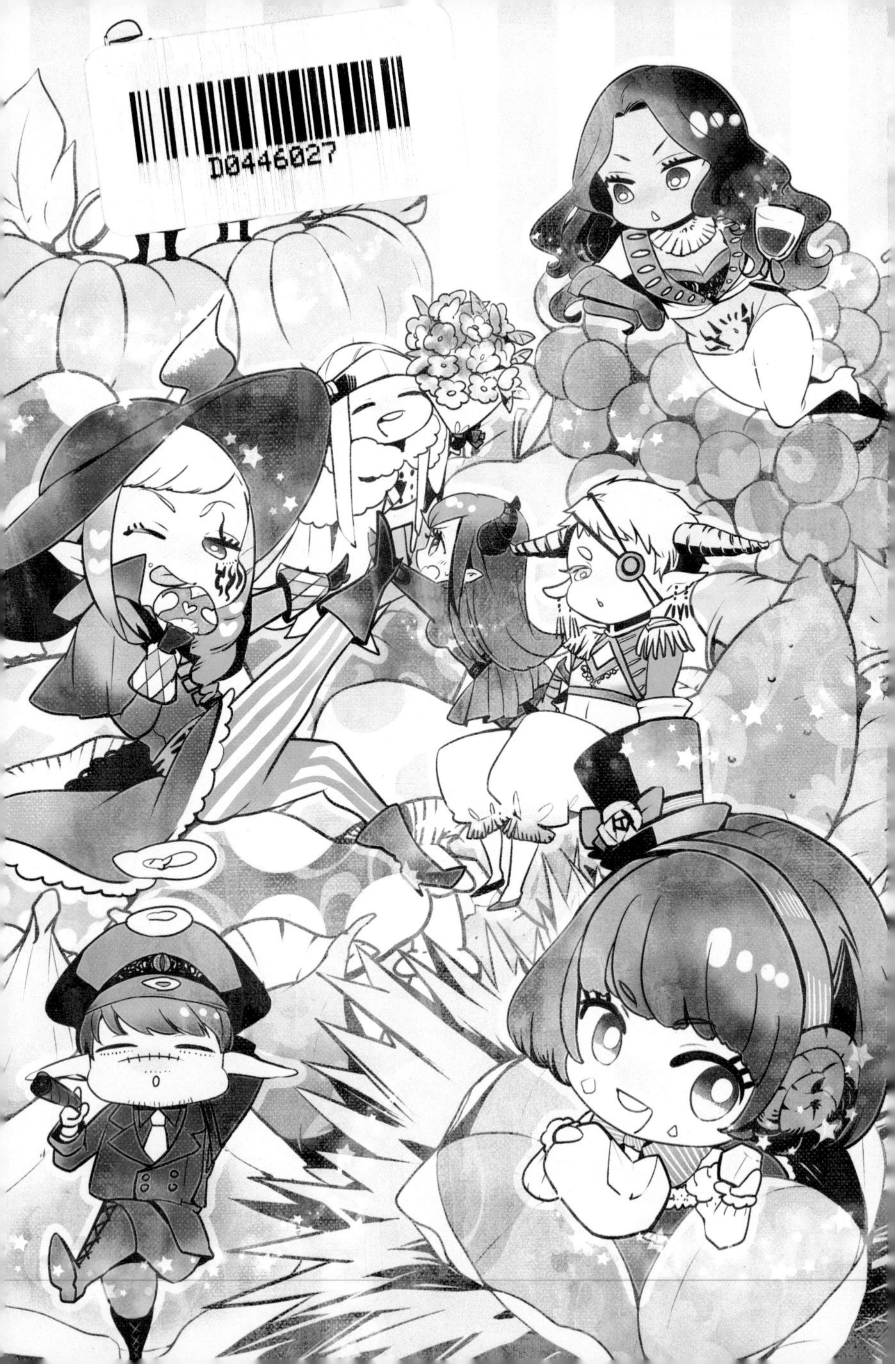

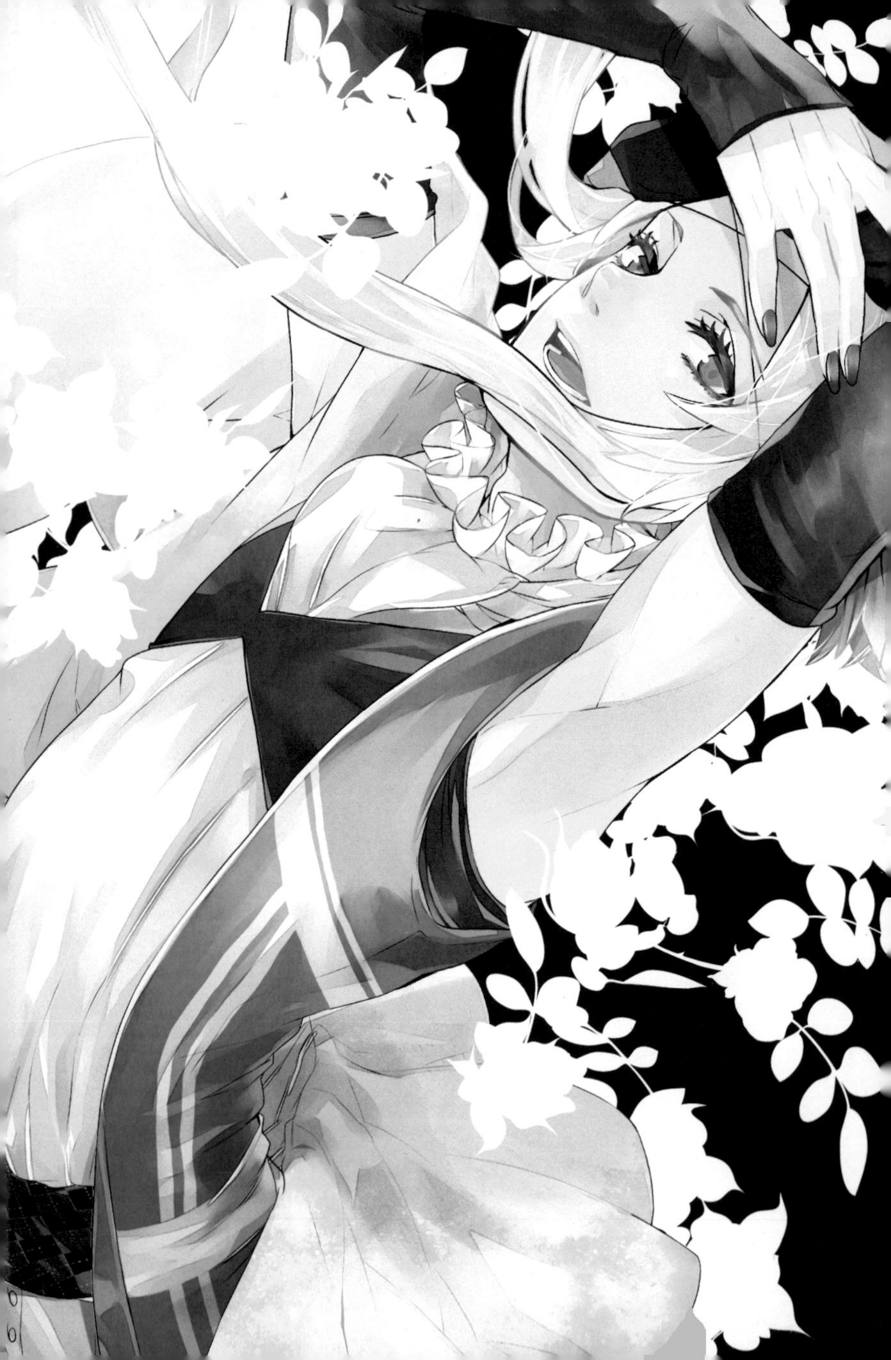

Devils and Realist
vol.4

story by Madoka Takadono
art by Utako Yukihiro

Cast of Characters

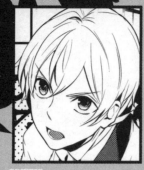

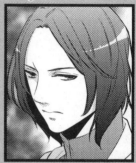

William

A brilliant realist from a famous noble family. As the descendant of King Solomon, he is the Elector with the authority to choose the representative of the king of Hell, although he is in denial of this fact.

Kevin

William's capable yet gambling-addicted butler. He has served the Twining family for generations and manages all of William's affairs. He has been appointed head pastor at Stradford School, but there's something more to him...

Dantalion

Seventy-first Pillar of Hell, who commands its leading thirty-six armies. He is Grand Duke of the Underworld and a candidate to represent the king. At school, students rely on him during sporting events.

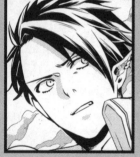

Sytry

Twelfth Pillar of Hell, who leads sixty armies. Sytry is Prince of Hell and a candidate to represent the king. He is treated like a princess at school because of his beautiful appearance.

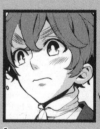

Isaac

William's classmate who is obsessed with supernatural phenomena.

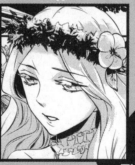

The Story So Far

The demons Dantalion and Sytry appear before William, claiming that William is the Elector with the power to select the representative king of Hell. Both insist they will not leave William's side until he chooses one of them, and the demons decide to enjoy their time masquerading as students. William isn't interested in having anything to do with either of them, but he gets dragged into one Hell-related incident after another. Shortly after William's butler, Kevin, is appointed to the academy as its pastor, William confirms that even the school representative is a demon. In the middle of all this, the Great Sabbat is being held in Hell, and the third candidate for representative king appears!

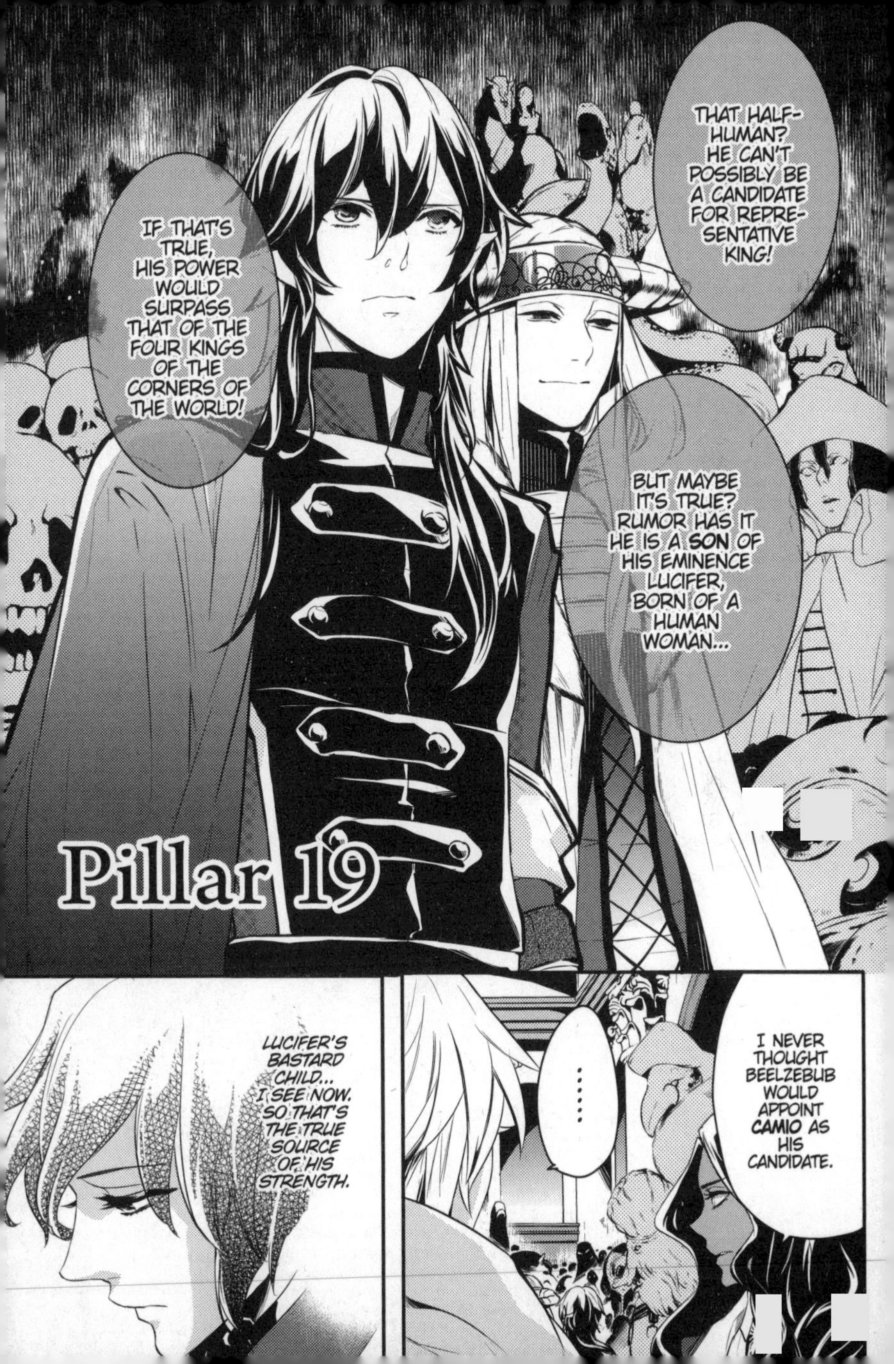
THAT HALF-HUMAN? HE CAN'T POSSIBLY BE A CANDIDATE FOR REPRE-SENTATIVE KING!
BUT MAYBE IT'S TRUE? RUMOR HAS IT HE IS A SON OF HIS EMINENCE LUCIFER, BORN OF A HUMAN WOMAN...
IF THAT'S TRUE, HIS POWER WOULD SURPASS THAT OF THE FOUR KINGS OF THE CORNERS OF THE WORLD!
Pillar 19
I NEVER THOUGHT BEELZEBUB WOULD APPOINT CAMIO AS HIS CANDIDATE.
......
LUCIFER'S BASTARD CHILD... I SEE NOW. SO THAT'S THE TRUE SOURCE OF HIS STRENGTH.

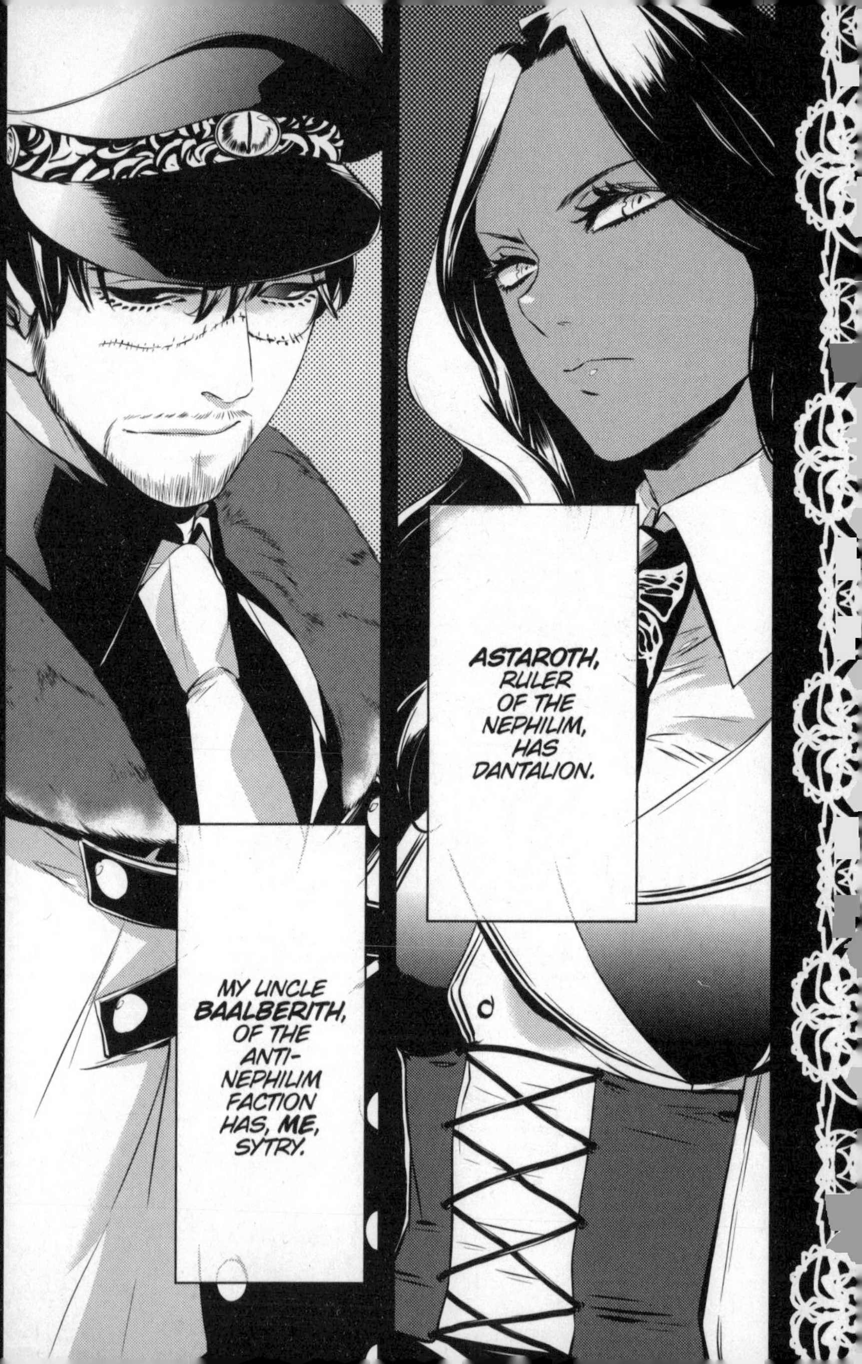
ASTAROTH, RULER OF THE NEPHILIM, HAS DANTALION.
MY UNCLE BAALBERITH, OF THE ANTI-NEPHILIM FACTION HAS, ME, SYTRY.

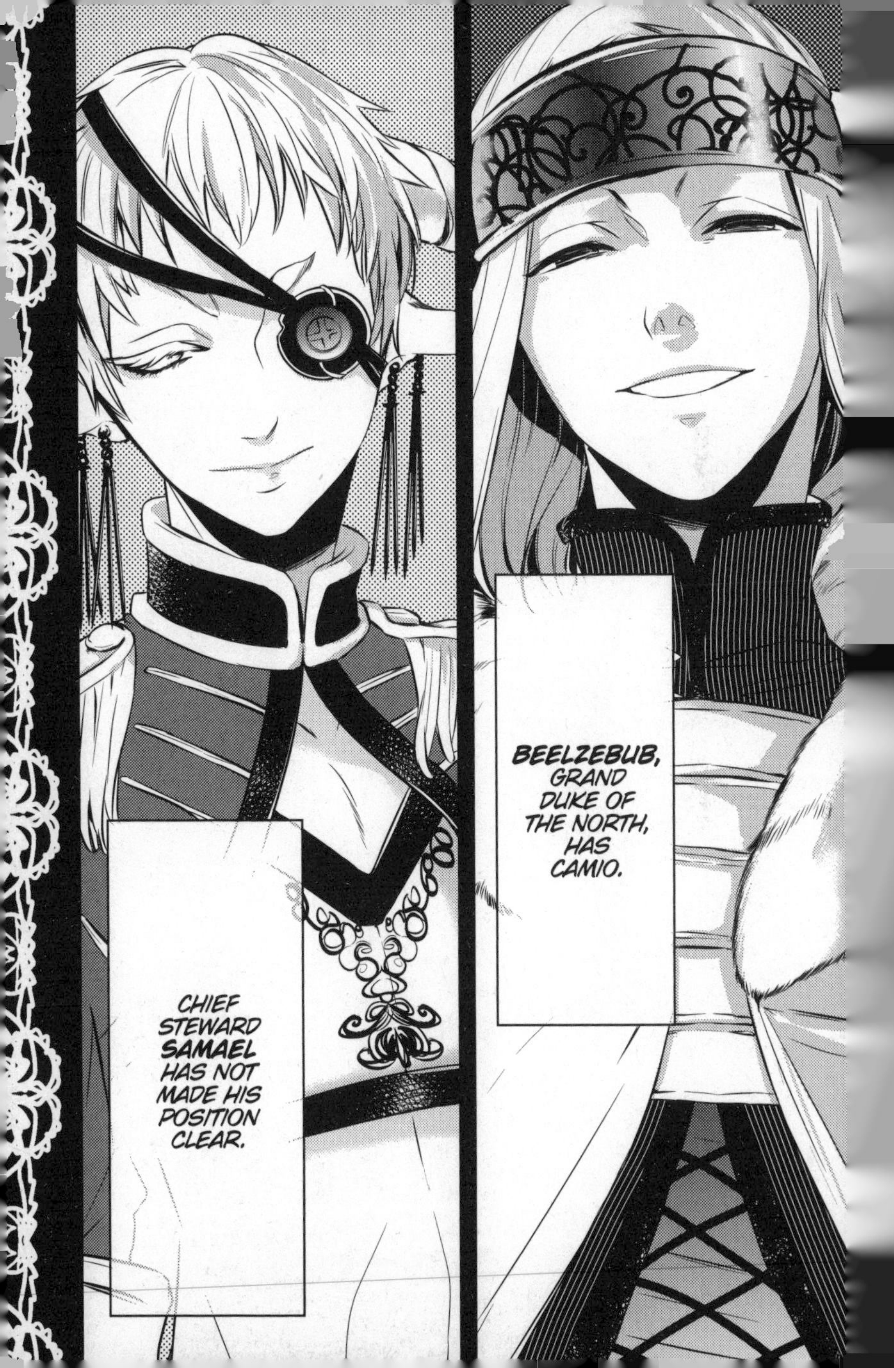
BEELZEBUB, GRAND DUKE OF THE NORTH, HAS CAMIO.
CHIEF STEWARD SAMAEL HAS NOT MADE HIS POSITION CLEAR.

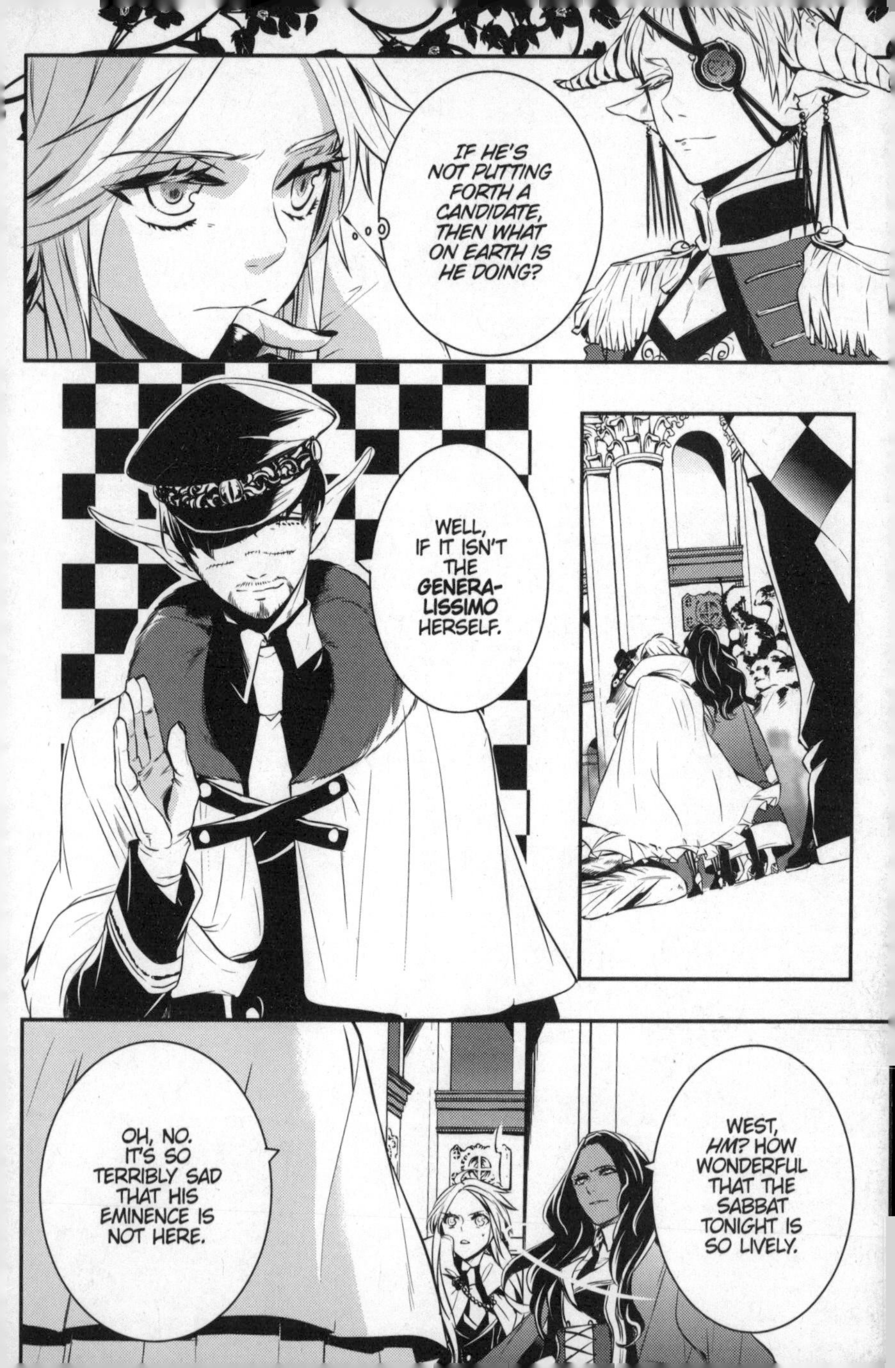
IF HE'S NOT PUTTING FORTH A CANDIDATE, THEN WHAT ON EARTH IS HE DOING?
WELL, IF IT ISN'T THE GENERA-LISSIMO HERSELF.
WEST, HM? HOW WONDERFUL THAT THE SABBAT TONIGHT IS SO LIVELY.
OH, NO. IT'S SO TERRIBLY SAD THAT HIS EMINENCE IS NOT HERE.

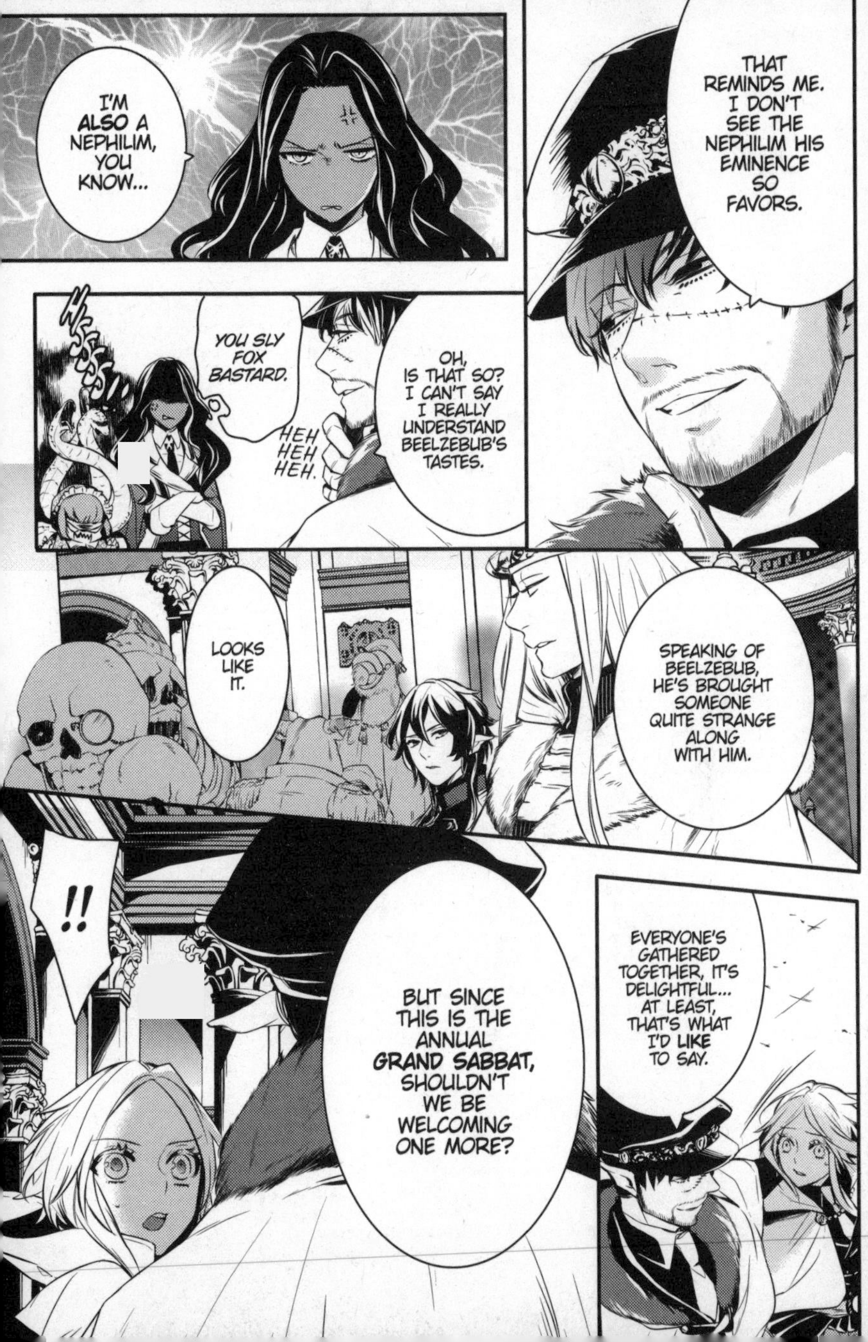
THAT REMINDS ME. I DON'T SEE THE NEPHILIM HIS EMINENCE SO FAVORS.
I'M ALSO A NEPHILIM, YOU KNOW...
OH, IS THAT SO? I CAN'T SAY I REALLY UNDERSTAND BEELZEBUB'S TASTES.
HEH HEH HEH.
YOU SLY FOX BASTARD.
HISSSS
SPEAKING OF BEELZEBUB, HE'S BROUGHT SOMEONE QUITE STRANGE ALONG WITH HIM.
LOOKS LIKE IT.
EVERYONE'S GATHERED TOGETHER, IT'S DELIGHTFUL... AT LEAST, THAT'S WHAT I'D LIKE TO SAY.
BUT SINCE THIS IS THE ANNUAL GRAND SABBAT, SHOULDN'T WE BE WELCOMING ONE MORE?
!!

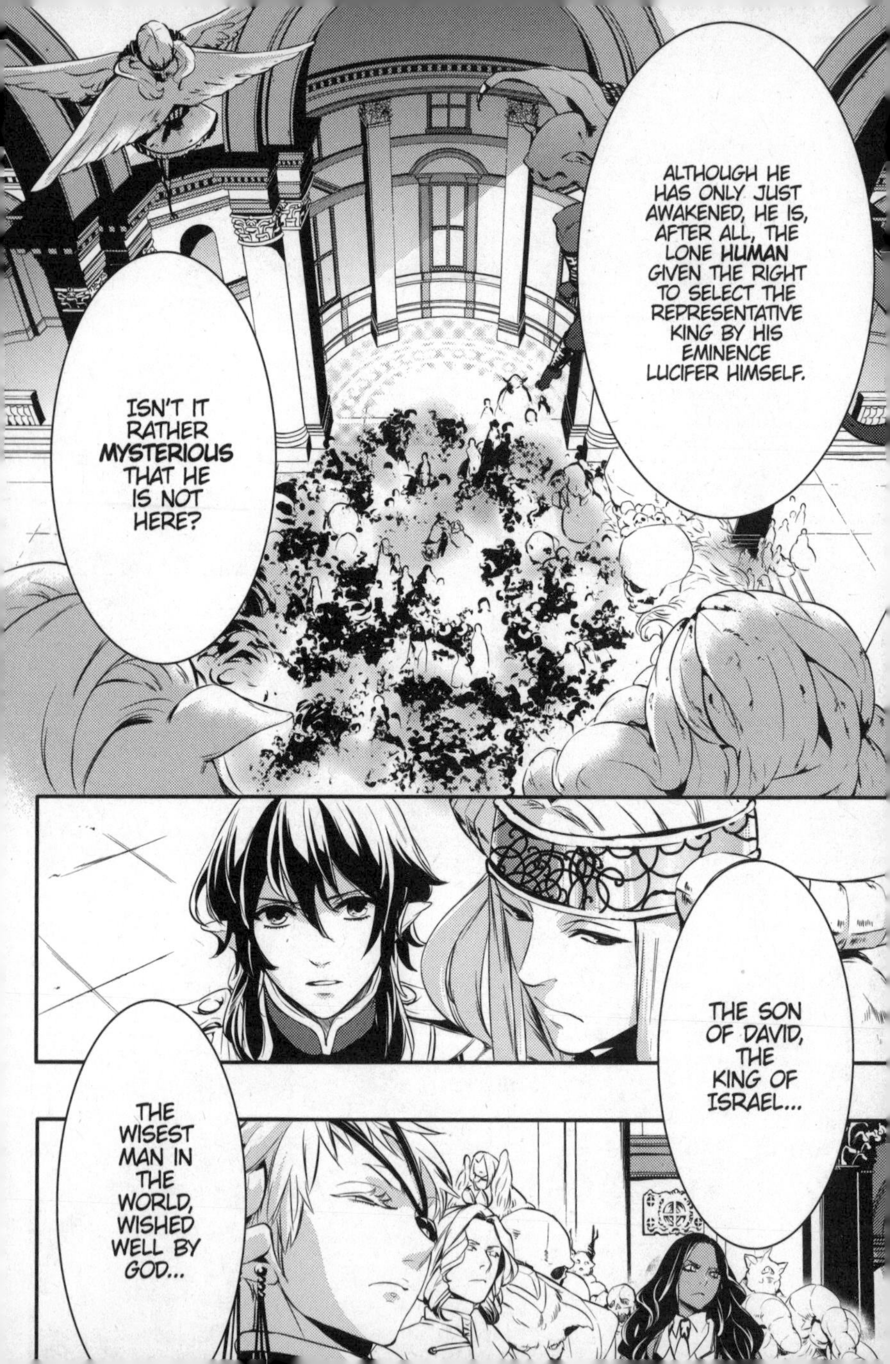
ALTHOUGH HE HAS ONLY JUST AWAKENED, HE IS, AFTER ALL, THE LONE HUMAN GIVEN THE RIGHT TO SELECT THE REPRESENTATIVE KING BY HIS EMINENCE LUCIFER HIMSELF.
ISN'T IT RATHER MYSTERIOUS THAT HE IS NOT HERE?
THE SON OF DAVID, THE KING OF ISRAEL...
THE WISEST MAN IN THE WORLD, WISHED WELL BY GOD...

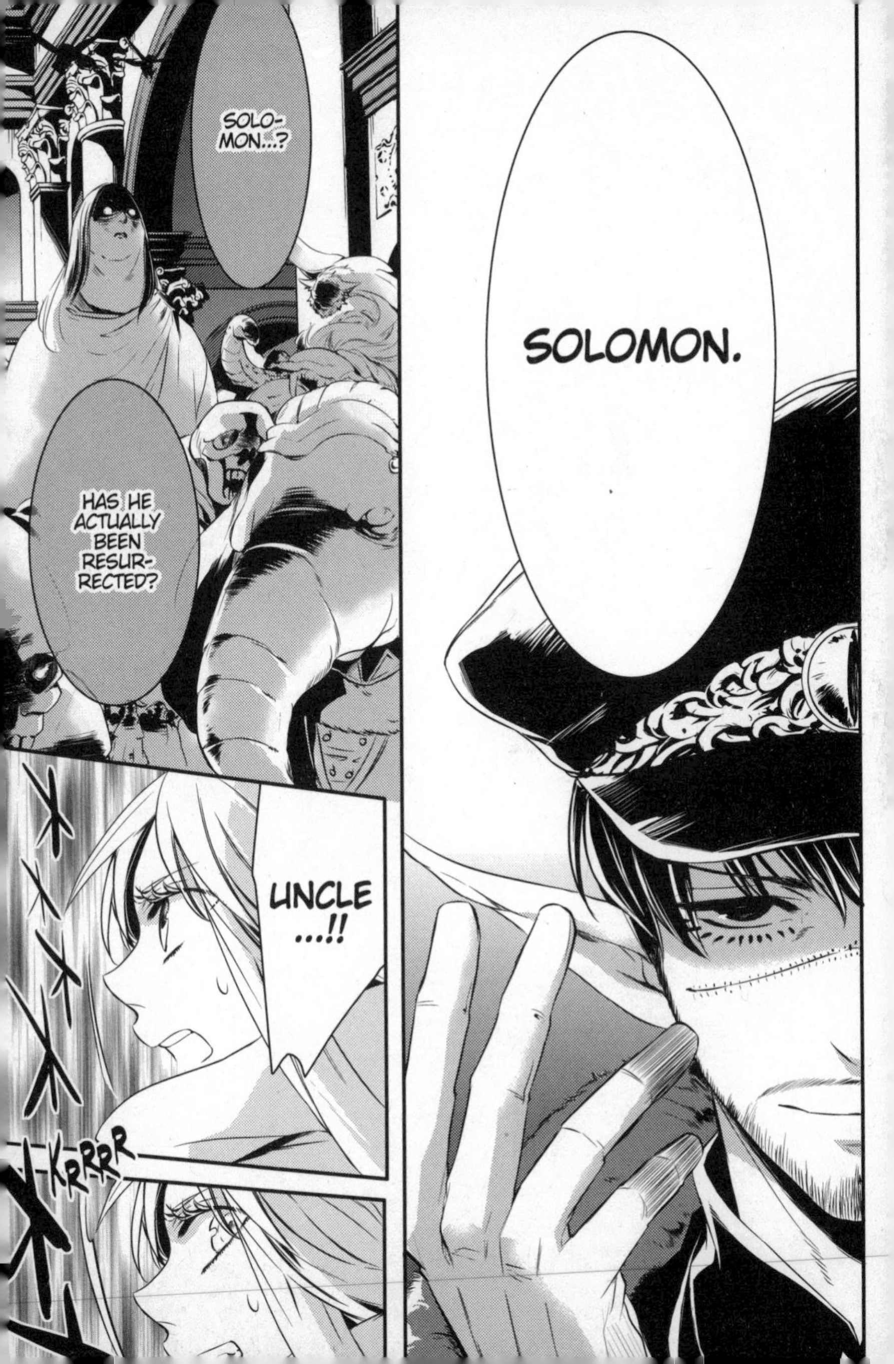
SOLOMON.
SOLO-MON...?
HAS HE ACTUALLY BEEN RESUR-RECTED?
UNCLE ...!!
KRRRR

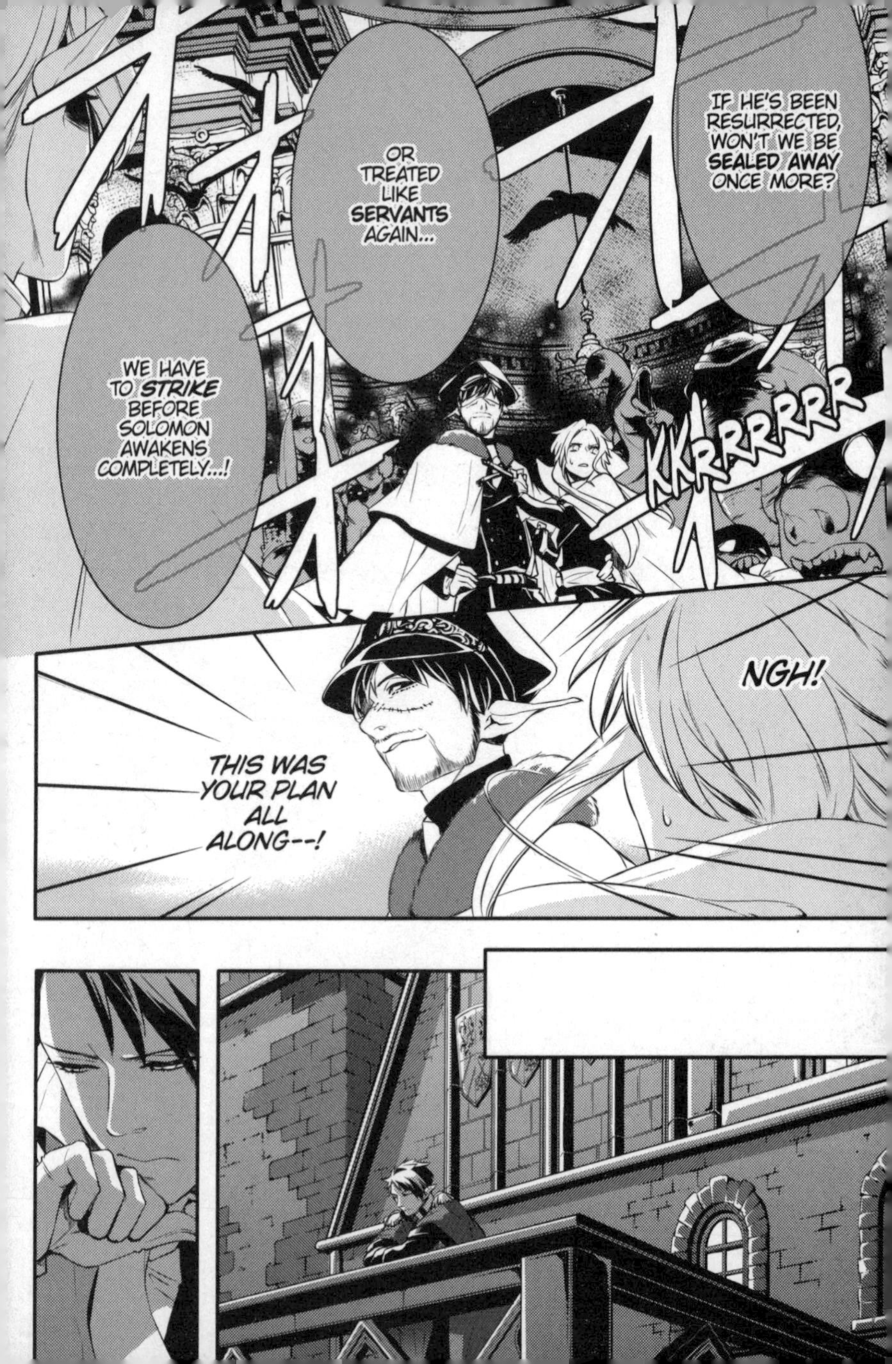
IF HE'S BEEN RESURRECTED, WON'T WE BE SEALED AWAY ONCE MORE?
OR TREATED LIKE SERVANTS AGAIN...
WE HAVE TO STRIKE BEFORE SOLOMON AWAKENS COMPLETELY...!
KKRRRRRR
NGH!
THIS WAS YOUR PLAN ALL ALONG--!

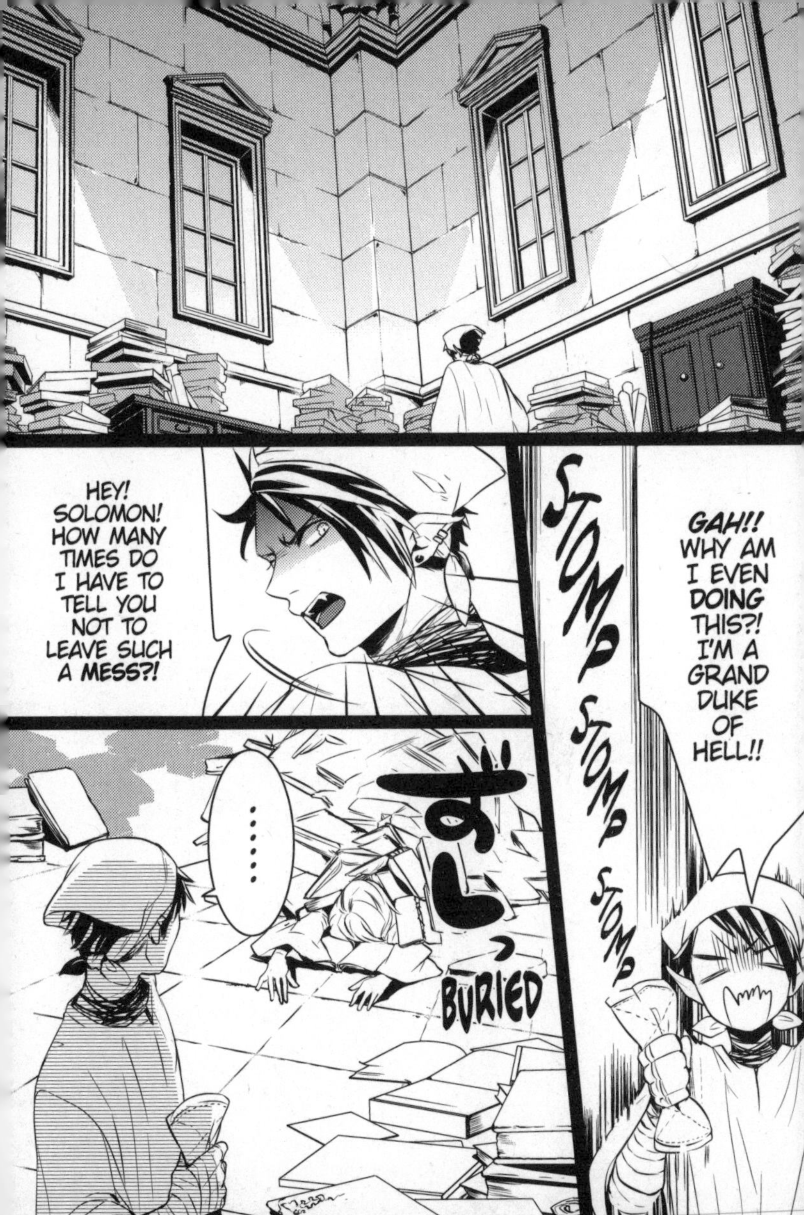
STOMP STOMP STOMP
GAH!! WHY AM I EVEN DOING THIS?! I'M A GRAND DUKE OF HELL!!
HEY! SOLOMON! HOW MANY TIMES DO I HAVE TO TELL YOU NOT TO LEAVE SUCH A MESS?!
ずし
BURIED
......

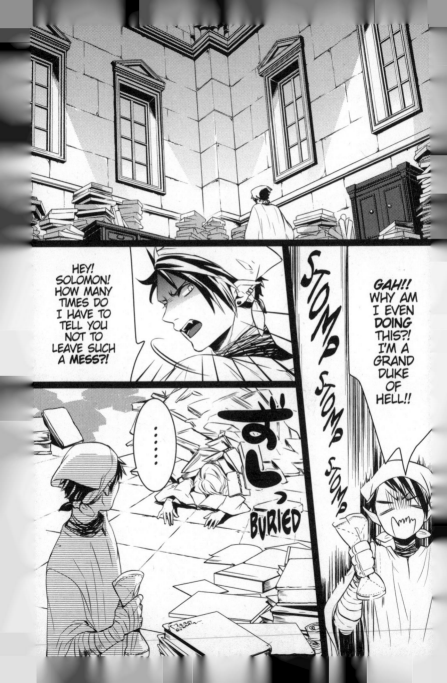

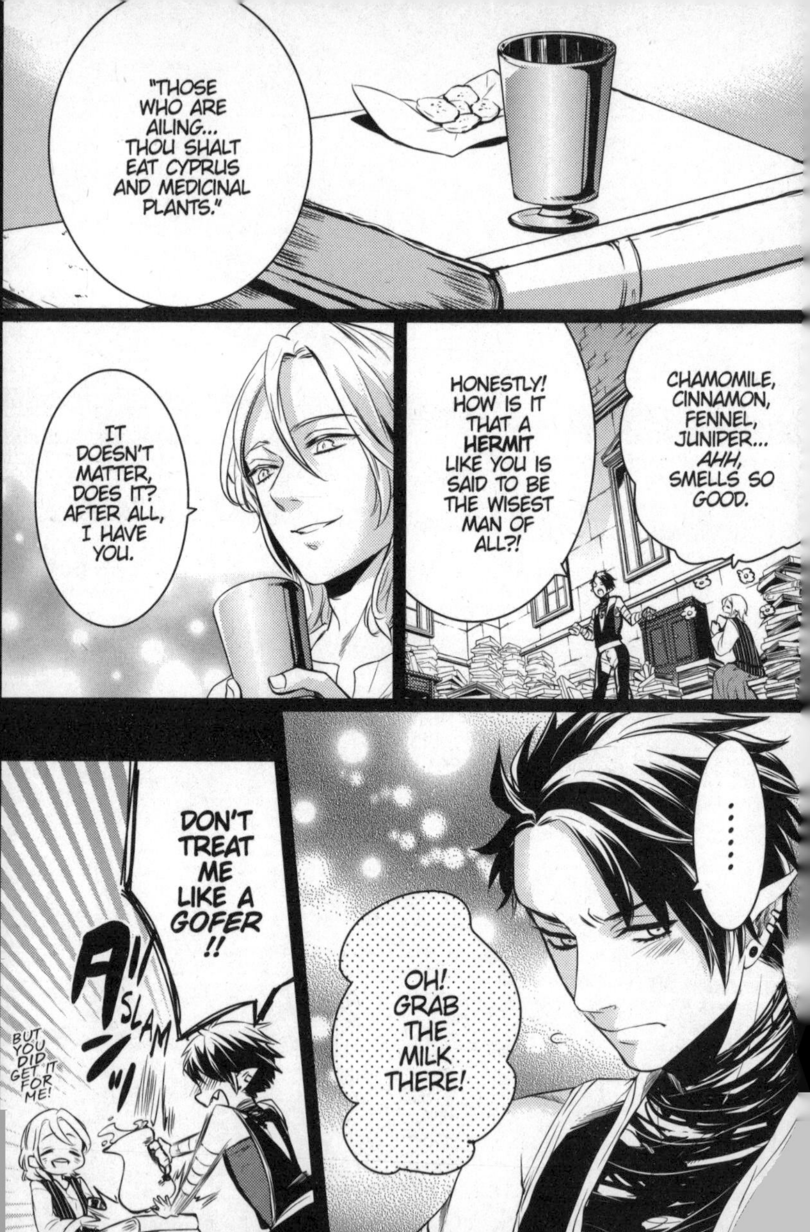
"THOSE WHO ARE AILING... THOU SHALT EAT CYPRUS AND MEDICINAL PLANTS."
CHAMOMILE, CINNAMON, FENNEL, JUNIPER... *AHH*, SMELLS SO GOOD.
HONESTLY! HOW IS IT THAT A **HERMIT** LIKE YOU IS SAID TO BE THE WISEST MAN OF ALL?!
IT DOESN'T MATTER, DOES IT? AFTER ALL, I HAVE YOU.
......
OH! GRAB THE MILK THERE!
DON'T TREAT ME LIKE A GOFER!!
SLAM
BUT YOU DID GET IT FOR ME!

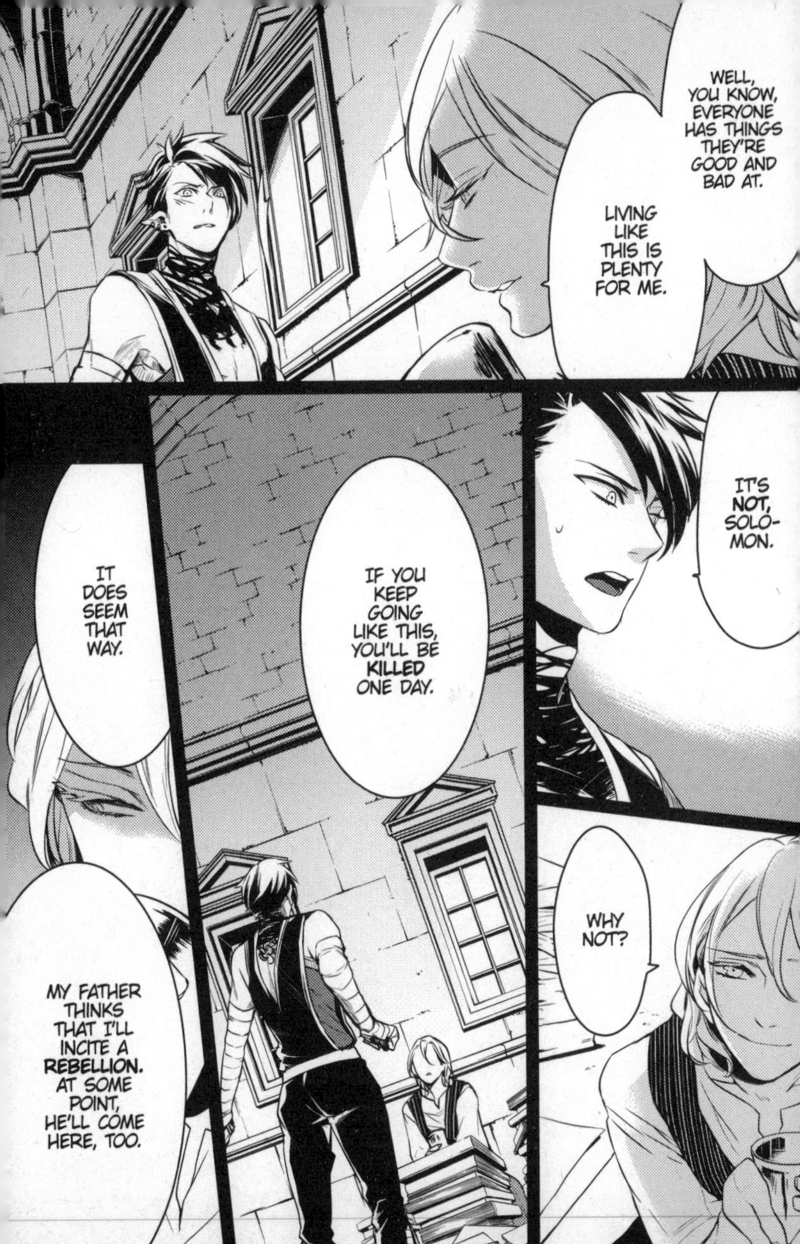
WELL, YOU KNOW, EVERYONE HAS THINGS THEY'RE GOOD AND BAD AT.
LIVING LIKE THIS IS PLENTY FOR ME.
IT'S NOT, SOLO-MON.
IF YOU KEEP GOING LIKE THIS, YOU'LL BE KILLED ONE DAY.
IT DOES SEEM THAT WAY.
WHY NOT?
MY FATHER THINKS THAT I'LL INCITE A REBELLION. AT SOME POINT, HE'LL COME HERE, TOO.

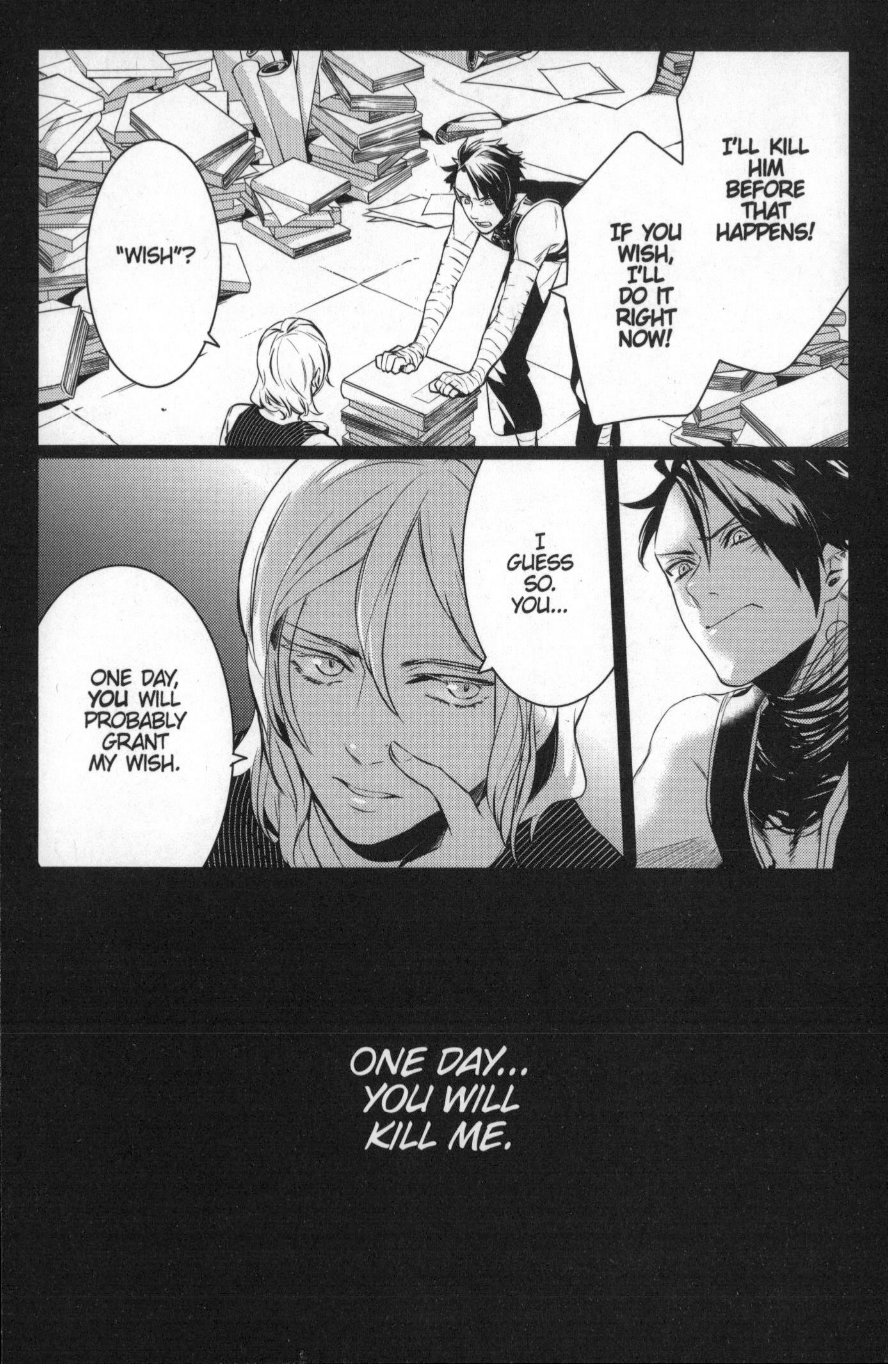
I'LL KILL HIM BEFORE THAT HAPPENS!
IF YOU WISH, I'LL DO IT RIGHT NOW!
"WISH"?
I GUESS SO. YOU...
ONE DAY, YOU WILL PROBABLY GRANT MY WISH.
ONE DAY... YOU WILL KILL ME.

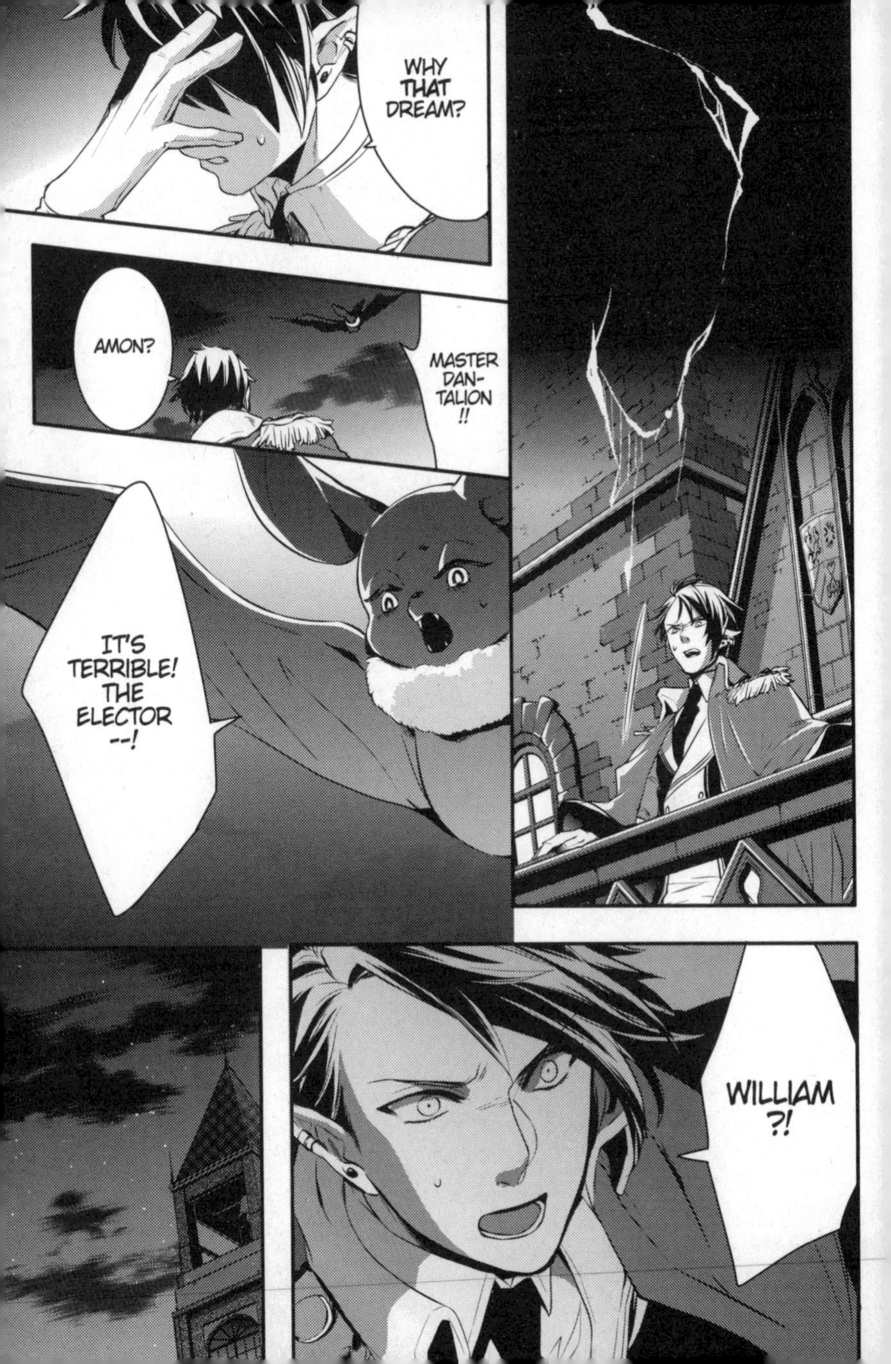
WHY THAT DREAM?
MASTER DAN-TALION !!
AMON?
IT'S TERRIBLE! THE ELECTOR --!
WILLIAM ?!

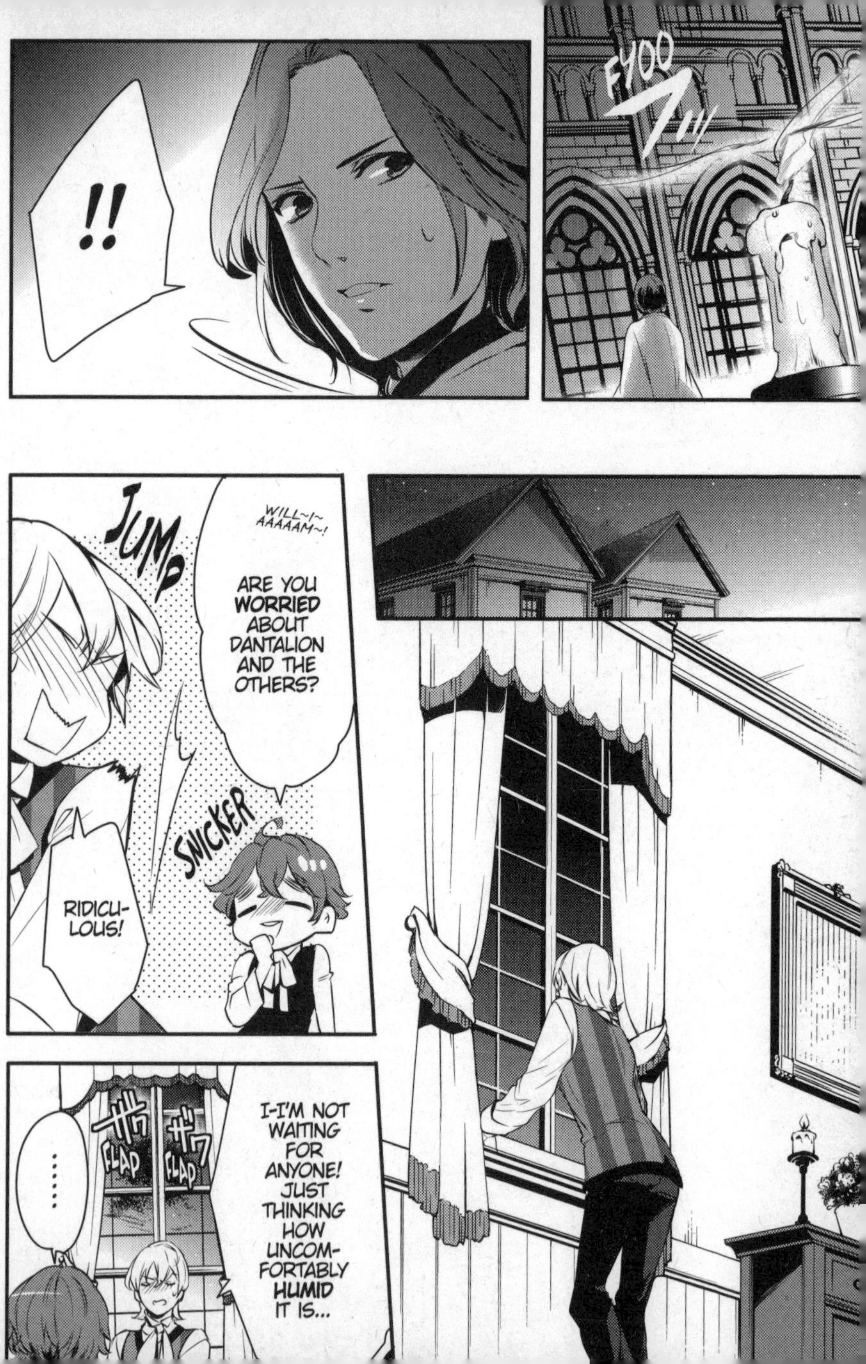
FYOO
!!
JUMP
WILL~I~ AAAAAM~!
ARE YOU WORRIED ABOUT DANTALION AND THE OTHERS?
SNICKER
RIDICU-LOUS!
I-I'M NOT WAITING FOR ANYONE! JUST THINKING HOW UNCOMFORTABLY HUMID IT IS...
FLAP
FLAP
......

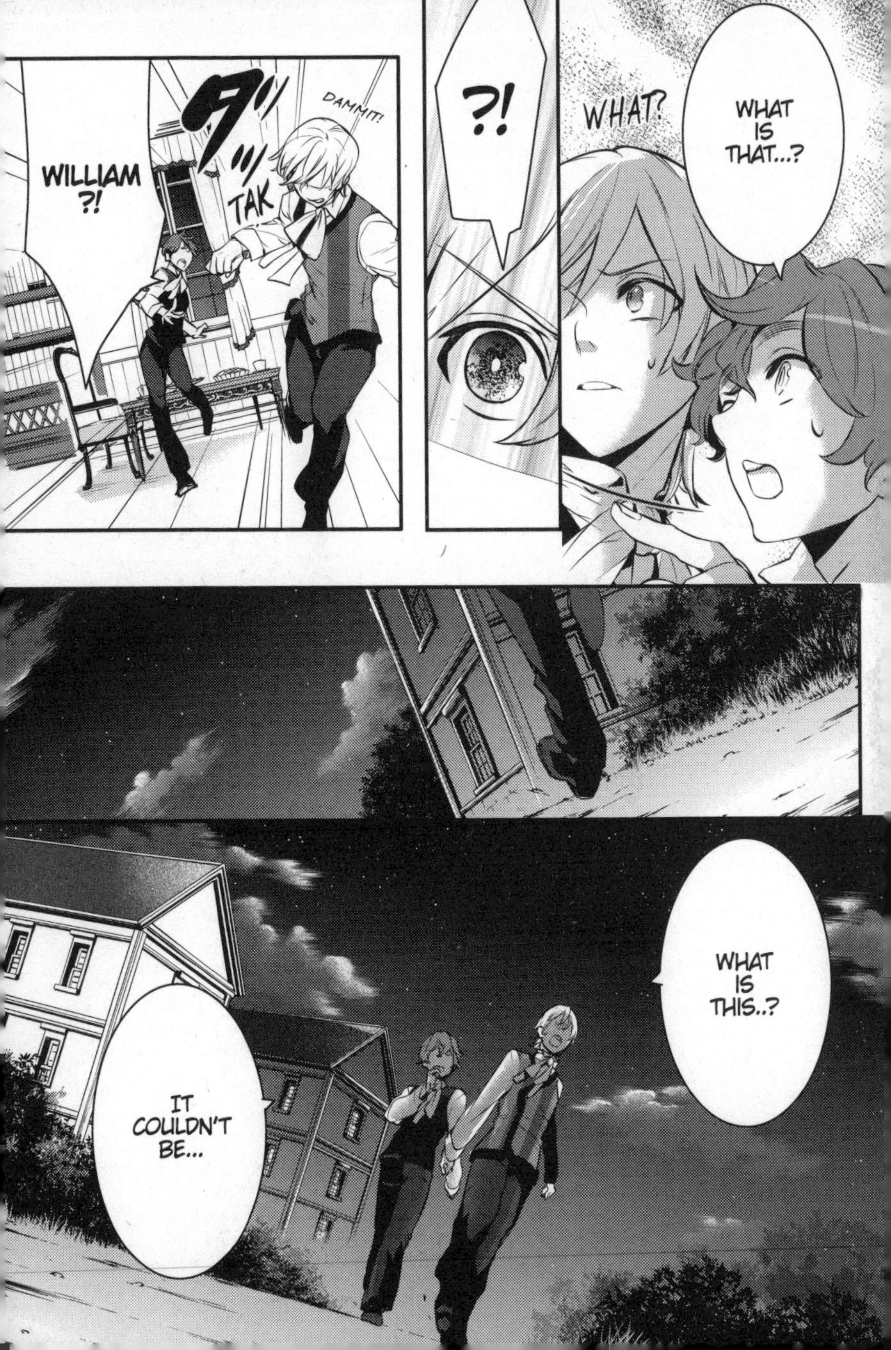
WHAT IS THAT...?
WHAT?
?!
DAMMIT!
TAK
WILLIAM ?!
WHAT IS THIS..?
IT COULDN'T BE...

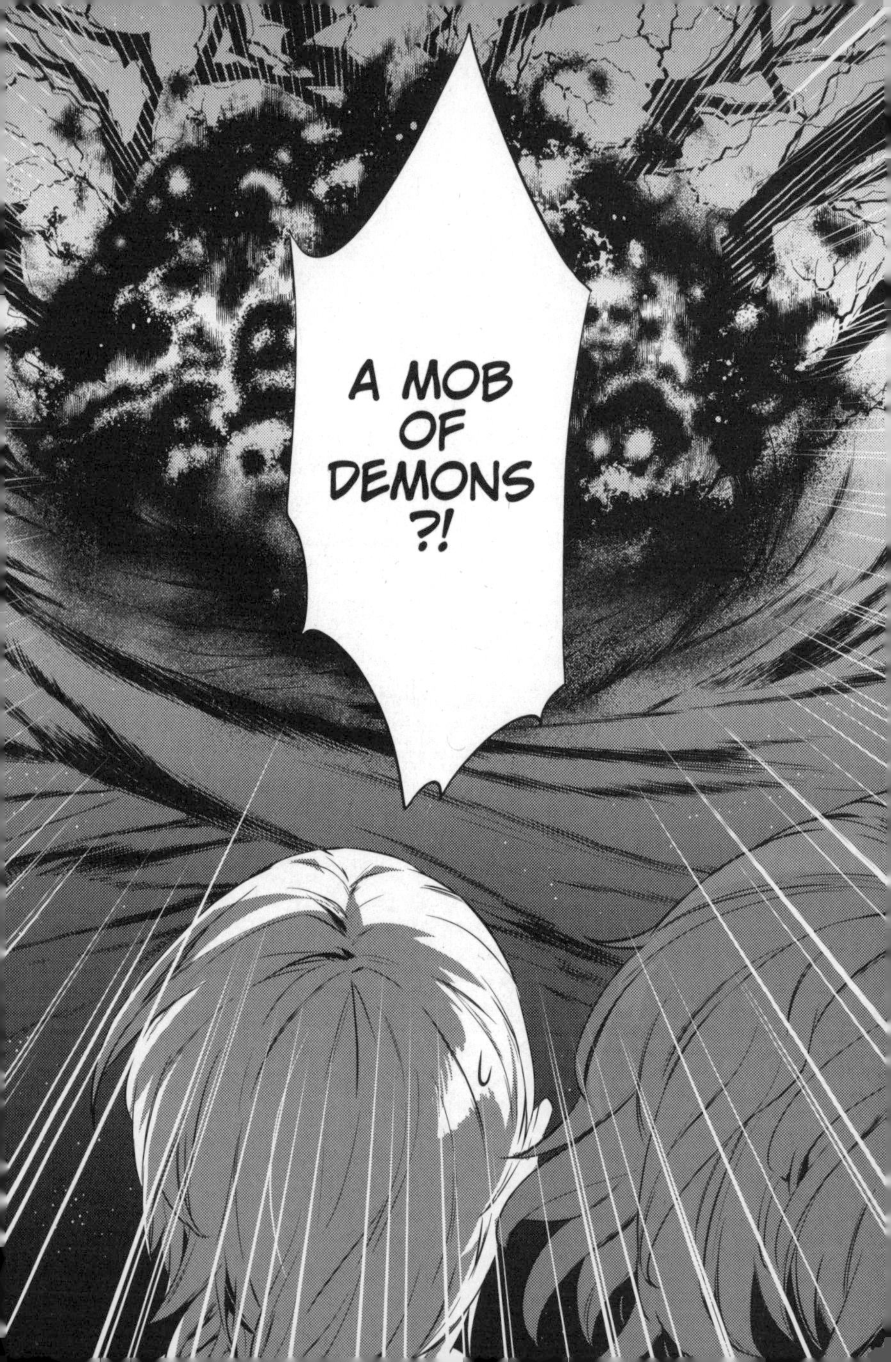
A MOB OF DEMONS ?!

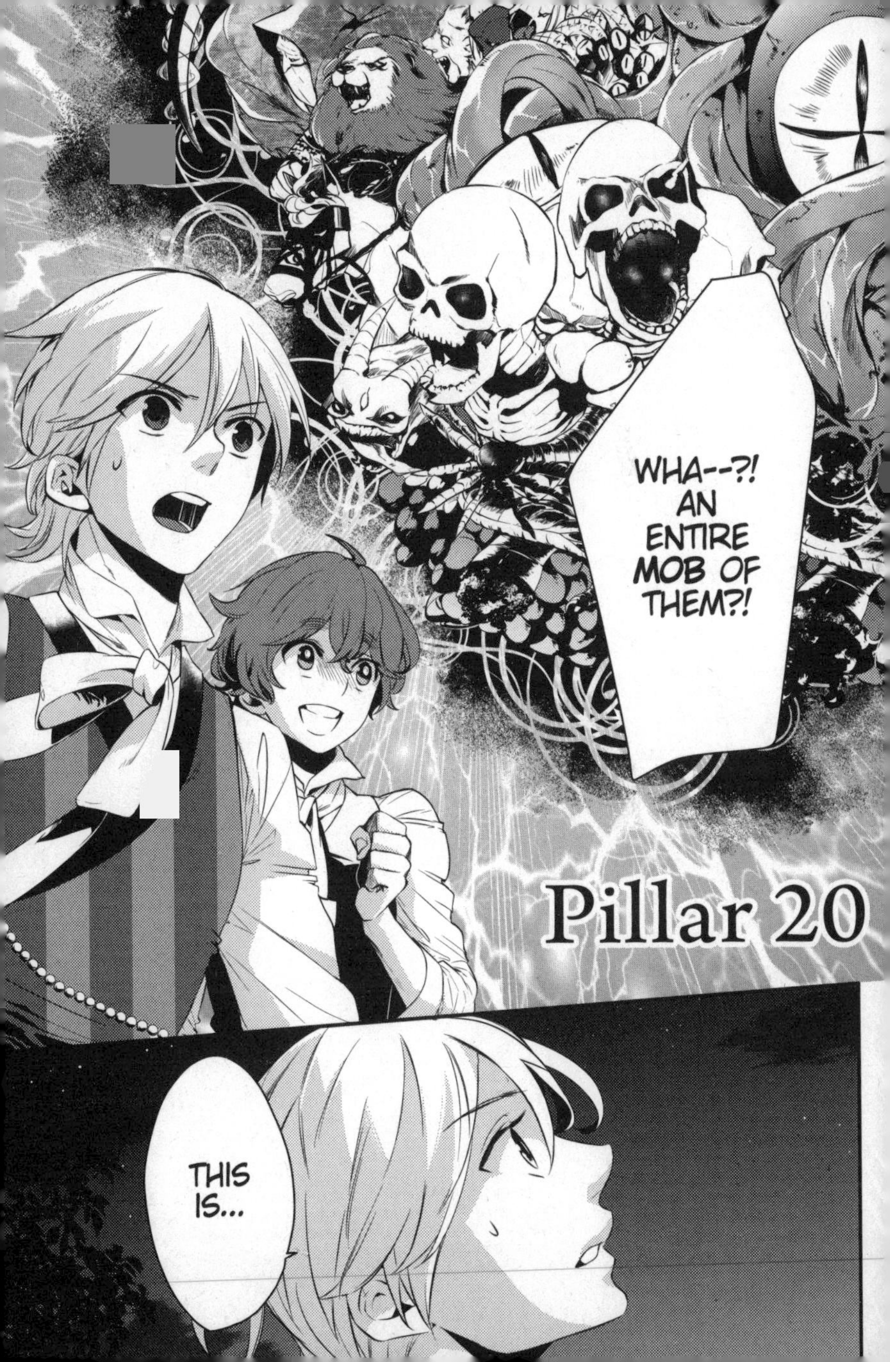
WHA--?! AN ENTIRE MOB OF THEM?!
Pillar 20
THIS IS...

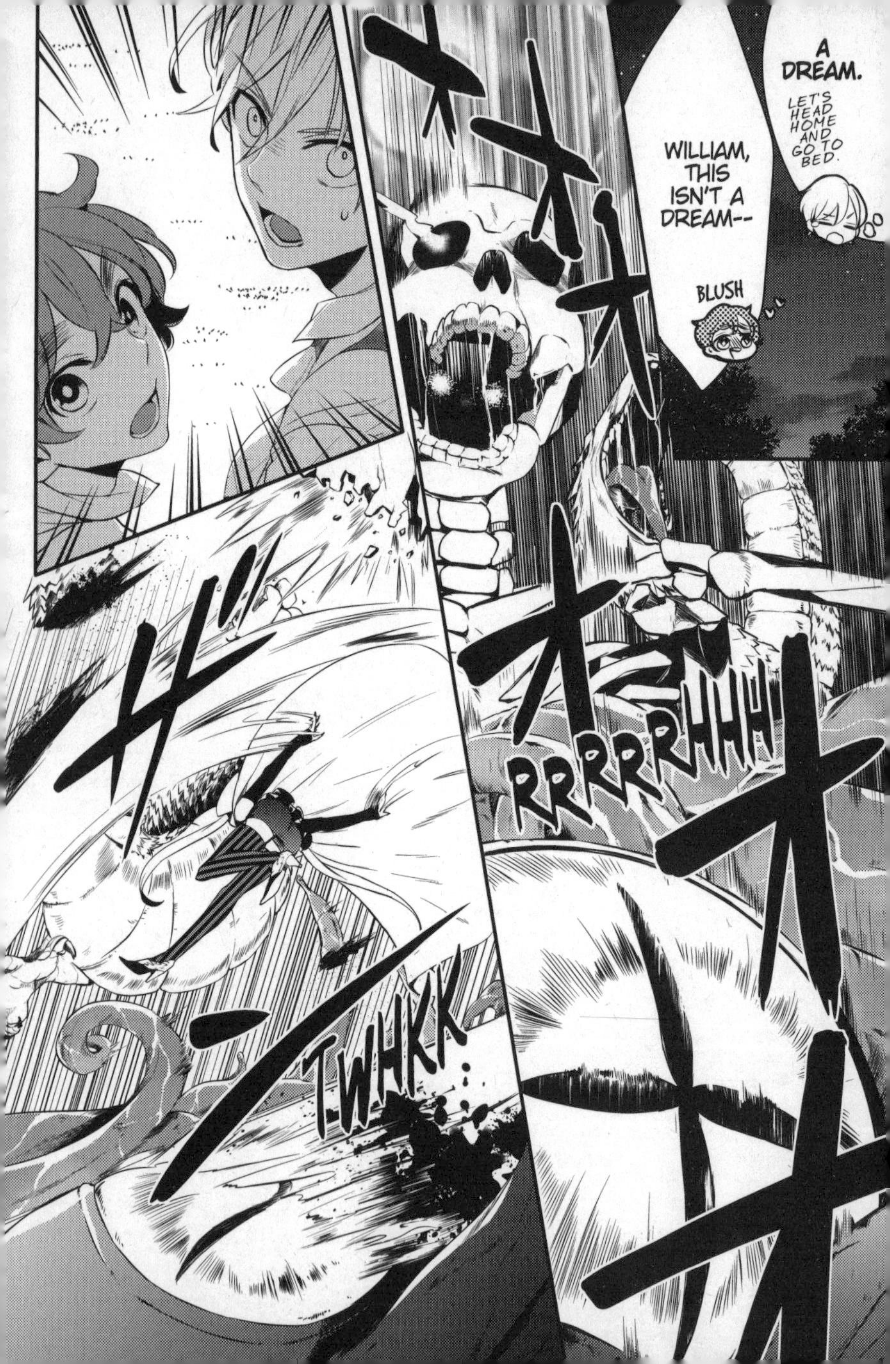
A DREAM.
LET'S HEAD HOME AND GO TO BED.
WILLIAM, THIS ISN'T A DREAM--
BLUSH
RRRRRRHHH!
TWHKK

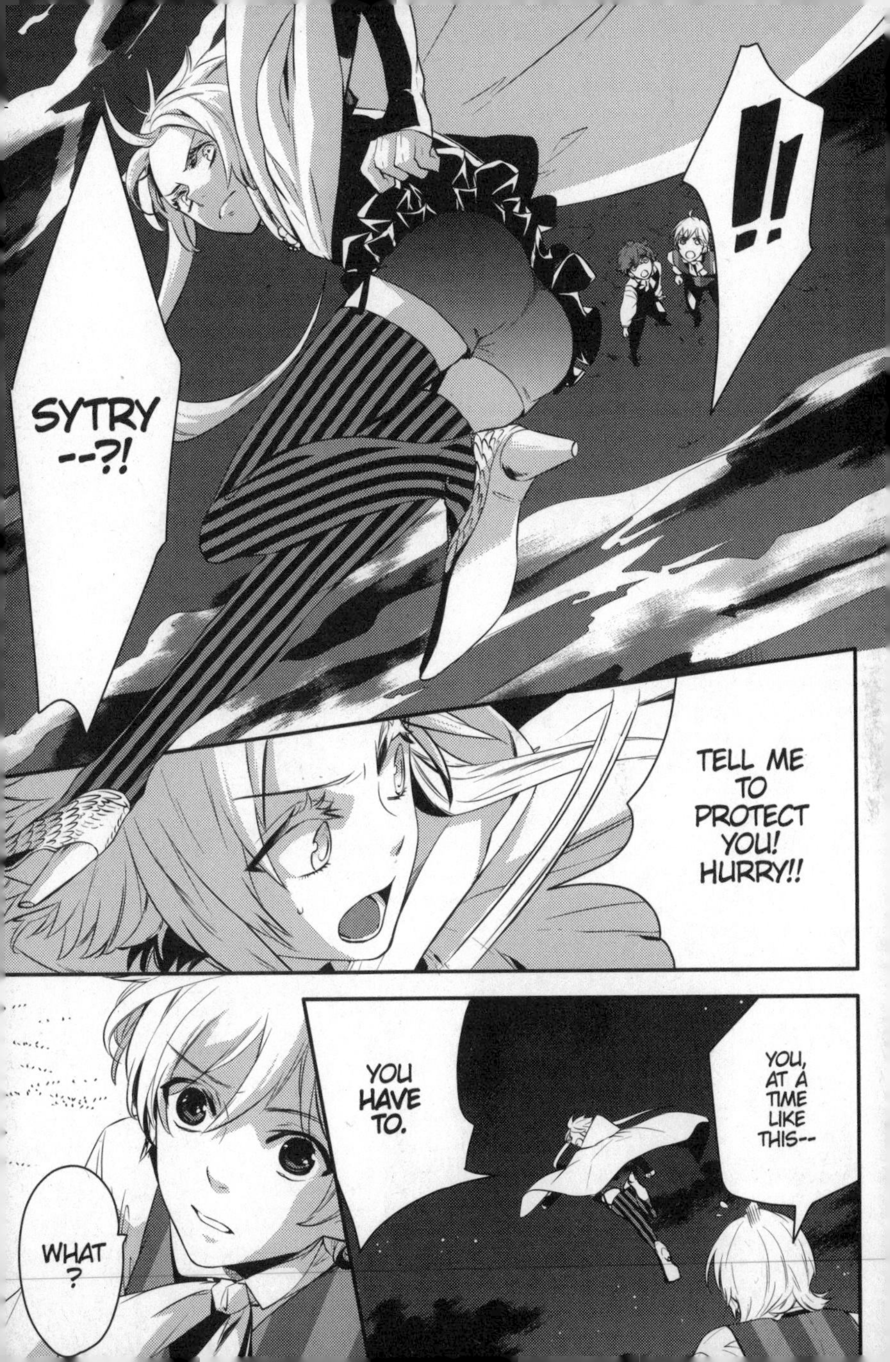
!!
SYTRY --?!
TELL ME TO PROTECT YOU! HURRY!!
YOU, AT A TIME LIKE THIS--
YOU HAVE TO.
WHAT?

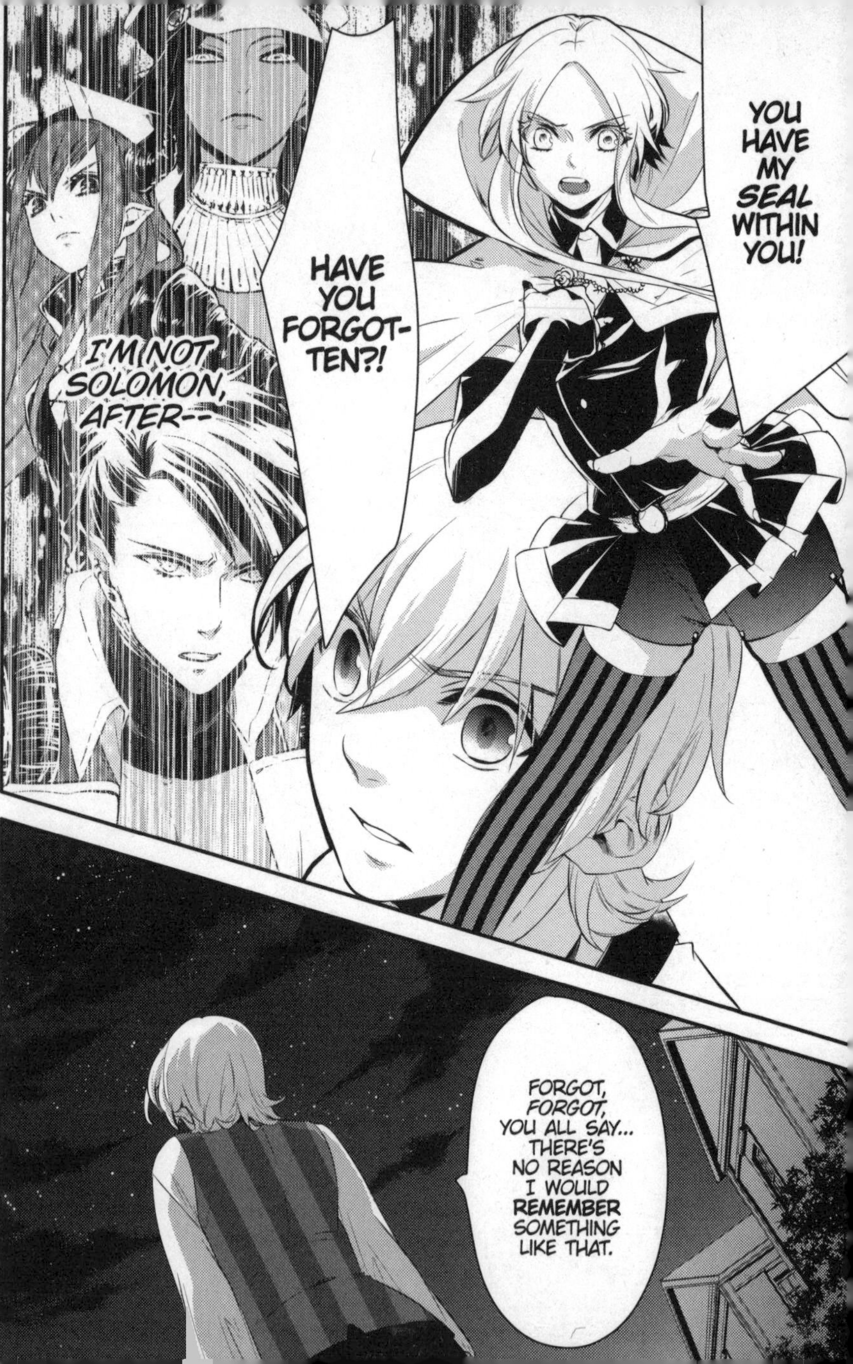

YOU HAVE MY SEAL WITHIN YOU!
HAVE YOU FORGOT-TEN?!
I'M NOT SOLOMON, AFTER--
FORGOT, FORGOT, YOU ALL SAY... THERE'S NO REASON I WOULD REMEMBER SOMETHING LIKE THAT.

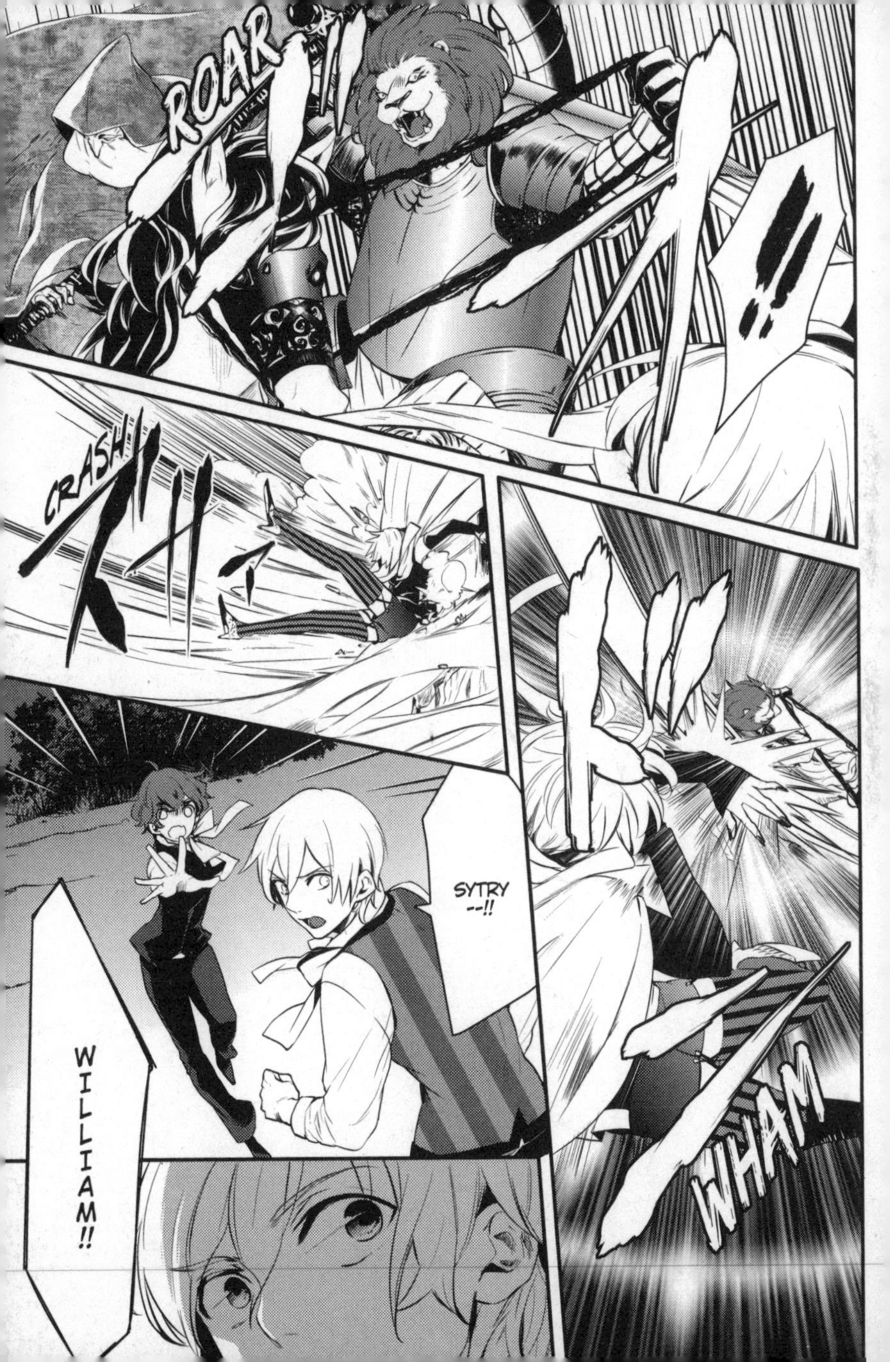
ROAR!!
!!
CRASH!!!
WHAM
SYTRY --!!
WILLIAM!!

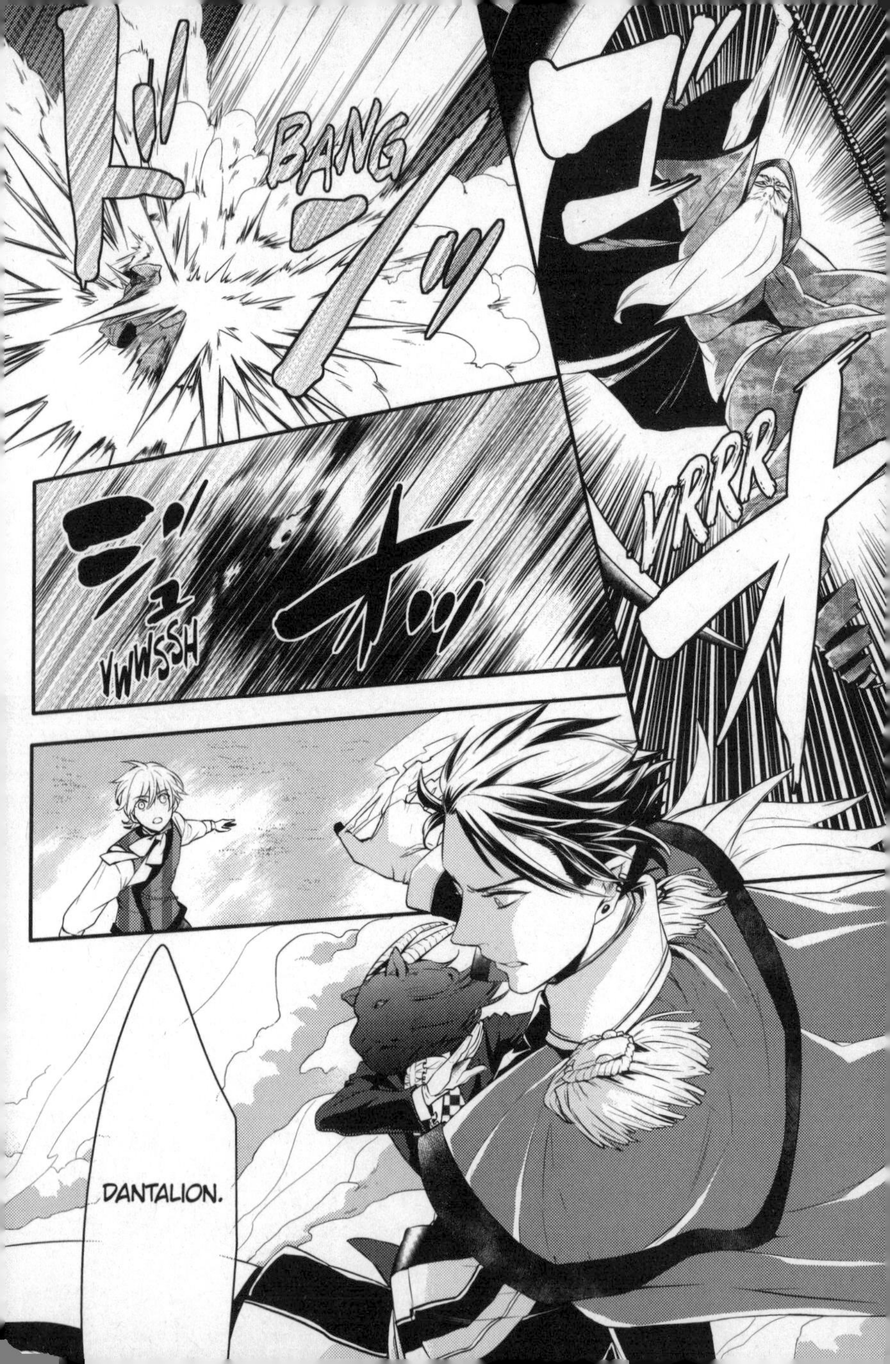
VRRR
BANG
VWWSSH
DANTALION.

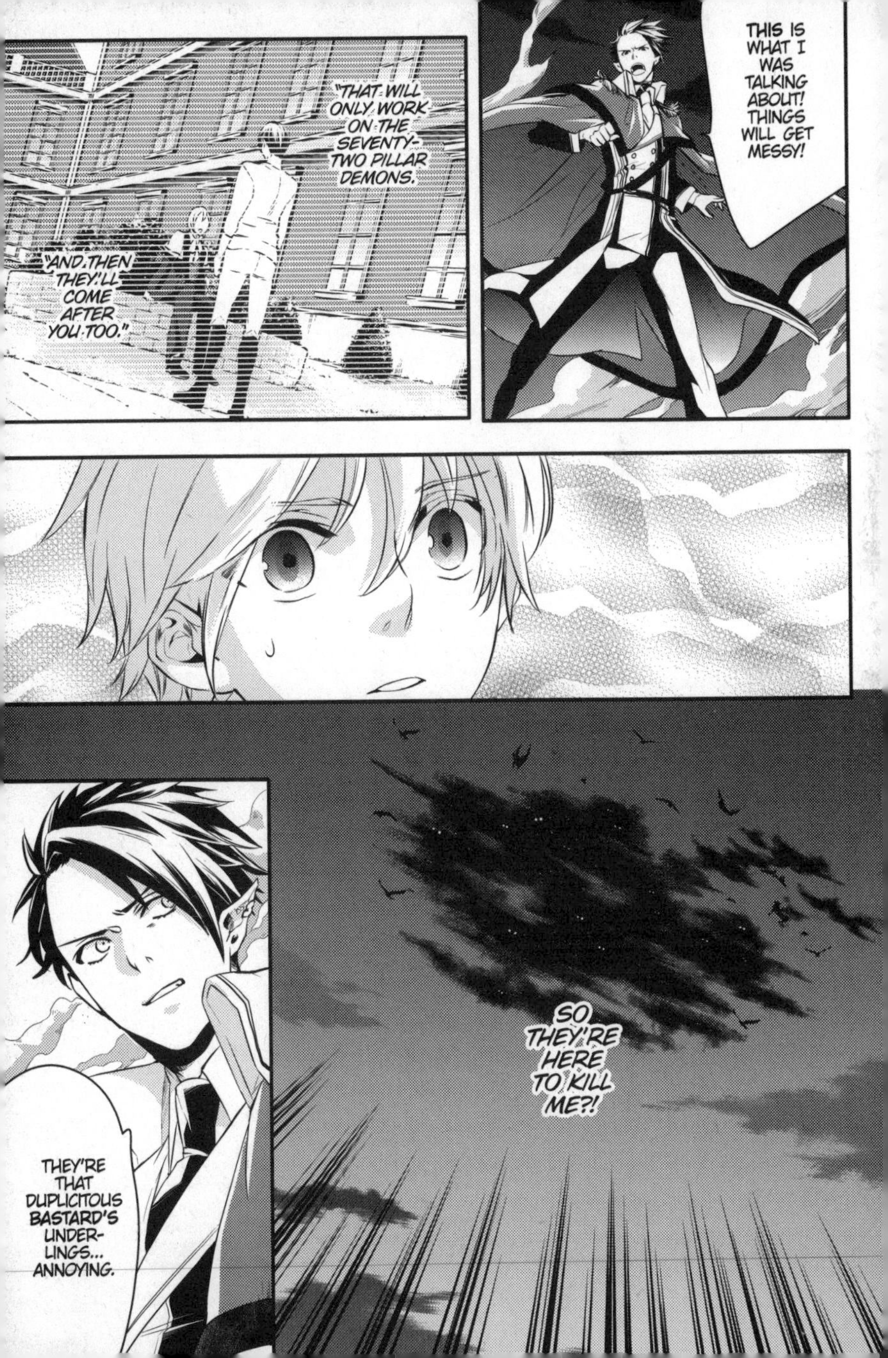
THIS IS WHAT I WAS TALKING ABOUT! THINGS WILL GET MESSY!
"THAT WILL ONLY WORK ON THE SEVENTY-TWO PILLAR DEMONS.
"AND THEN THEY'LL COME AFTER YOU TOO."
SO THEY'RE HERE TO KILL ME?!
THEY'RE THAT DUPLICITOUS BASTARD'S UNDER-LINGS... ANNOYING.

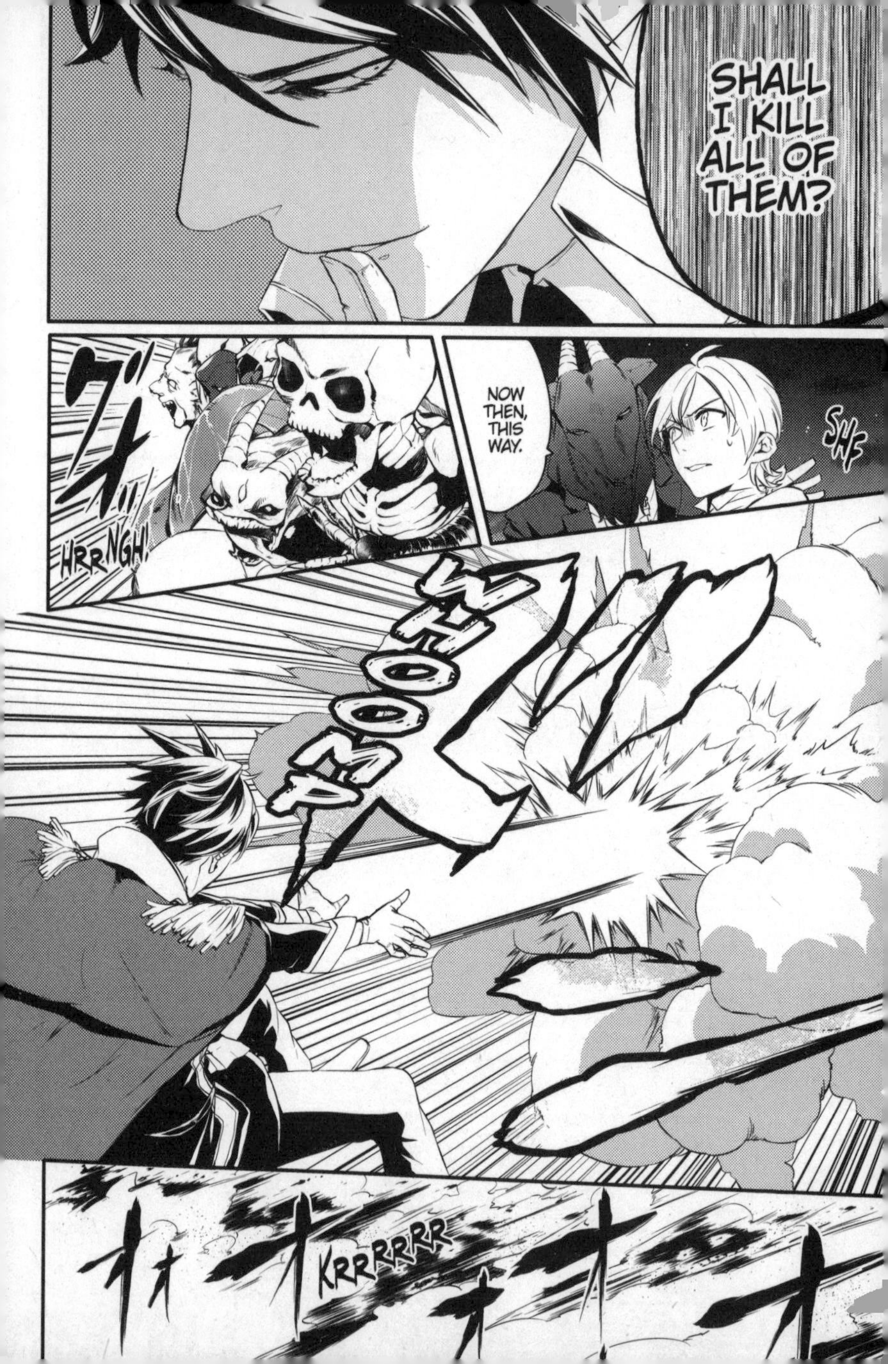
SHALL I KILL ALL OF THEM?
SHF
NOW THEN, THIS WAY.
HRR NGH!
WHOOMP
KRRRRRR

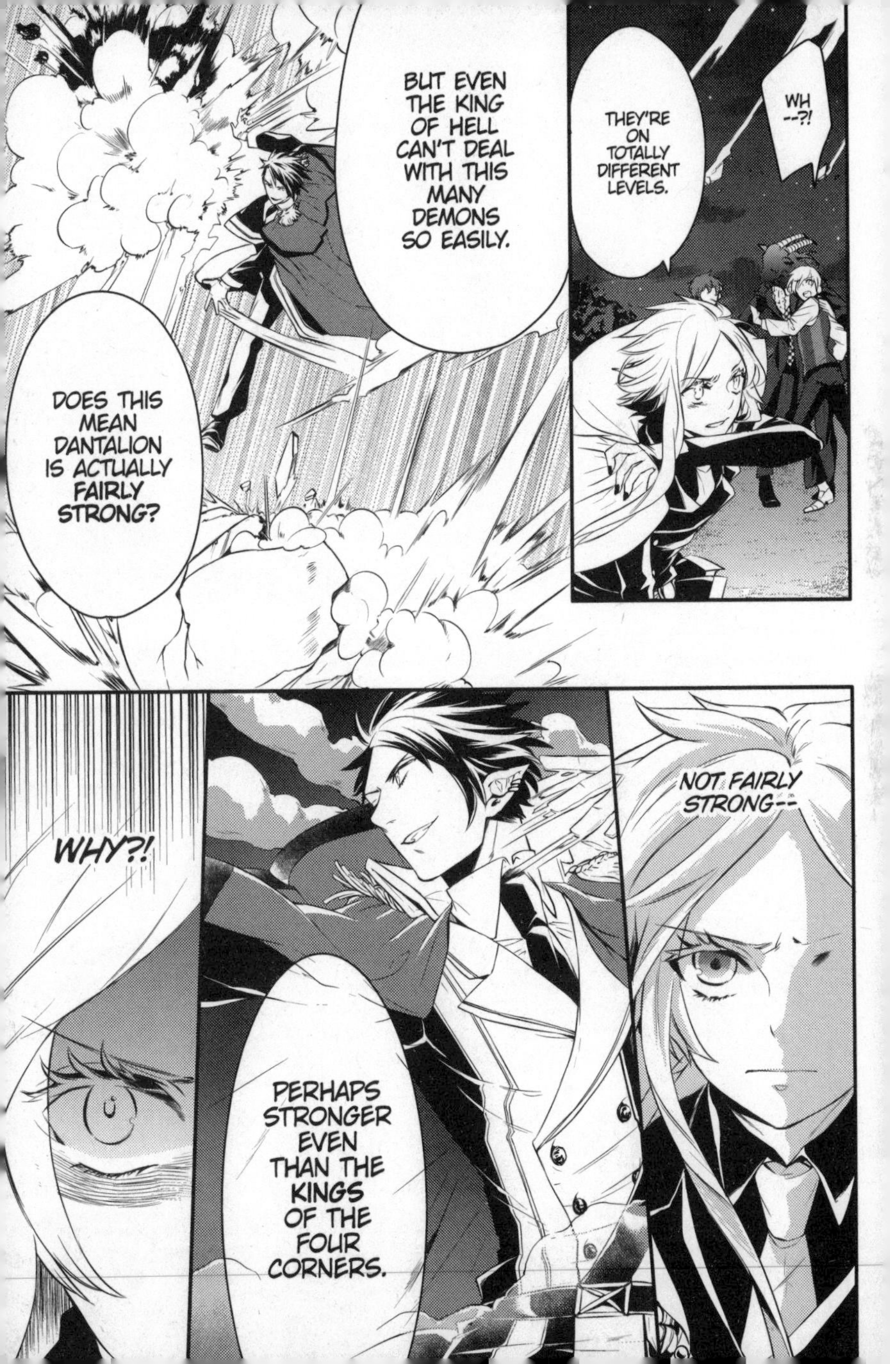
WH--?!
THEY'RE ON TOTALLY DIFFERENT LEVELS.
BUT EVEN THE KING OF HELL CAN'T DEAL WITH THIS MANY DEMONS SO EASILY.
DOES THIS MEAN DANTALION IS ACTUALLY FAIRLY STRONG?
NOT FAIRLY STRONG--
PERHAPS STRONGER EVEN THAN THE KINGS OF THE FOUR CORNERS.
WHY?!

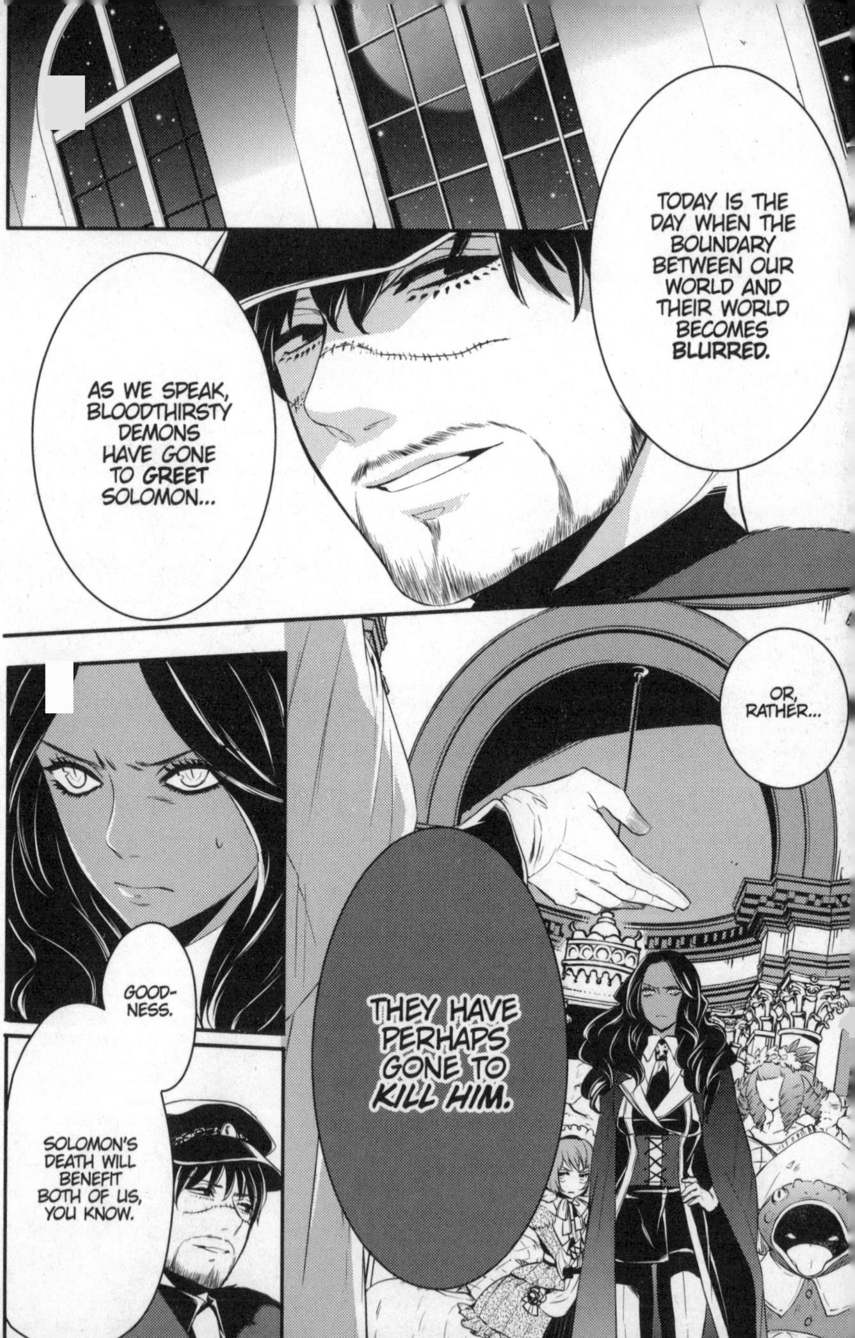
TODAY IS THE DAY WHEN THE BOUNDARY BETWEEN OUR WORLD AND THEIR WORLD BECOMES BLURRED.
AS WE SPEAK, BLOODTHIRSTY DEMONS HAVE GONE TO GREET SOLOMON...
OR, RATHER...
THEY HAVE PERHAPS GONE TO KILL HIM.
GOOD-NESS.
SOLOMON'S DEATH WILL BENEFIT BOTH OF US, YOU KNOW.

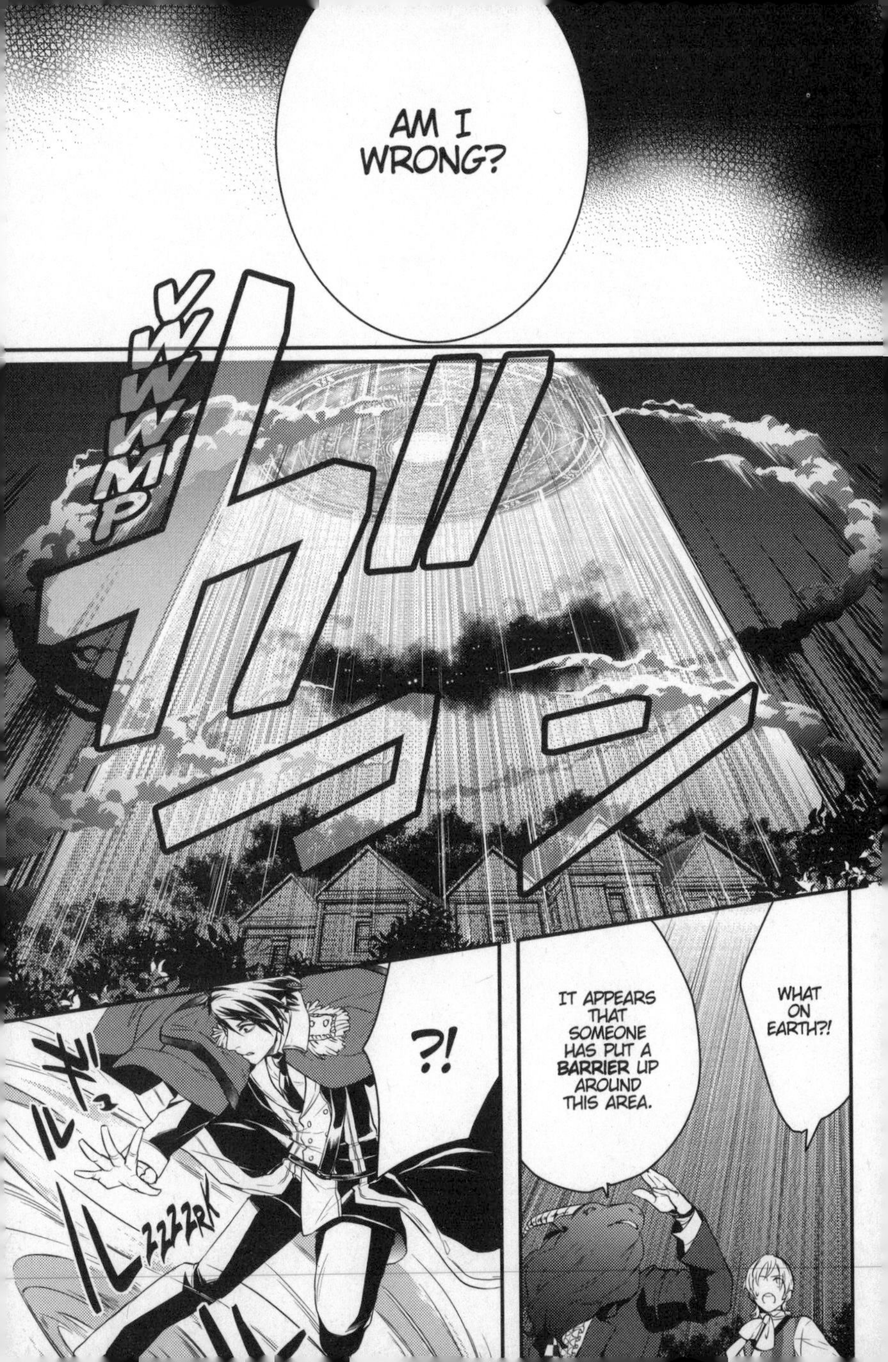
AM I WRONG?
VWWWMP
WHAT ON EARTH?!
IT APPEARS THAT SOMEONE HAS PUT A BARRIER UP AROUND THIS AREA.
?!
ZZZZRK

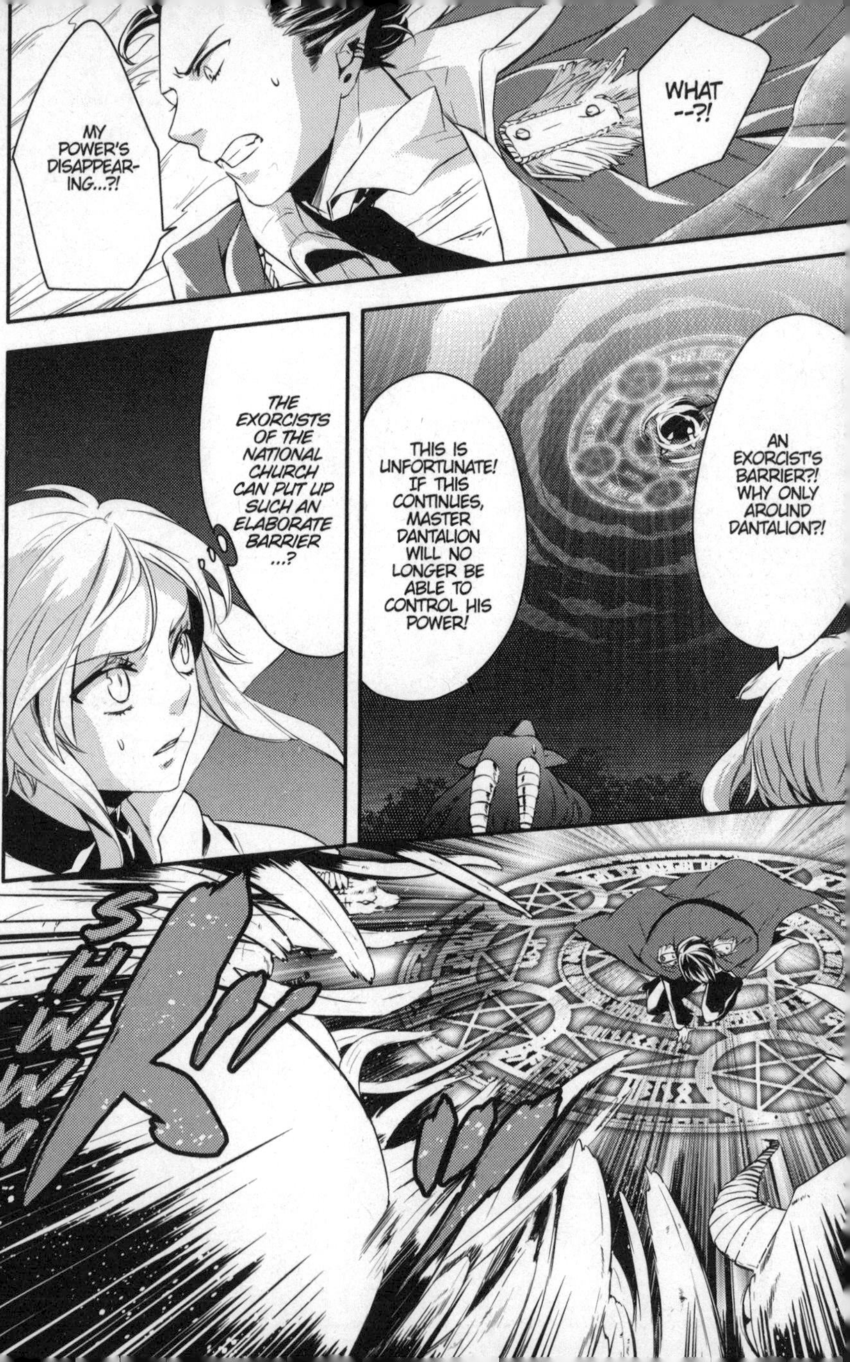
WHAT --?!
MY POWER'S DISAPPEARING...?!
AN EXORCIST'S BARRIER?! WHY ONLY AROUND DANTALION?!
THIS IS UNFORTUNATE! IF THIS CONTINUES, MASTER DANTALION WILL NO LONGER BE ABLE TO CONTROL HIS POWER!
THE EXORCISTS OF THE NATIONAL CHURCH CAN PUT UP SUCH AN ELABORATE BARRIER ...?
SHWWM

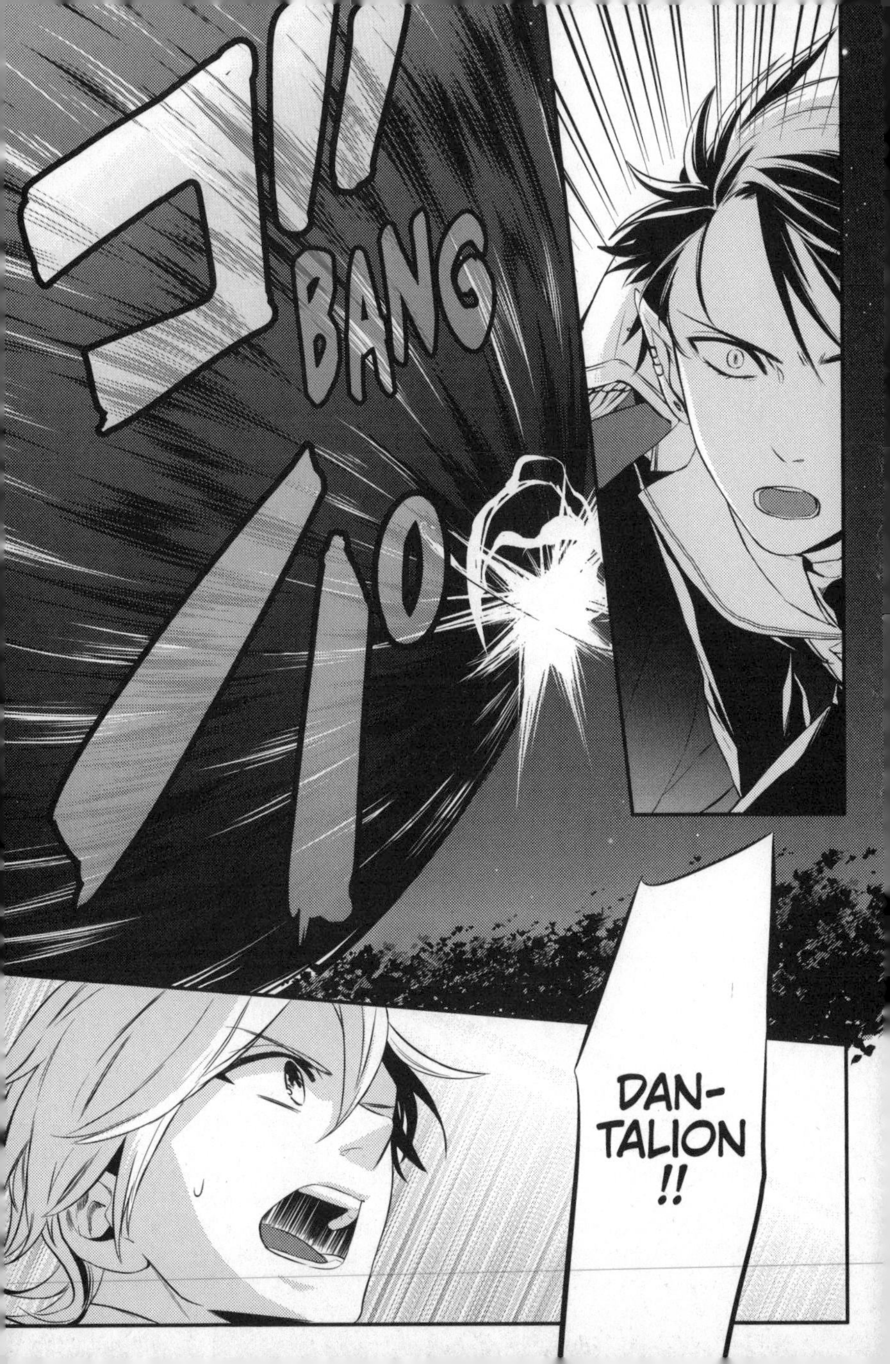
BANG
DAN-
TALION
!!

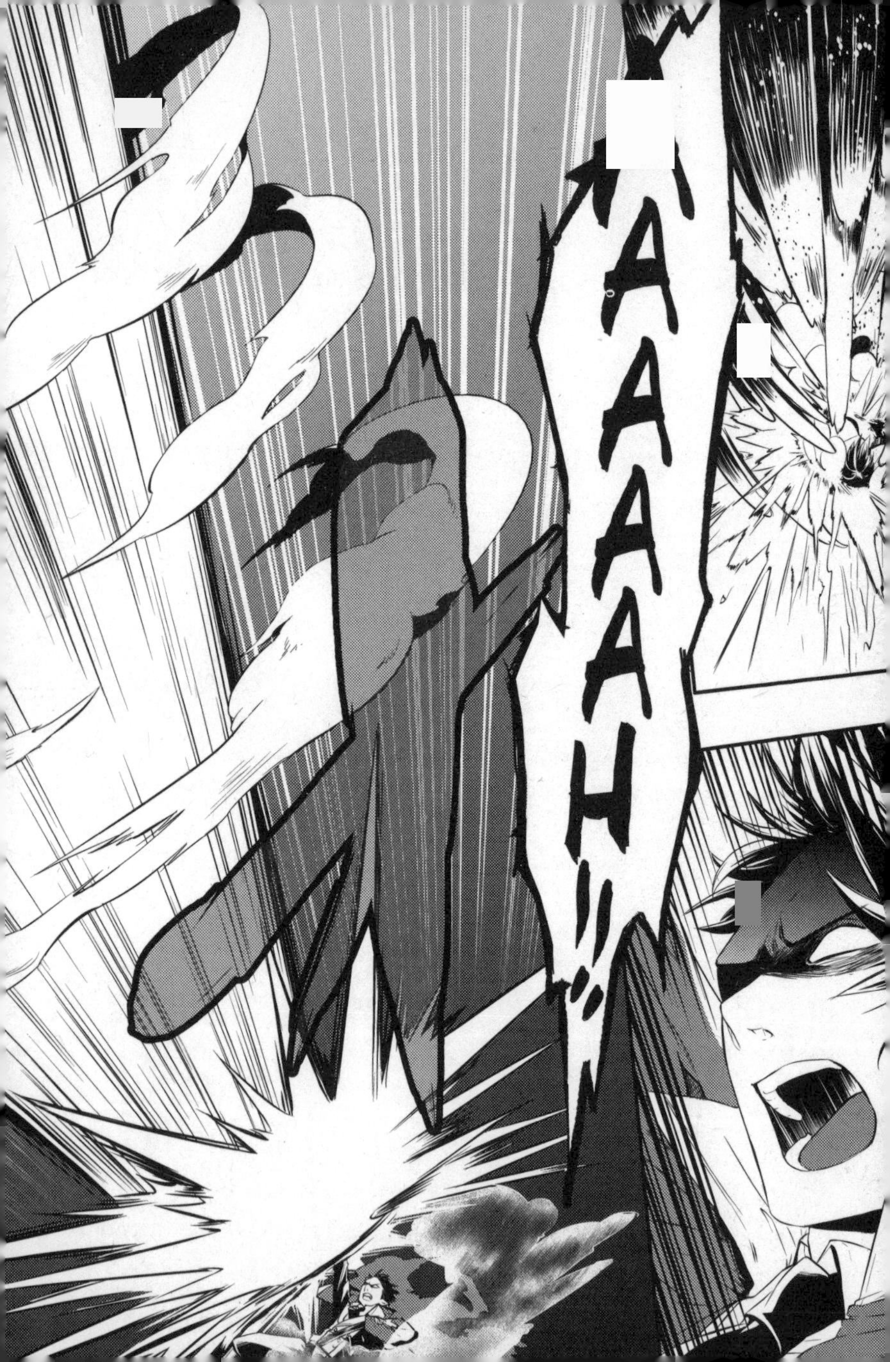
AAAAAH!!..

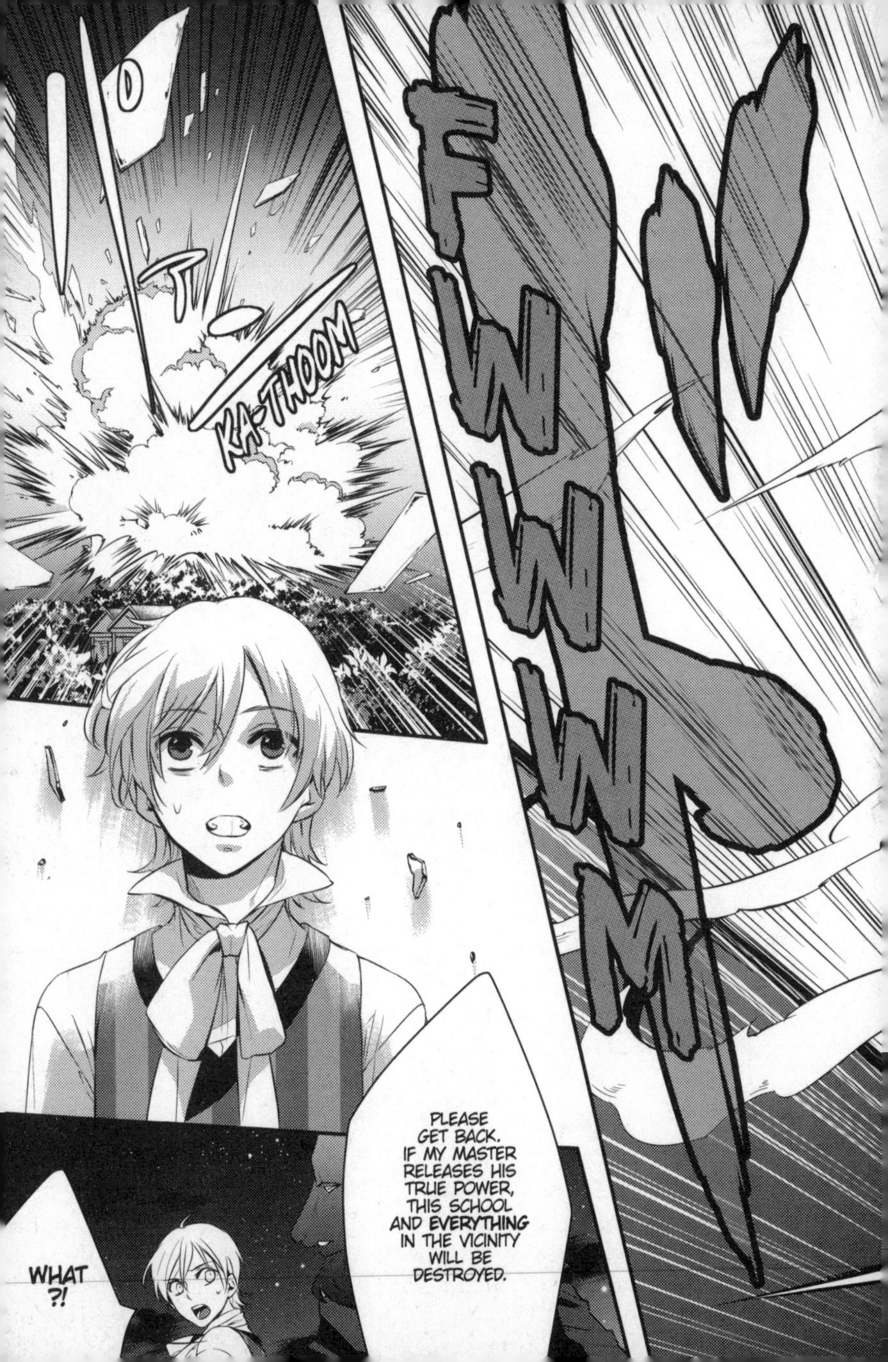
FWWWWM
DTO
KA-THOOM
PLEASE GET BACK. IF MY MASTER RELEASES HIS TRUE POWER, THIS SCHOOL AND EVERYTHING IN THE VICINITY WILL BE DESTROYED.
WHAT ?!

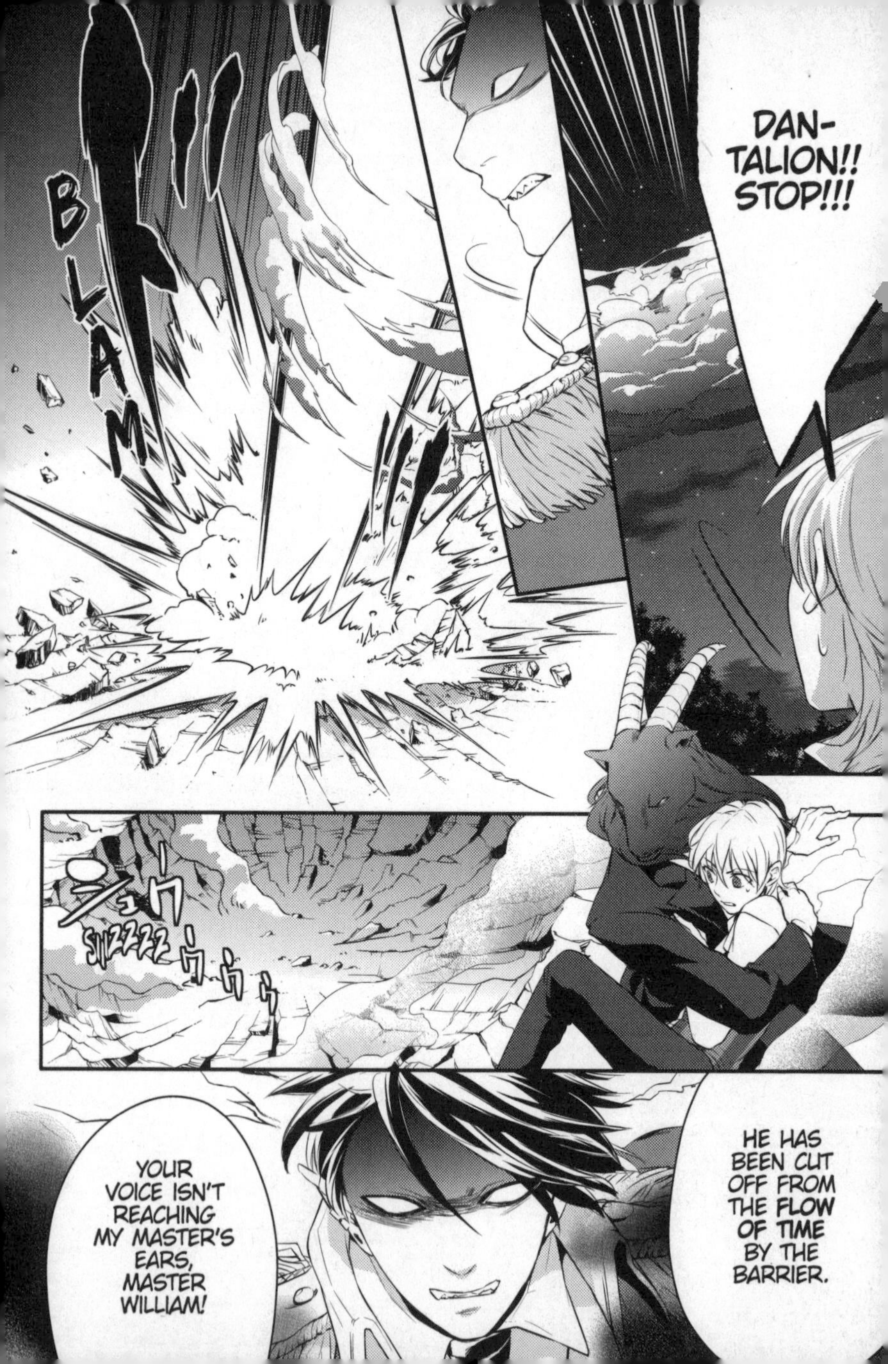
DAN-TALION!! STOP!!!
BLAM
SHZZZZ
HE HAS BEEN CUT OFF FROM THE FLOW OF TIME BY THE BARRIER.
YOUR VOICE ISN'T REACHING MY MASTER'S EARS, MASTER WILLIAM!

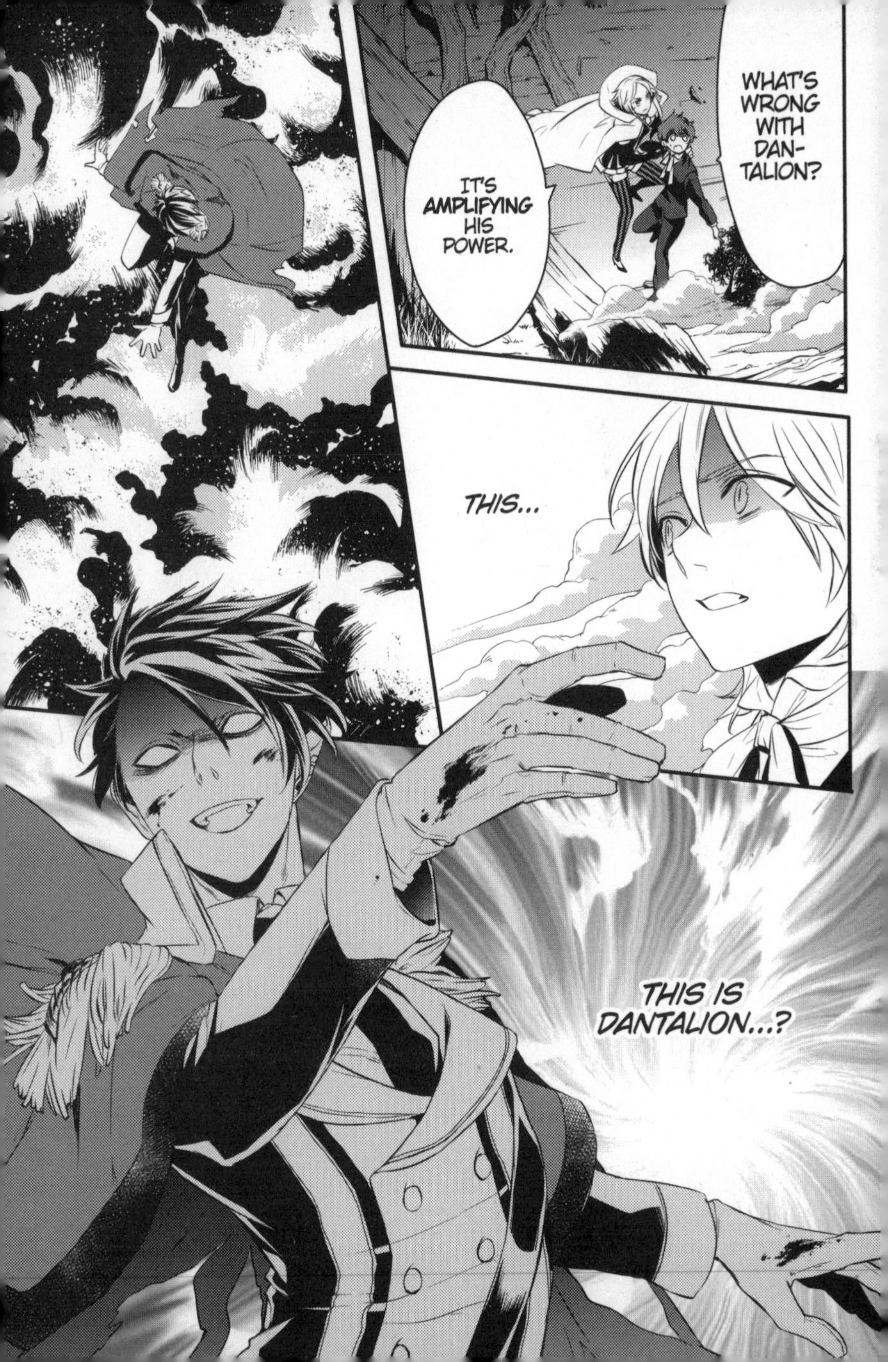
WHAT'S WRONG WITH DAN-TALION?
IT'S AMPLIFYING HIS POWER.
THIS...
THIS IS DANTALION...?

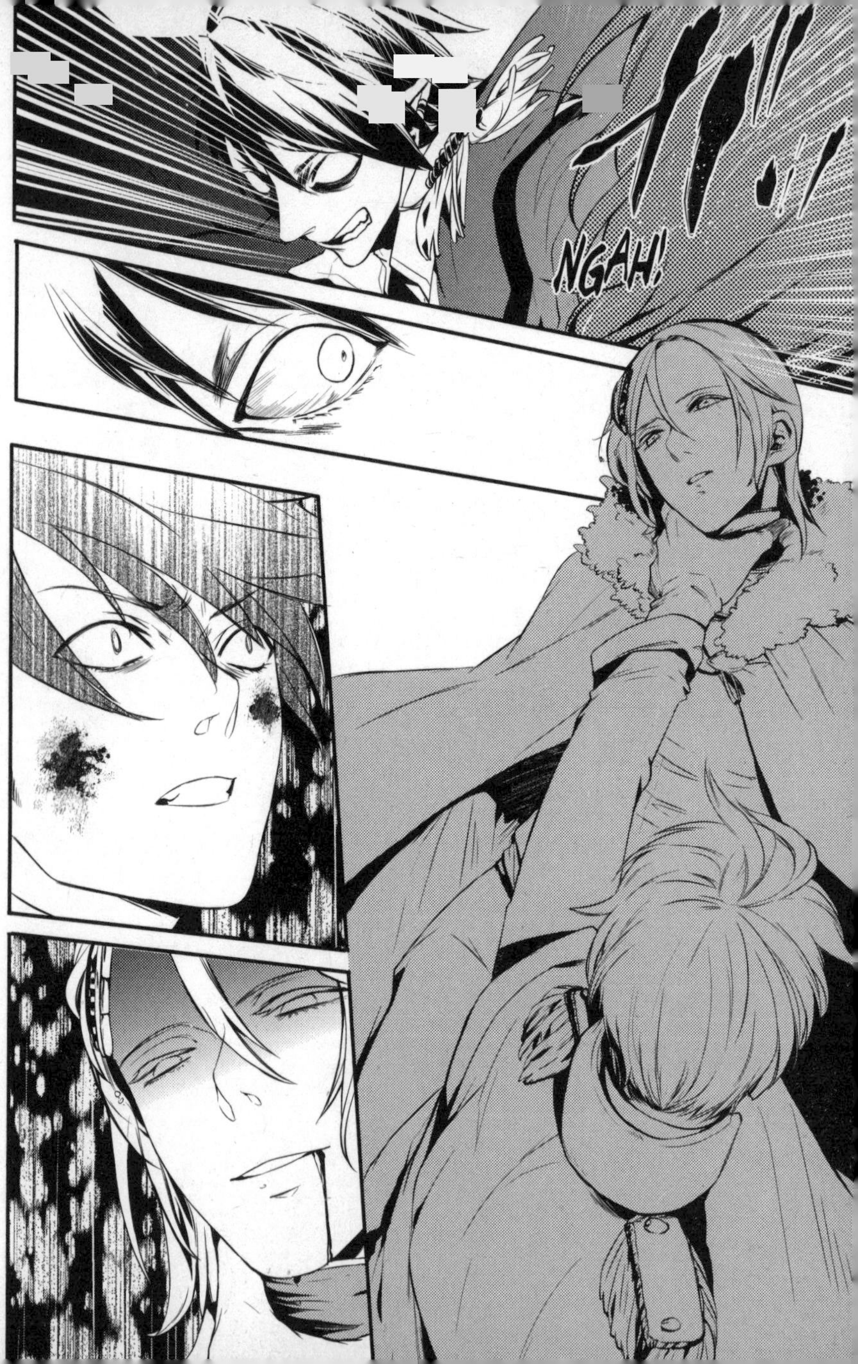
NGAH!

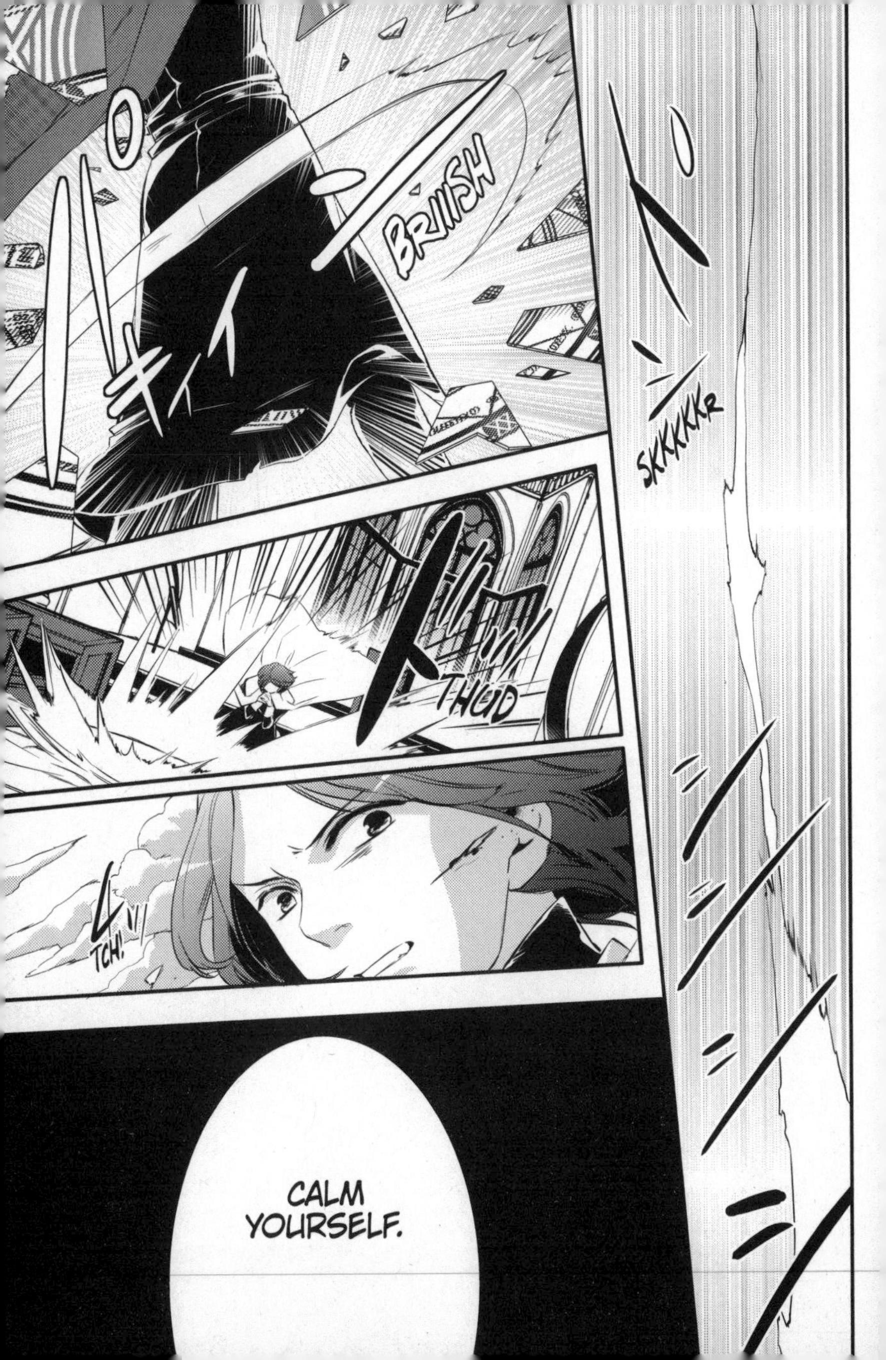
SKKKKKR
BRIIISH
THUD
TCH!
CALM YOURSELF.

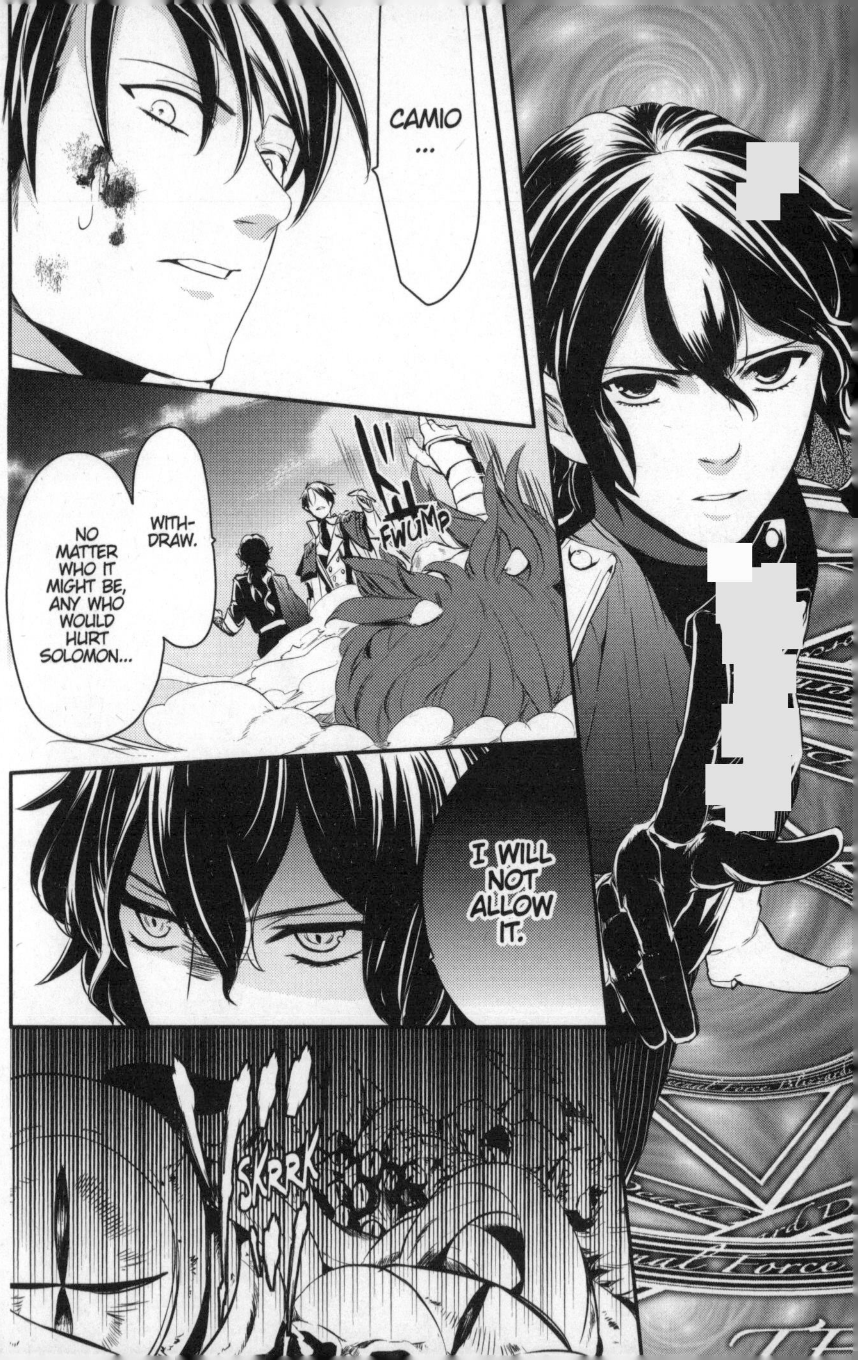
CAMIO ...
WITH-DRAW.
FWUMP
NO MATTER WHO IT MIGHT BE, ANY WHO WOULD HURT SOLOMON...
I WILL NOT ALLOW IT.
SKRRK

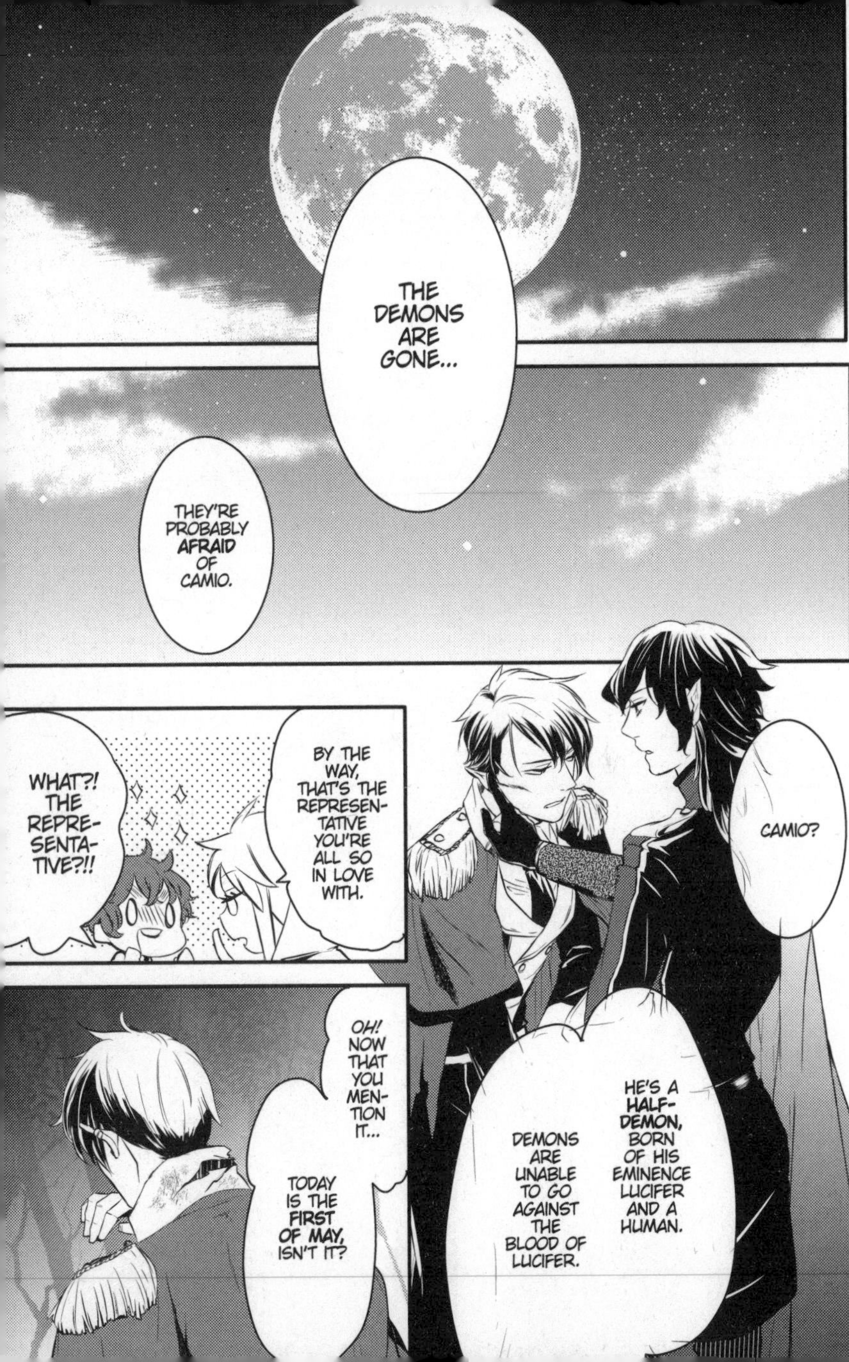
THE DEMONS ARE GONE...
THEY'RE PROBABLY AFRAID OF CAMIO.
CAMIO?
BY THE WAY, THAT'S THE REPRESEN-TATIVE YOU'RE ALL SO IN LOVE WITH.
WHAT?! THE REPRE-SENTA-TIVE?!!
HE'S A HALF-DEMON, BORN OF HIS EMINENCE LUCIFER AND A HUMAN.
DEMONS ARE UNABLE TO GO AGAINST THE BLOOD OF LUCIFER.
OH! NOW THAT YOU MEN-TION IT...
TODAY IS THE FIRST OF MAY, ISN'T IT?

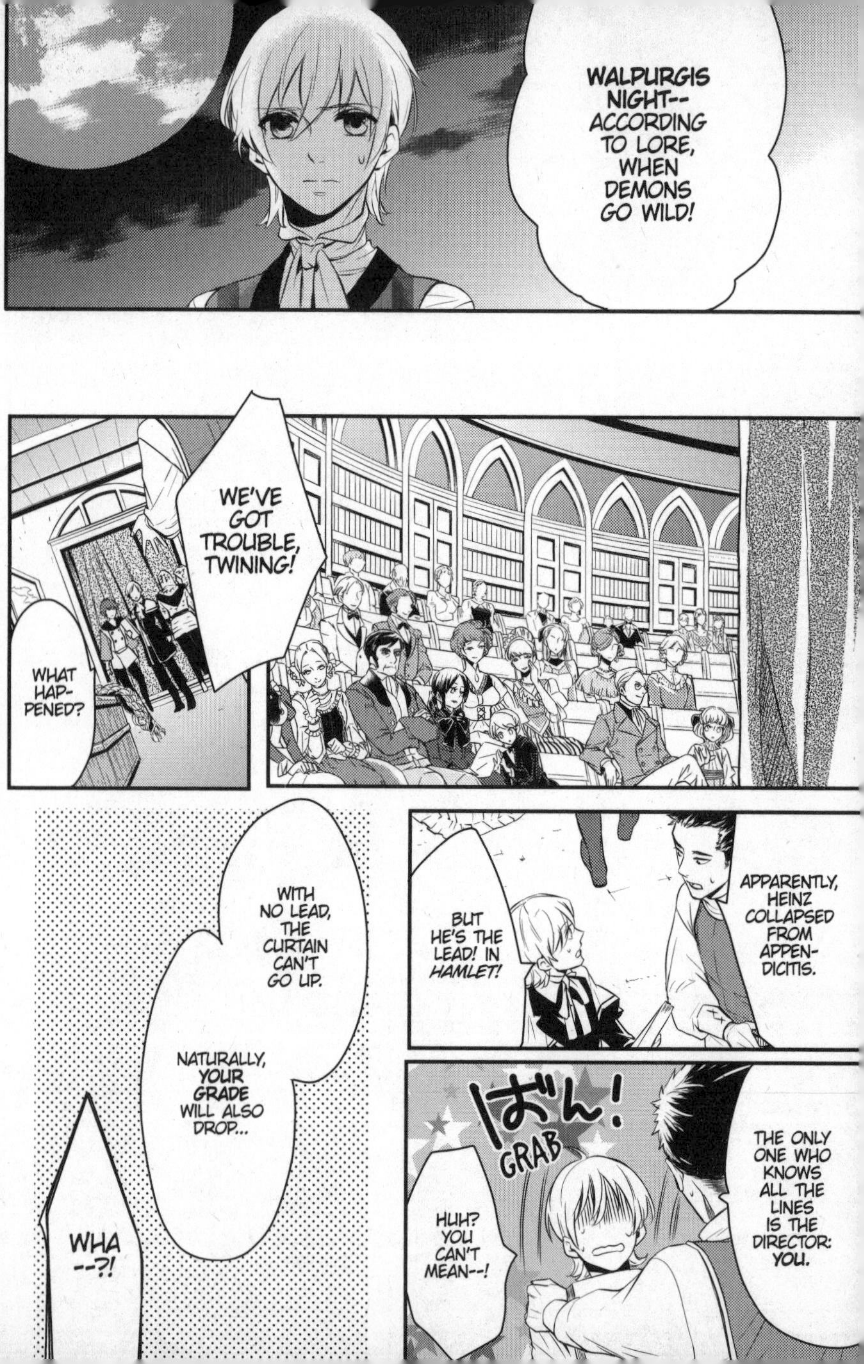

WALPURGIS NIGHT-- ACCORDING TO LORE, WHEN DEMONS GO WILD!
WE'VE GOT TROUBLE, TWINING!
WHAT HAP-PENED?
APPARENTLY, HEINZ COLLAPSED FROM APPEN-DICITIS.
BUT HE'S THE LEAD! IN *HAMLET*!
WITH NO LEAD, THE CURTAIN CAN'T GO UP.
NATURALLY, YOUR GRADE WILL ALSO DROP...
THE ONLY ONE WHO KNOWS ALL THE LINES IS THE DIRECTOR: YOU.
GRAB
HUH? YOU CAN'T MEAN--!
WHA--?!

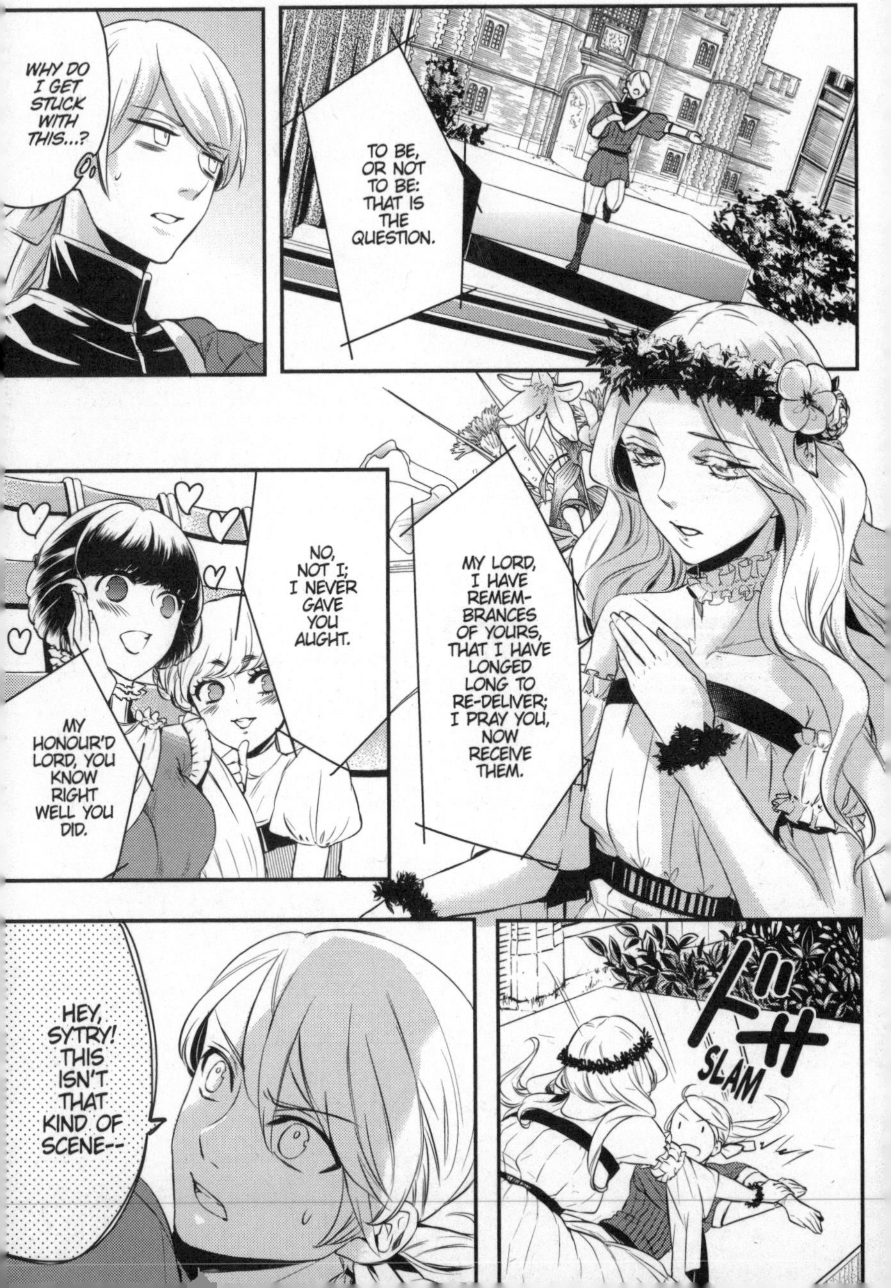
TO BE, OR NOT TO BE: THAT IS THE QUESTION.
WHY DO I GET STUCK WITH THIS...?
MY LORD, I HAVE REMEMBRANCES OF YOURS, THAT I HAVE LONGED LONG TO RE-DELIVER; I PRAY YOU, NOW RECEIVE THEM.
NO, NOT I; I NEVER GAVE YOU AUGHT.
MY HONOUR'D LORD, YOU KNOW RIGHT WELL YOU DID.
SLAM
HEY, SYTRY! THIS ISN'T THAT KIND OF SCENE--

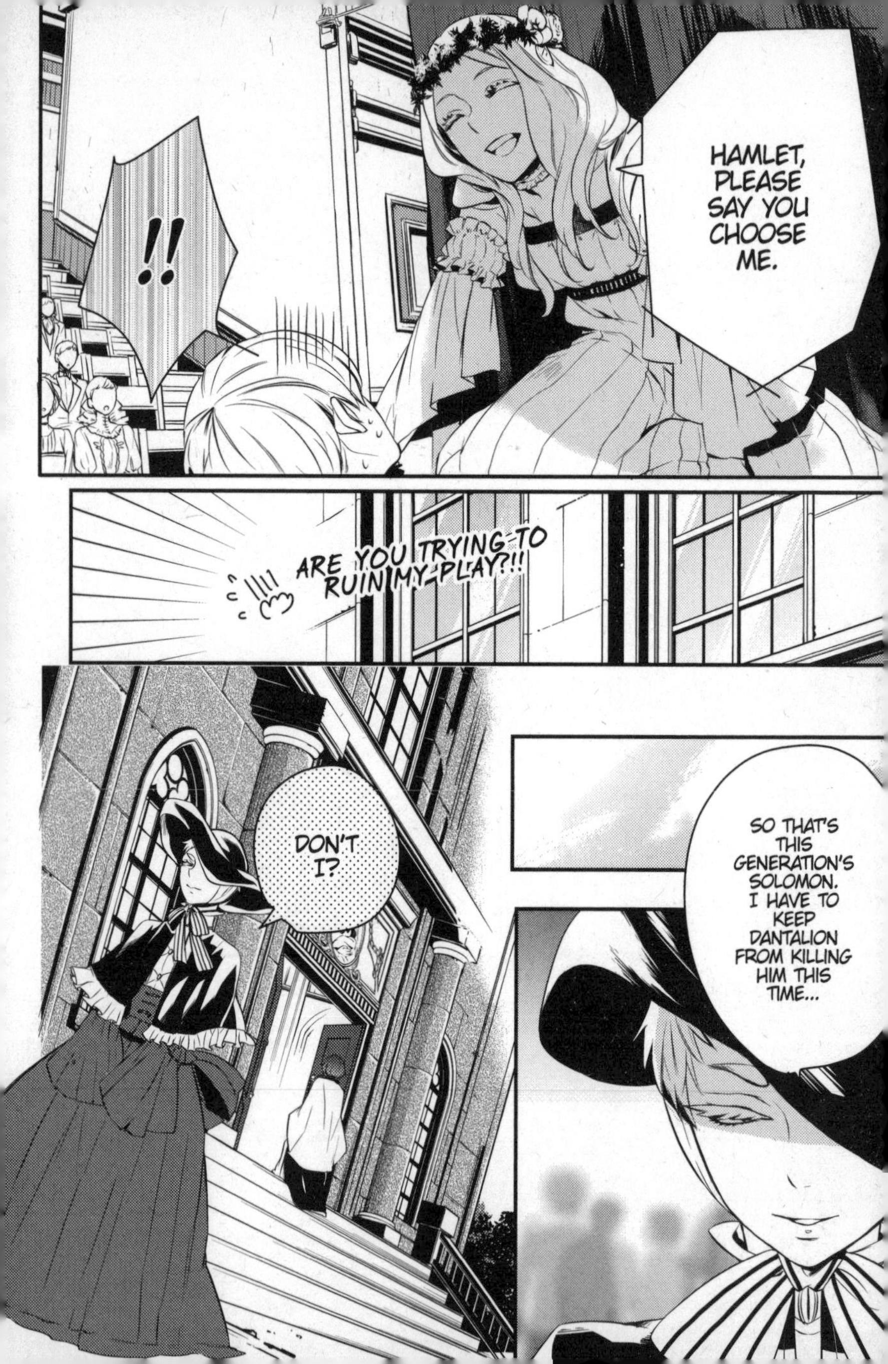
HAMLET, PLEASE SAY YOU CHOOSE ME.
!!
ARE YOU TRYING TO RUIN MY PLAY?!!
SO THAT'S THIS GENERATION'S SOLOMON. I HAVE TO KEEP DANTALION FROM KILLING HIM THIS TIME...
DON'T I?

Pillar 21

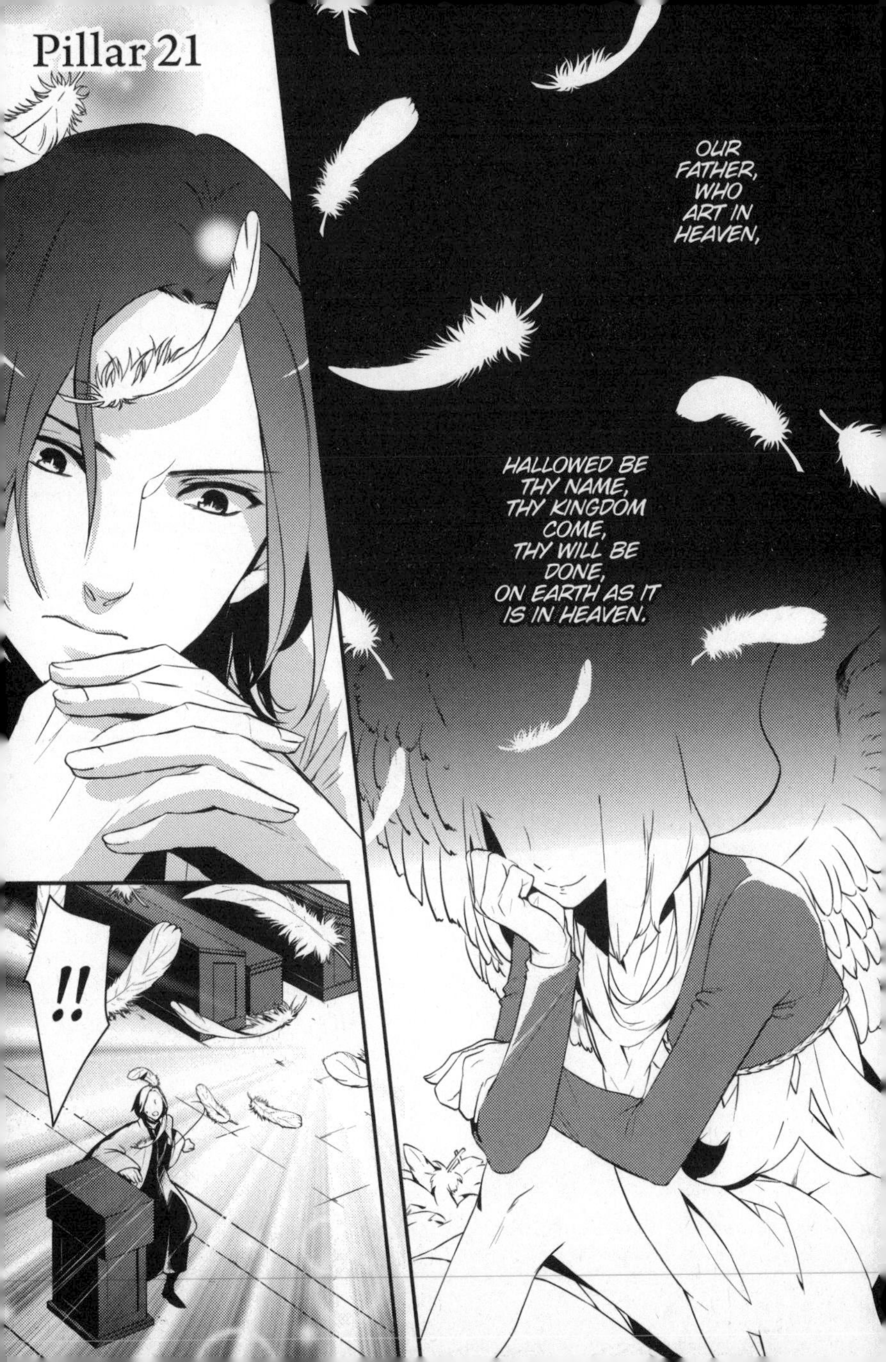
OUR FATHER, WHO ART IN HEAVEN,
HALLOWED BE THY NAME, THY KINGDOM COME, THY WILL BE DONE, ON EARTH AS IT IS IN HEAVEN.
!!

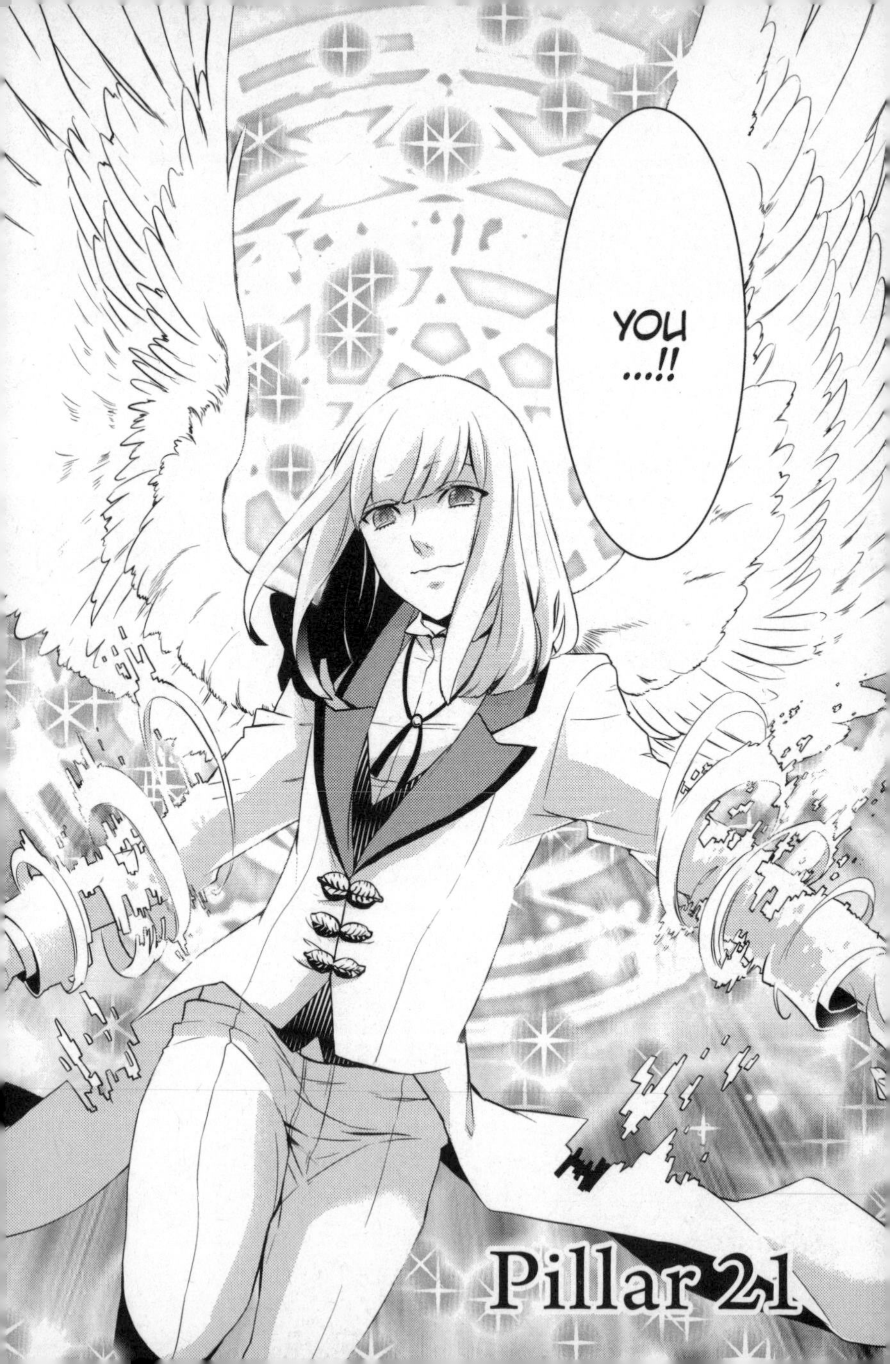
YOU ...!!
Pillar 21

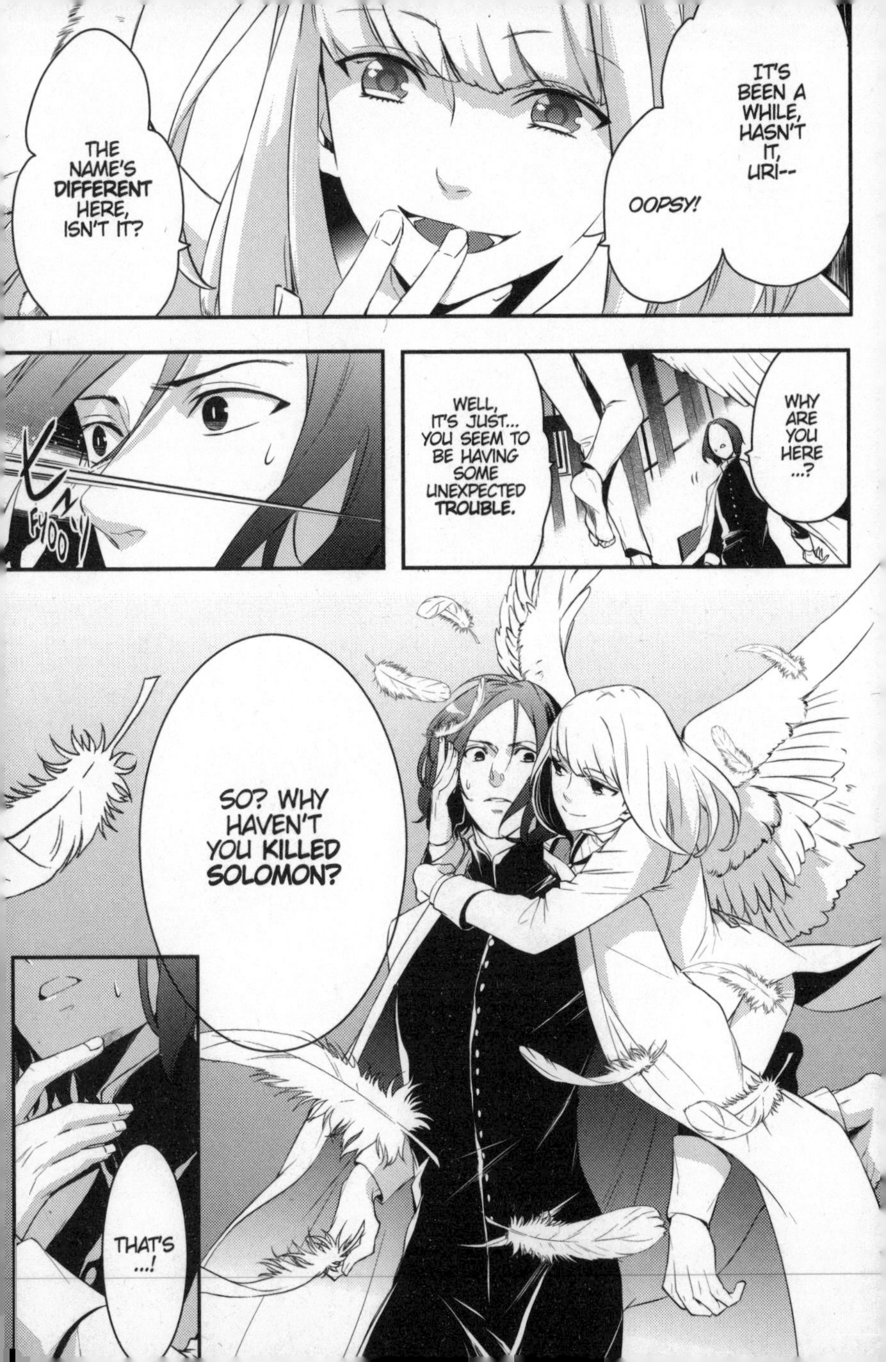
IT'S BEEN A WHILE, HASN'T IT, URI--
OOPSY!
THE NAME'S DIFFERENT HERE, ISN'T IT?
WHY ARE YOU HERE ...?
WELL, IT'S JUST... YOU SEEM TO BE HAVING SOME UNEXPECTED TROUBLE.
FYOO
SO? WHY HAVEN'T YOU KILLED SOLOMON?
THAT'S ...!

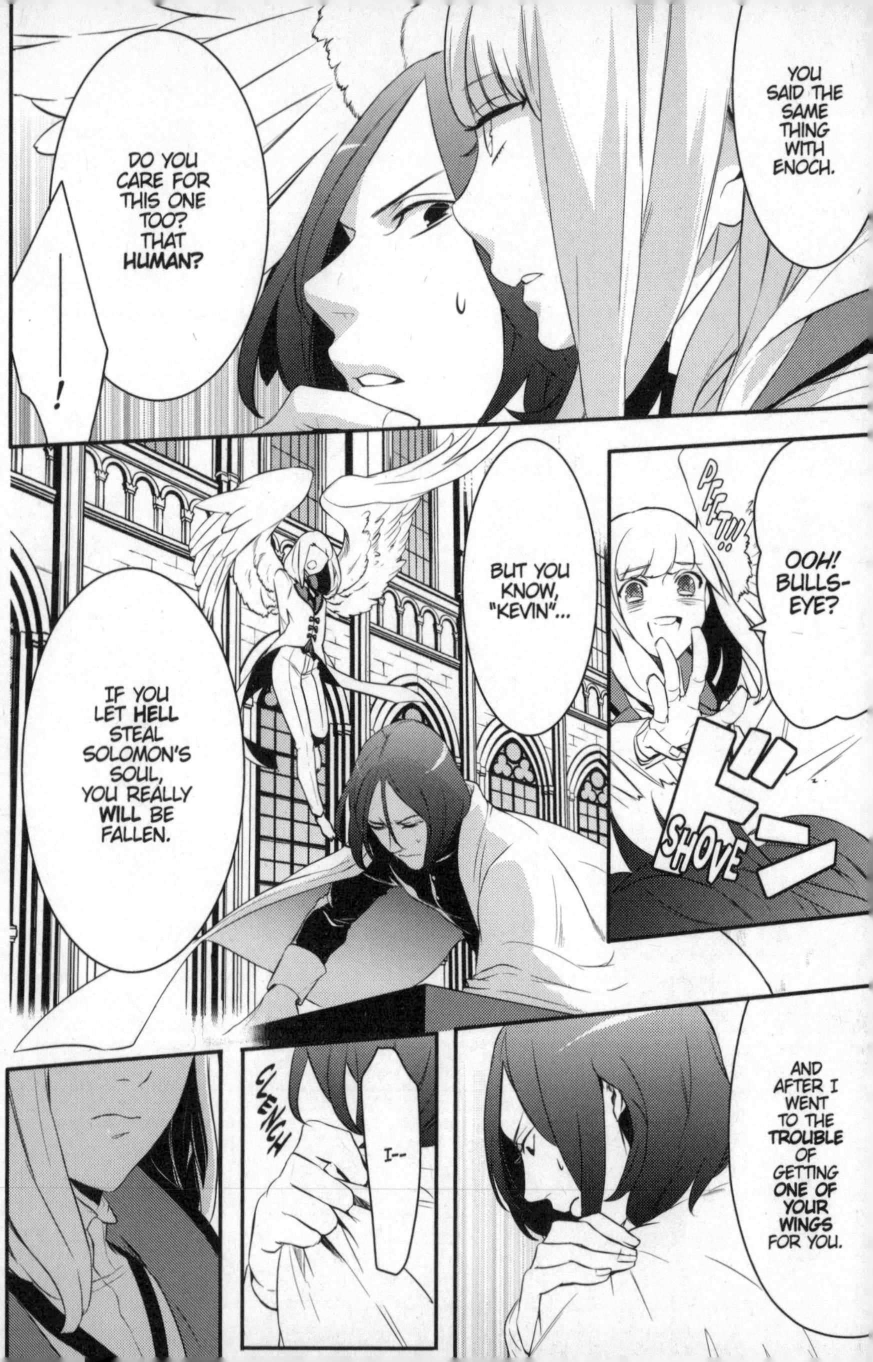
YOU SAID THE SAME THING WITH ENOCH.
DO YOU CARE FOR THIS ONE TOO? THAT HUMAN?
——!
PFFT!!
OOH! BULLS-EYE?
SHOVE
BUT YOU KNOW, "KEVIN"...
IF YOU LET HELL STEAL SOLOMON'S SOUL, YOU REALLY WILL BE FALLEN.
AND AFTER I WENT TO THE TROUBLE OF GETTING ONE OF YOUR WINGS FOR YOU.
CLENCH
I--

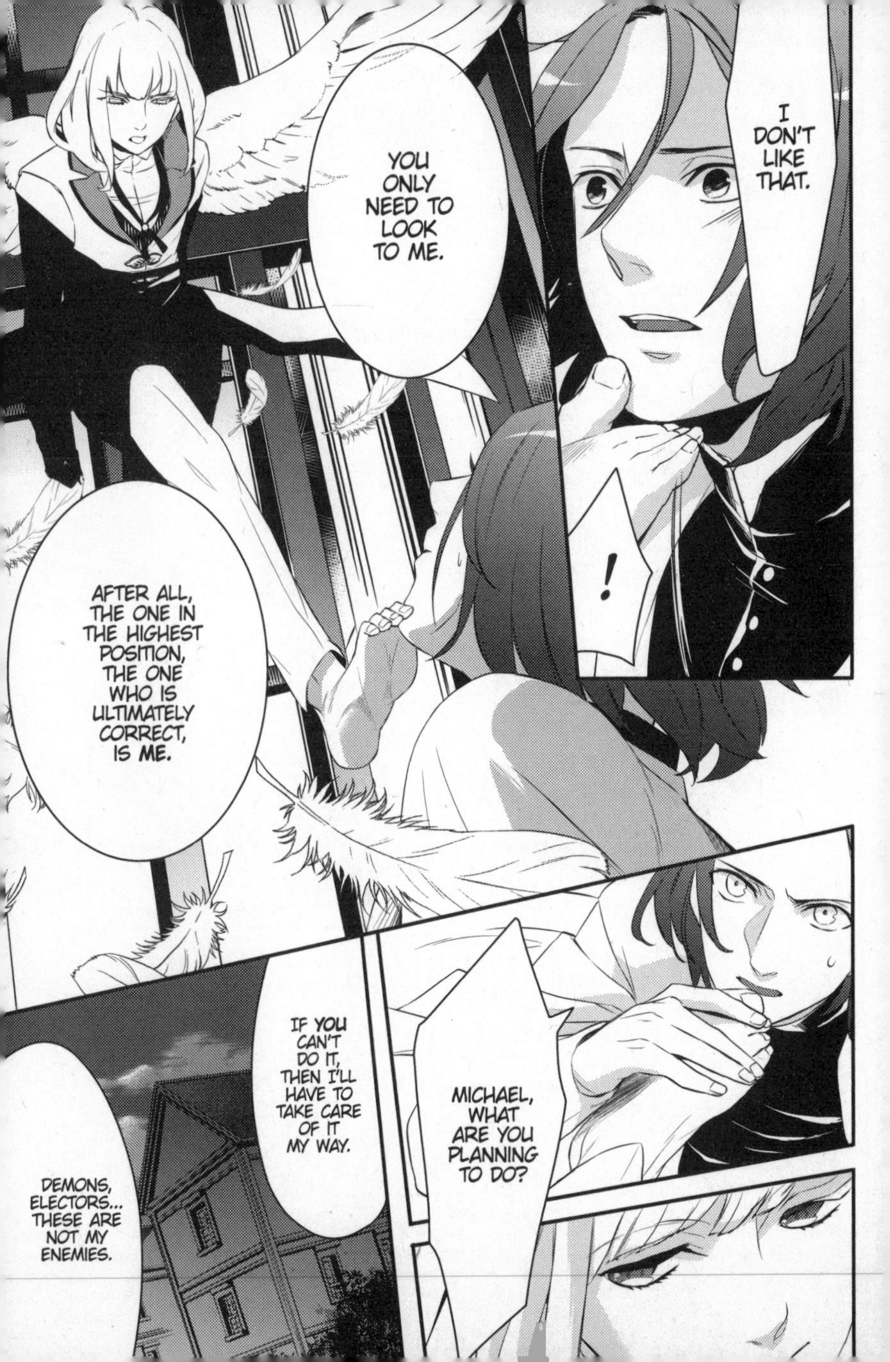
I DON'T LIKE THAT.
YOU ONLY NEED TO LOOK TO ME.
!
AFTER ALL, THE ONE IN THE HIGHEST POSITION, THE ONE WHO IS ULTIMATELY CORRECT, IS ME.
MICHAEL, WHAT ARE YOU PLANNING TO DO?
IF YOU CAN'T DO IT, THEN I'LL HAVE TO TAKE CARE OF IT MY WAY.
DEMONS, ELECTORS... THESE ARE NOT MY ENEMIES.

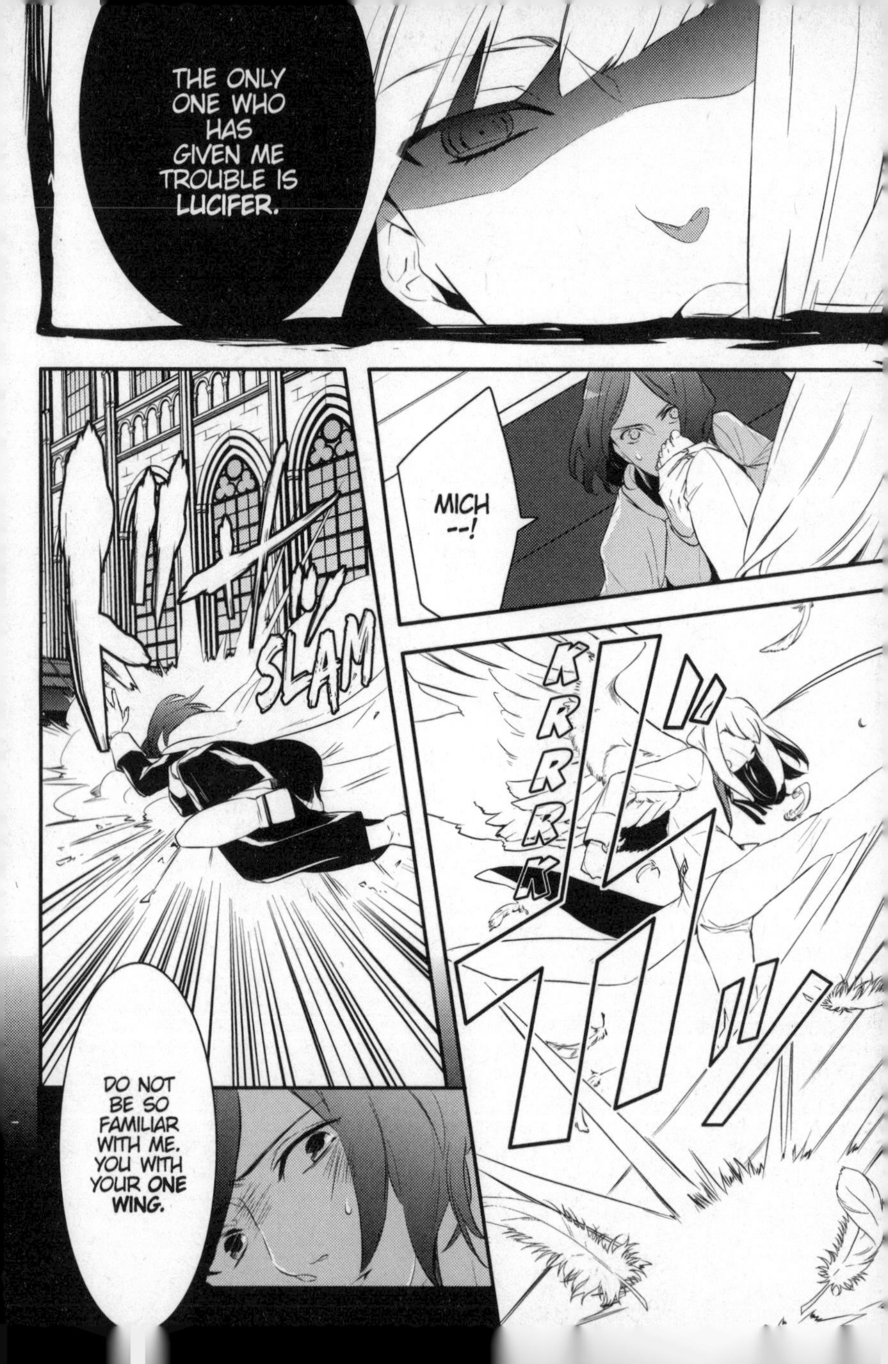
THE ONLY ONE WHO HAS GIVEN ME TROUBLE IS LUCIFER.
MICH--!
SLAM
KRRRRK
DO NOT BE SO FAMILIAR WITH ME. YOU WITH YOUR ONE WING.

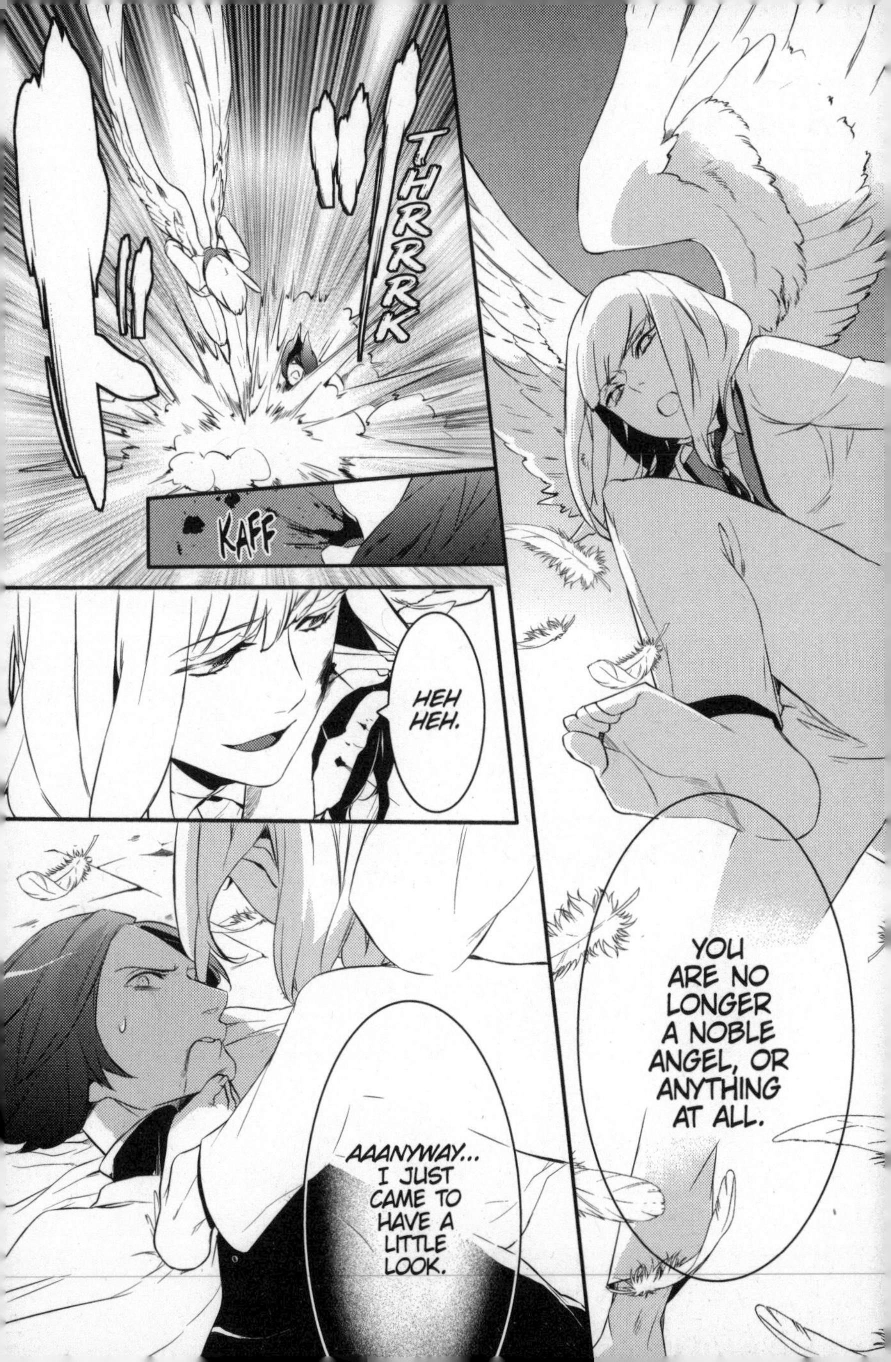
THRRRK
KAFF
HEH HEH.
YOU ARE NO LONGER A NOBLE ANGEL, OR ANYTHING AT ALL.
AAANYWAY... I JUST CAME TO HAVE A LITTLE LOOK.

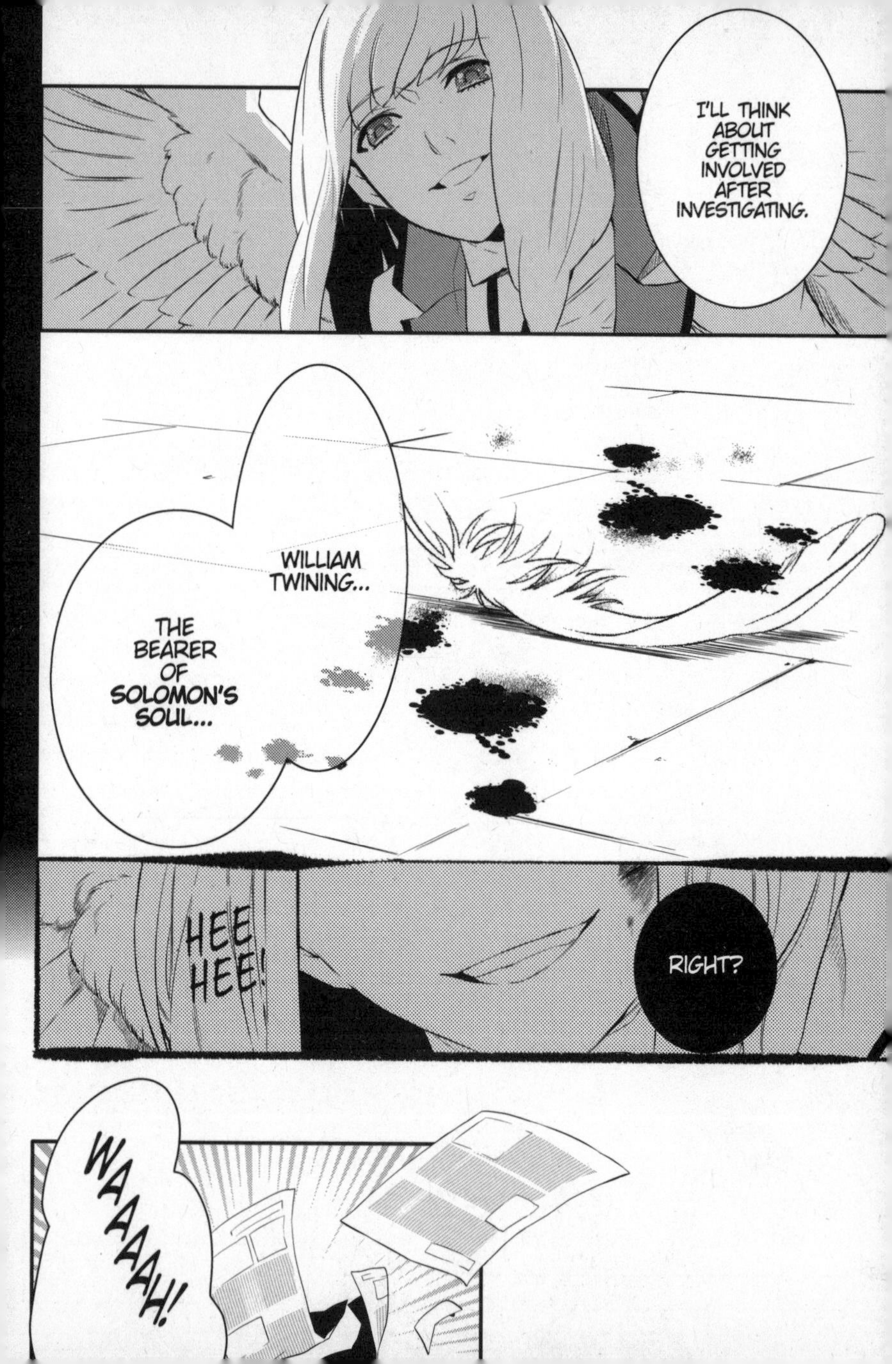
I'LL THINK ABOUT GETTING INVOLVED AFTER INVESTIGATING.
WILLIAM TWINING...
THE BEARER OF SOLOMON'S SOUL...
RIGHT?
HEE HEE!
WAAAAH!

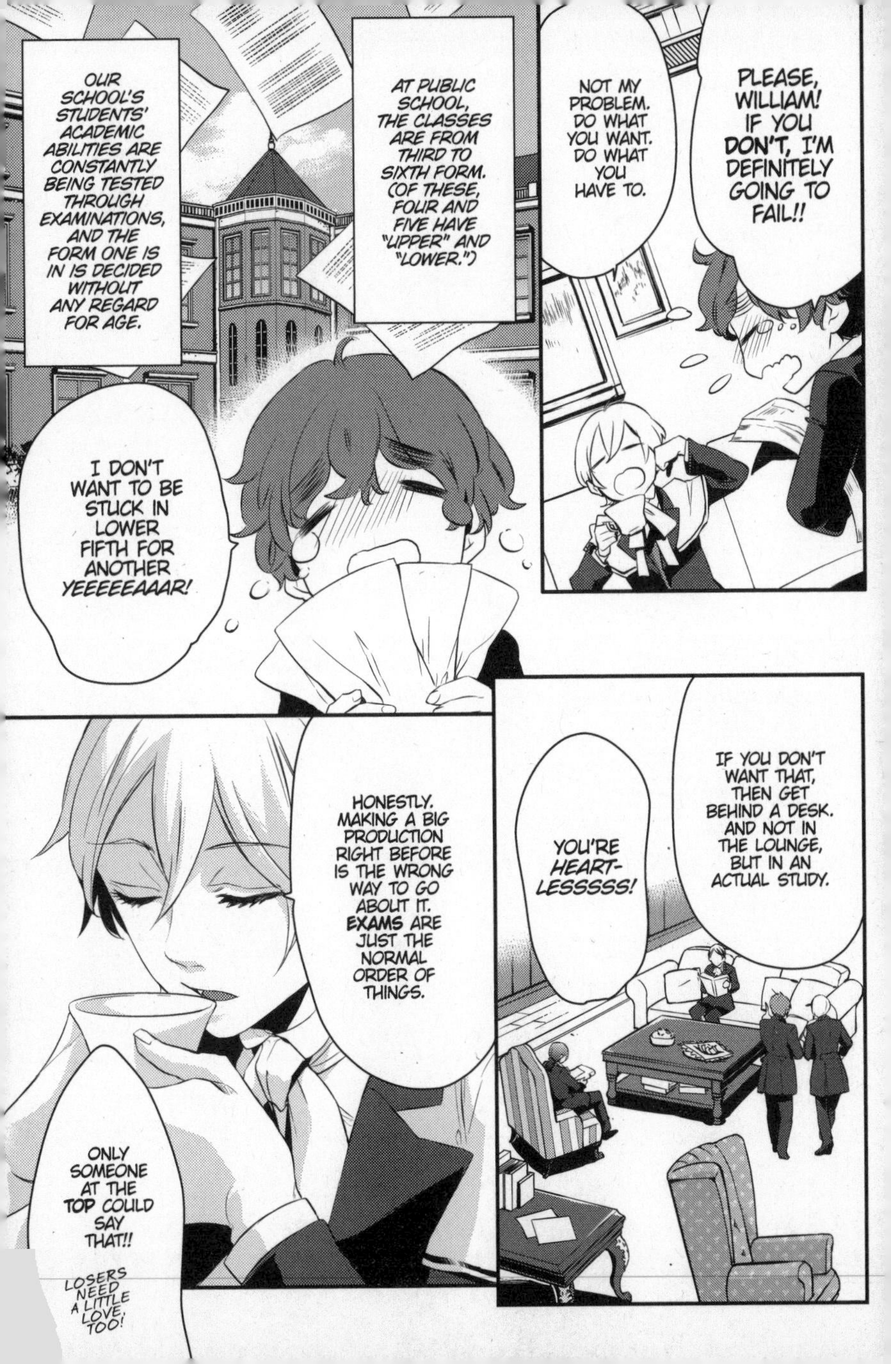

PLEASE, WILLIAM! IF YOU DON'T, I'M DEFINITELY GOING TO FAIL!!
NOT MY PROBLEM. DO WHAT YOU WANT. DO WHAT YOU HAVE TO.
AT PUBLIC SCHOOL, THE CLASSES ARE FROM THIRD TO SIXTH FORM. (OF THESE, FOUR AND FIVE HAVE "UPPER" AND "LOWER.")
OUR SCHOOL'S STUDENTS' ACADEMIC ABILITIES ARE CONSTANTLY BEING TESTED THROUGH EXAMINATIONS, AND THE FORM ONE IS IN IS DECIDED WITHOUT ANY REGARD FOR AGE.
I DON'T WANT TO BE STUCK IN LOWER FIFTH FOR ANOTHER YEEEEEAAAR!
IF YOU DON'T WANT THAT, THEN GET BEHIND A DESK. AND NOT IN THE LOUNGE, BUT IN AN ACTUAL STUDY.
YOU'RE HEART-LESSSSS!
HONESTLY. MAKING A BIG PRODUCTION RIGHT BEFORE IS THE WRONG WAY TO GO ABOUT IT. EXAMS ARE JUST THE NORMAL ORDER OF THINGS.
ONLY SOMEONE AT THE TOP COULD SAY THAT!!
LOSERS NEED A LITTLE LOVE, TOO!

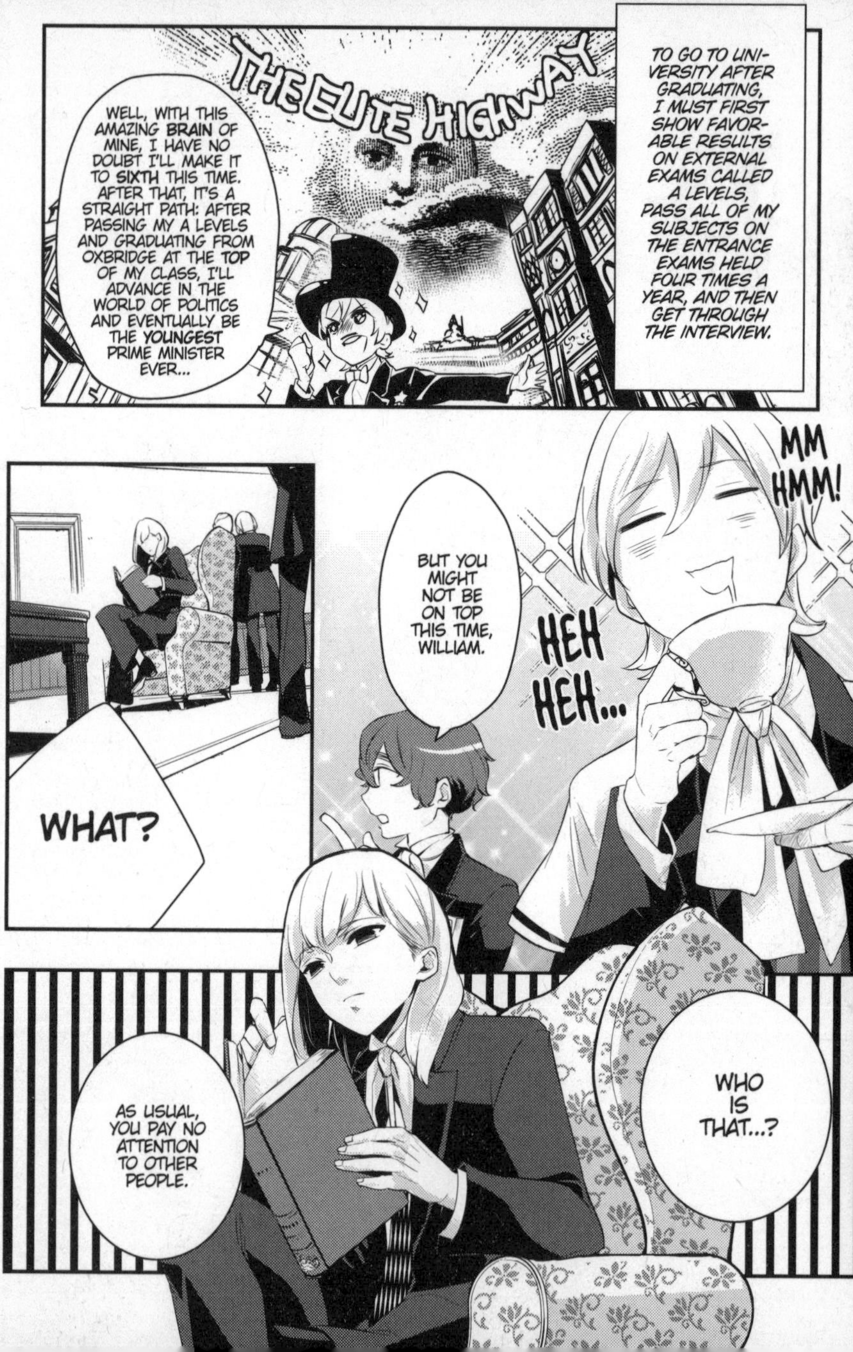

TO GO TO UNIVERSITY AFTER GRADUATING, I MUST FIRST SHOW FAVORABLE RESULTS ON EXTERNAL EXAMS CALLED A LEVELS, PASS ALL OF MY SUBJECTS ON THE ENTRANCE EXAMS HELD FOUR TIMES A YEAR, AND THEN GET THROUGH THE INTERVIEW.
THE ELITE HIGHWAY
WELL, WITH THIS AMAZING BRAIN OF MINE, I HAVE NO DOUBT I'LL MAKE IT TO SIXTH THIS TIME. AFTER THAT, IT'S A STRAIGHT PATH: AFTER PASSING MY A LEVELS AND GRADUATING FROM OXBRIDGE AT THE TOP OF MY CLASS, I'LL ADVANCE IN THE WORLD OF POLITICS AND EVENTUALLY BE THE YOUNGEST PRIME MINISTER EVER...
MM HMM!
HEH HEH...
BUT YOU MIGHT NOT BE ON TOP THIS TIME, WILLIAM.
WHAT?
WHO IS THAT...?
AS USUAL, YOU PAY NO ATTENTION TO OTHER PEOPLE.

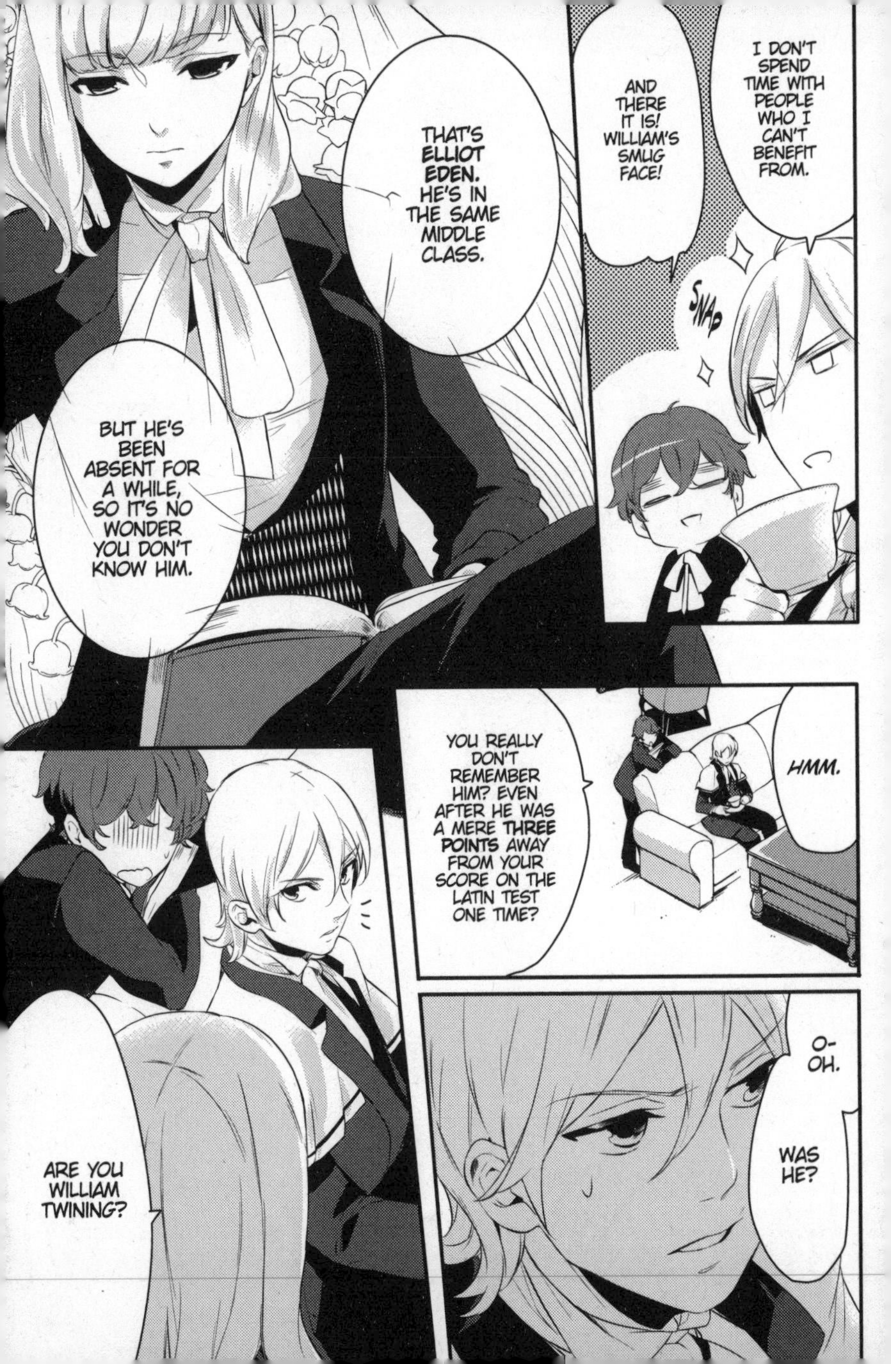
I DON'T SPEND TIME WITH PEOPLE WHO I CAN'T BENEFIT FROM.
AND THERE IT IS! WILLIAM'S SMUG FACE!
SNAP
THAT'S ELLIOT EDEN. HE'S IN THE SAME MIDDLE CLASS.
BUT HE'S BEEN ABSENT FOR A WHILE, SO IT'S NO WONDER YOU DON'T KNOW HIM.
HMM.
YOU REALLY DON'T REMEMBER HIM? EVEN AFTER HE WAS A MERE THREE POINTS AWAY FROM YOUR SCORE ON THE LATIN TEST ONE TIME?
O-OH.
WAS HE?
ARE YOU WILLIAM TWINING?

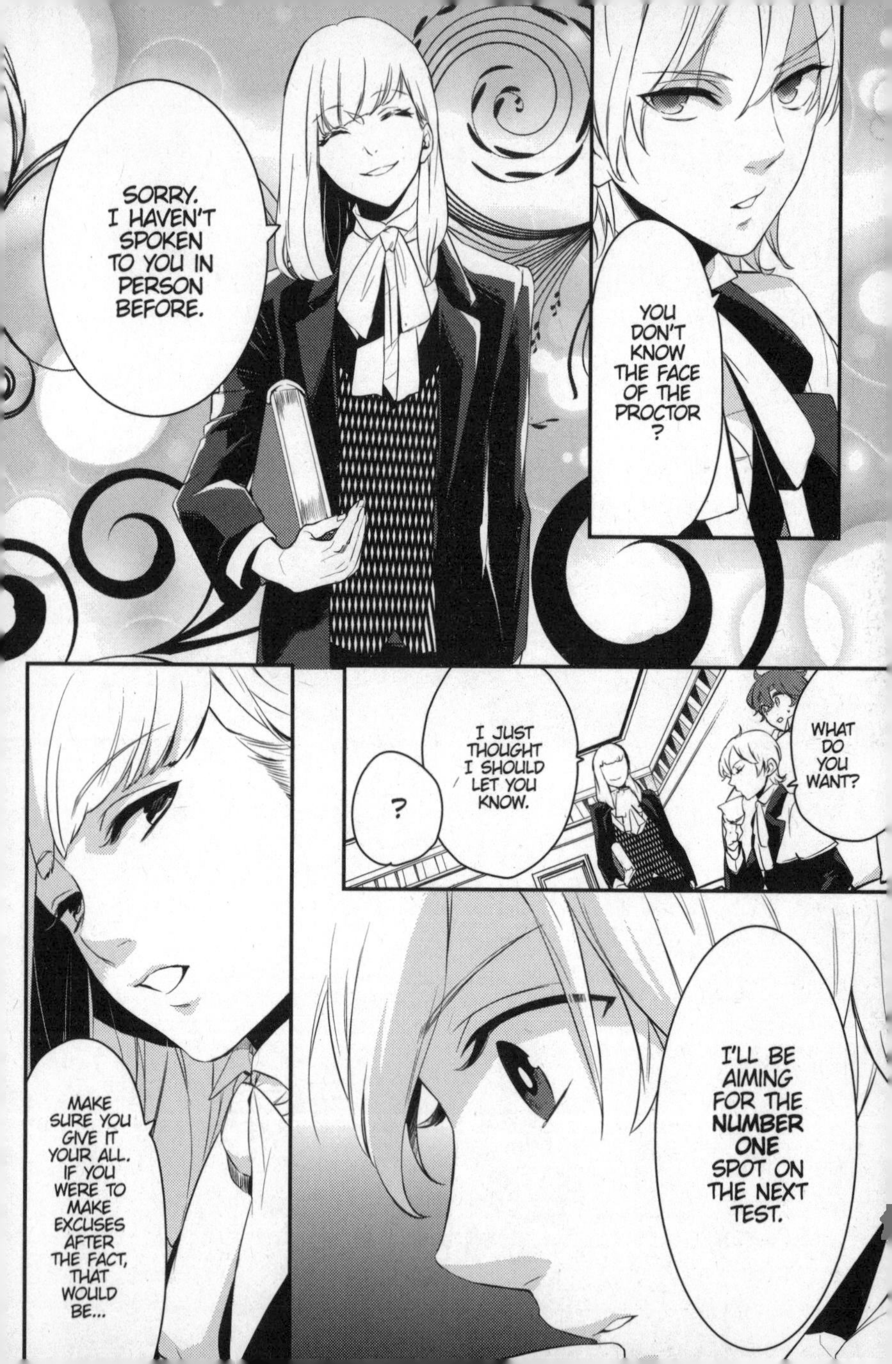
YOU DON'T KNOW THE FACE OF THE PROCTOR ?
SORRY. I HAVEN'T SPOKEN TO YOU IN PERSON BEFORE.
WHAT DO YOU WANT?
I JUST THOUGHT I SHOULD LET YOU KNOW.
?
I'LL BE AIMING FOR THE NUMBER ONE SPOT ON THE NEXT TEST.
MAKE SURE YOU GIVE IT YOUR ALL. IF YOU WERE TO MAKE EXCUSES AFTER THE FACT, THAT WOULD BE...

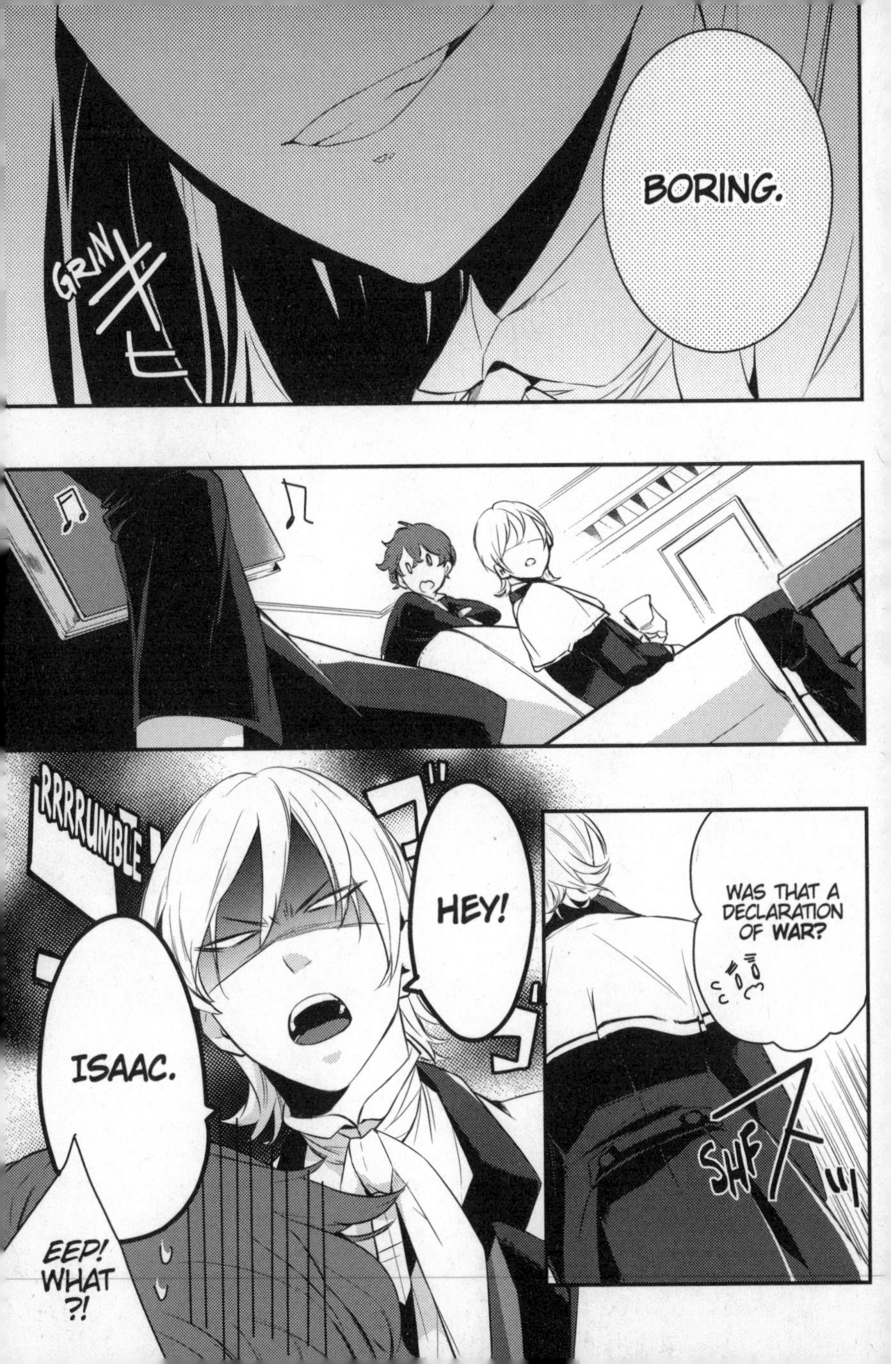
BORING.
GRIN
RRRRUMBLE
HEY!
WAS THAT A DECLARATION OF WAR?
ISAAC.
SHF
EEP! WHAT ?!

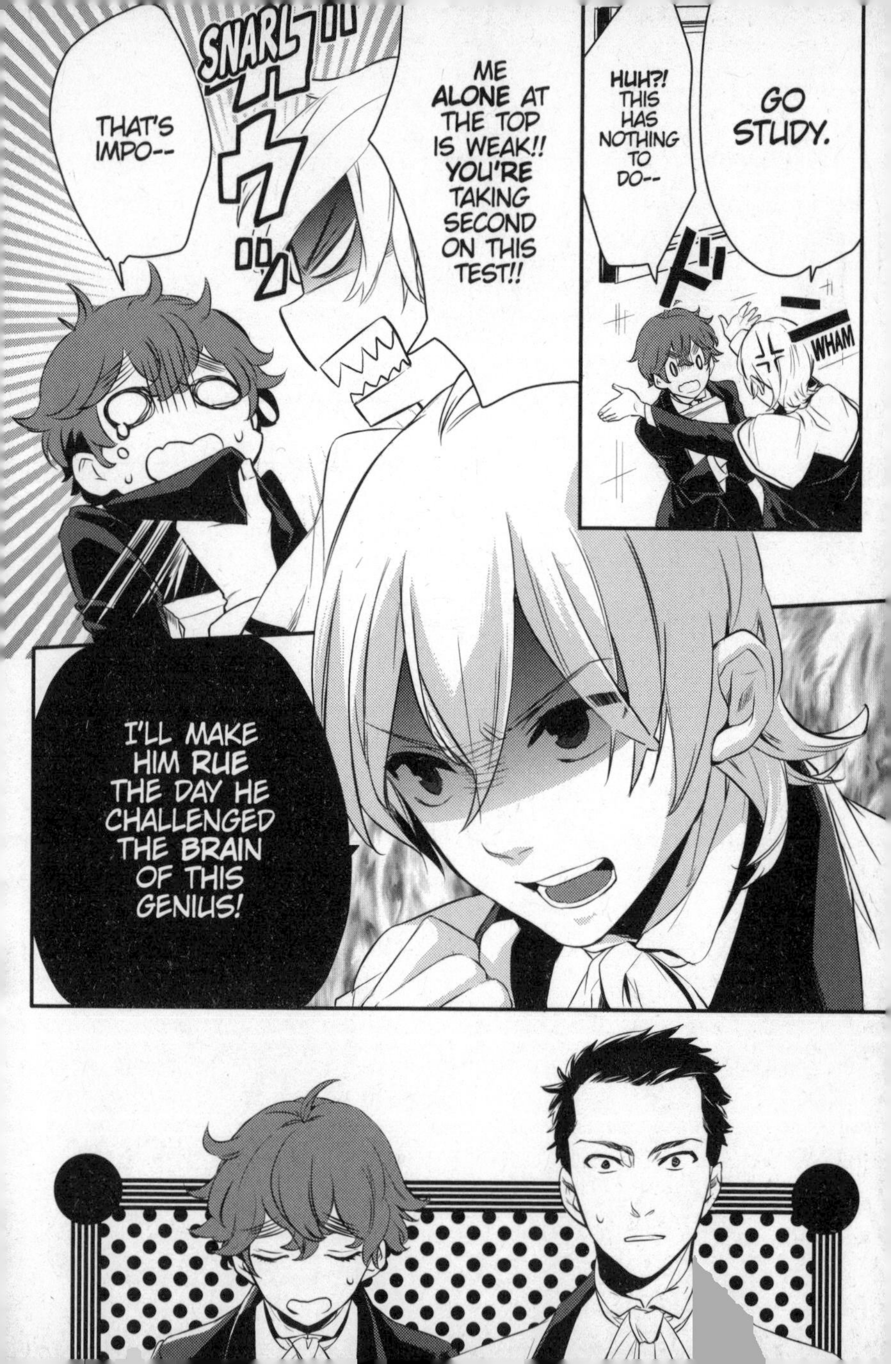
GO STUDY.
HUH?! THIS HAS NOTHING TO DO--
WHAM
ME ALONE AT THE TOP IS WEAK!! YOU'RE TAKING SECOND ON THIS TEST!!
SNARL
THAT'S IMPO--
I'LL MAKE HIM RUE THE DAY HE CHALLENGED THE BRAIN OF THIS GENIUS!

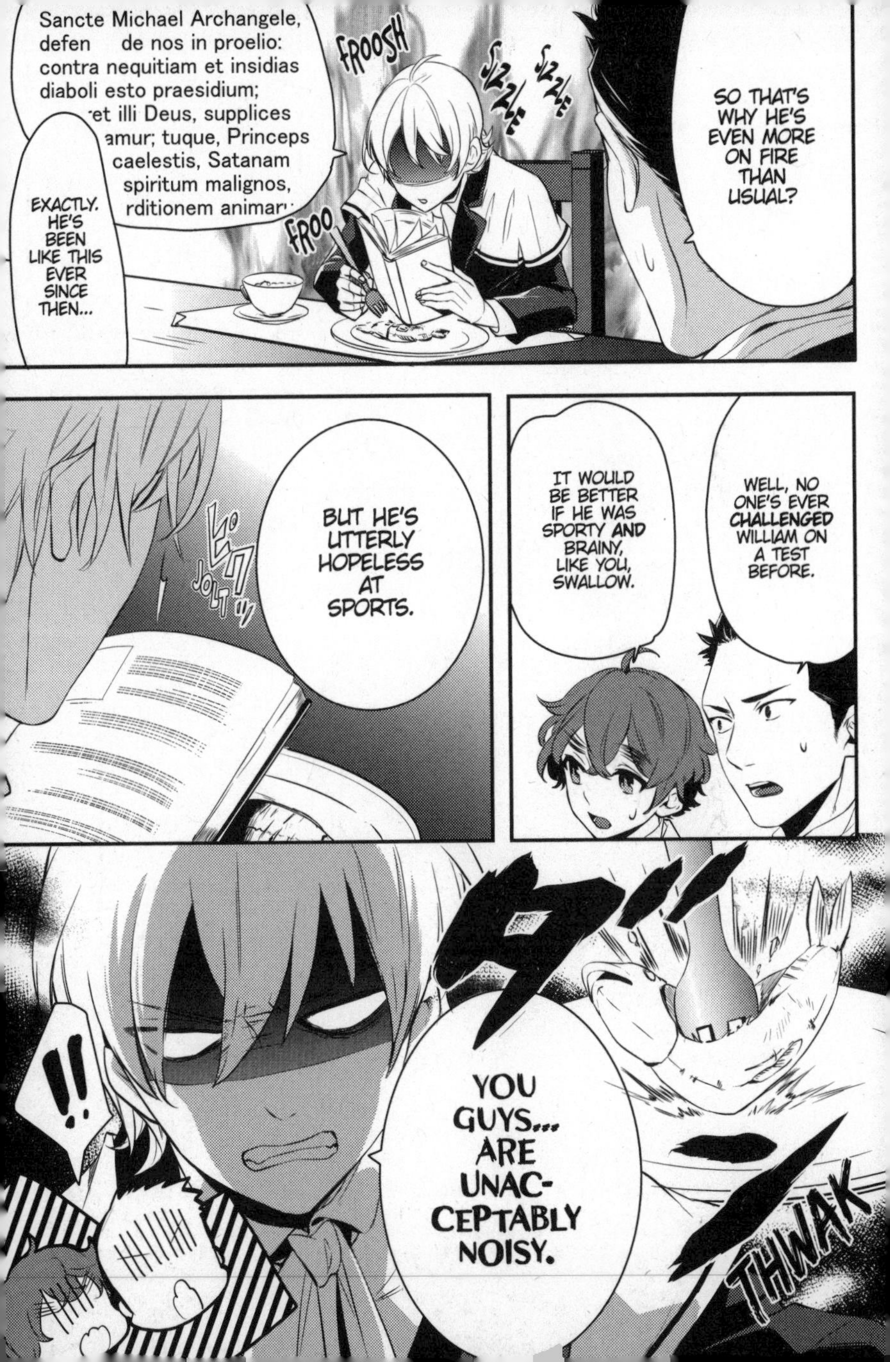
SO THAT'S WHY HE'S EVEN MORE ON FIRE THAN USUAL?
SIZZLE
SIZZLE
FROOSH
Sancte Michael Archangele,
defen de nos in proelio:
contra nequitiam et insidias
diaboli esto praesidium;
et illi Deus, supplices
amur; tuque, Princeps
caelestis, Satanam
spiritum malignos,
rditionem animaru
FROO
EXACTLY. HE'S BEEN LIKE THIS EVER SINCE THEN...
WELL, NO ONE'S EVER CHALLENGED WILLIAM ON A TEST BEFORE.
IT WOULD BE BETTER IF HE WAS SPORTY AND BRAINY, LIKE YOU, SWALLOW.
BUT HE'S UTTERLY HOPELESS AT SPORTS.
JOLT
THWAK
YOU GUYS... ARE UNAC- CEPTABLY NOISY.
!!

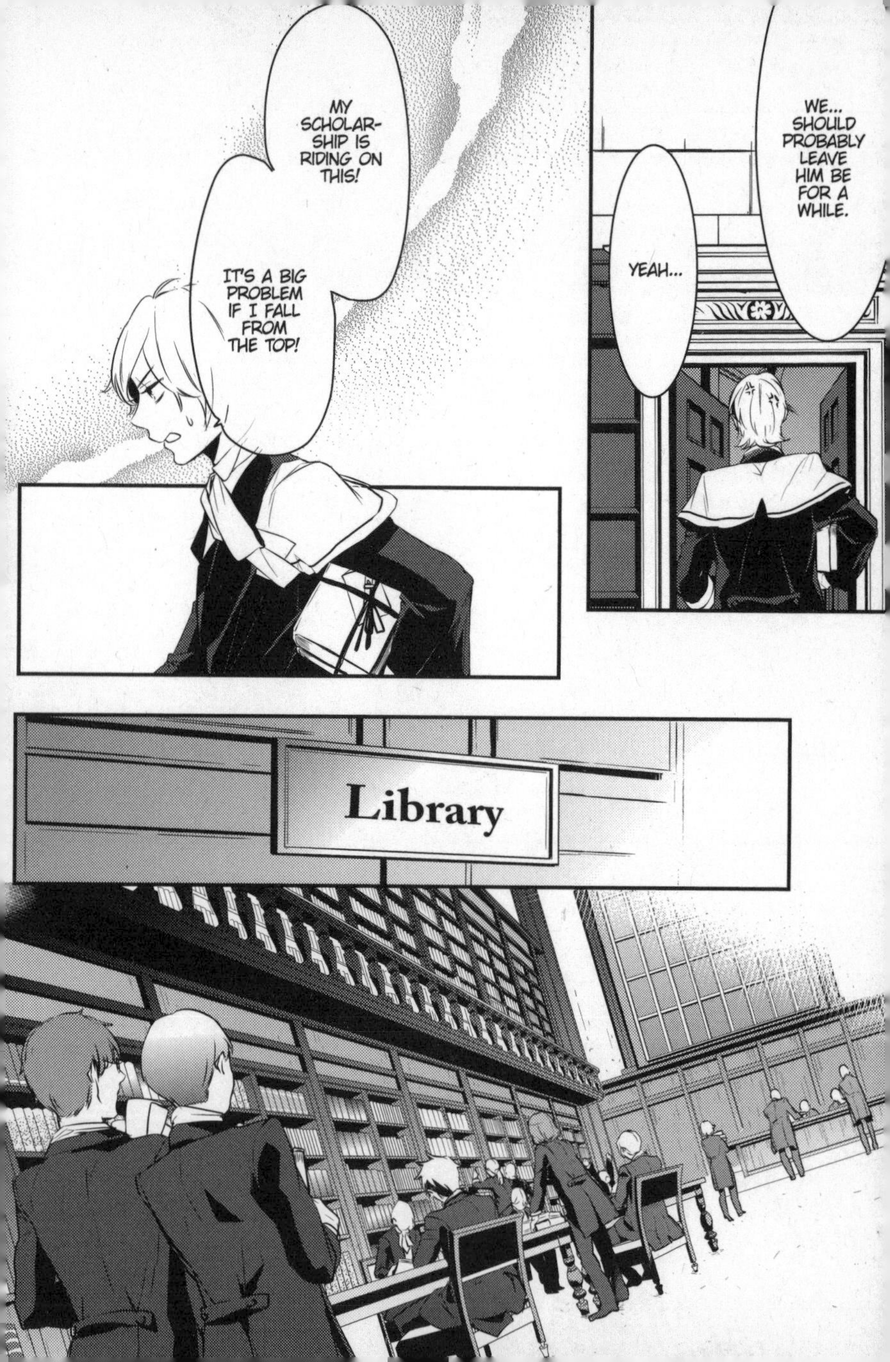
WE... SHOULD PROBABLY LEAVE HIM BE FOR A WHILE.
YEAH...
MY SCHOLAR-SHIP IS RIDING ON THIS!
IT'S A BIG PROBLEM IF I FALL FROM THE TOP!
Library

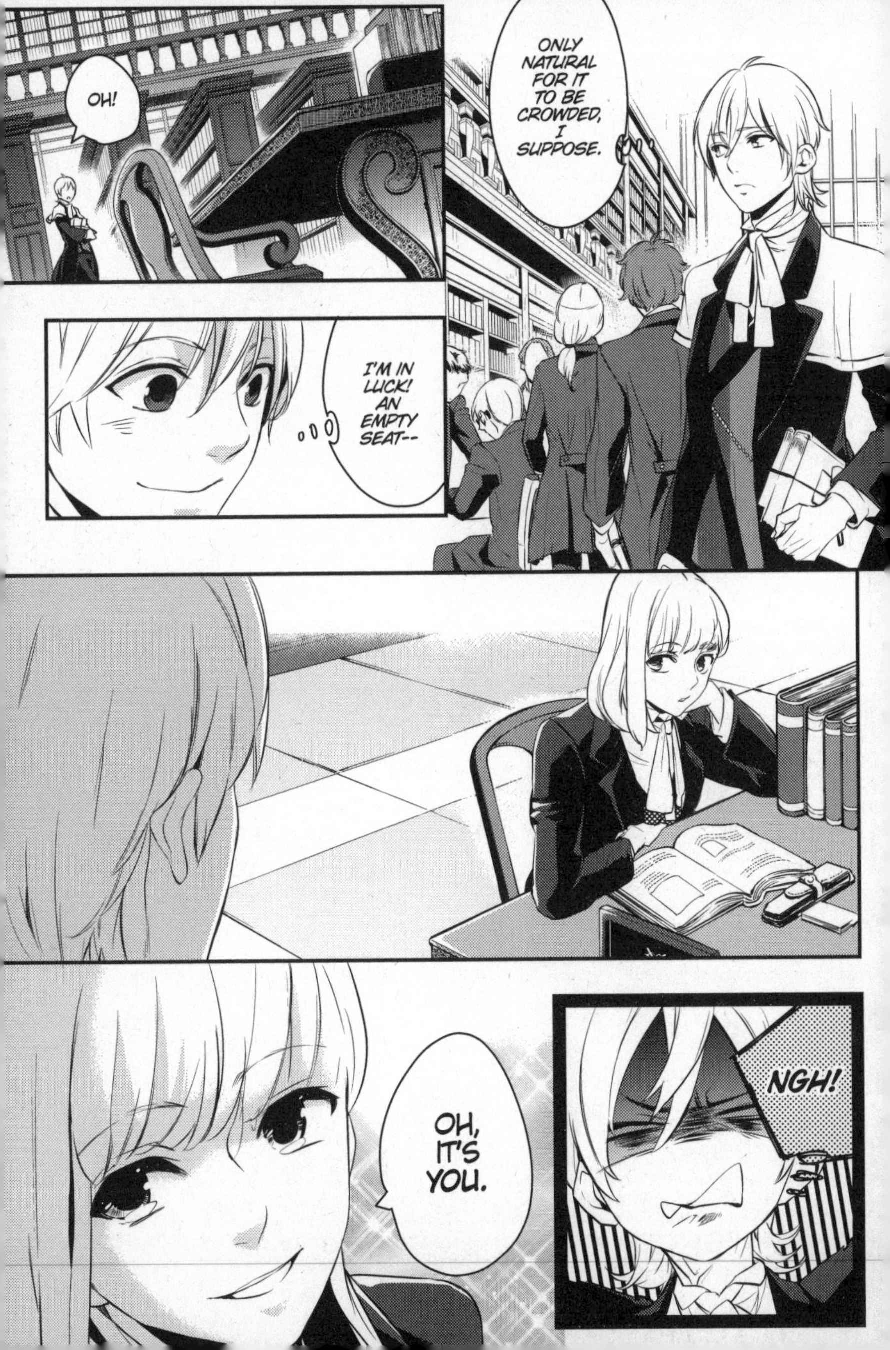
ONLY NATURAL FOR IT TO BE CROWDED, I SUPPOSE.
OH!
I'M IN LUCK! AN EMPTY SEAT--
OH, IT'S YOU.
NGH!

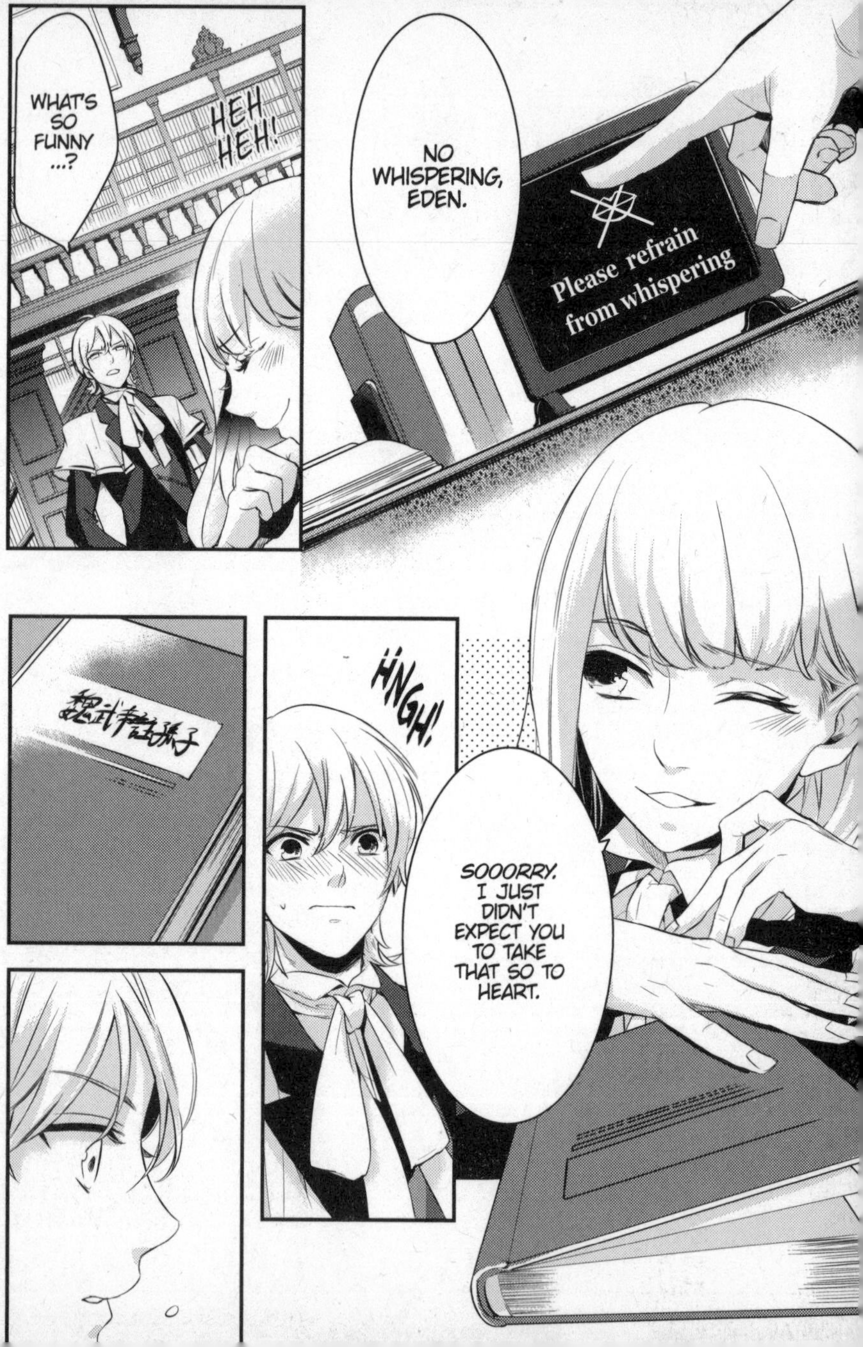
NO WHISPERING, EDEN.
Please refrain from whispering
HEH HEH!
WHAT'S SO FUNNY ...?
SOOORRY. I JUST DIDN'T EXPECT YOU TO TAKE THAT SO TO HEART.
HNGH!

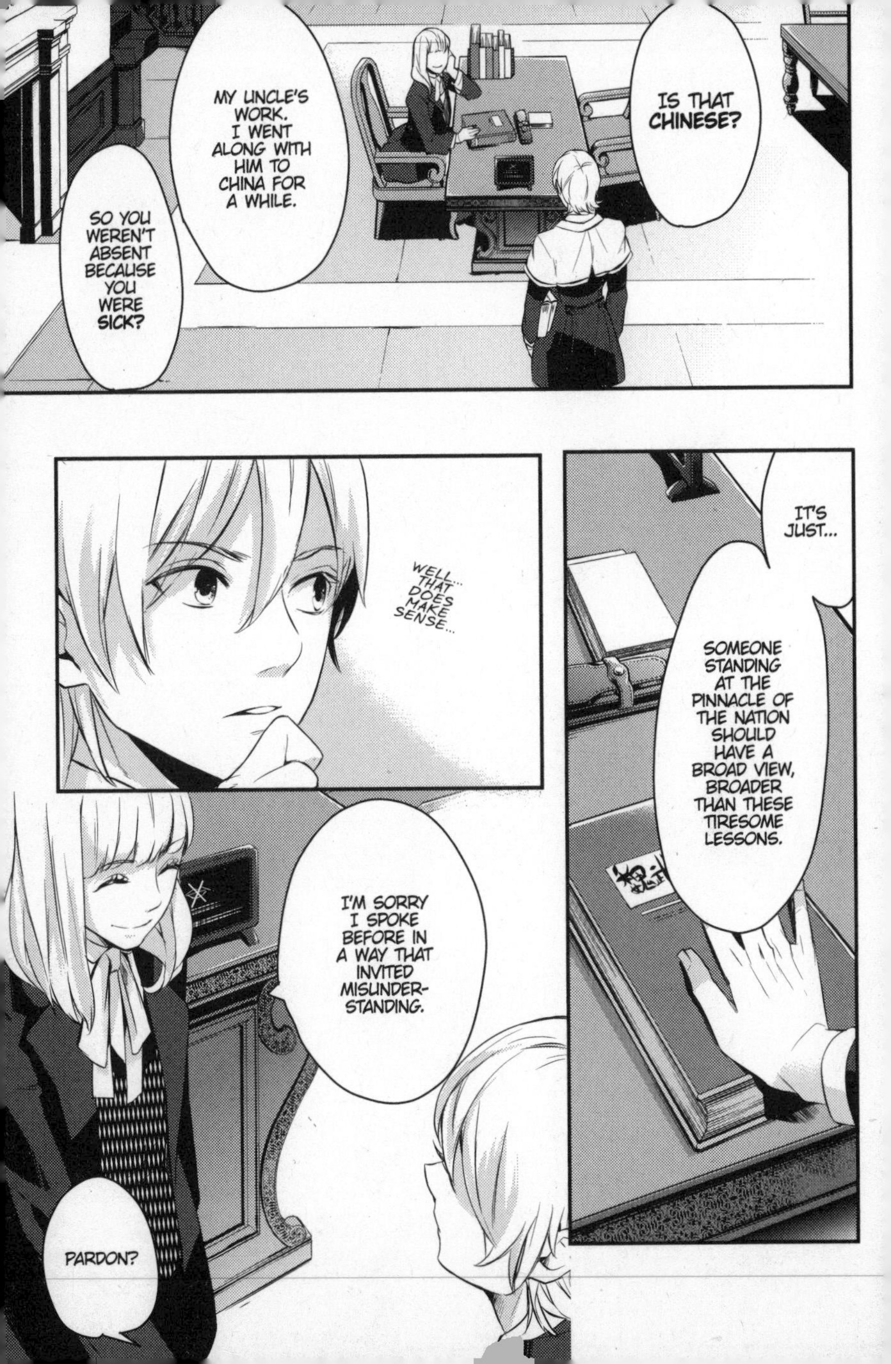
IS THAT CHINESE?
MY UNCLE'S WORK. I WENT ALONG WITH HIM TO CHINA FOR A WHILE.
SO YOU WEREN'T ABSENT BECAUSE YOU WERE SICK?
IT'S JUST...
SOMEONE STANDING AT THE PINNACLE OF THE NATION SHOULD HAVE A BROAD VIEW, BROADER THAN THESE TIRESOME LESSONS.
WELL... THAT DOES MAKE SENSE...
I'M SORRY I SPOKE BEFORE IN A WAY THAT INVITED MISUNDER-STANDING.
PARDON?

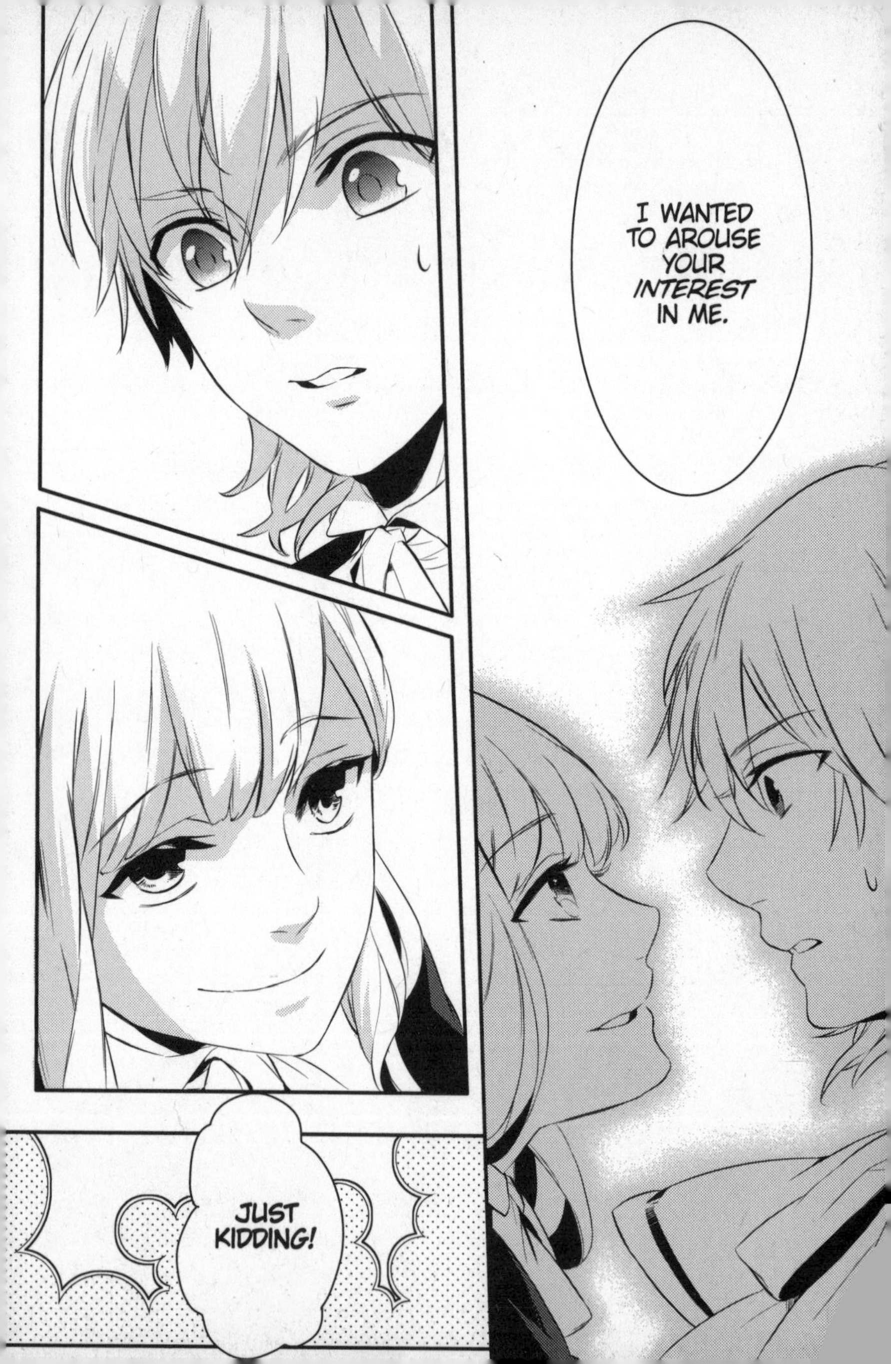
I WANTED TO AROUSE YOUR *INTEREST* IN ME.
JUST KIDDING!

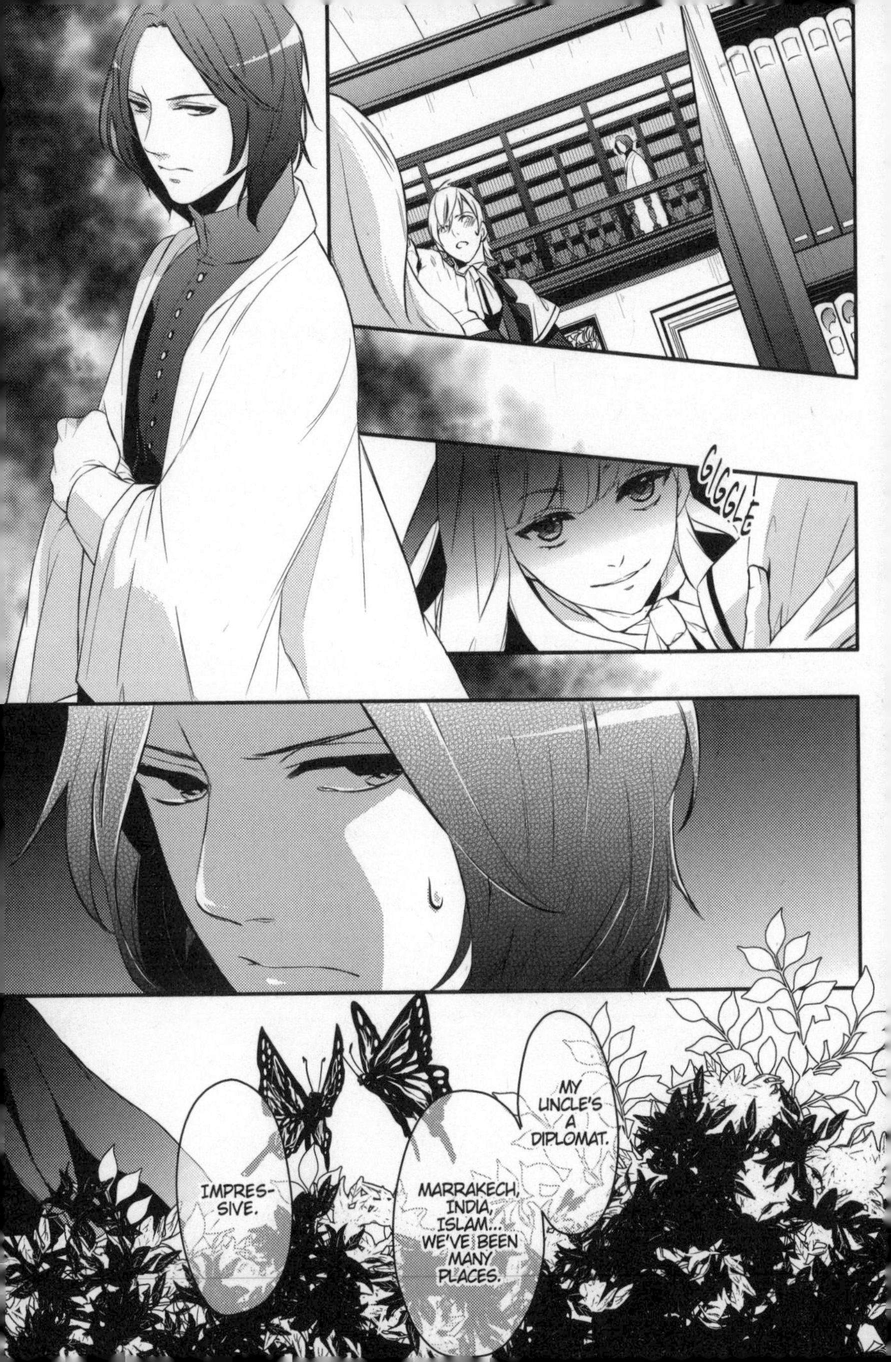
GIGGLE
MY UNCLE'S A DIPLOMAT.
MARRAKECH, INDIA, ISLAM... WE'VE BEEN MANY PLACES.
IMPRES-SIVE.

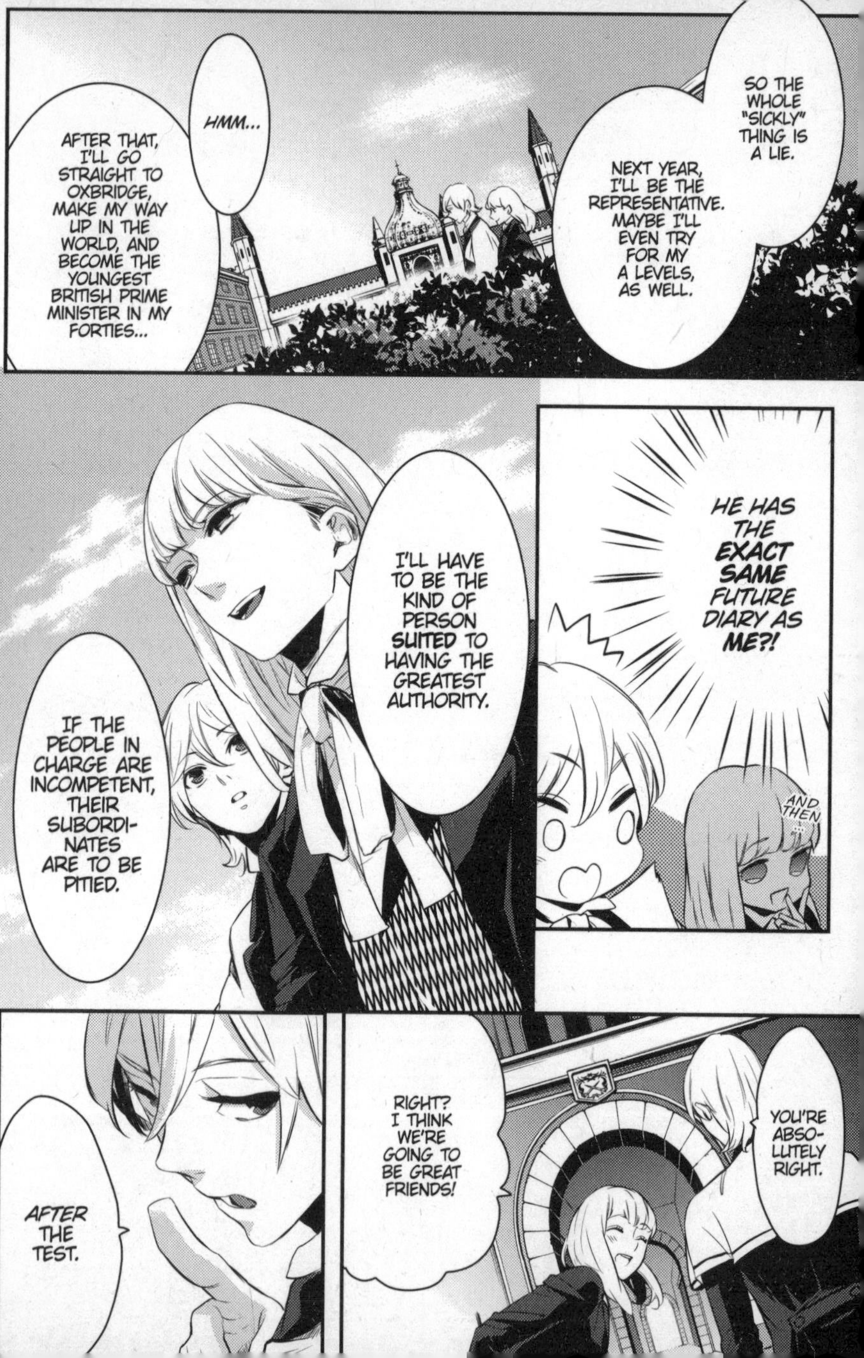
SO THE WHOLE "SICKLY" THING IS A LIE.
NEXT YEAR, I'LL BE THE REPRESENTATIVE. MAYBE I'LL EVEN TRY FOR MY A LEVELS, AS WELL.
HMM...
AFTER THAT, I'LL GO STRAIGHT TO OXBRIDGE, MAKE MY WAY UP IN THE WORLD, AND BECOME THE YOUNGEST BRITISH PRIME MINISTER IN MY FORTIES...
HE HAS THE **EXACT SAME** FUTURE DIARY AS **ME?!**
AND THEN...
I'LL HAVE TO BE THE KIND OF PERSON **SUITED** TO HAVING THE GREATEST AUTHORITY.
IF THE PEOPLE IN CHARGE ARE INCOMPETENT, THEIR SUBORDI-NATES ARE TO BE PITIED.
YOU'RE ABSO-LUTELY RIGHT.
RIGHT? I THINK WE'RE GOING TO BE GREAT FRIENDS!
AFTER THE TEST.

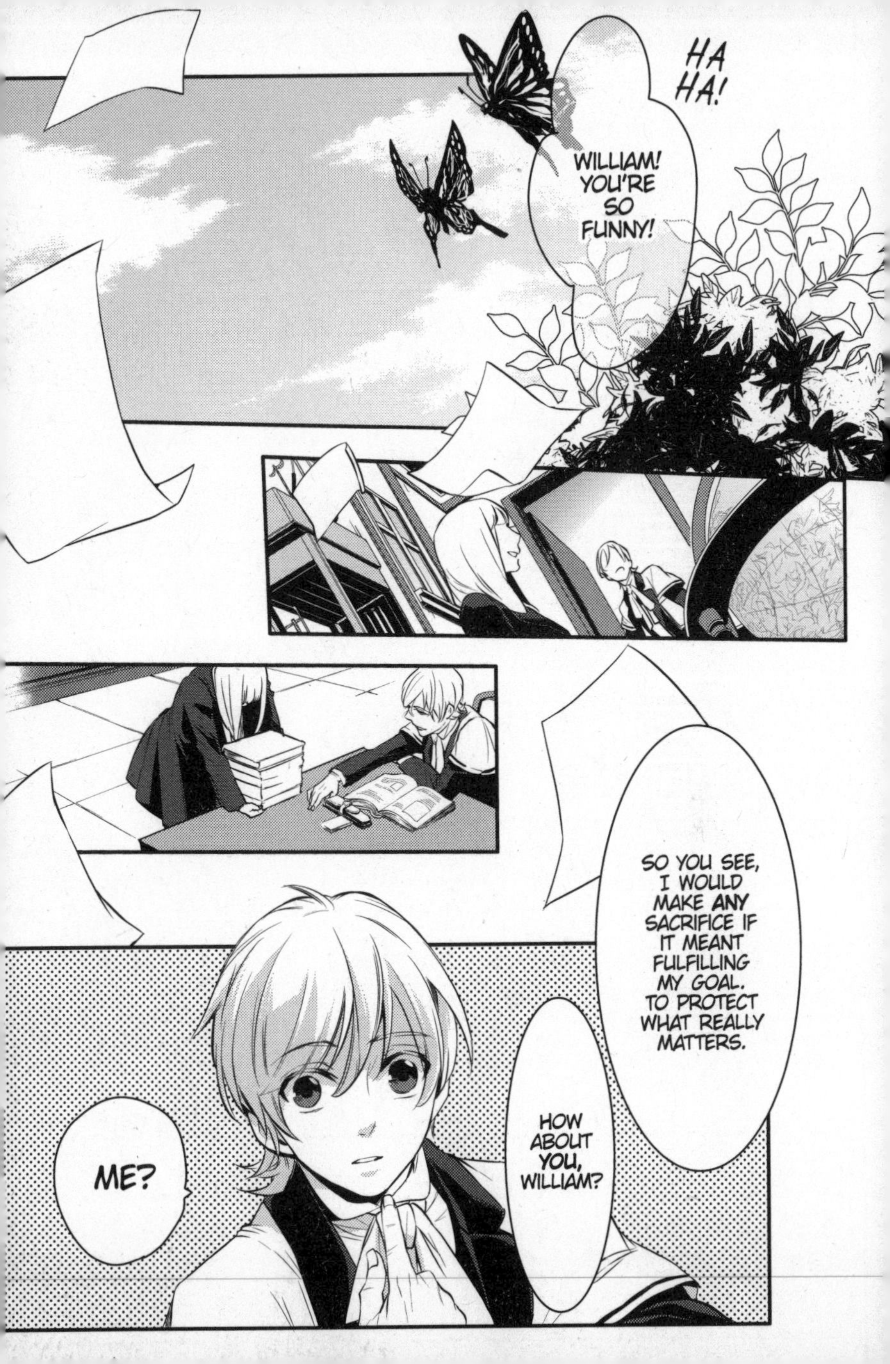

HA HA!
WILLIAM! YOU'RE SO FUNNY!
SO YOU SEE, I WOULD MAKE ANY SACRIFICE IF IT MEANT FULFILLING MY GOAL. TO PROTECT WHAT REALLY MATTERS.
HOW ABOUT YOU, WILLIAM?
ME?

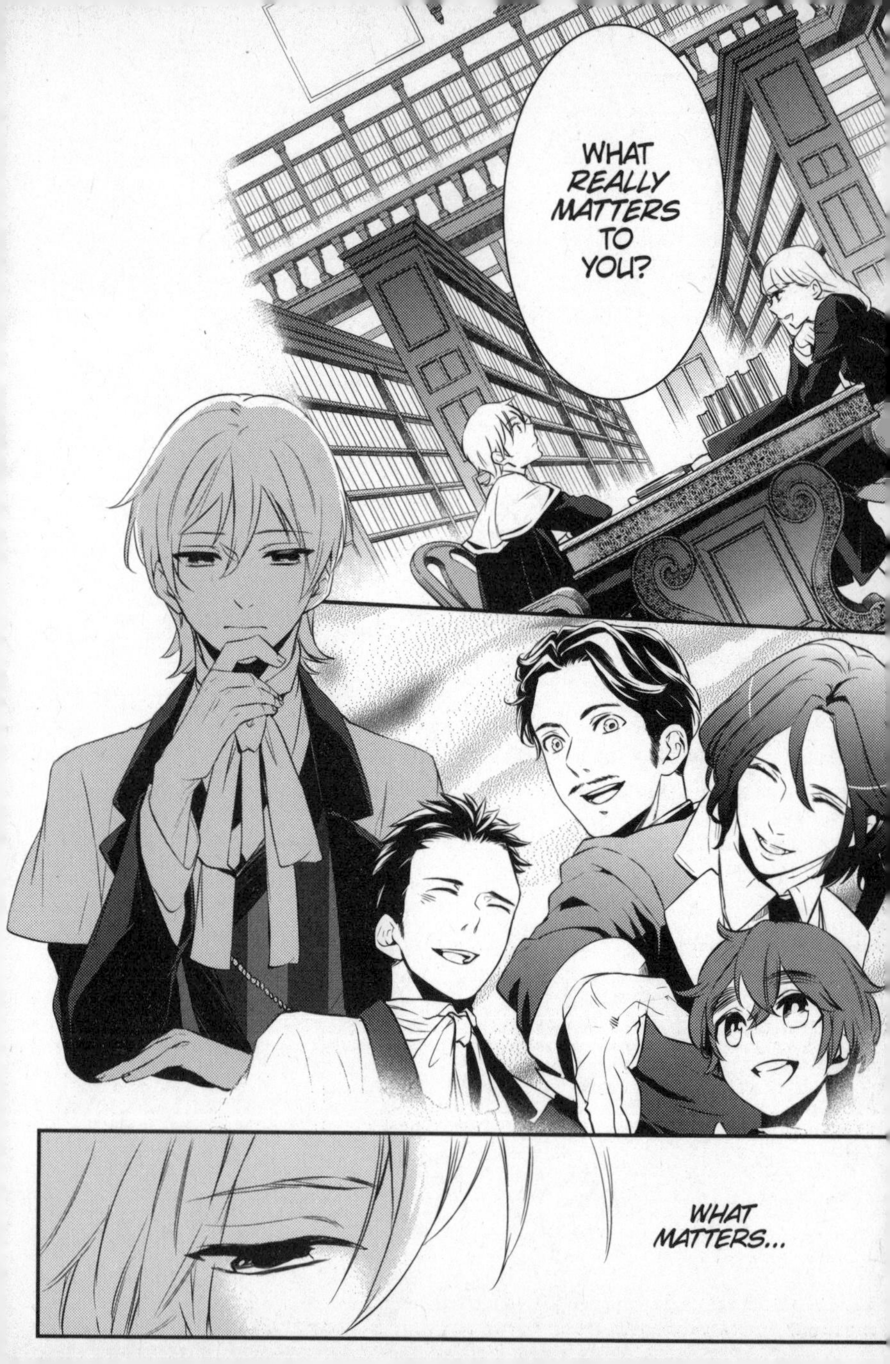
WHAT REALLY MATTERS TO YOU?
WHAT MATTERS...

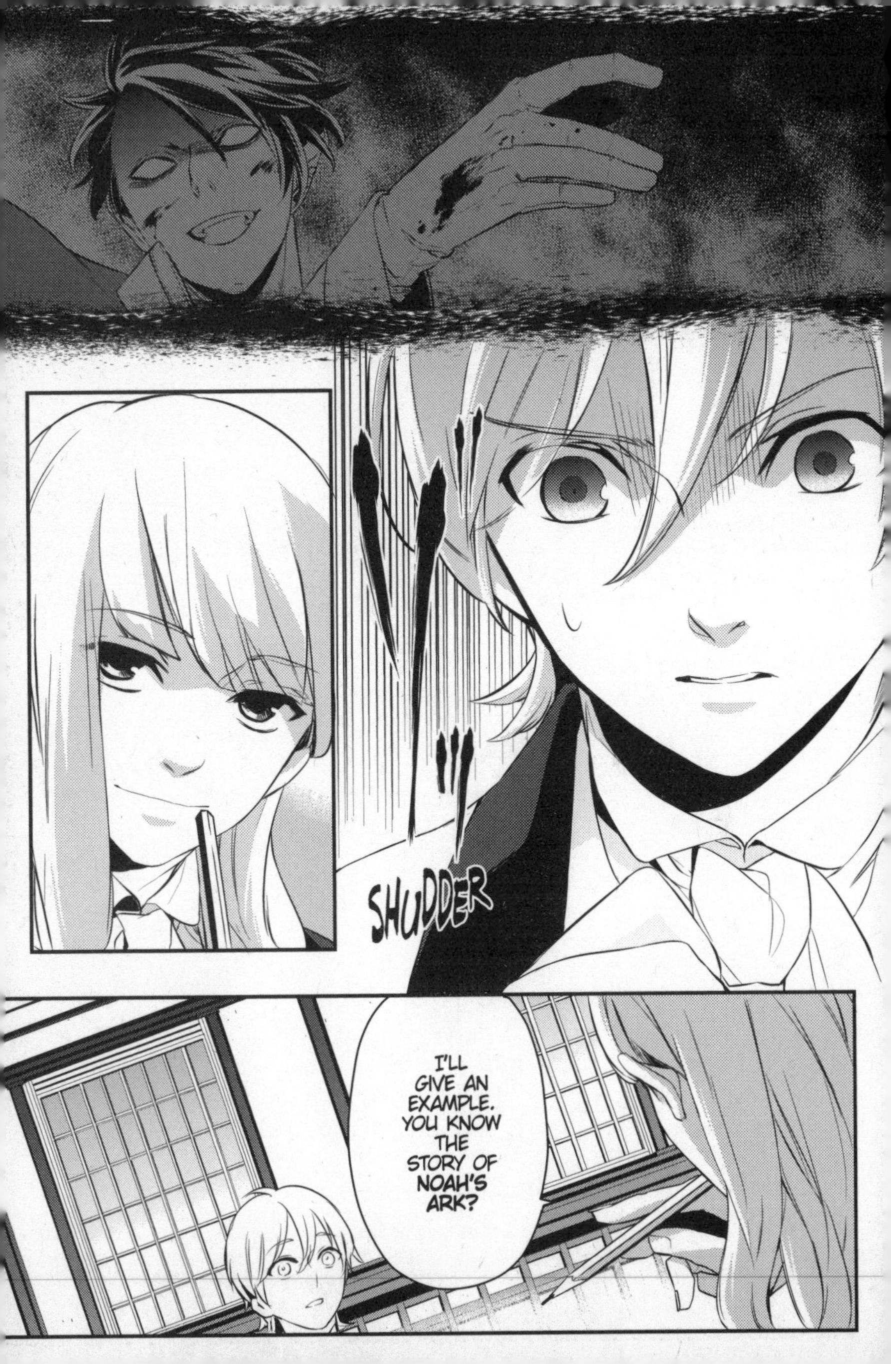
SHUDDER
I'LL GIVE AN EXAMPLE. YOU KNOW THE STORY OF NOAH'S ARK?

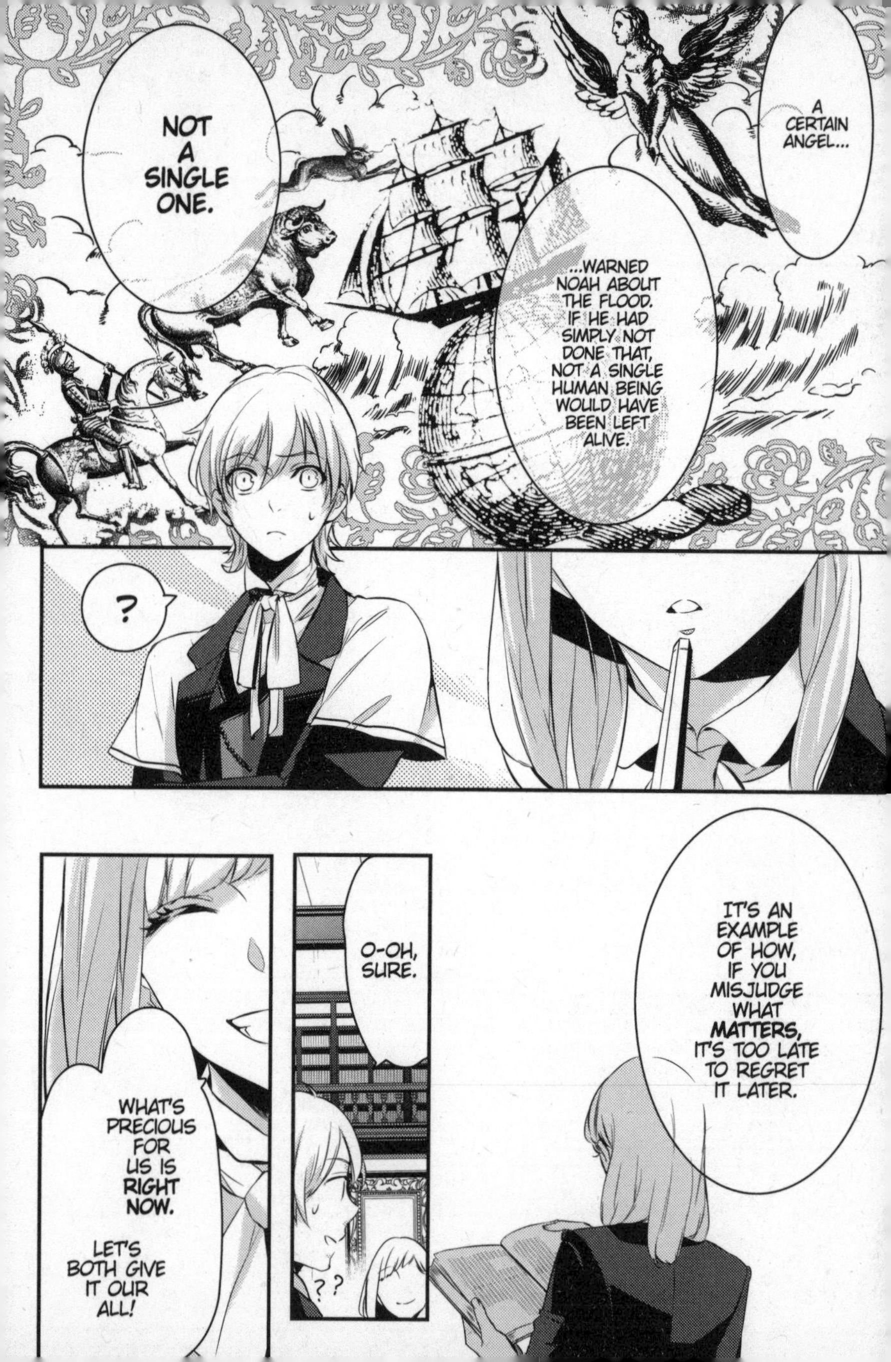
A CERTAIN ANGEL...
...WARNED NOAH ABOUT THE FLOOD. IF HE HAD SIMPLY NOT DONE THAT, NOT A SINGLE HUMAN BEING WOULD HAVE BEEN LEFT ALIVE.
NOT A SINGLE ONE.
?
IT'S AN EXAMPLE OF HOW, IF YOU MISJUDGE WHAT MATTERS, IT'S TOO LATE TO REGRET IT LATER.
O-OH, SURE.
??
WHAT'S PRECIOUS FOR US IS RIGHT NOW.
LET'S BOTH GIVE IT OUR ALL!

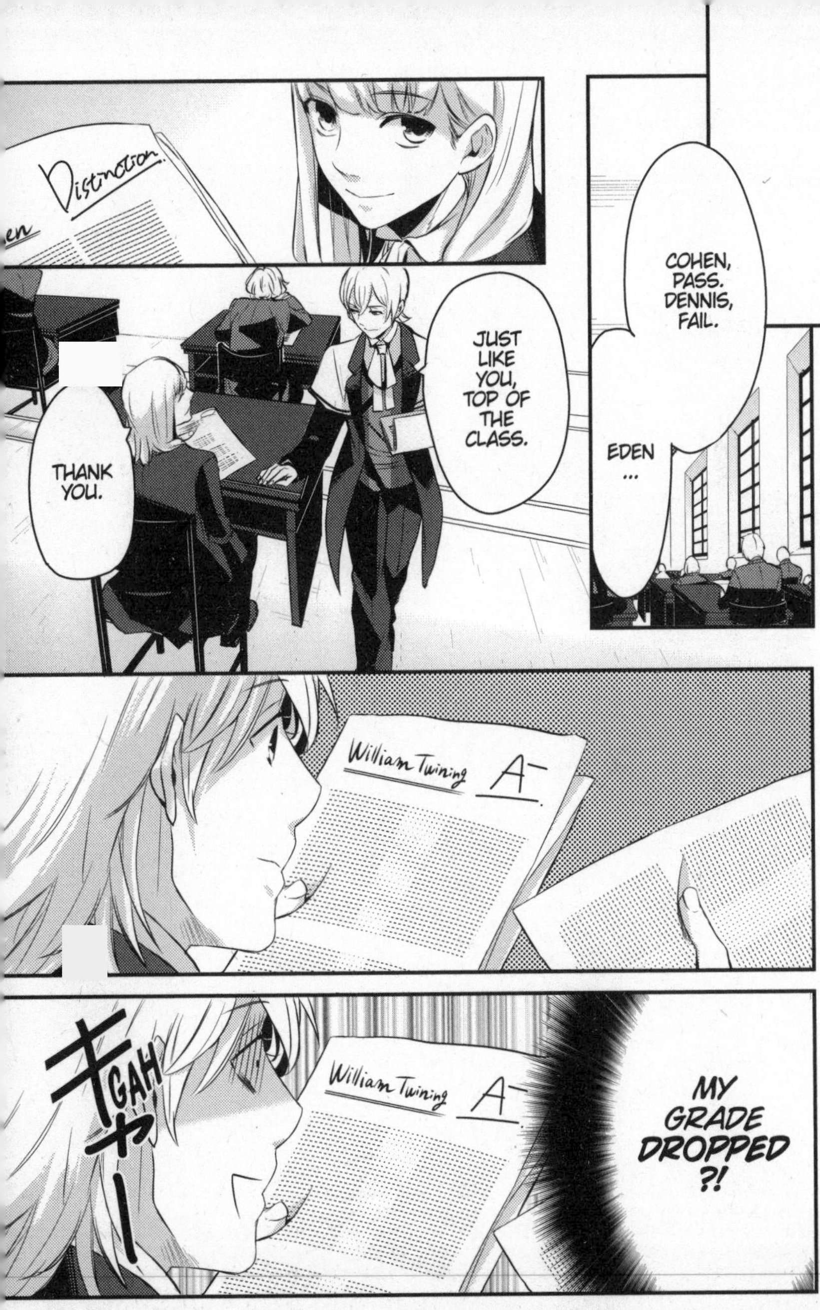
COHEN, PASS. DENNIS, FAIL.
EDEN ...
Distinction
JUST LIKE YOU, TOP OF THE CLASS.
THANK YOU.
William Twining A−
ギャー GAH
William Twining A−
MY GRADE DROPPED ?!

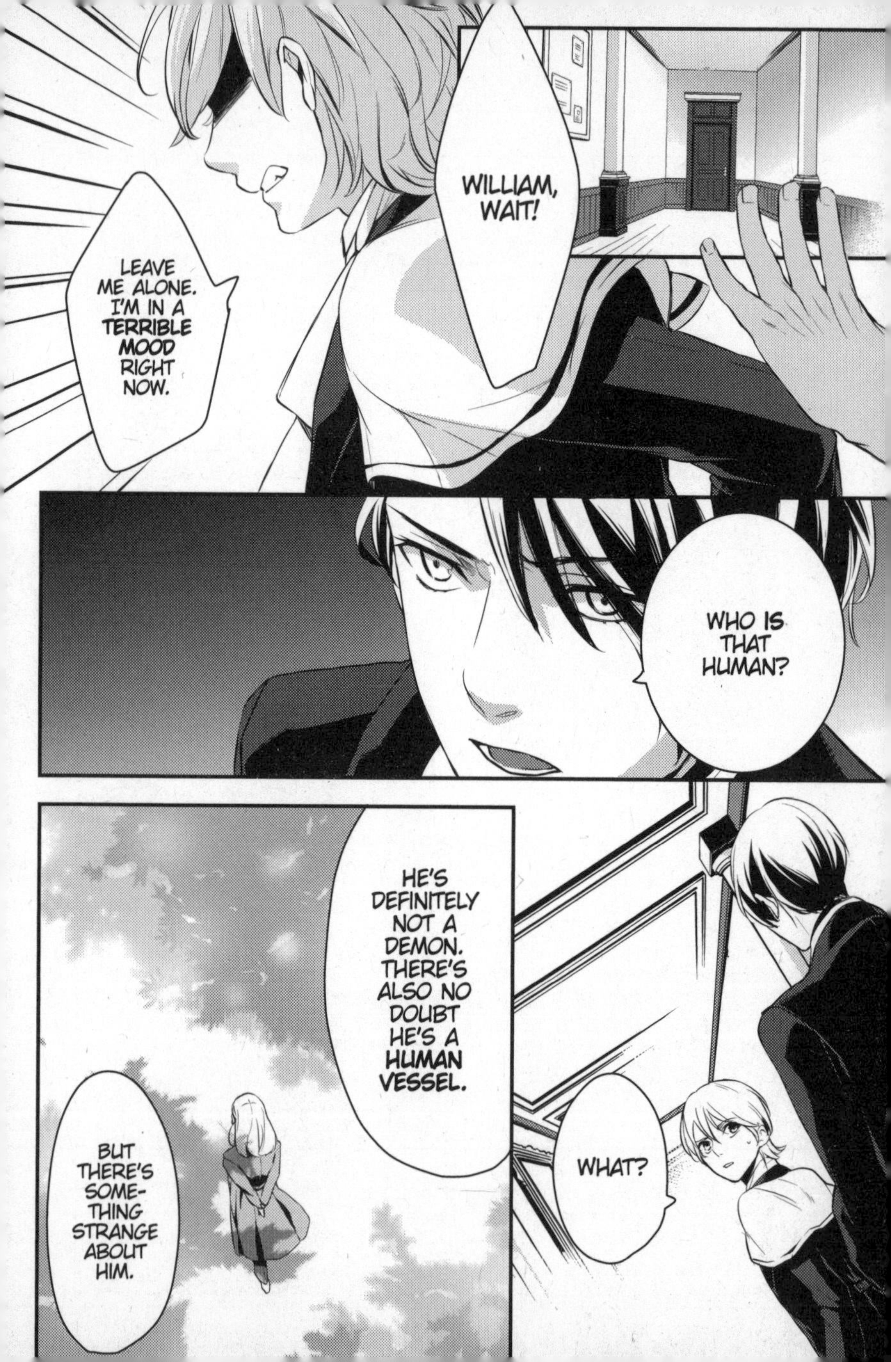
WILLIAM, WAIT!
LEAVE ME ALONE. I'M IN A TERRIBLE MOOD RIGHT NOW.
WHO IS THAT HUMAN?
WHAT?
HE'S DEFINITELY NOT A DEMON. THERE'S ALSO NO DOUBT HE'S A HUMAN VESSEL.
BUT THERE'S SOME-THING STRANGE ABOUT HIM.

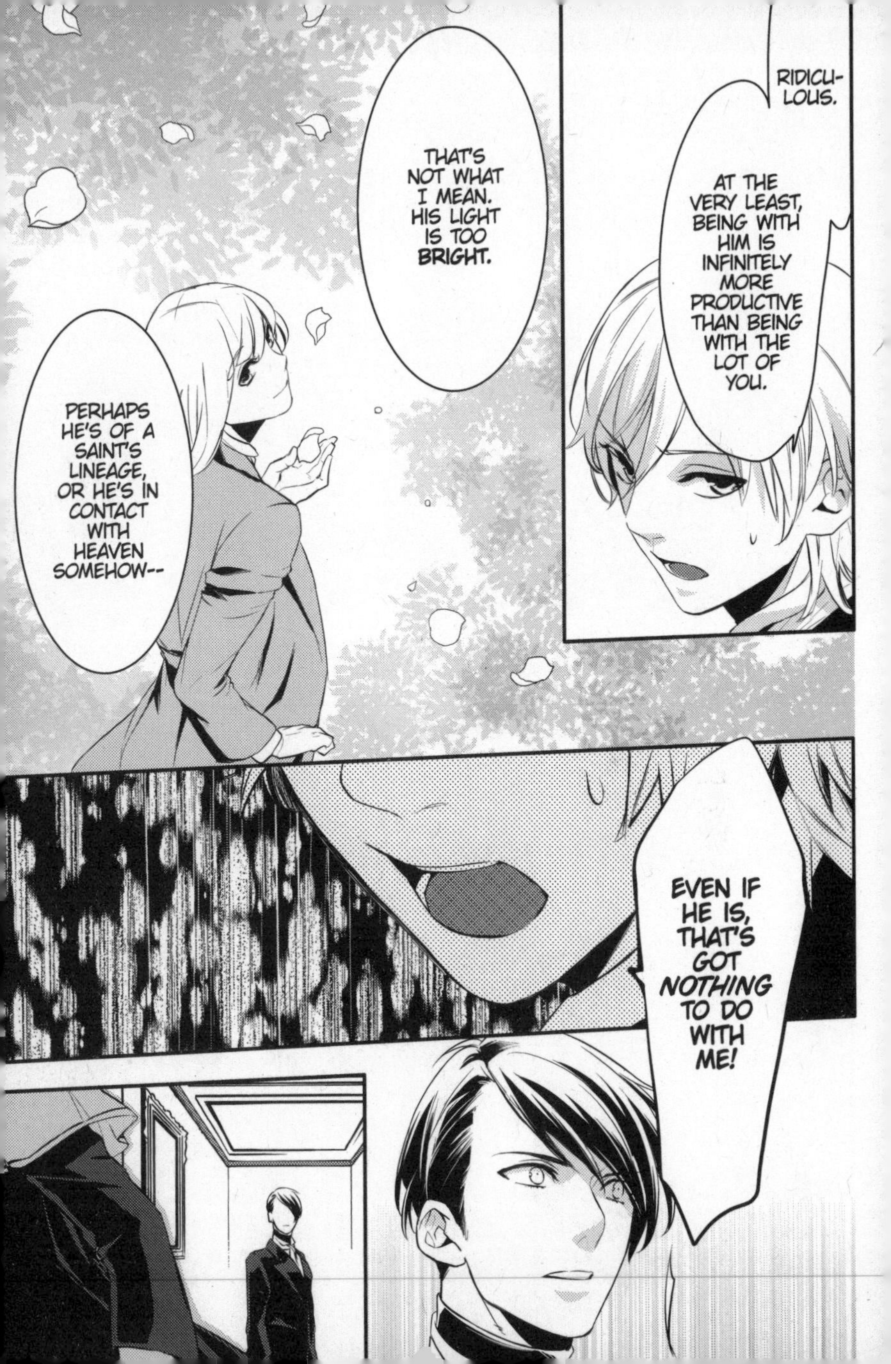
RIDICULOUS.
AT THE VERY LEAST, BEING WITH HIM IS INFINITELY MORE PRODUCTIVE THAN BEING WITH THE LOT OF YOU.
THAT'S NOT WHAT I MEAN. HIS LIGHT IS TOO BRIGHT.
PERHAPS HE'S OF A SAINT'S LINEAGE, OR HE'S IN CONTACT WITH HEAVEN SOMEHOW--
EVEN IF HE IS, THAT'S GOT *NOTHING* TO DO WITH ME!

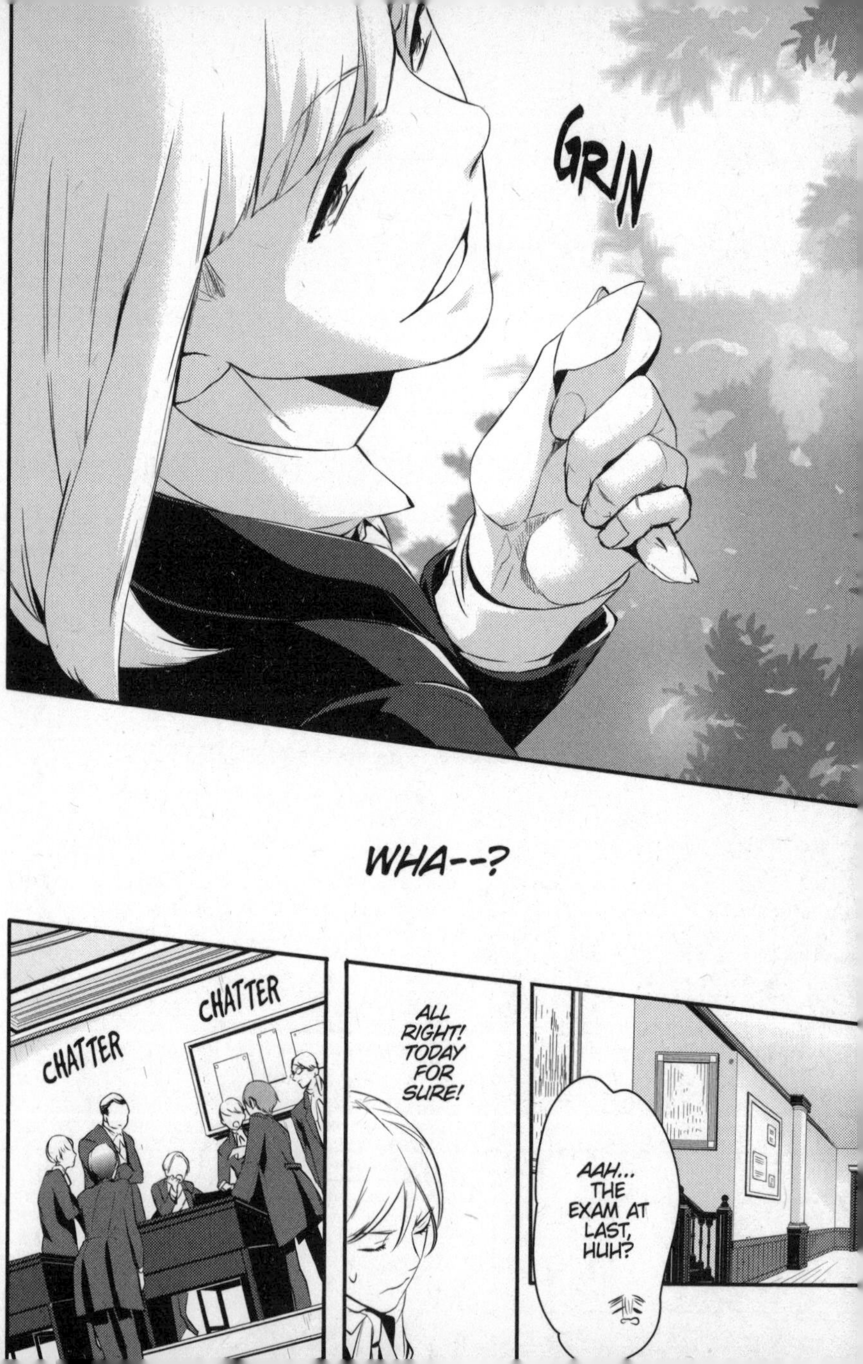
GRIN
WHA--?
AAH... THE EXAM AT LAST, HUH?
ALL RIGHT! TODAY FOR SURE!
CHATTER
CHATTER

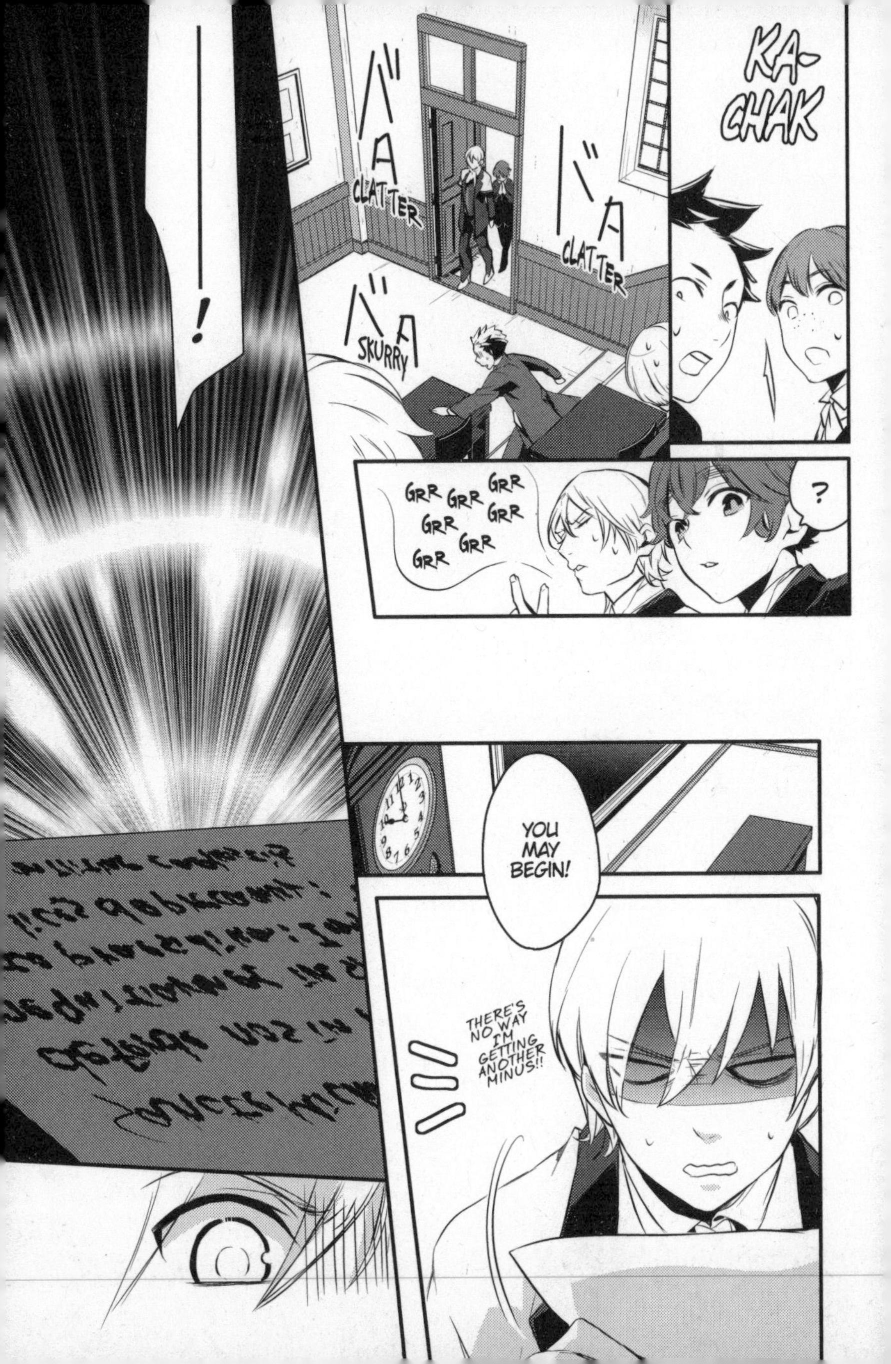

KA-CHAK
バ
CLATTER
バ
CLATTER
バ
SKURRY
?
GRR GRR GRR GRR GRR GRR GRR
YOU MAY BEGIN!
THERE'S NO WAY I'M GETTING ANOTHER MINUS!!
——!

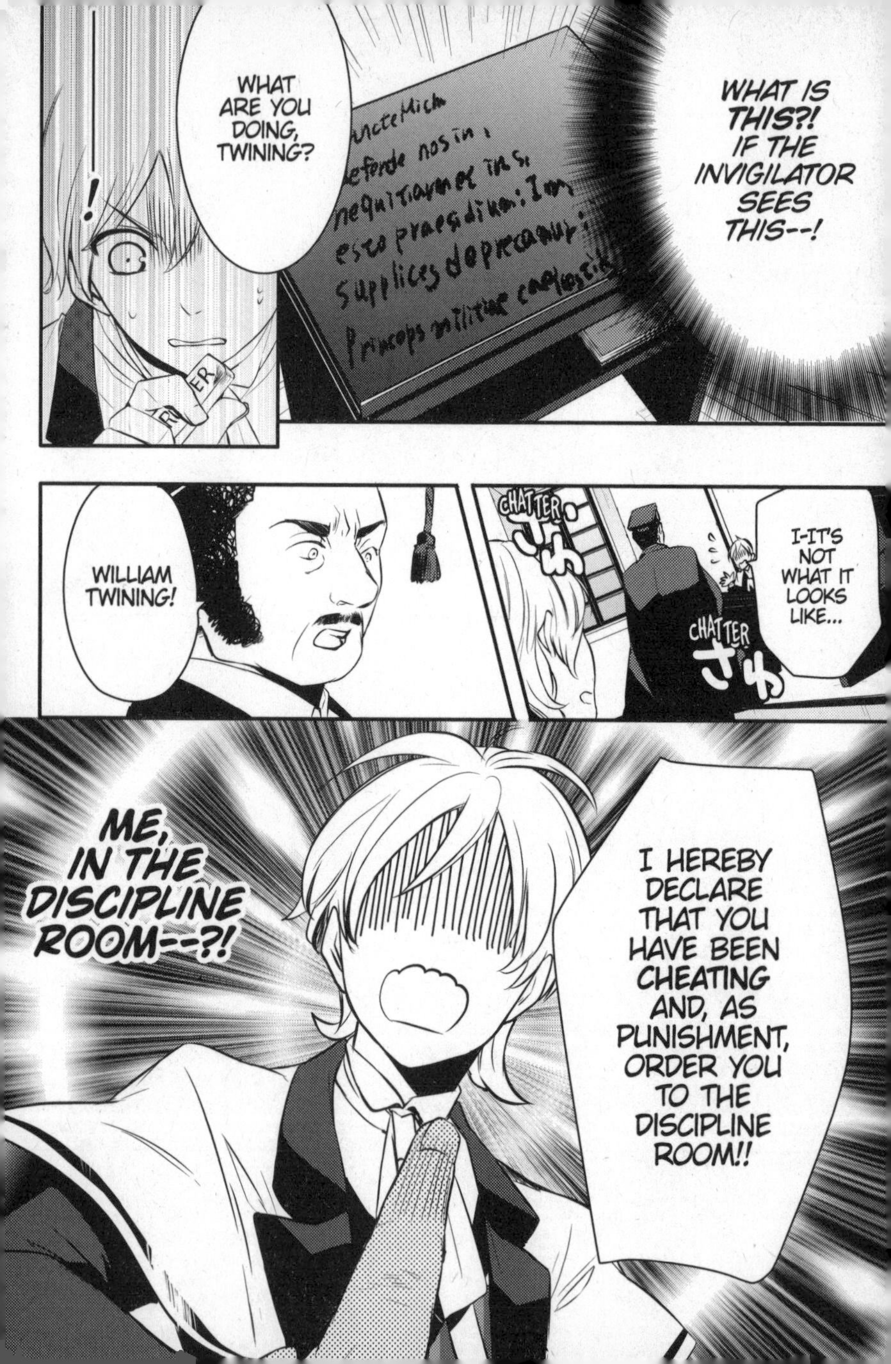
WHAT IS THIS?! IF THE INVIGILATOR SEES THIS--!
WHAT ARE YOU DOING, TWINING?
CHATTER
I-IT'S NOT WHAT IT LOOKS LIKE...
CHATTER
WILLIAM TWINING!
I HEREBY DECLARE THAT YOU HAVE BEEN CHEATING AND, AS PUNISHMENT, ORDER YOU TO THE DISCIPLINE ROOM!!
ME, IN THE DISCIPLINE ROOM--?!

Pillar 22

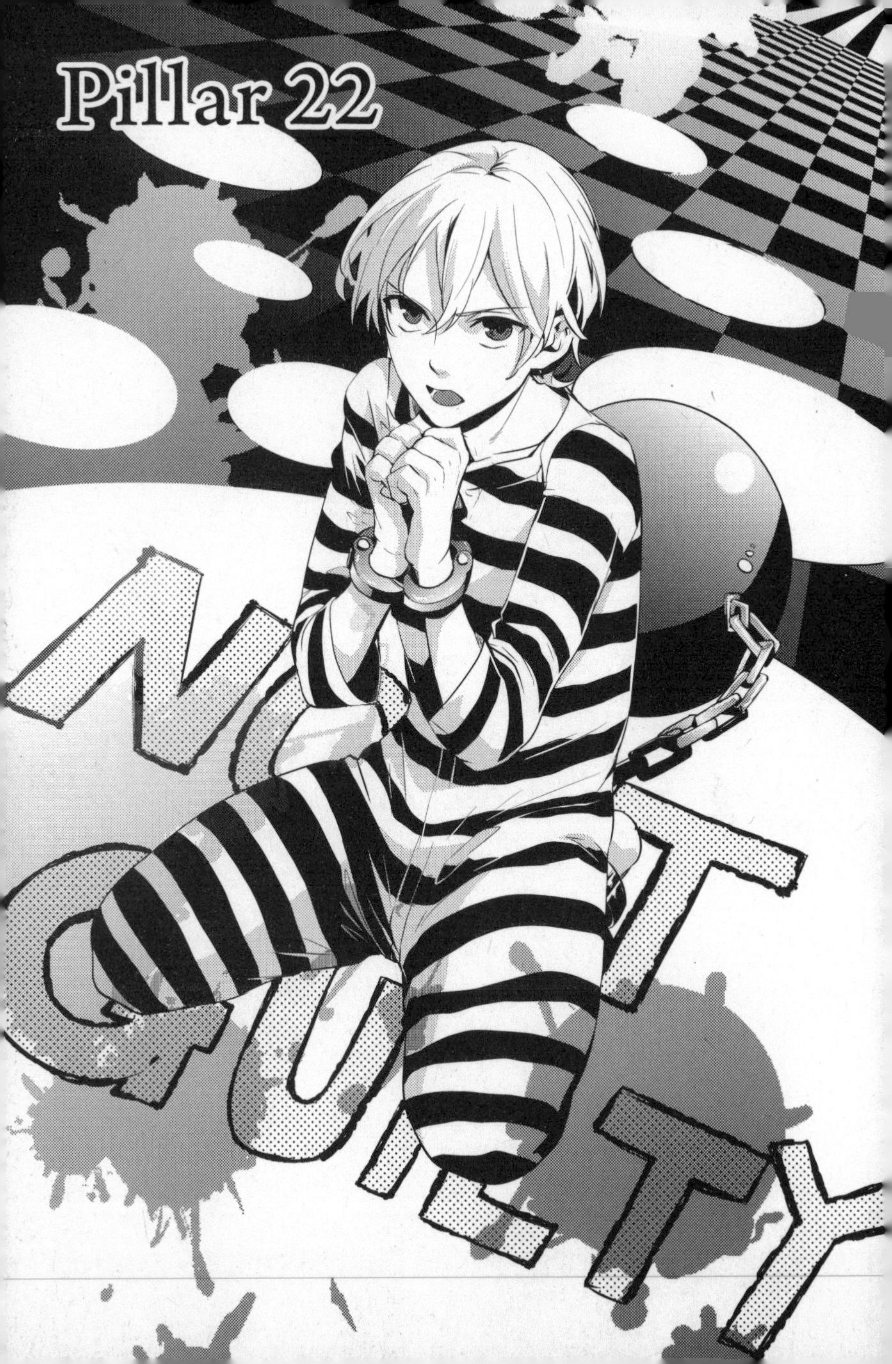
NOT GUILTY

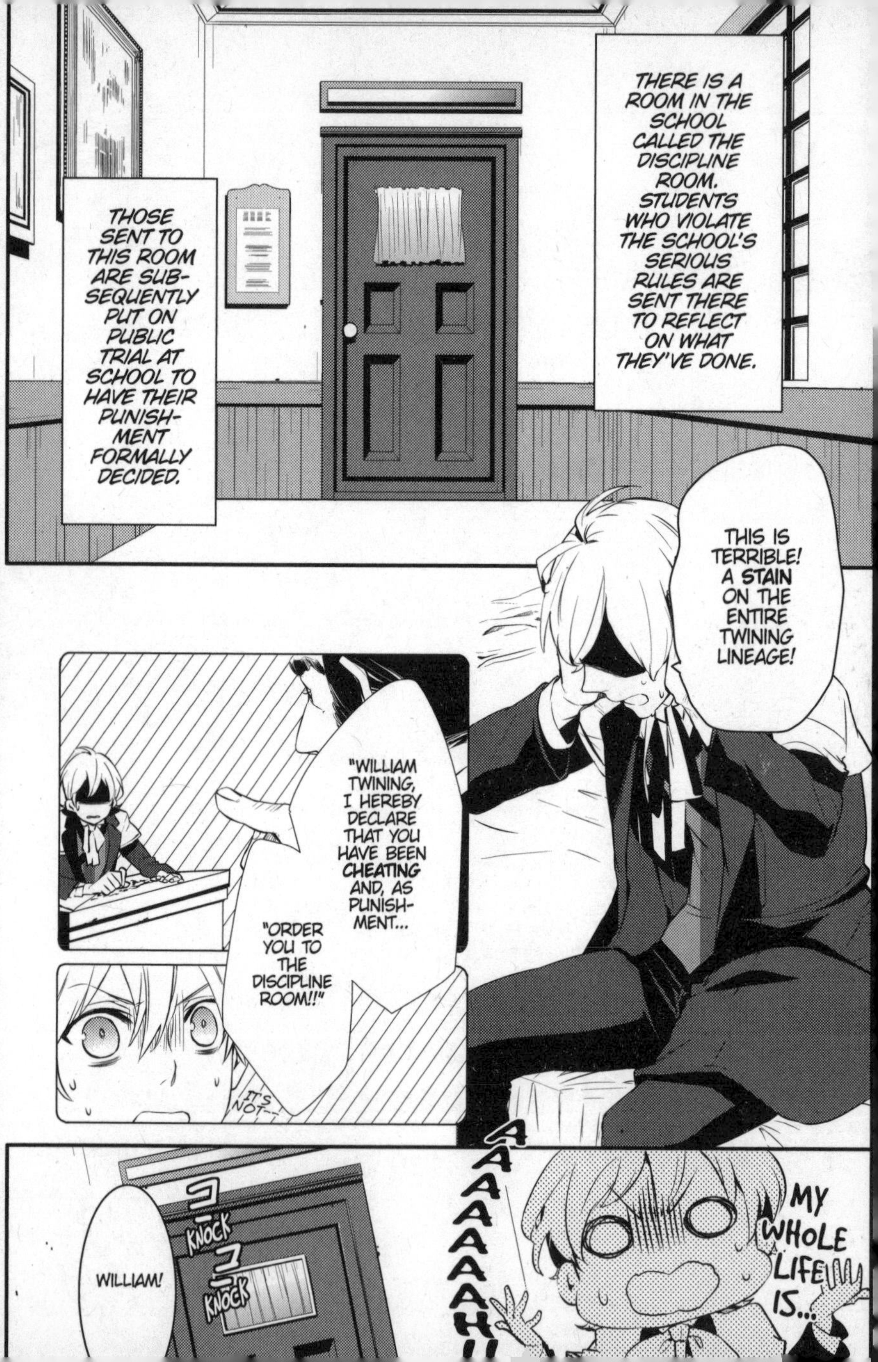
THERE IS A ROOM IN THE SCHOOL CALLED THE DISCIPLINE ROOM. STUDENTS WHO VIOLATE THE SCHOOL'S SERIOUS RULES ARE SENT THERE TO REFLECT ON WHAT THEY'VE DONE.
THOSE SENT TO THIS ROOM ARE SUB-SEQUENTLY PUT ON PUBLIC TRIAL AT SCHOOL TO HAVE THEIR PUNISH-MENT FORMALLY DECIDED.
THIS IS TERRIBLE! A STAIN ON THE ENTIRE TWINING LINEAGE!
"WILLIAM TWINING, I HEREBY DECLARE THAT YOU HAVE BEEN CHEATING AND, AS PUNISH-MENT...
"ORDER YOU TO THE DISCIPLINE ROOM!!"
IT'S NOT--!
MY WHOLE LIFE IS...
AAAAAAAAH!!
KNOCK
KNOCK
WILLIAM!

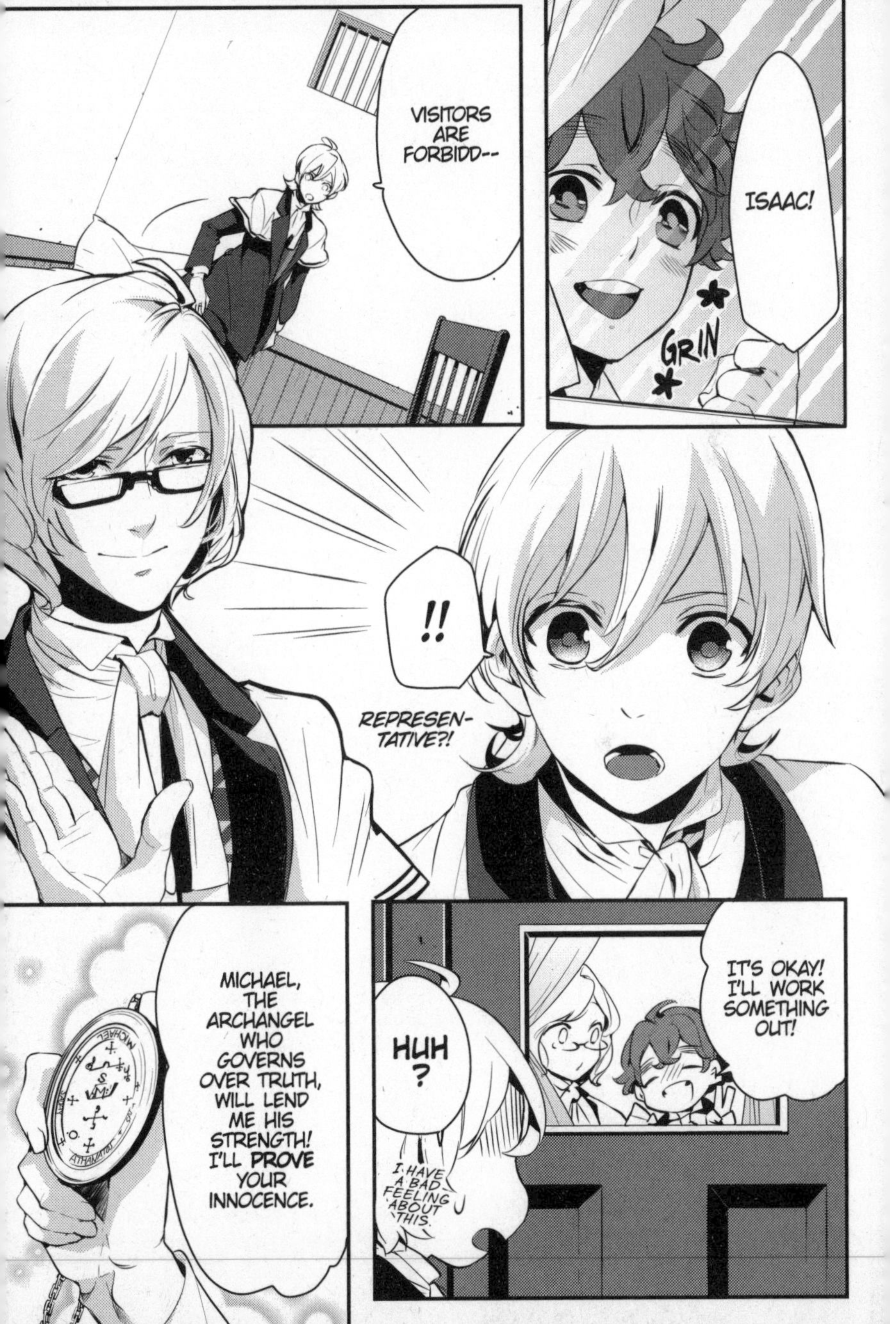
ISAAC!
GRIN
VISITORS ARE FORBIDD--
!!
REPRESEN-TATIVE?!
IT'S OKAY! I'LL WORK SOMETHING OUT!
HUH?
I HAVE A BAD FEELING ABOUT THIS.
MICHAEL, THE ARCHANGEL WHO GOVERNS OVER TRUTH, WILL LEND ME HIS STRENGTH! I'LL PROVE YOUR INNOCENCE.

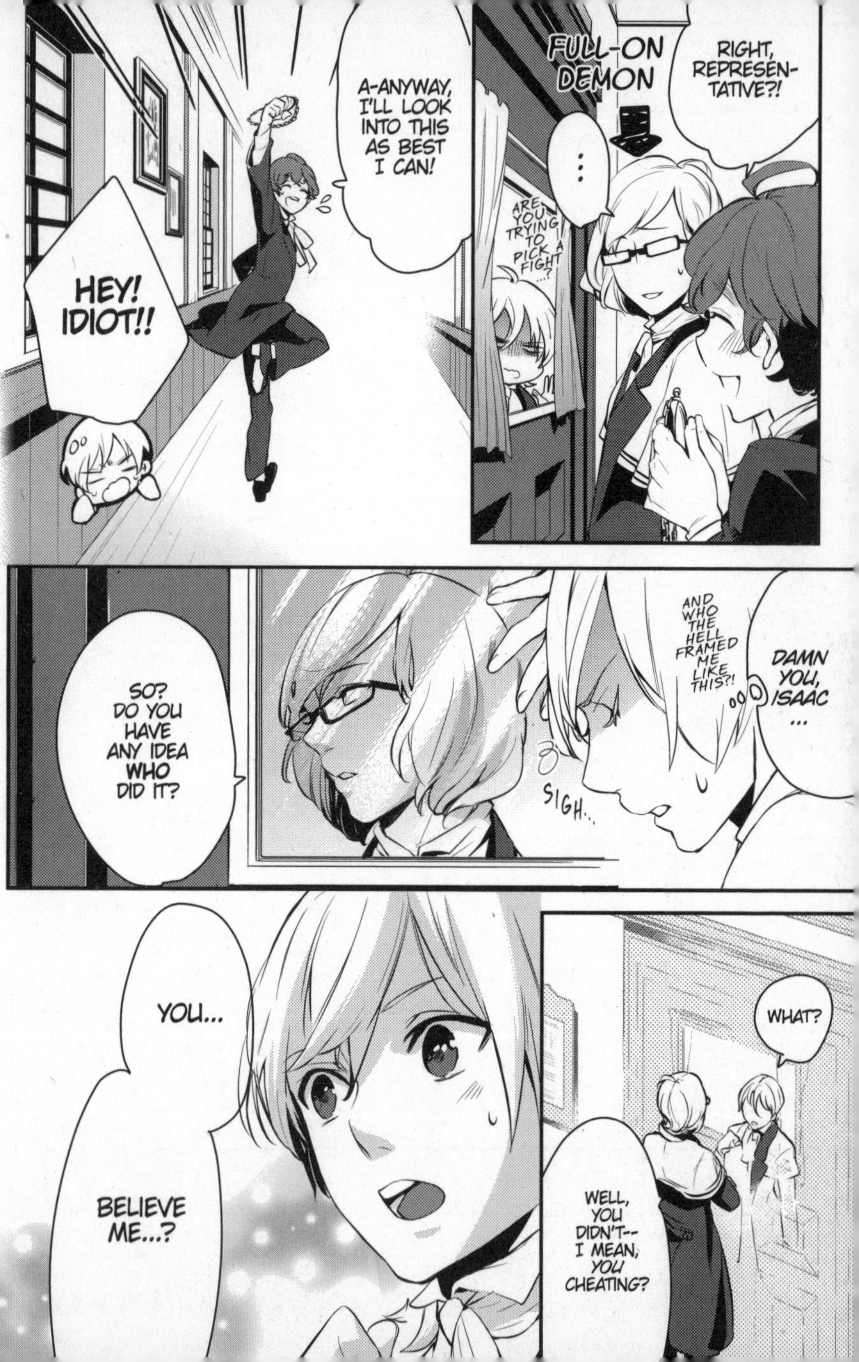
RIGHT, REPRESEN-TATIVE?!
FULL-ON DEMON
...
ARE YOU TRYING TO PICK A FIGHT...?
A-ANYWAY, I'LL LOOK INTO THIS AS BEST I CAN!
HEY! IDIOT!!
DAMN YOU, ISAAC...
AND WHO THE HELL FRAMED ME LIKE THIS?!
SIGH...
SO? DO YOU HAVE ANY IDEA WHO DID IT?
WHAT?
WELL, YOU DIDN'T-- I MEAN, YOU CHEATING?
YOU...
BELIEVE ME...?

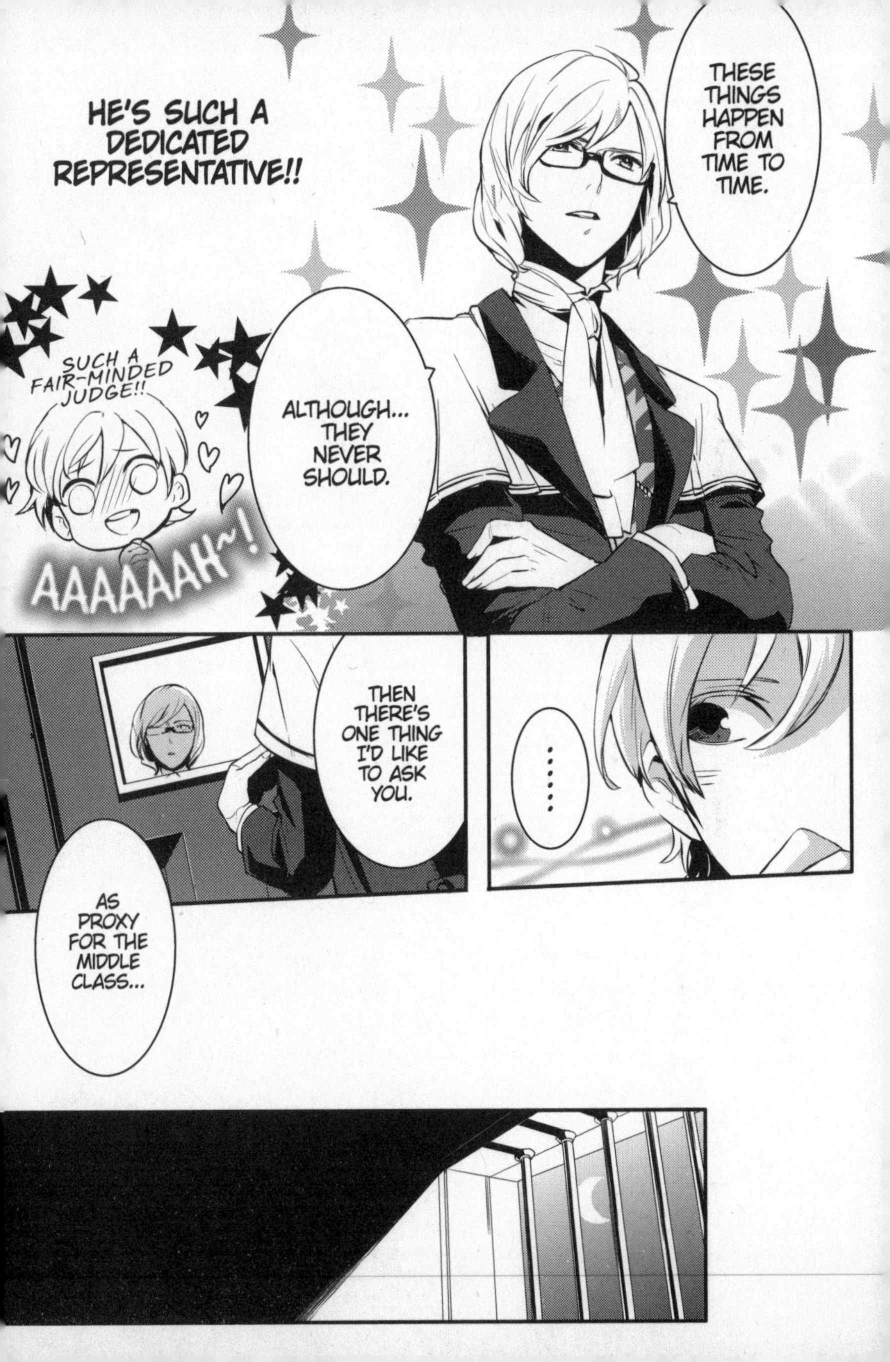
THESE THINGS HAPPEN FROM TIME TO TIME.
HE'S SUCH A DEDICATED REPRESENTATIVE!!
ALTHOUGH... THEY NEVER SHOULD.
SUCH A FAIR-MINDED JUDGE!!
AAAAAAH~!
......
THEN THERE'S ONE THING I'D LIKE TO ASK YOU.
AS PROXY FOR THE MIDDLE CLASS...

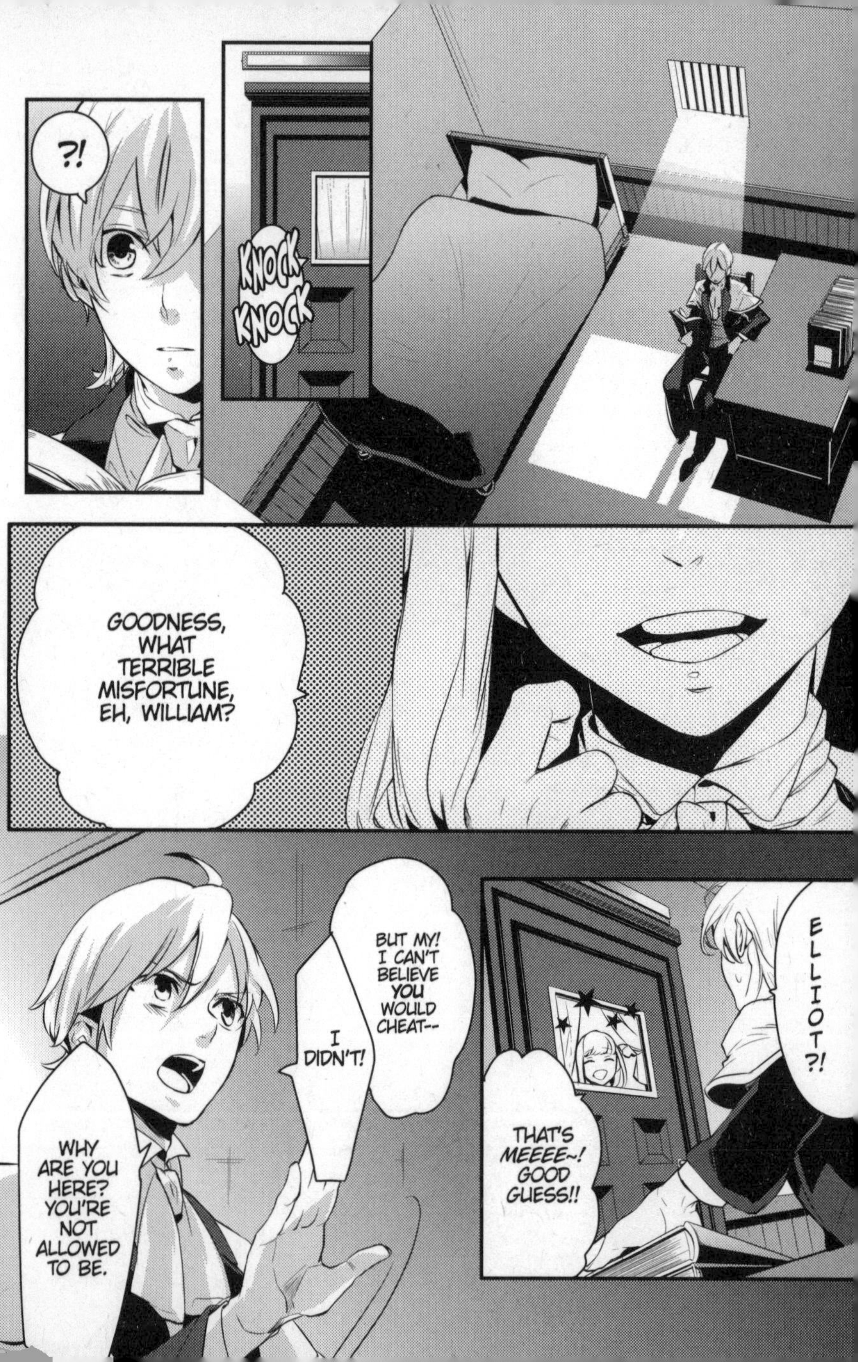
KNOCK KNOCK
?!
GOODNESS, WHAT TERRIBLE MISFORTUNE, EH, WILLIAM?
ELLIOT?!
THAT'S MEEEE~! GOOD GUESS!!
BUT MY! I CAN'T BELIEVE YOU WOULD CHEAT--
I DIDN'T!
WHY ARE YOU HERE? YOU'RE NOT ALLOWED TO BE.

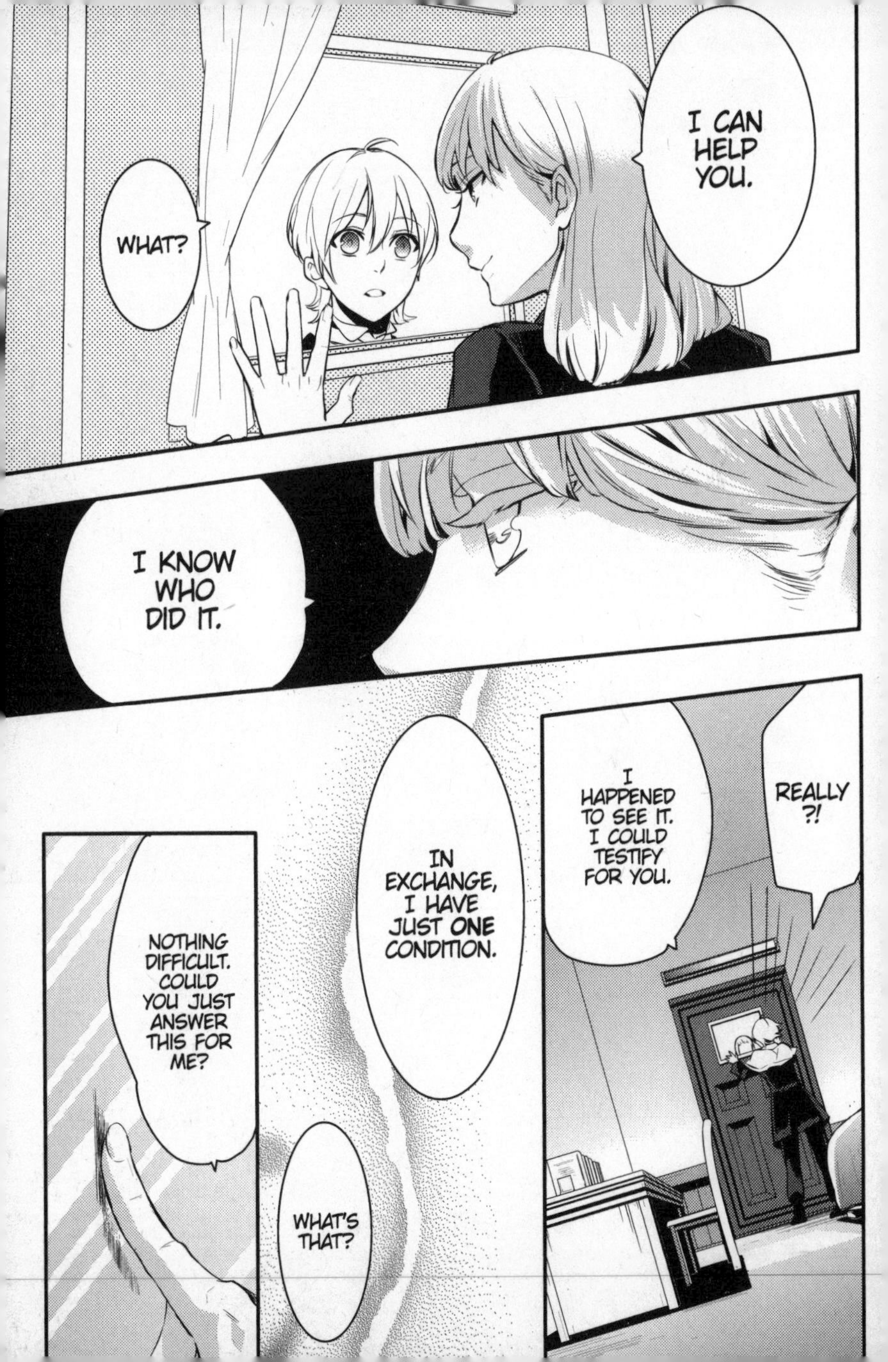
I CAN HELP YOU.
WHAT?
I KNOW WHO DID IT.
REALLY?!
I HAPPENED TO SEE IT. I COULD TESTIFY FOR YOU.
IN EXCHANGE, I HAVE JUST ONE CONDITION.
WHAT'S THAT?
NOTHING DIFFICULT. COULD YOU JUST ANSWER THIS FOR ME?

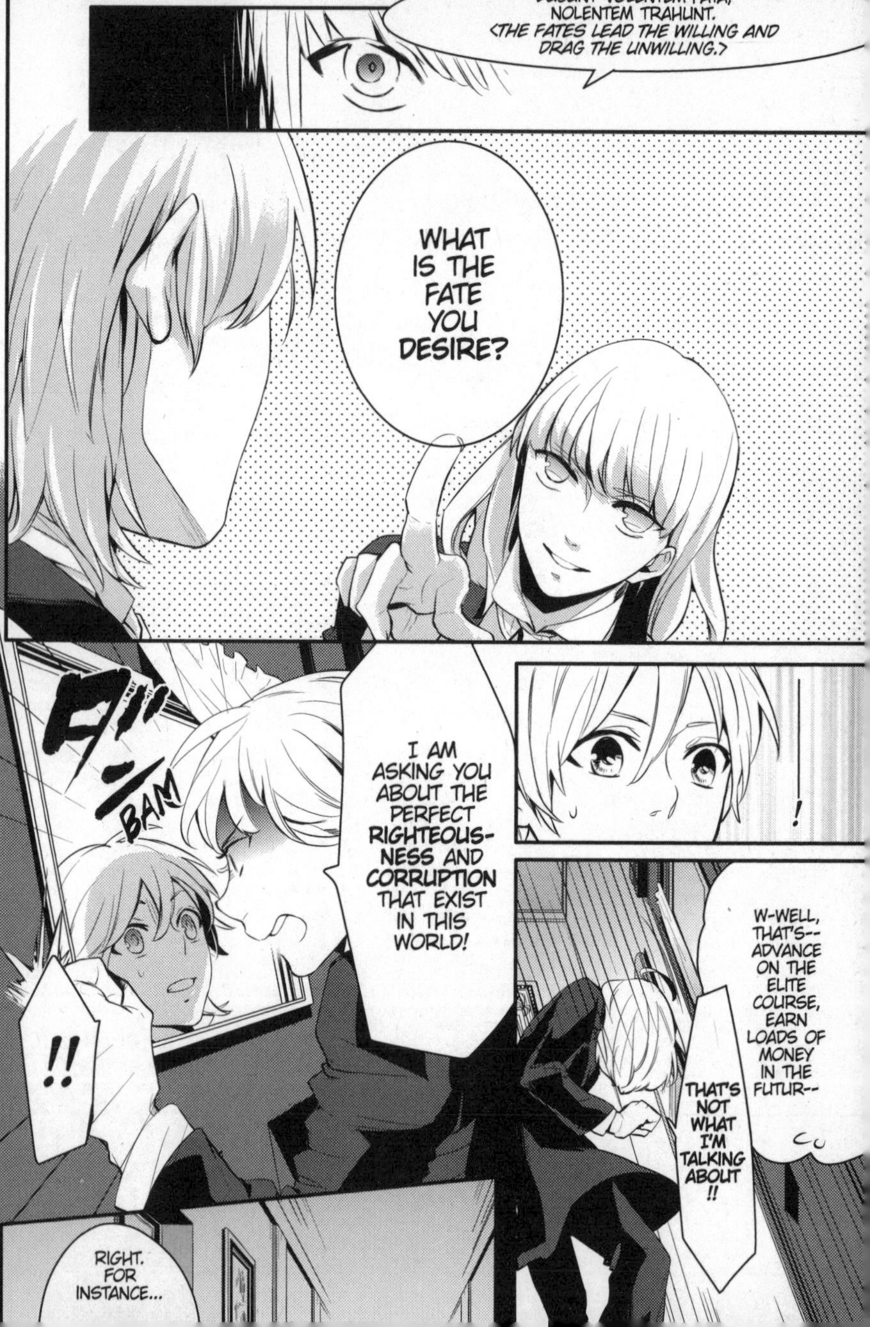
DUCUNT VOLENTEM FATA, NOLENTEM TRAHUNT. <THE FATES LEAD THE WILLING AND DRAG THE UNWILLING.>
WHAT IS THE FATE YOU DESIRE?
!
W-WELL, THAT'S-- ADVANCE ON THE ELITE COURSE, EARN LOADS OF MONEY IN THE FUTUR--
BAM
I AM ASKING YOU ABOUT THE PERFECT RIGHTEOUSNESS AND CORRUPTION THAT EXIST IN THIS WORLD!
THAT'S NOT WHAT I'M TALKING ABOUT !!
!!
RIGHT. FOR INSTANCE...

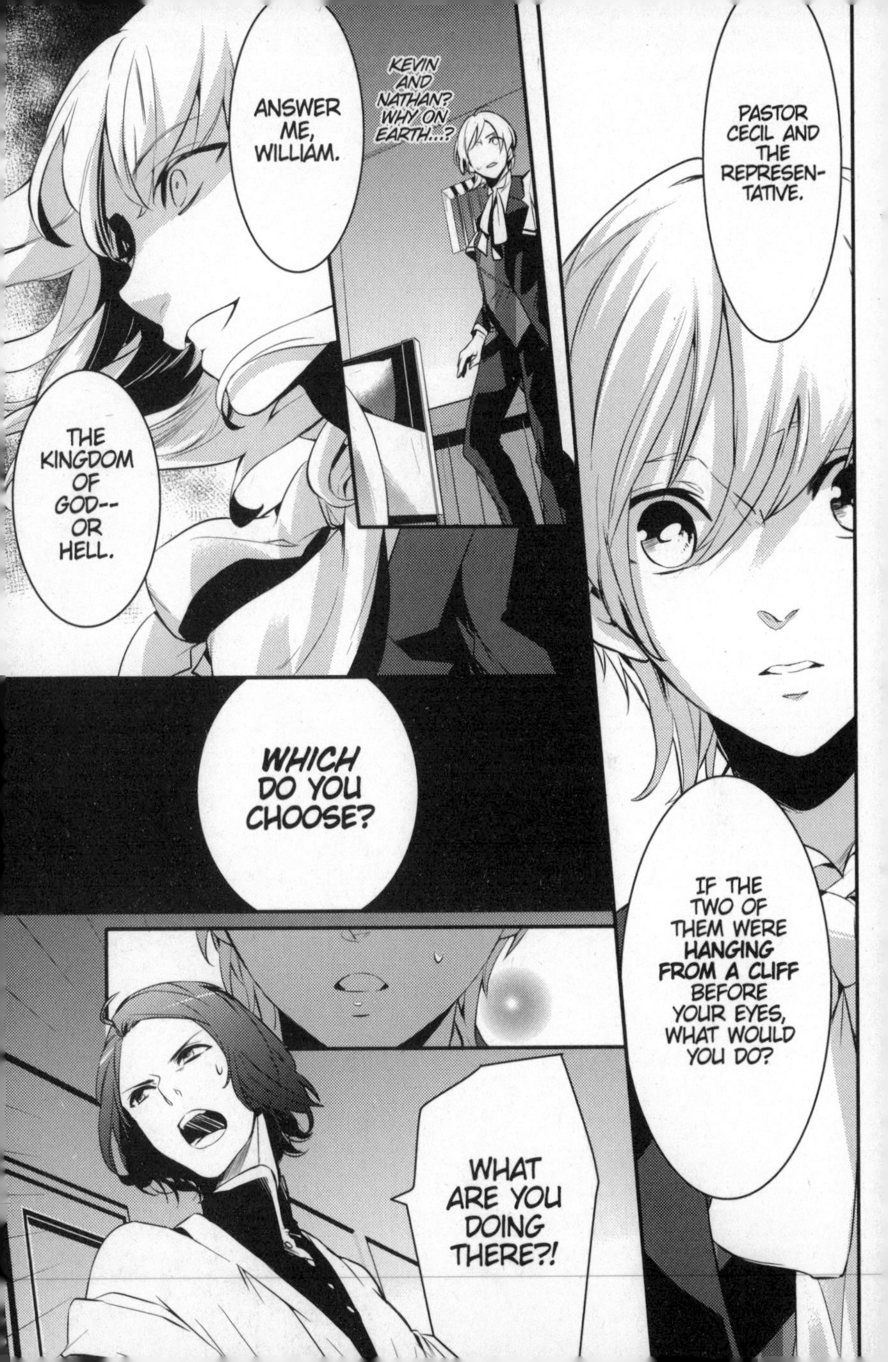
PASTOR CECIL AND THE REPRESEN-TATIVE.
IF THE TWO OF THEM WERE HANGING FROM A CLIFF BEFORE YOUR EYES, WHAT WOULD YOU DO?
ANSWER ME, WILLIAM.
THE KINGDOM OF GOD-- OR HELL.
WHICH DO YOU CHOOSE?
KEVIN AND NATHAN? WHY ON EARTH...?
WHAT ARE YOU DOING THERE?!

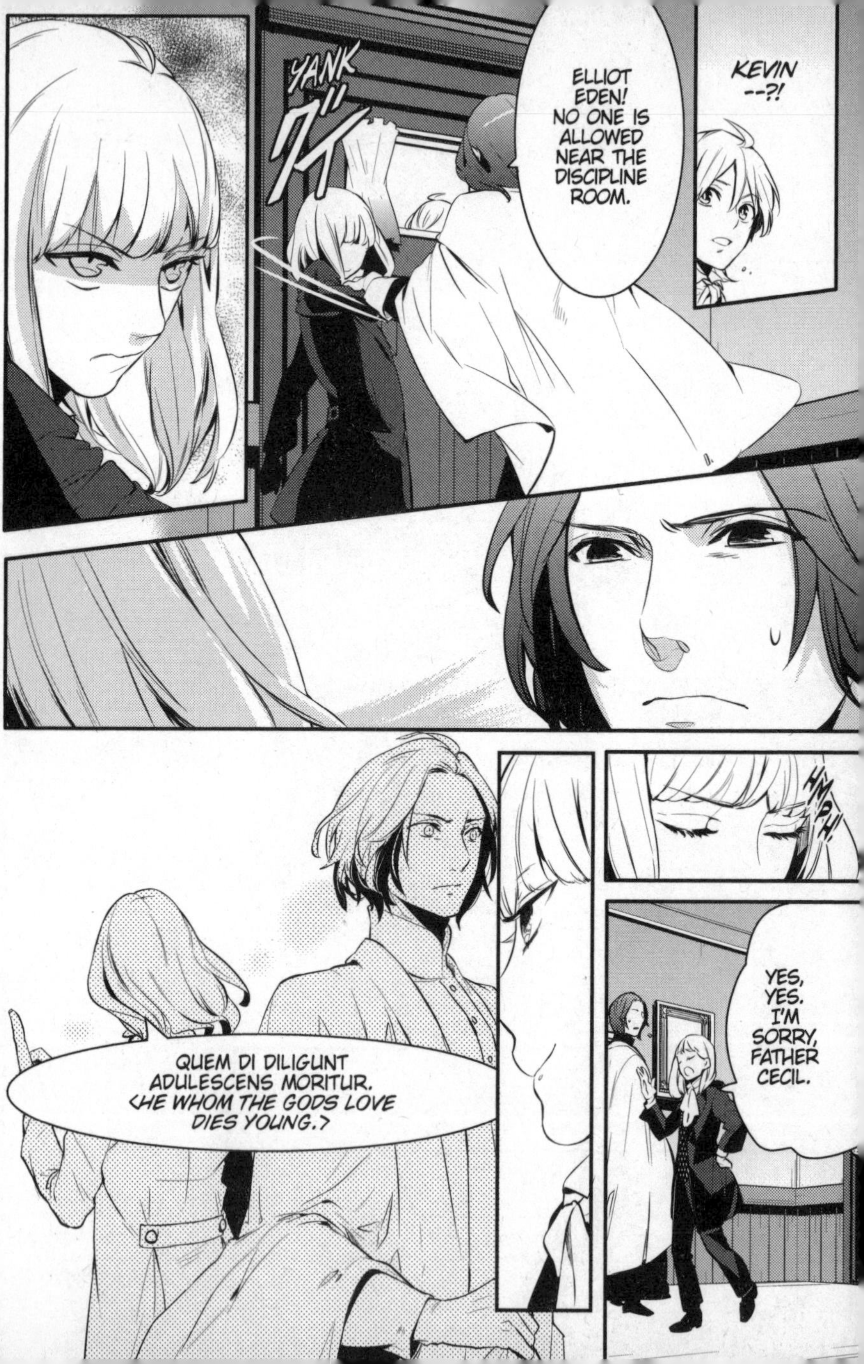
KEVIN --?!
ELLIOT EDEN! NO ONE IS ALLOWED NEAR THE DISCIPLINE ROOM.
YANK
グイ
HMPH!
YES, YES. I'M SORRY, FATHER CECIL.
QUEM DI DILIGUNT ADULESCENS MORITUR. <HE WHOM THE GODS LOVE DIES YOUNG.>

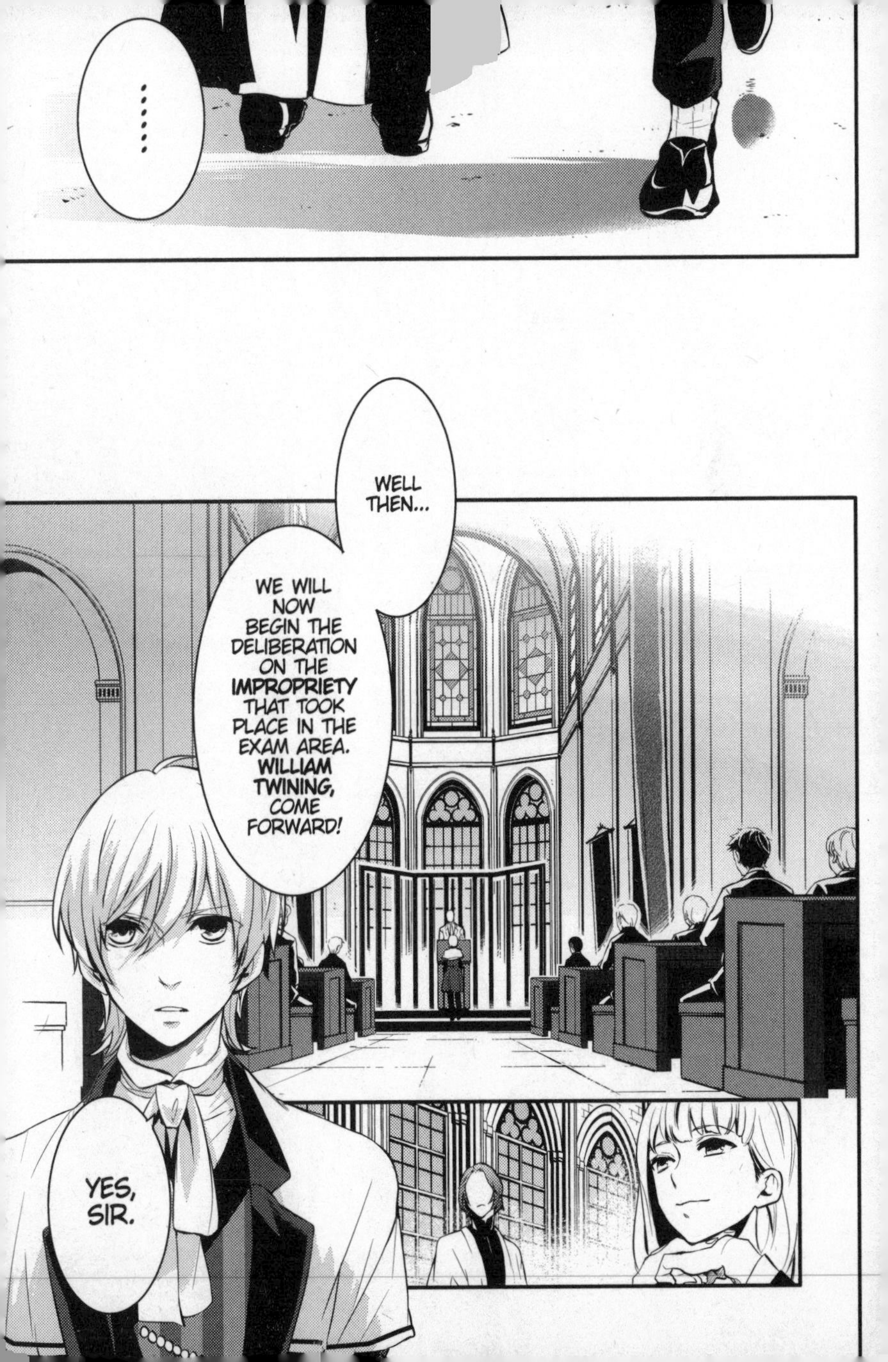
......
WELL THEN...
WE WILL NOW BEGIN THE DELIBERATION ON THE IMPROPRIETY THAT TOOK PLACE IN THE EXAM AREA. WILLIAM TWINING, COME FORWARD!
YES, SIR.

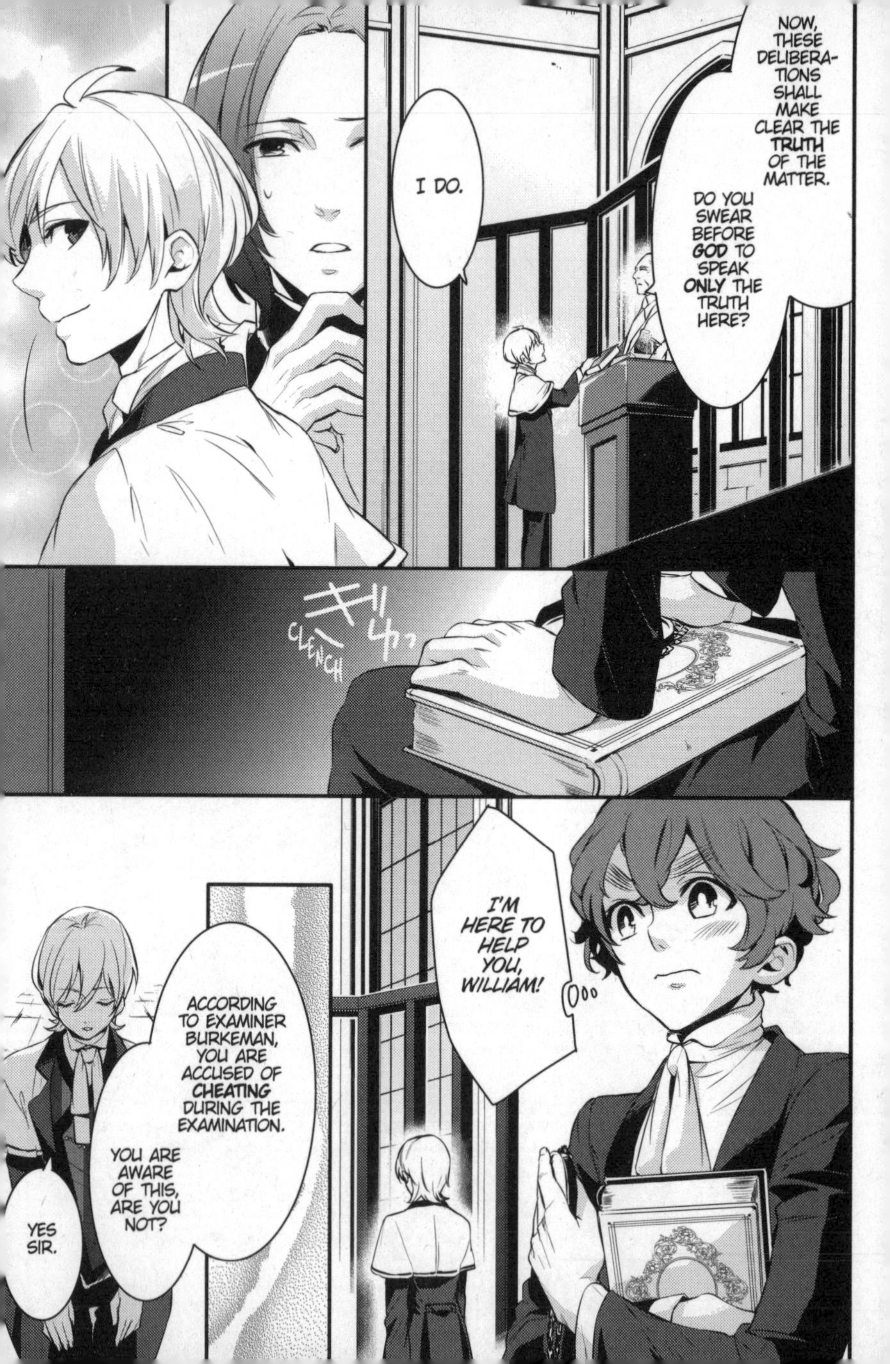
NOW, THESE DELIBERATIONS SHALL MAKE CLEAR THE **TRUTH** OF THE MATTER.
DO YOU SWEAR BEFORE **GOD** TO SPEAK **ONLY** THE TRUTH HERE?
I DO.
ぎゅっ
CLENCH
I'M HERE TO HELP YOU, WILLIAM!
ACCORDING TO EXAMINER BURKEMAN, YOU ARE ACCUSED OF **CHEATING** DURING THE EXAMINATION.
YOU ARE AWARE OF THIS, ARE YOU NOT?
YES SIR.

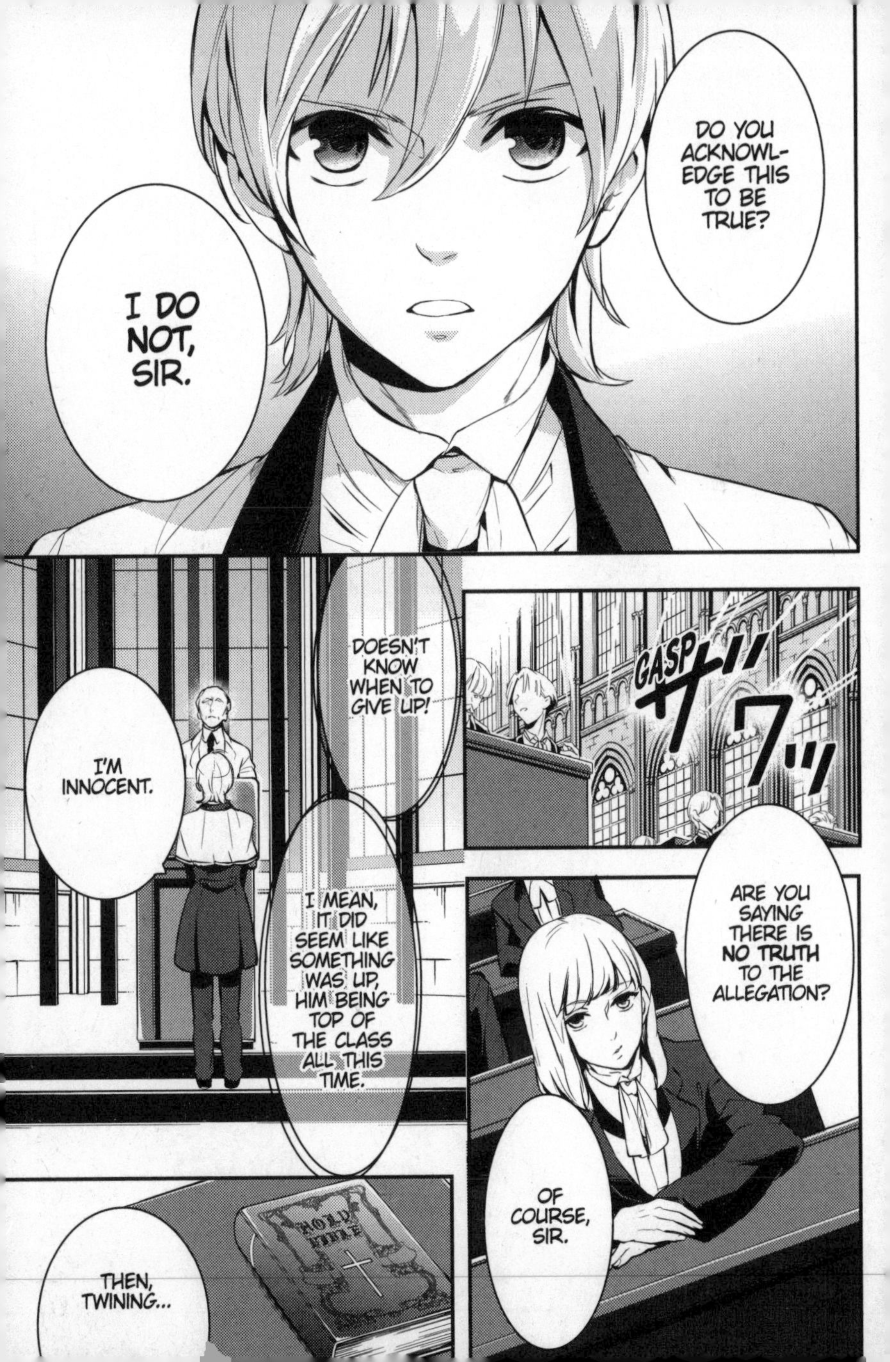
DO YOU ACKNOWL-EDGE THIS TO BE TRUE?
I DO NOT, SIR.
GASP
DOESN'T KNOW WHEN TO GIVE UP!
I MEAN, IT DID SEEM LIKE SOMETHING WAS UP, HIM BEING TOP OF THE CLASS ALL THIS TIME.
I'M INNOCENT.
ARE YOU SAYING THERE IS NO TRUTH TO THE ALLEGATION?
OF COURSE, SIR.
THEN, TWINING...

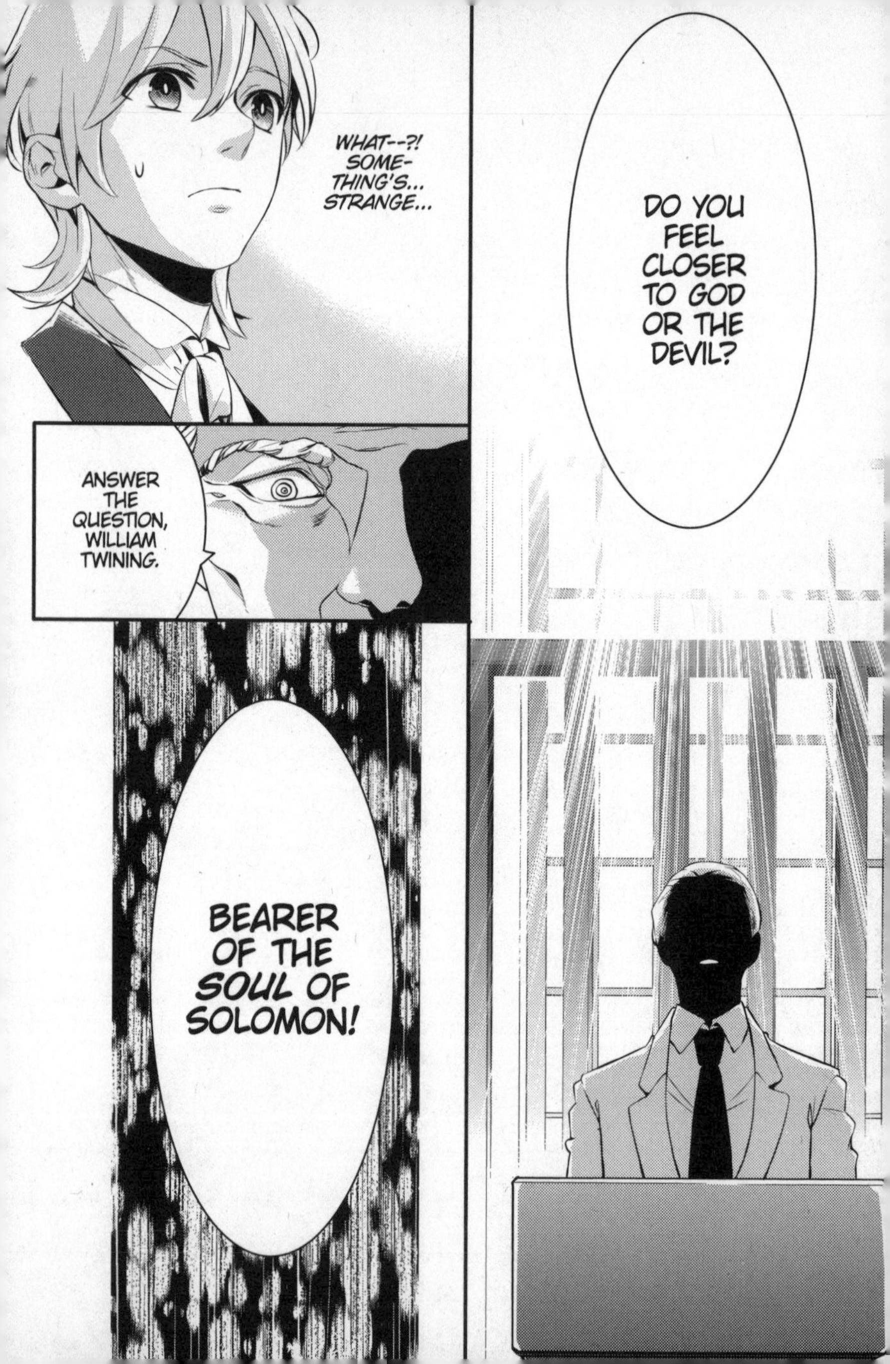
DO YOU FEEL CLOSER TO GOD OR THE DEVIL?
WHAT--?! SOME-THING'S... STRANGE...
ANSWER THE QUESTION, WILLIAM TWINING.
BEARER OF THE *SOUL* OF SOLOMON!

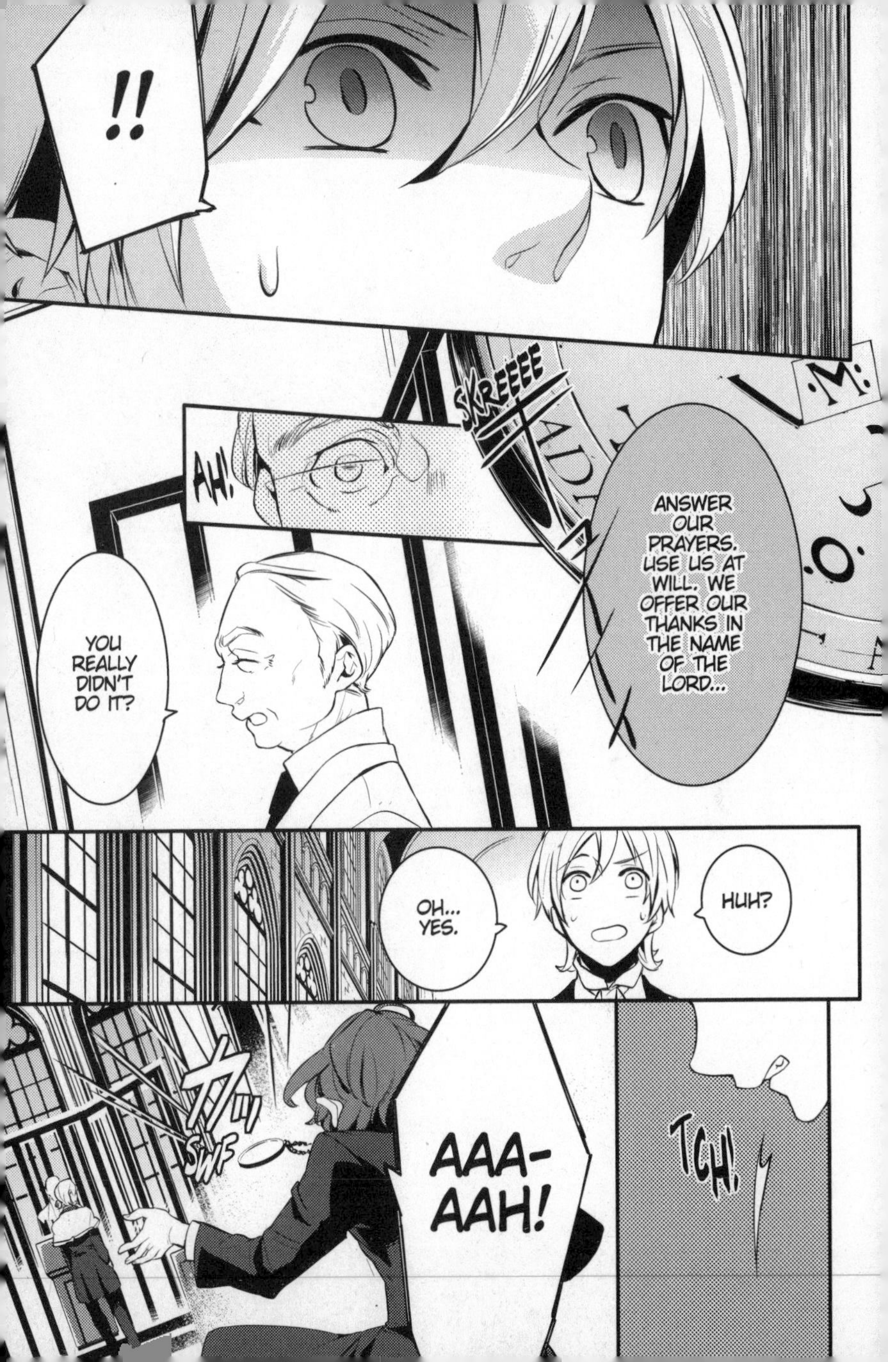
!!
SKREEEE
AH!
ANSWER OUR PRAYERS. USE US AT WILL. WE OFFER OUR THANKS IN THE NAME OF THE LORD...
YOU REALLY DIDN'T DO IT?
HUH?
OH... YES.
TCH.
AAA-AAH!
SWF

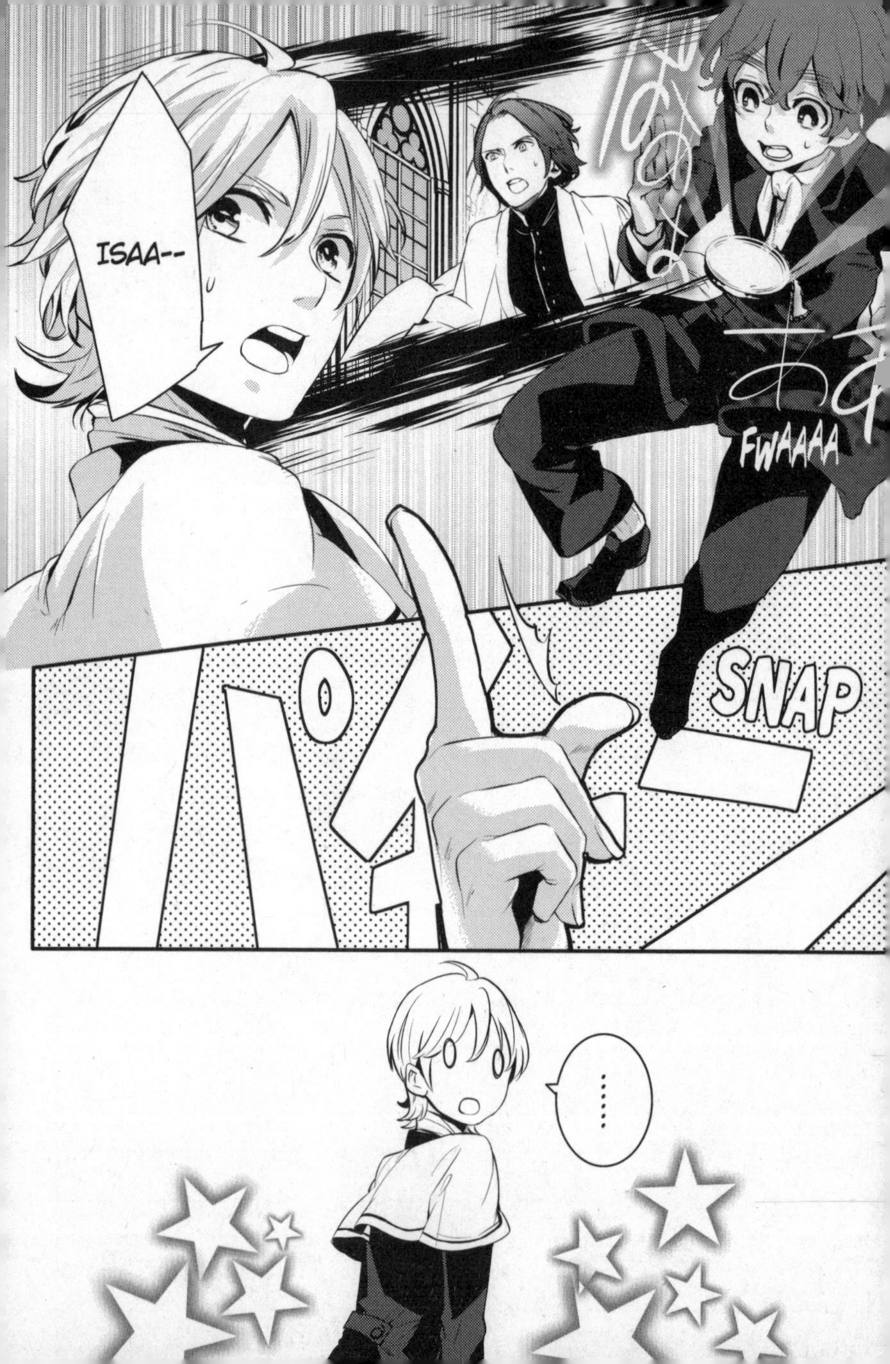
FWAAAA
ISAA--
SNAP
......

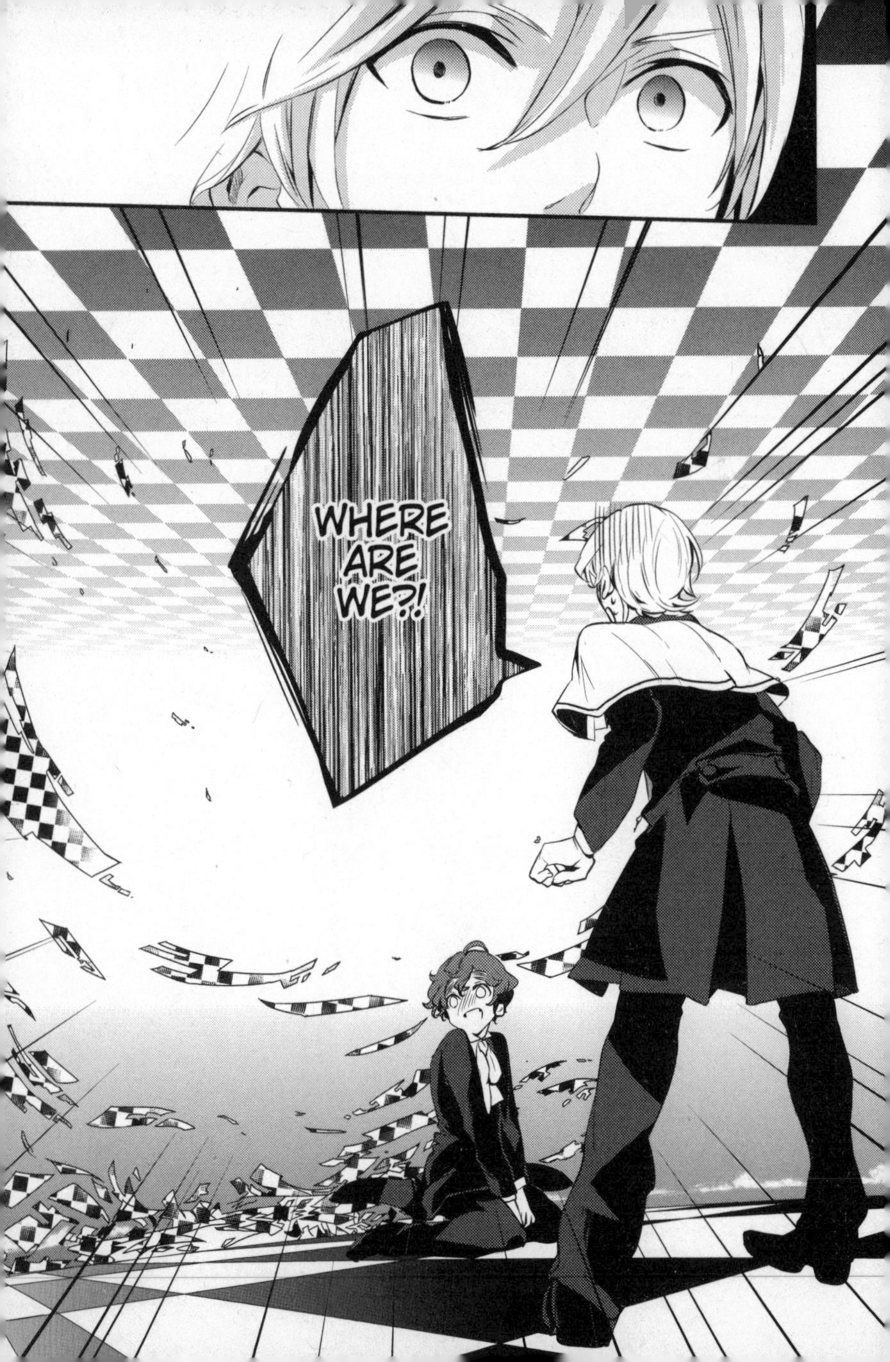
WHERE ARE WE?!

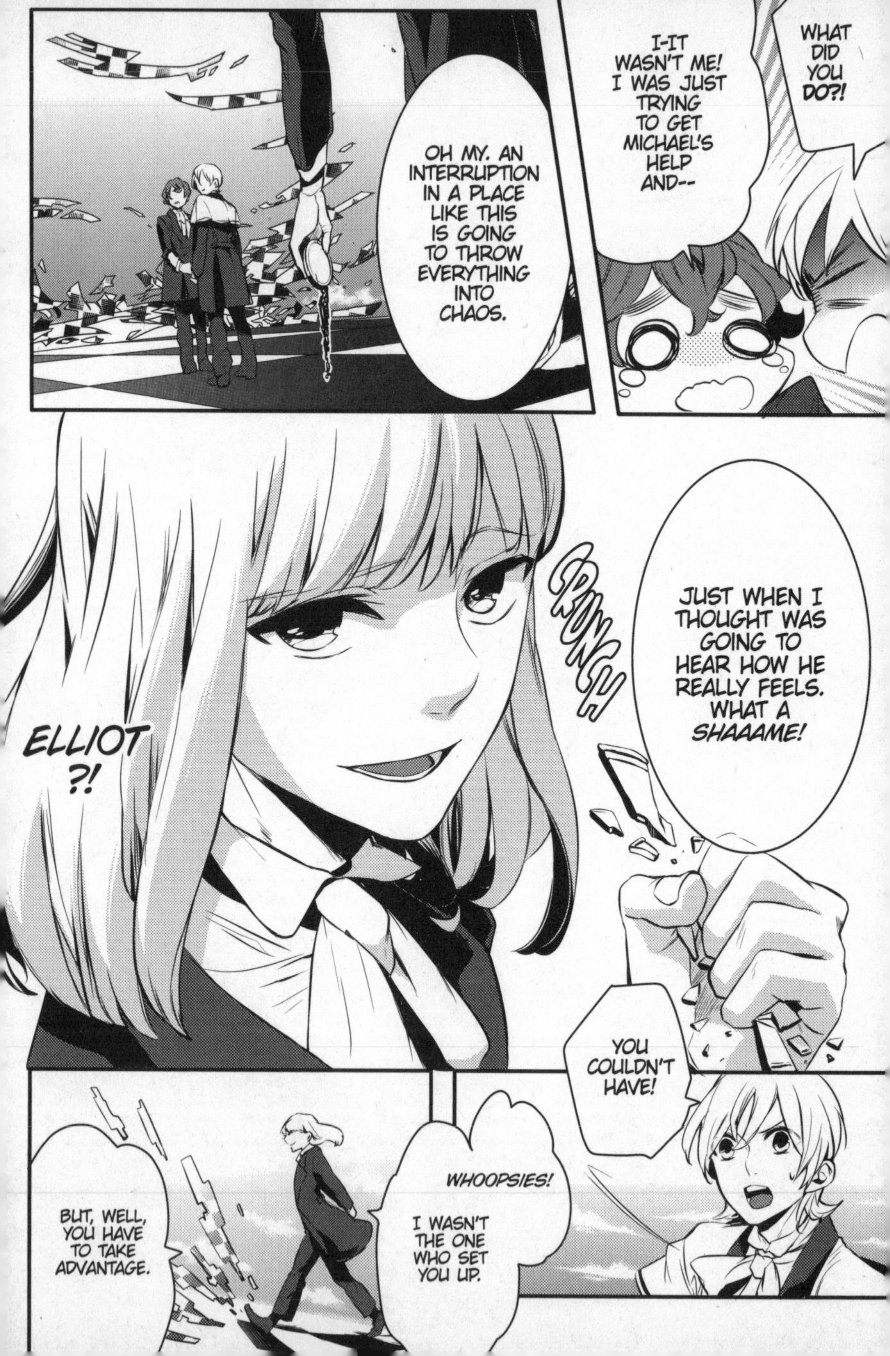
WHAT DID YOU DO?!
I-IT WASN'T ME! I WAS JUST TRYING TO GET MICHAEL'S HELP AND--
OH MY. AN INTERRUPTION IN A PLACE LIKE THIS IS GOING TO THROW EVERYTHING INTO CHAOS.
JUST WHEN I THOUGHT WAS GOING TO HEAR HOW HE REALLY FEELS. WHAT A *SHAAAME!*
CRUNCH
ELLIOT ?!
YOU COULDN'T HAVE!
WHOOPSIES!
I WASN'T THE ONE WHO SET YOU UP.
BUT, WELL, YOU HAVE TO TAKE ADVANTAGE.

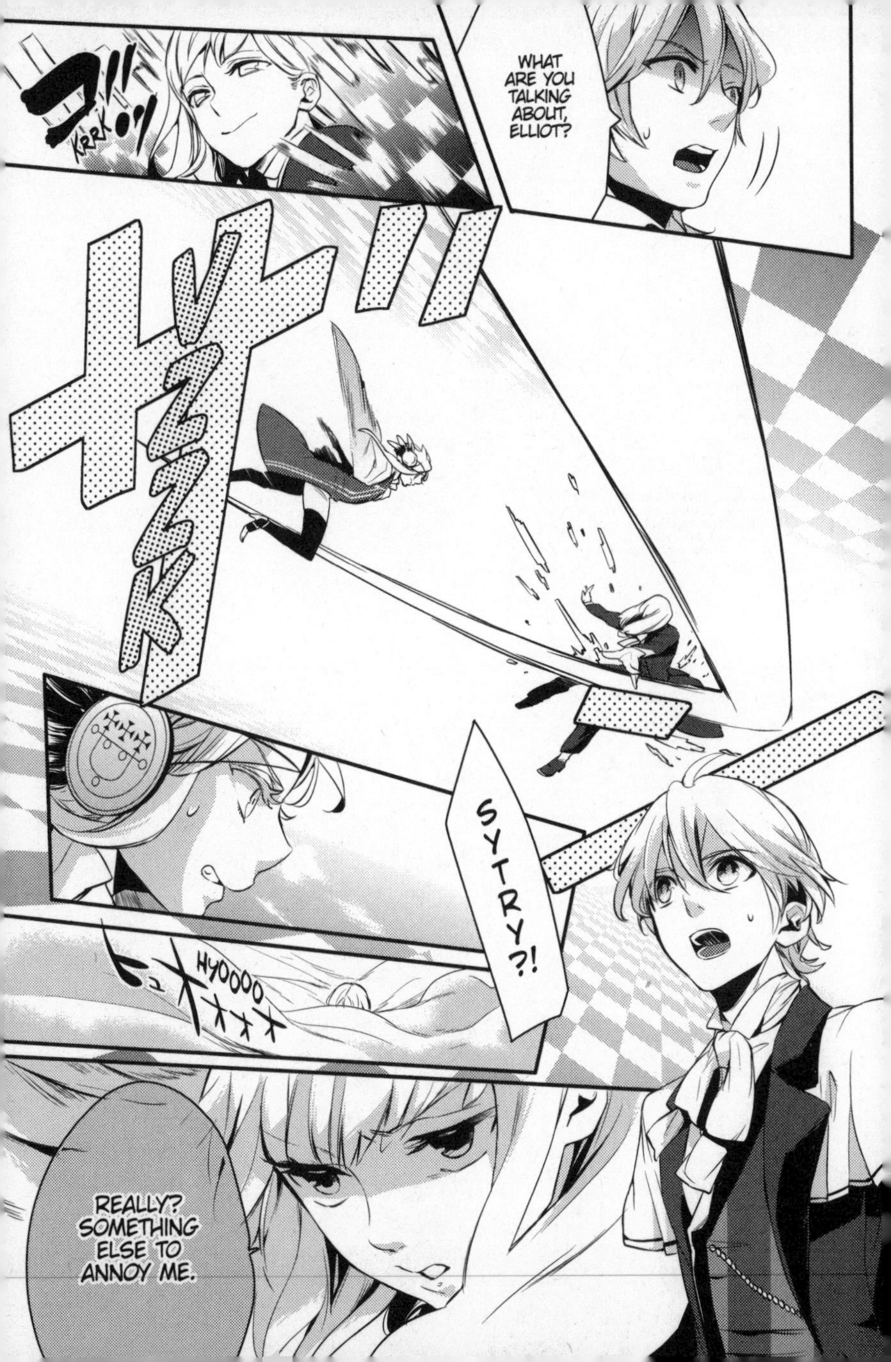
WHAT ARE YOU TALKING ABOUT, ELLIOT?
KRRK
SYTRY?!
HYOOOO
REALLY? SOMETHING ELSE TO ANNOY ME.

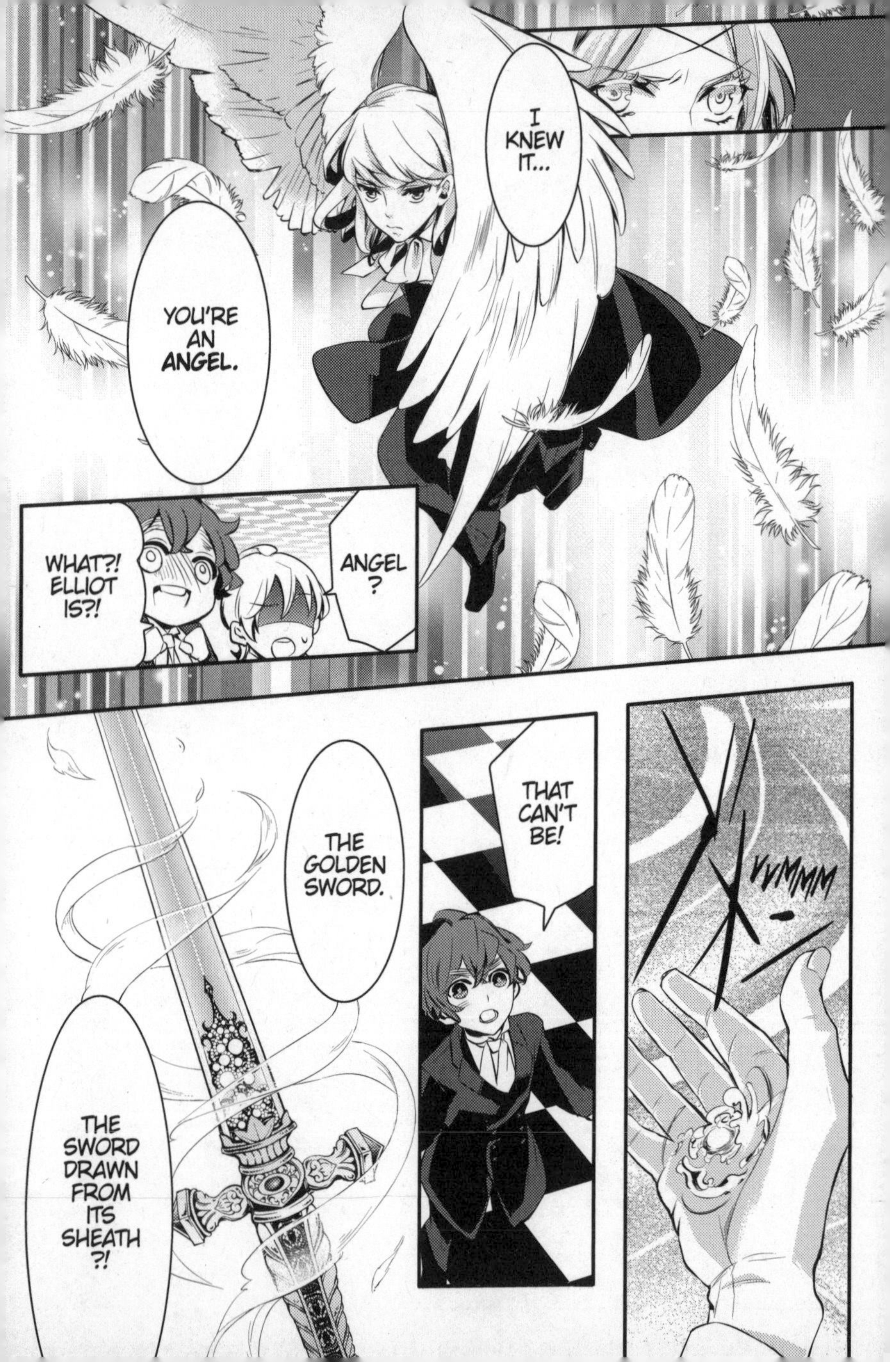
I KNEW IT...
YOU'RE AN ANGEL.
ANGEL?
WHAT?! ELLIOT IS?!
VVMMM
THAT CAN'T BE!
THE GOLDEN SWORD.
THE SWORD DRAWN FROM ITS SHEATH?!

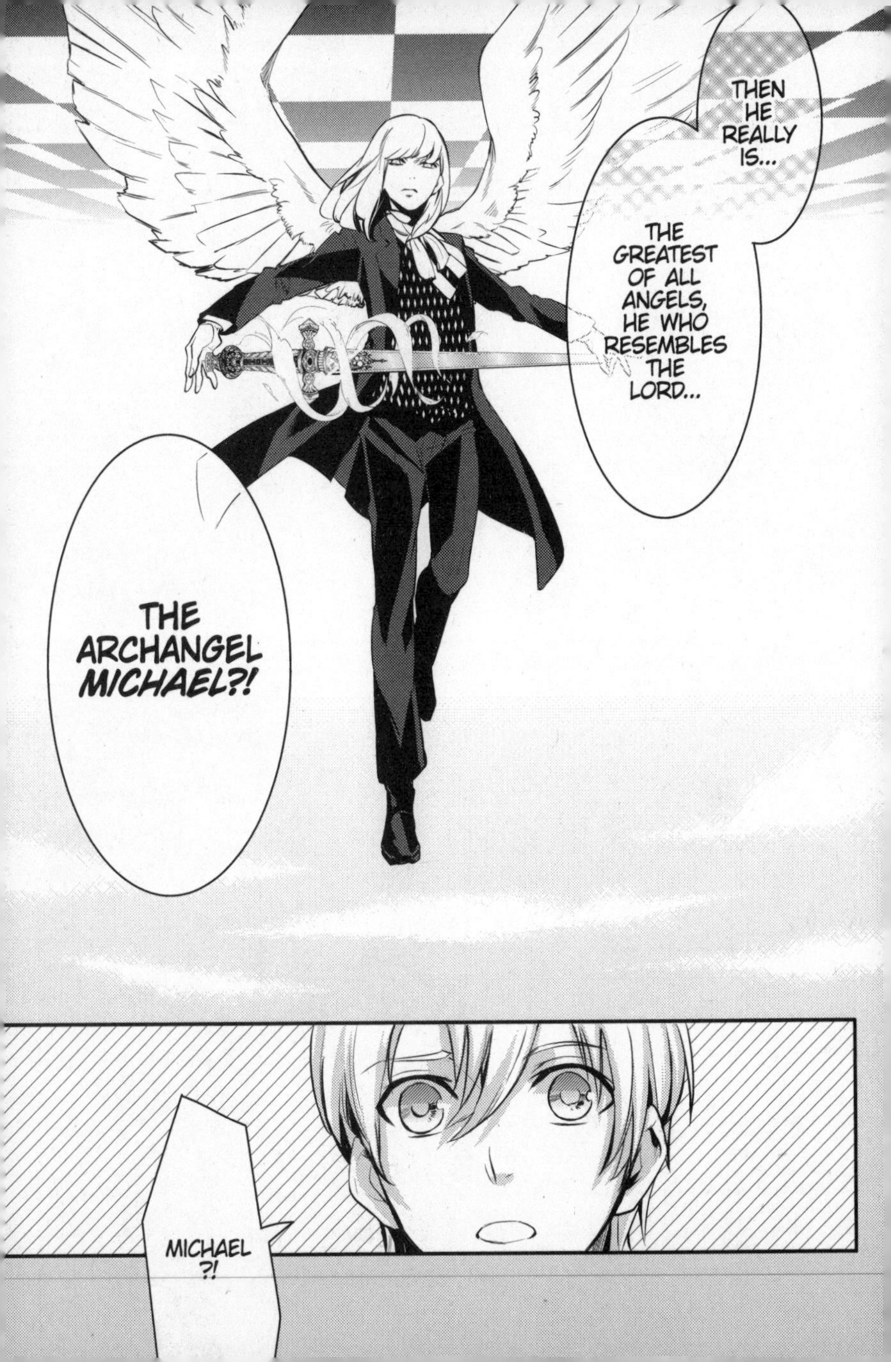
THEN HE REALLY IS...
THE GREATEST OF ALL ANGELS, HE WHO RESEMBLES THE LORD...
THE ARCHANGEL MICHAEL?!
MICHAEL ?!

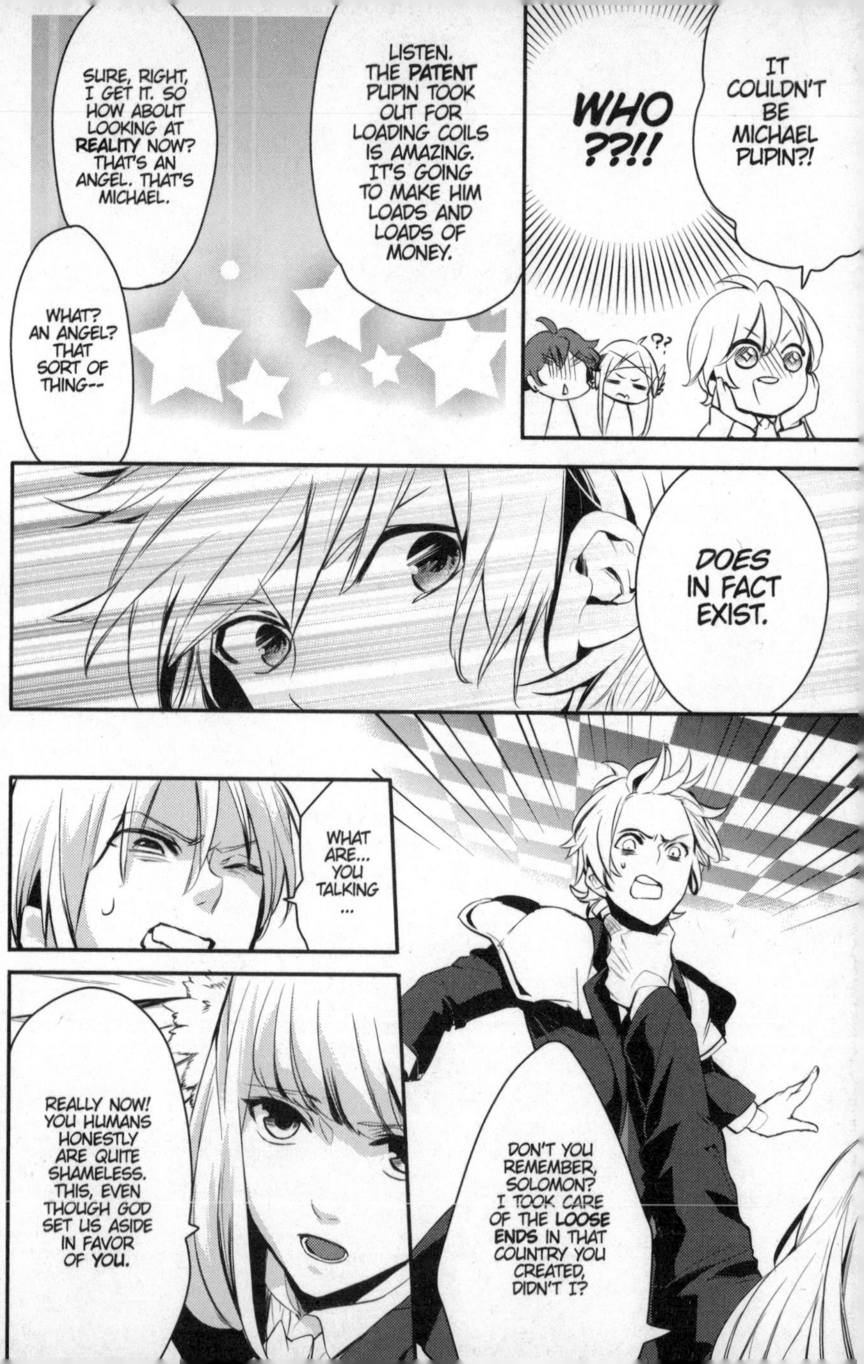
IT COULDN'T BE MICHAEL PUPIN?!
WHO ??!!
LISTEN. THE PATENT PUPIN TOOK OUT FOR LOADING COILS IS AMAZING. IT'S GOING TO MAKE HIM LOADS AND LOADS OF MONEY.
SURE, RIGHT, I GET IT. SO HOW ABOUT LOOKING AT REALITY NOW? THAT'S AN ANGEL. THAT'S MICHAEL.
WHAT? AN ANGEL? THAT SORT OF THING--
??
DOES IN FACT EXIST.
WHAT ARE... YOU TALKING ...
DON'T YOU REMEMBER, SOLOMON? I TOOK CARE OF THE LOOSE ENDS IN THAT COUNTRY YOU CREATED, DIDN'T I?
REALLY NOW! YOU HUMANS HONESTLY ARE QUITE SHAMELESS. THIS, EVEN THOUGH GOD SET US ASIDE IN FAVOR OF YOU.

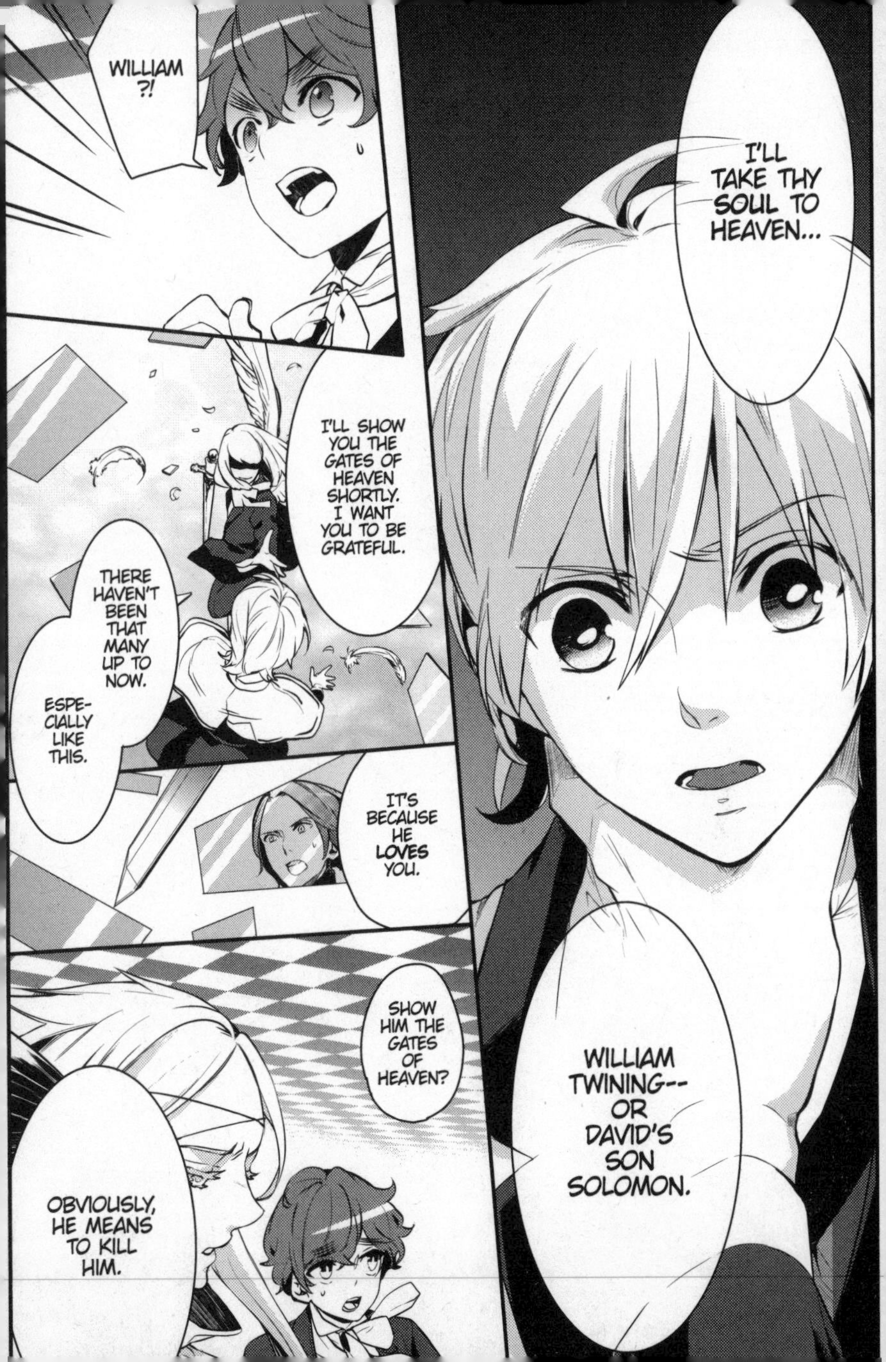
I'LL TAKE THY SOUL TO HEAVEN...
WILLIAM TWINING-- OR DAVID'S SON SOLOMON.
WILLIAM ?!
I'LL SHOW YOU THE GATES OF HEAVEN SHORTLY. I WANT YOU TO BE GRATEFUL.
THERE HAVEN'T BEEN THAT MANY UP TO NOW.
ESPE-CIALLY LIKE THIS.
IT'S BECAUSE HE LOVES YOU.
SHOW HIM THE GATES OF HEAVEN?
OBVIOUSLY, HE MEANS TO KILL HIM.

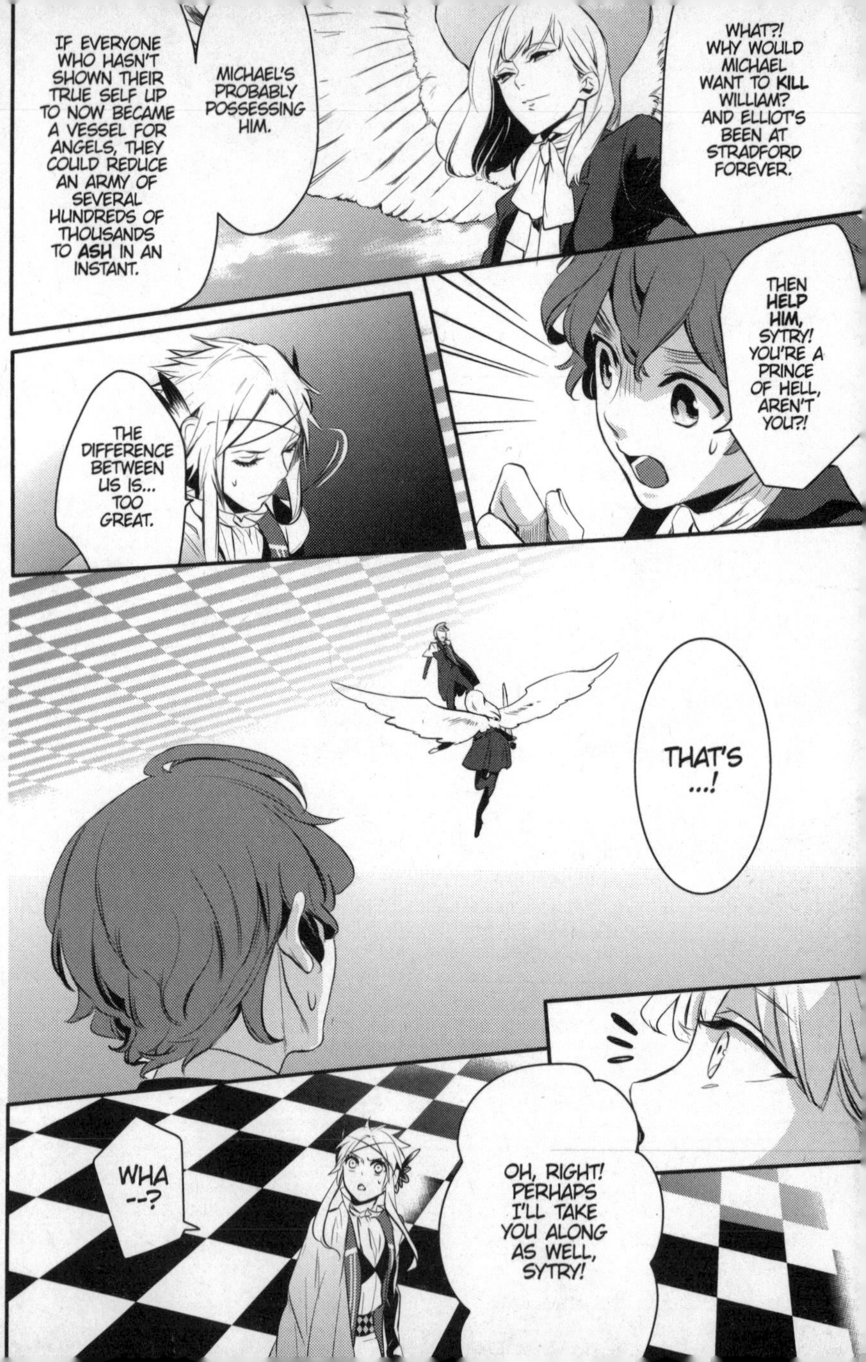
WHAT?! WHY WOULD MICHAEL WANT TO KILL WILLIAM? AND ELLIOT'S BEEN AT STRADFORD FOREVER.
MICHAEL'S PROBABLY POSSESSING HIM.
IF EVERYONE WHO HASN'T SHOWN THEIR TRUE SELF UP TO NOW BECAME A VESSEL FOR ANGELS, THEY COULD REDUCE AN ARMY OF SEVERAL HUNDREDS OF THOUSANDS TO ASH IN AN INSTANT.
THEN HELP HIM, SYTRY! YOU'RE A PRINCE OF HELL, AREN'T YOU?!
THE DIFFERENCE BETWEEN US IS... TOO GREAT.
THAT'S ...!
OH, RIGHT! PERHAPS I'LL TAKE YOU ALONG AS WELL, SYTRY!
WHA --?

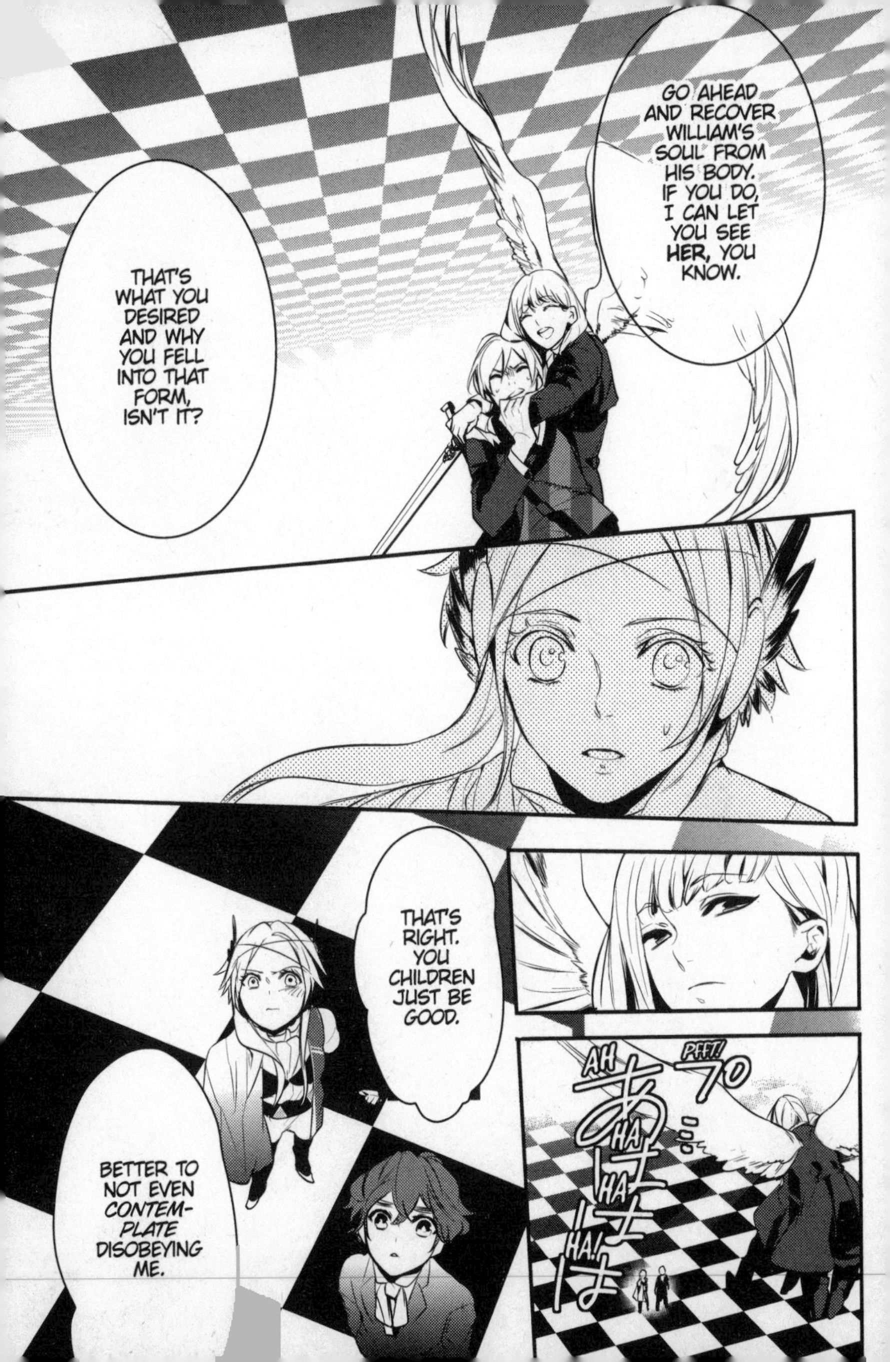
GO AHEAD AND RECOVER WILLIAM'S SOUL FROM HIS BODY. IF YOU DO, I CAN LET YOU SEE HER, YOU KNOW.
THAT'S WHAT YOU DESIRED AND WHY YOU FELL INTO THAT FORM, ISN'T IT?
THAT'S RIGHT. YOU CHILDREN JUST BE GOOD.
BETTER TO NOT EVEN CONTEMPLATE DISOBEYING ME.
PFFT!
AH
HA
HA
HA!

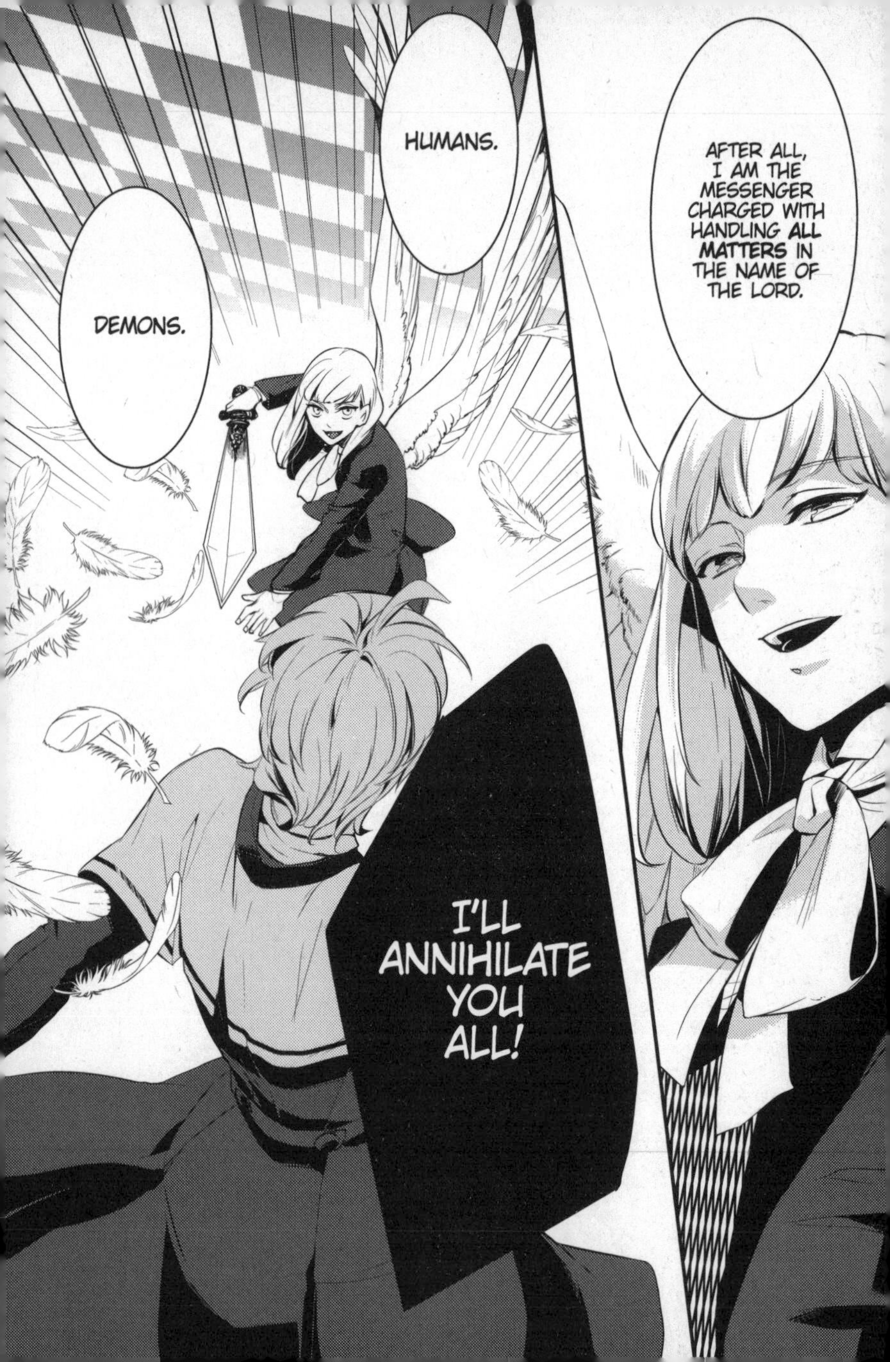
AFTER ALL, I AM THE MESSENGER CHARGED WITH HANDLING ALL MATTERS IN THE NAME OF THE LORD.
HUMANS.
DEMONS.
I'LL ANNIHILATE YOU ALL!

魔界王子

devils and realist

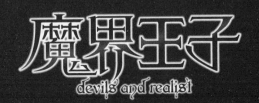

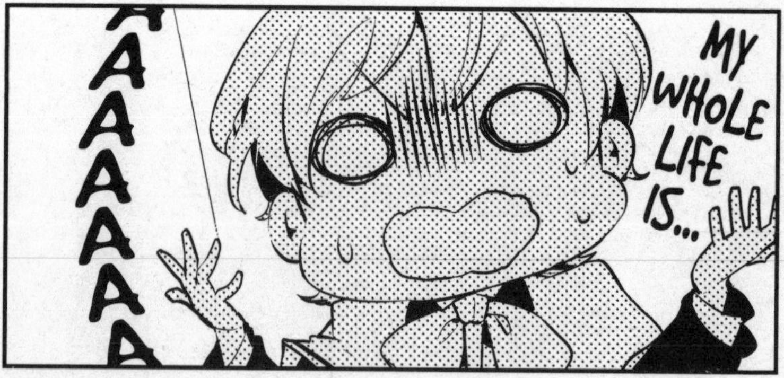
MY WHOLE LIFE IS...
AAAAAAA

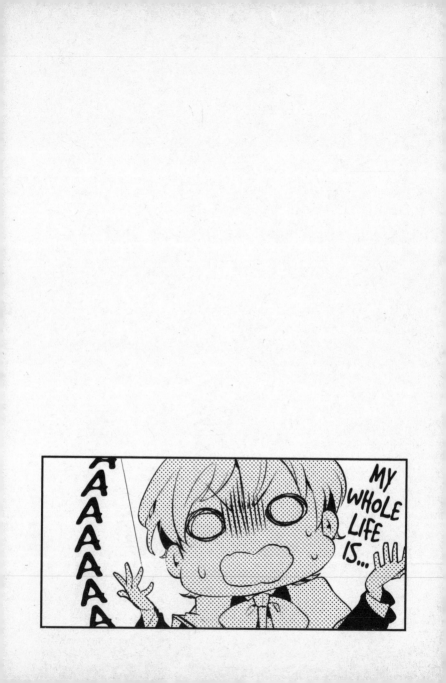

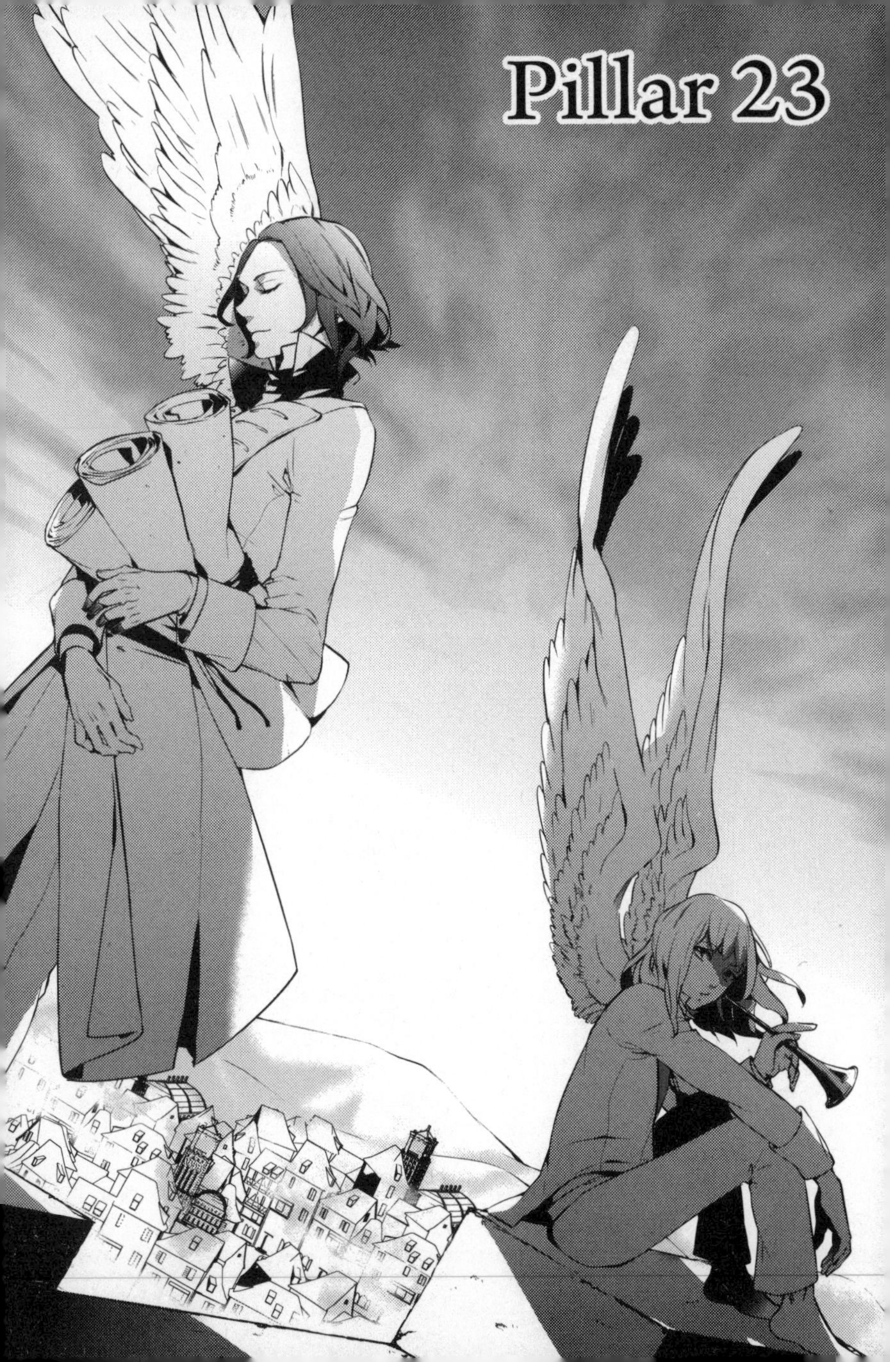
Pillar 23

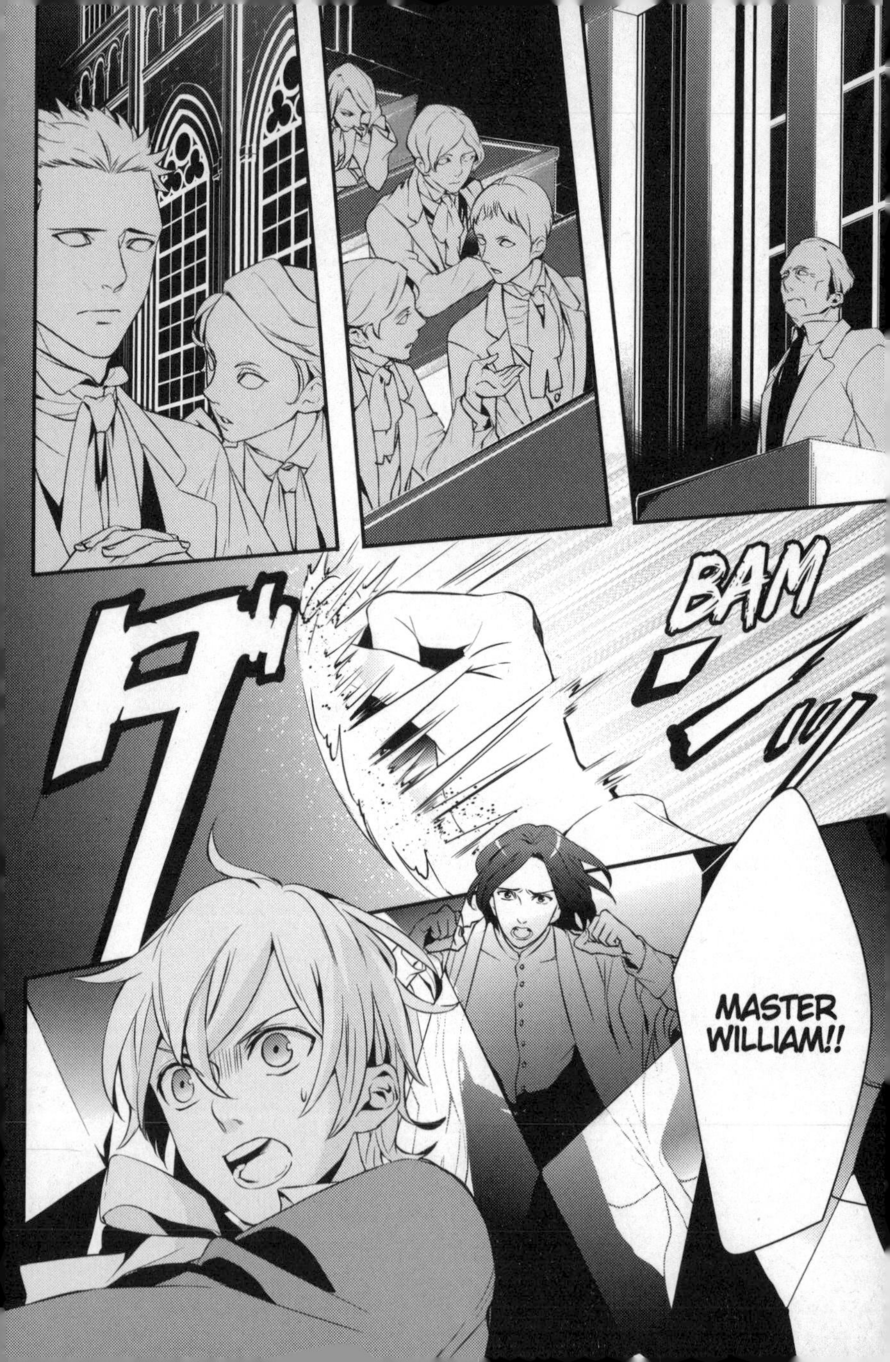
BAM
MASTER WILLIAM!!

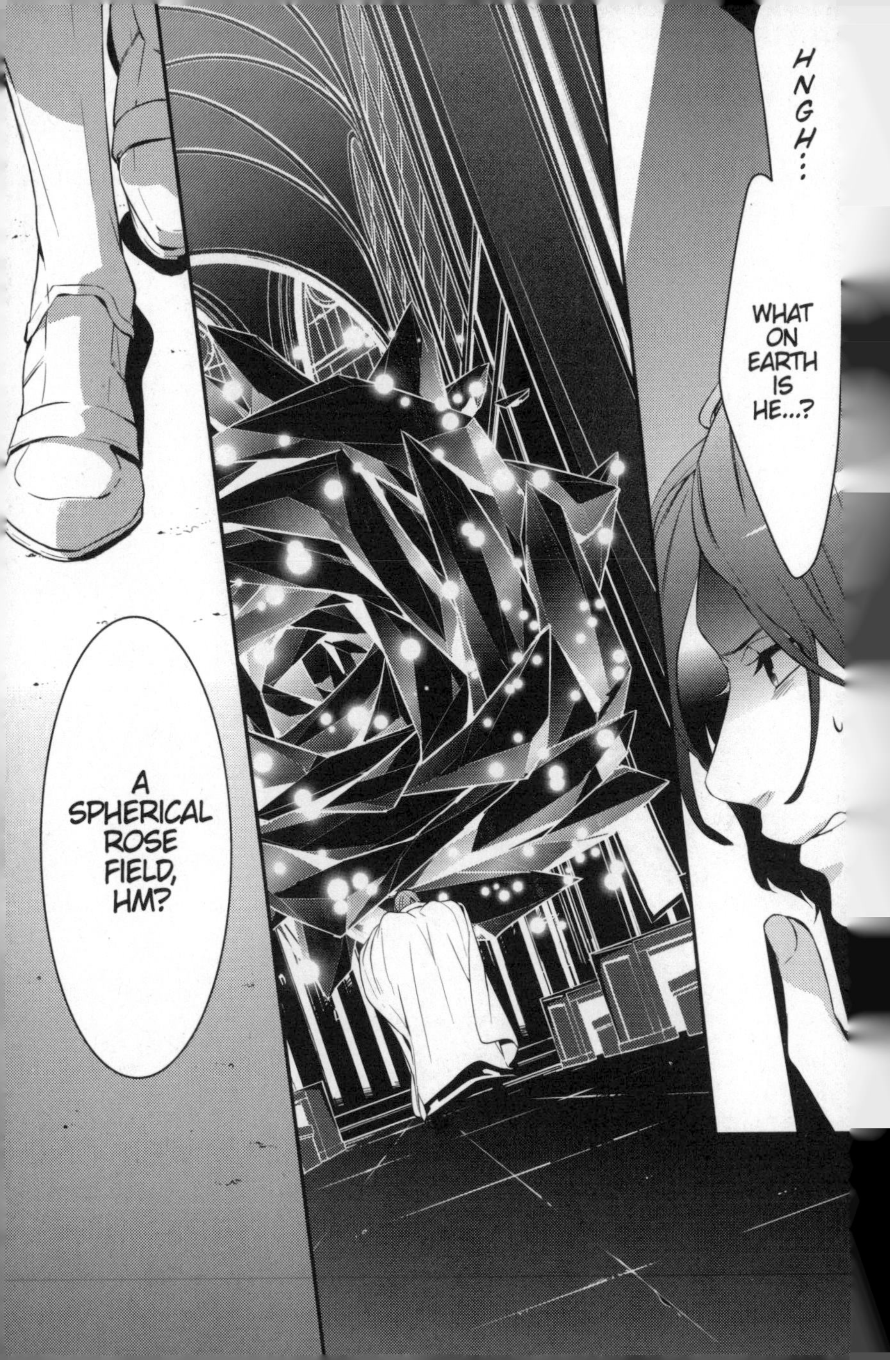
HNGH...
WHAT ON EARTH IS HE...?
A SPHERICAL ROSE FIELD, HM?

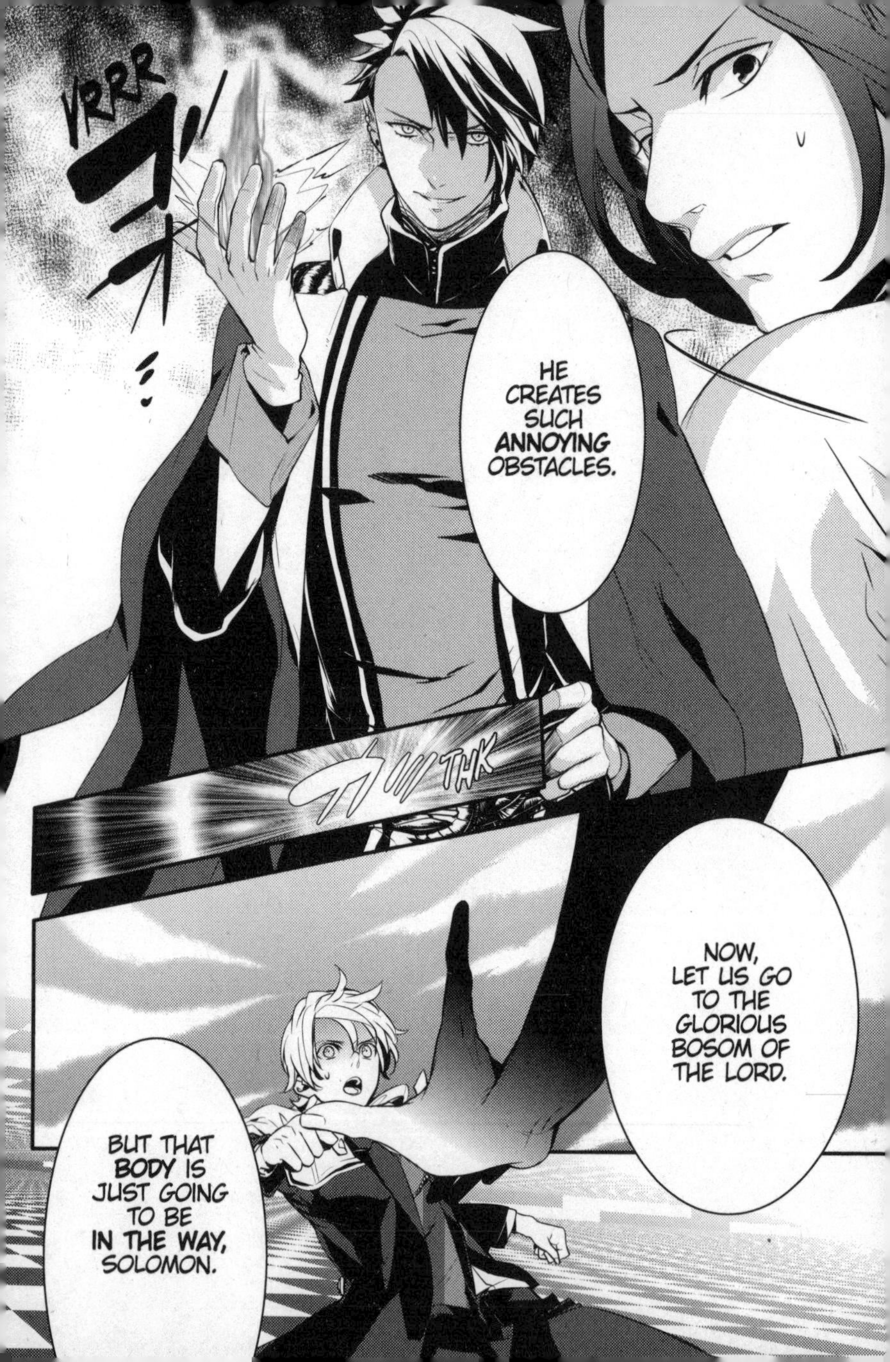

VRRR
HE CREATES SUCH ANNOYING OBSTACLES.
THK
NOW, LET US GO TO THE GLORIOUS BOSOM OF THE LORD.
BUT THAT BODY IS JUST GOING TO BE IN THE WAY, SOLOMON.

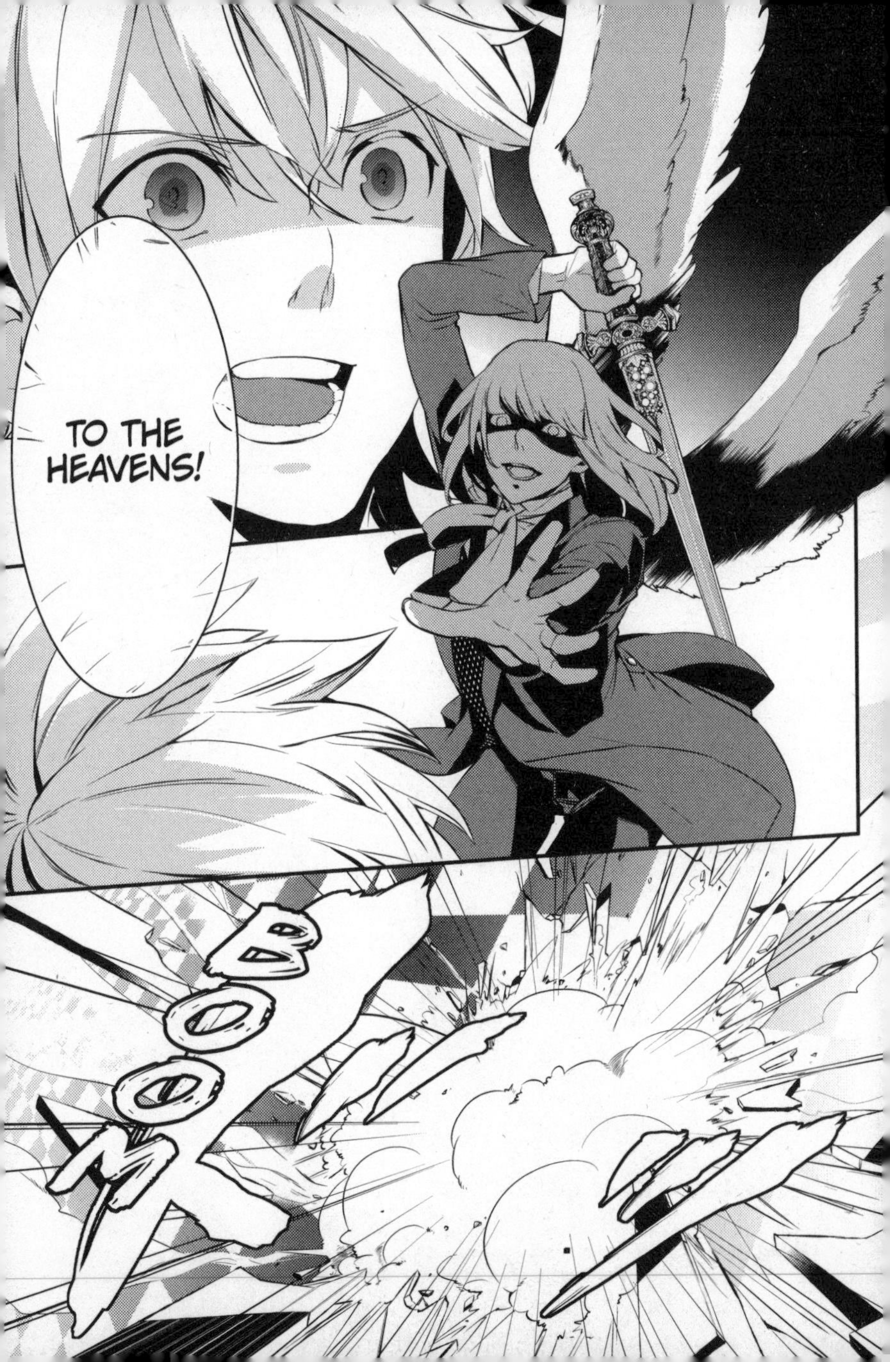
TO THE HEAVENS!
BOOM

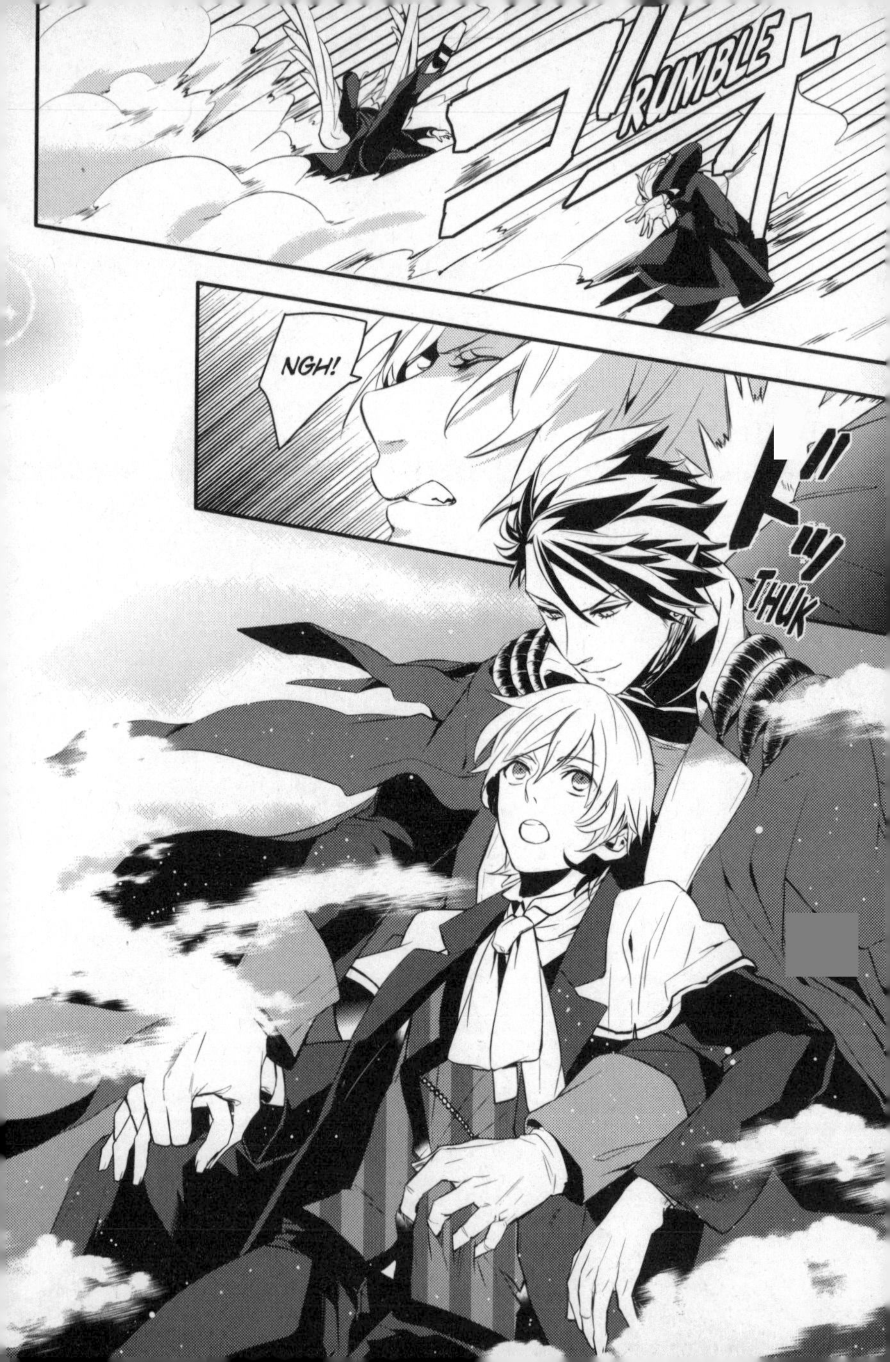
RUMBLE
NGH!
THUK

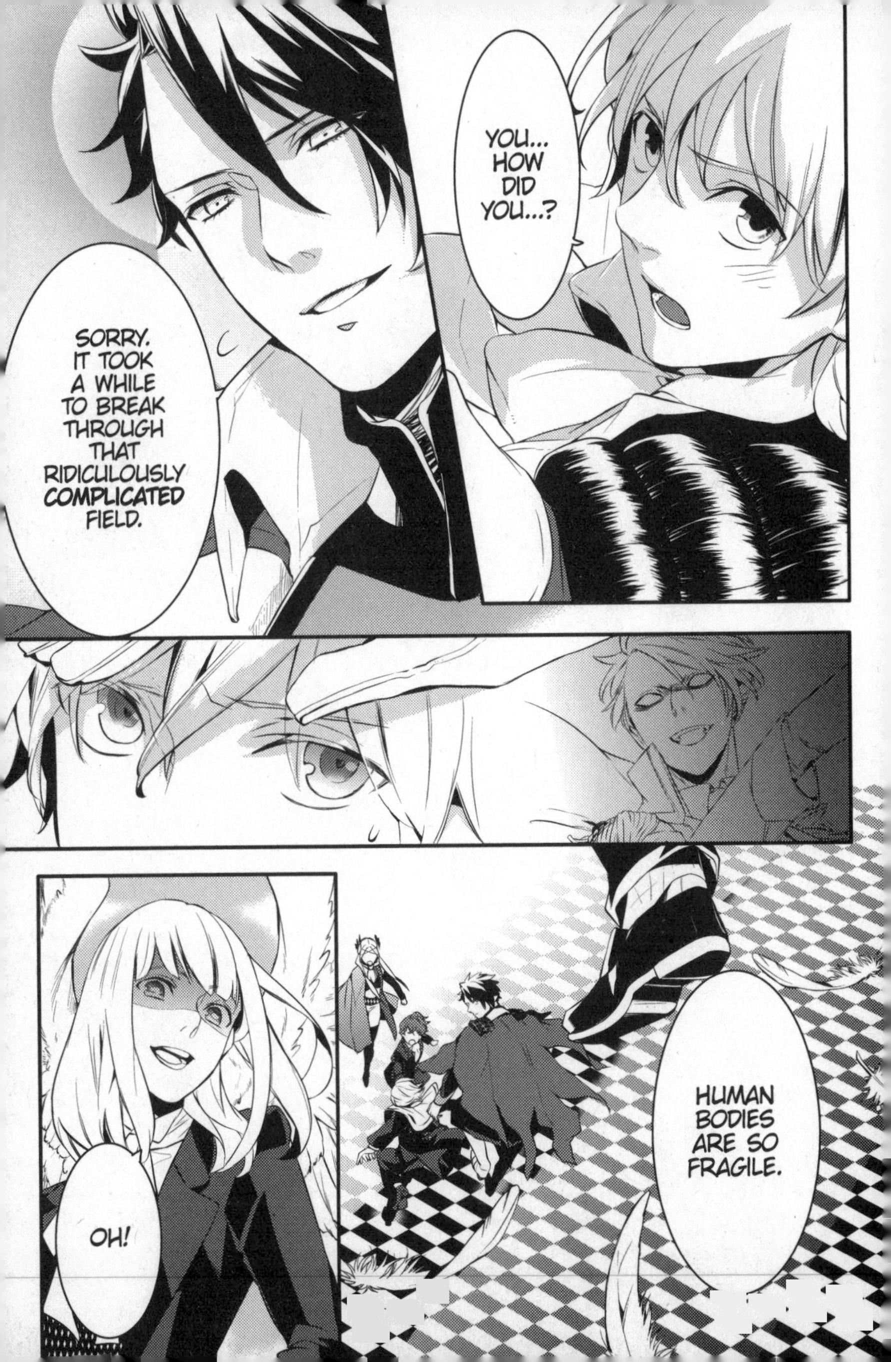
YOU... HOW DID YOU...?
SORRY. IT TOOK A WHILE TO BREAK THROUGH THAT RIDICULOUSLY COMPLICATED FIELD.
HUMAN BODIES ARE SO FRAGILE.
OH!

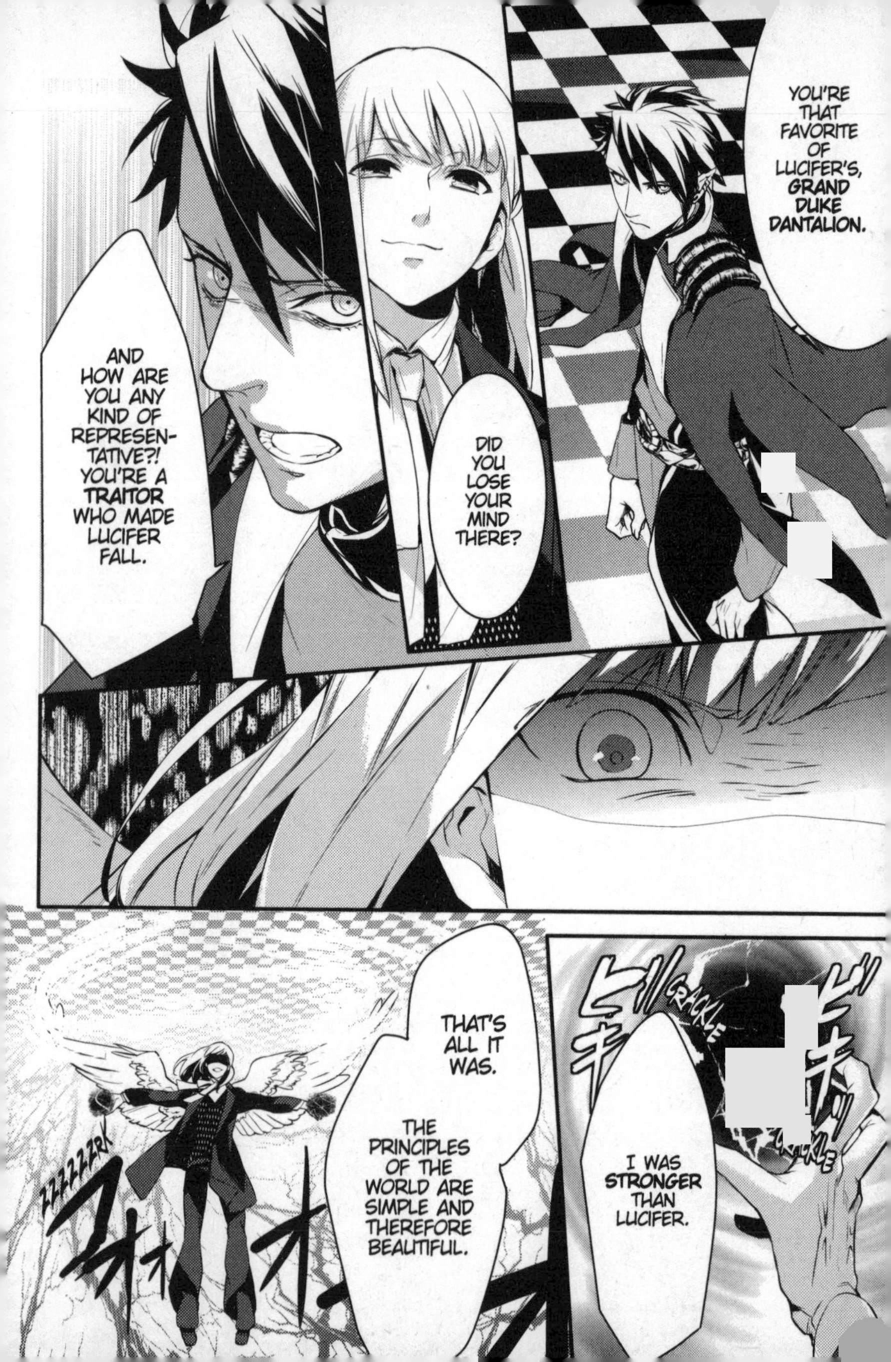
YOU'RE THAT FAVORITE OF LUCIFER'S, GRAND DUKE DANTALION.
DID YOU LOSE YOUR MIND THERE?
AND HOW ARE YOU ANY KIND OF REPRESENTATIVE?! YOU'RE A TRAITOR WHO MADE LUCIFER FALL.
CRACKLE
CRACKLE
I WAS STRONGER THAN LUCIFER.
THAT'S ALL IT WAS.
THE PRINCIPLES OF THE WORLD ARE SIMPLE AND THEREFORE BEAUTIFUL.

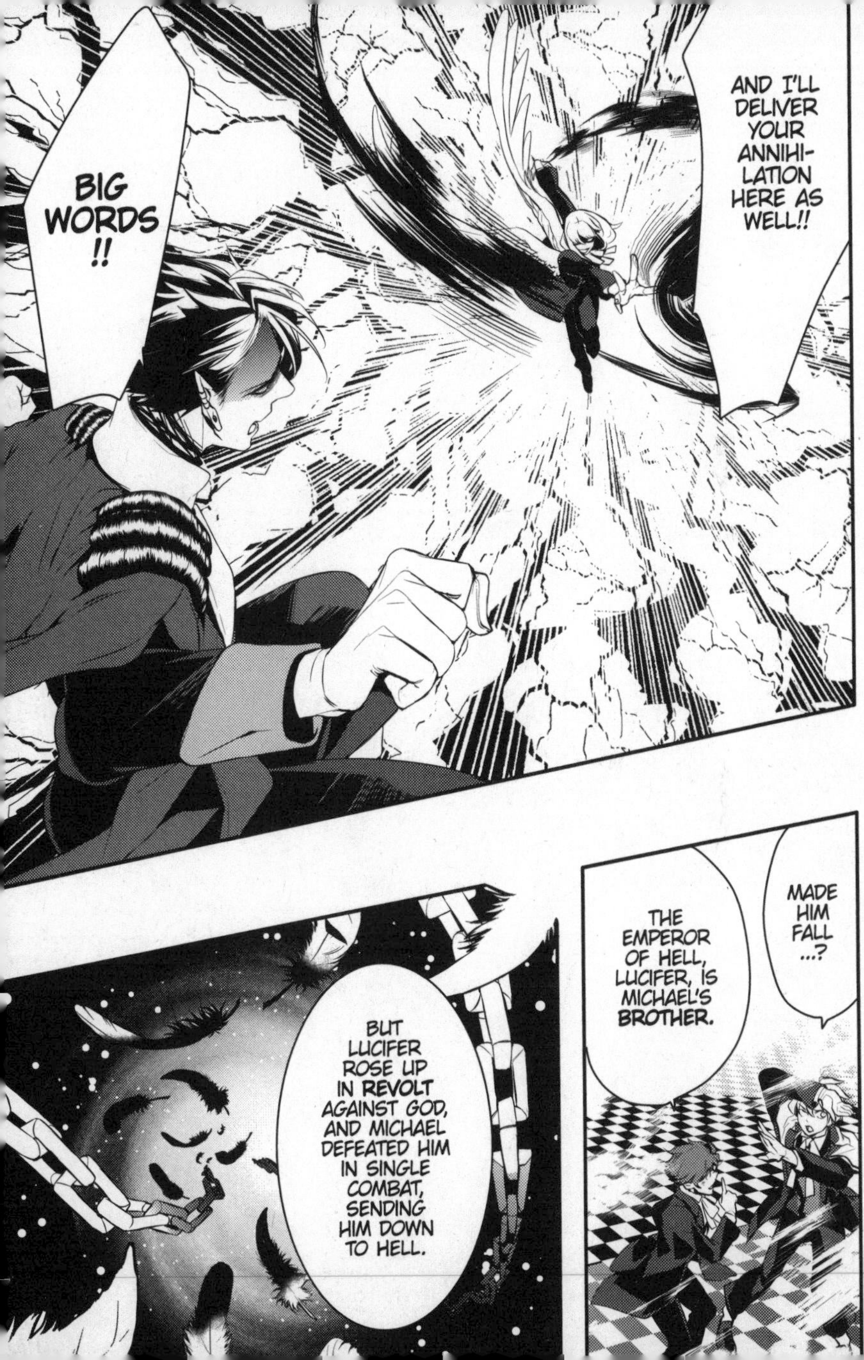
AND I'LL DELIVER YOUR ANNIHILATION HERE AS WELL!!
BIG WORDS!!
MADE HIM FALL...?
THE EMPEROR OF HELL, LUCIFER, IS MICHAEL'S BROTHER.
BUT LUCIFER ROSE UP IN REVOLT AGAINST GOD, AND MICHAEL DEFEATED HIM IN SINGLE COMBAT, SENDING HIM DOWN TO HELL.

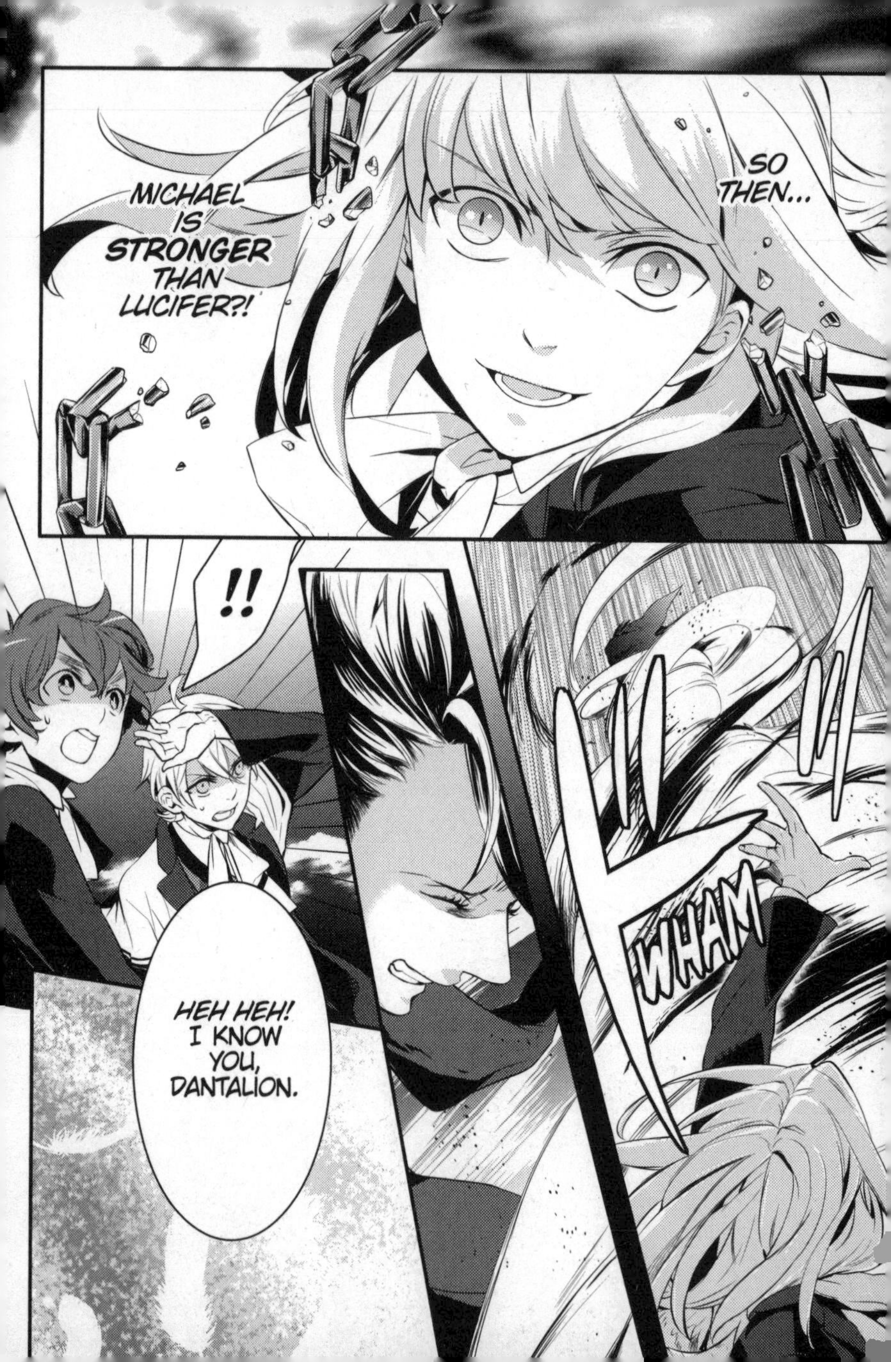
SO THEN...
MICHAEL IS STRONGER THAN LUCIFER?!
WHAM
!!
HEH HEH! I KNOW YOU, DANTALION.

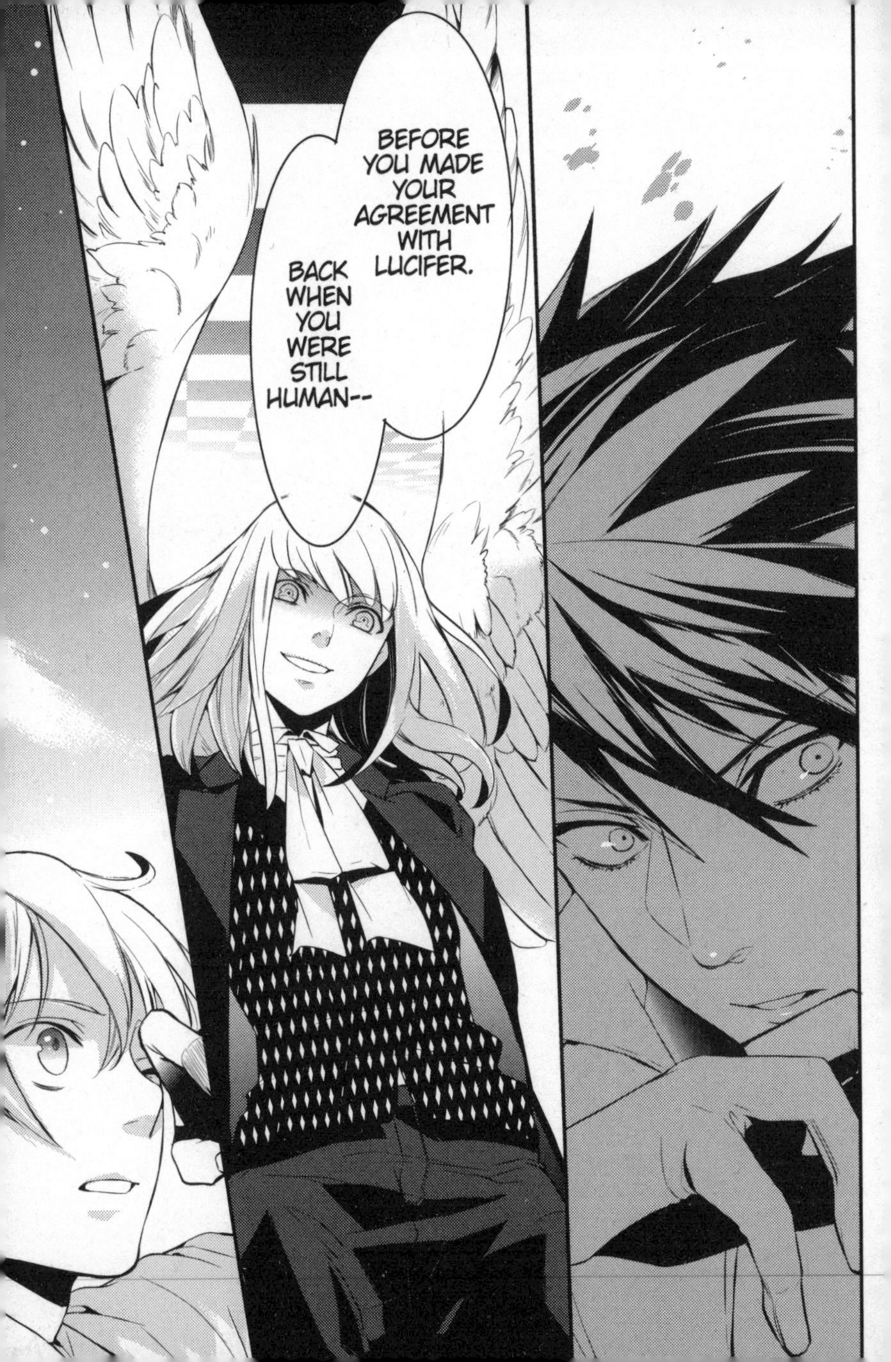
BEFORE YOU MADE YOUR AGREEMENT WITH LUCIFER.
BACK WHEN YOU WERE STILL HUMAN--

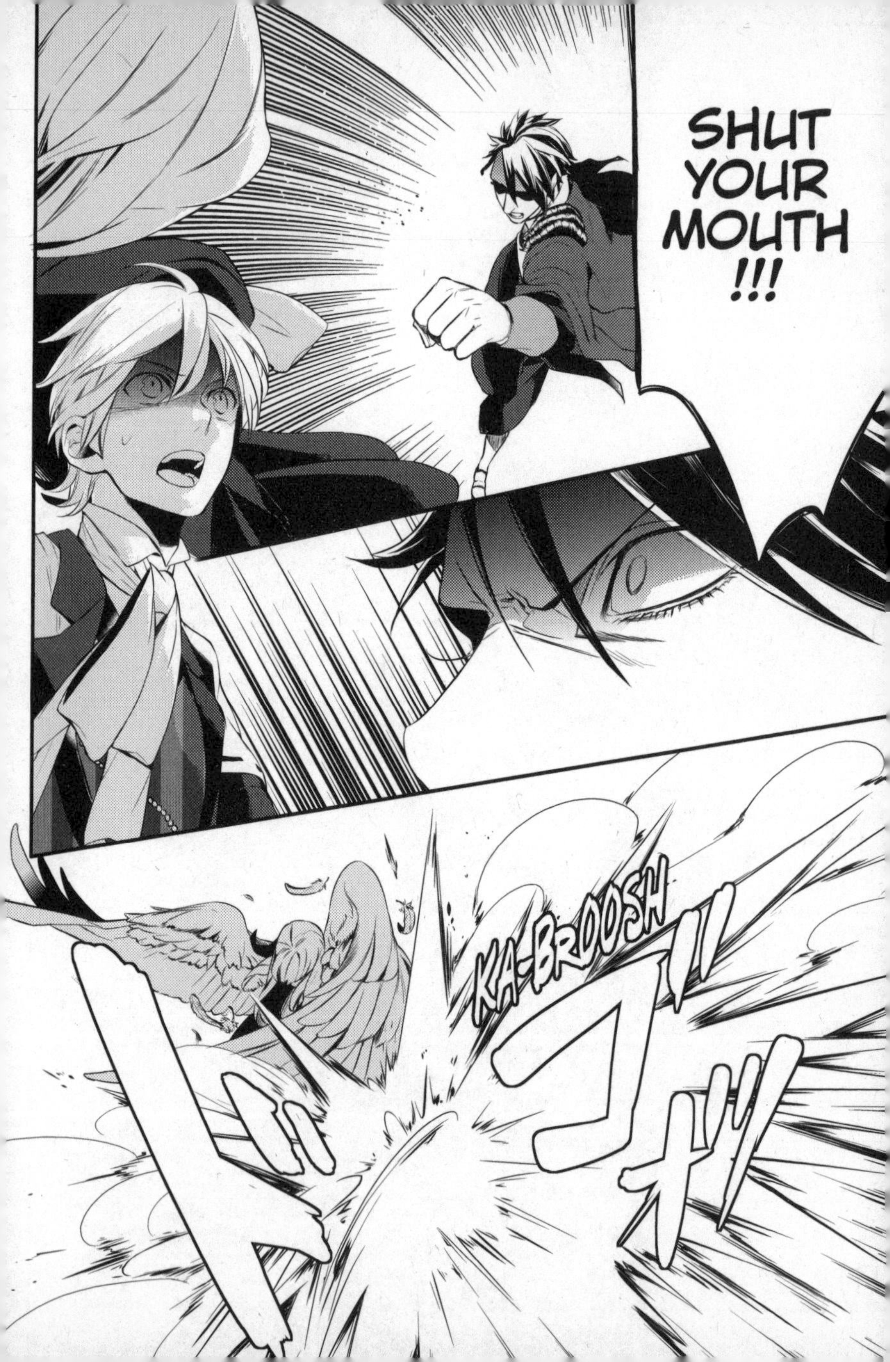
SHUT YOUR MOUTH !!!
KA-BROOSH !!

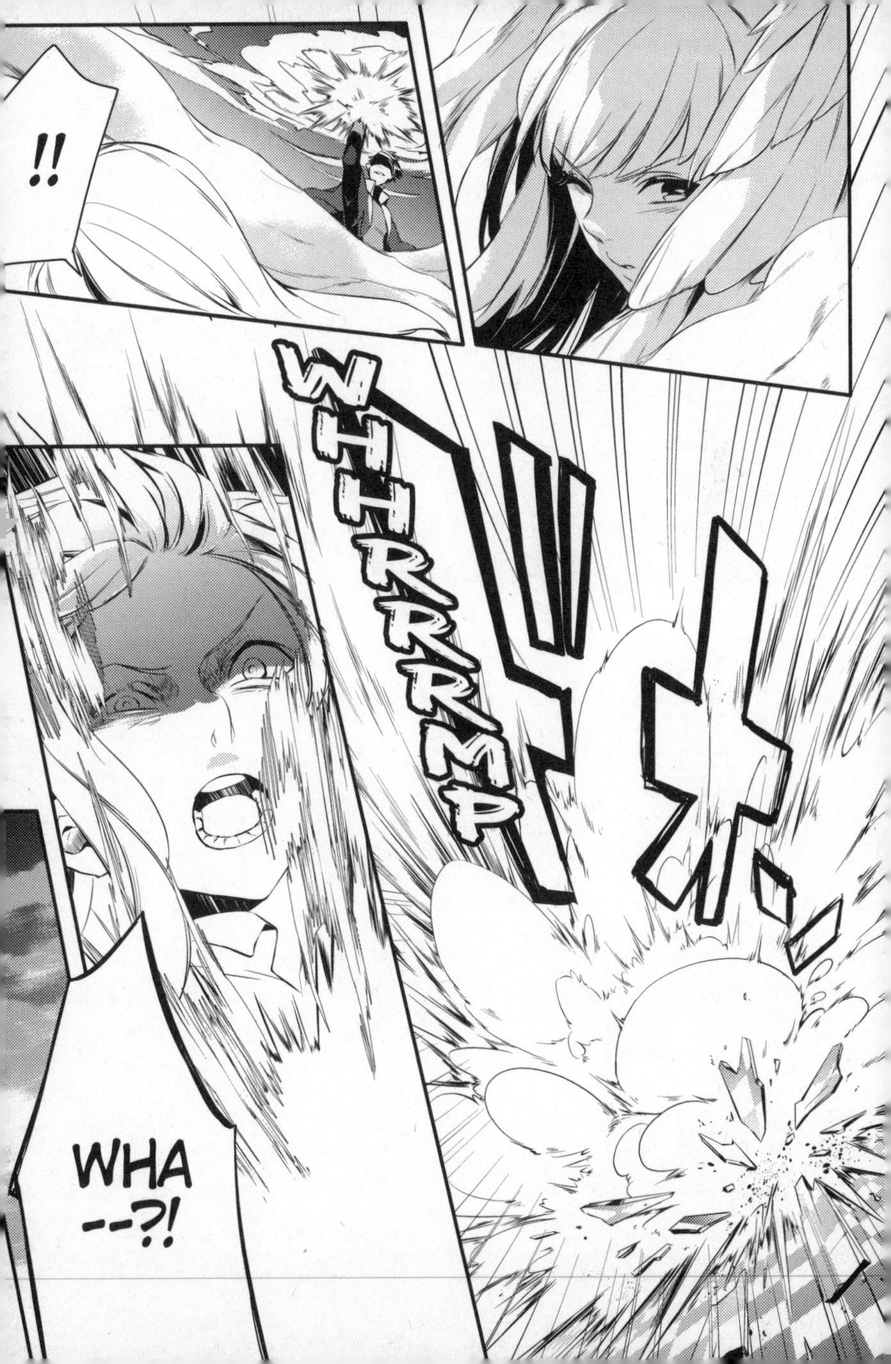
!!
WHHRRRMP
WHA --?!

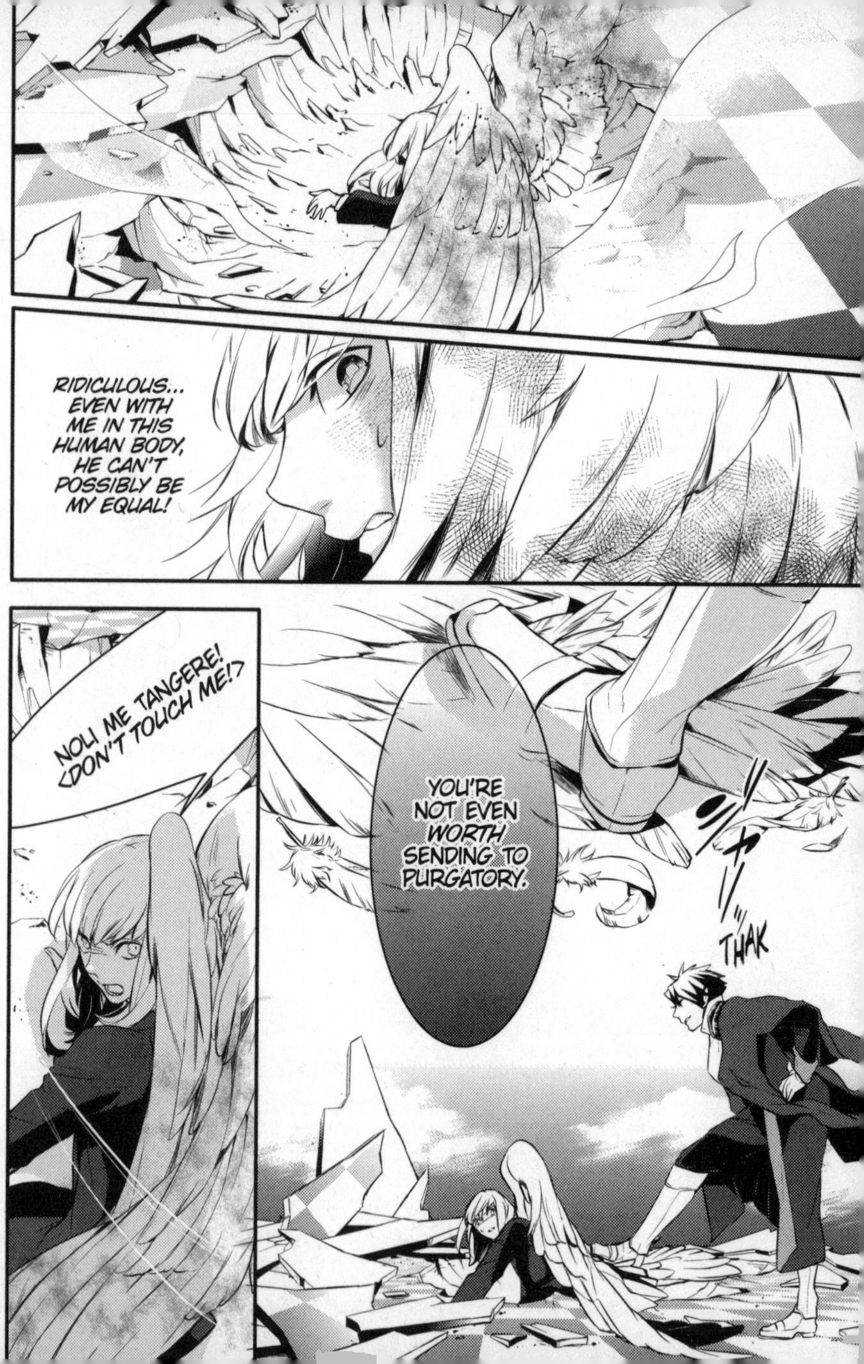
RIDICULOUS... EVEN WITH ME IN THIS HUMAN BODY, HE CAN'T POSSIBLY BE MY EQUAL!
YOU'RE NOT EVEN WORTH SENDING TO PURGATORY.
NOLI ME TANGERE! <DON'T TOUCH ME!>
THAK

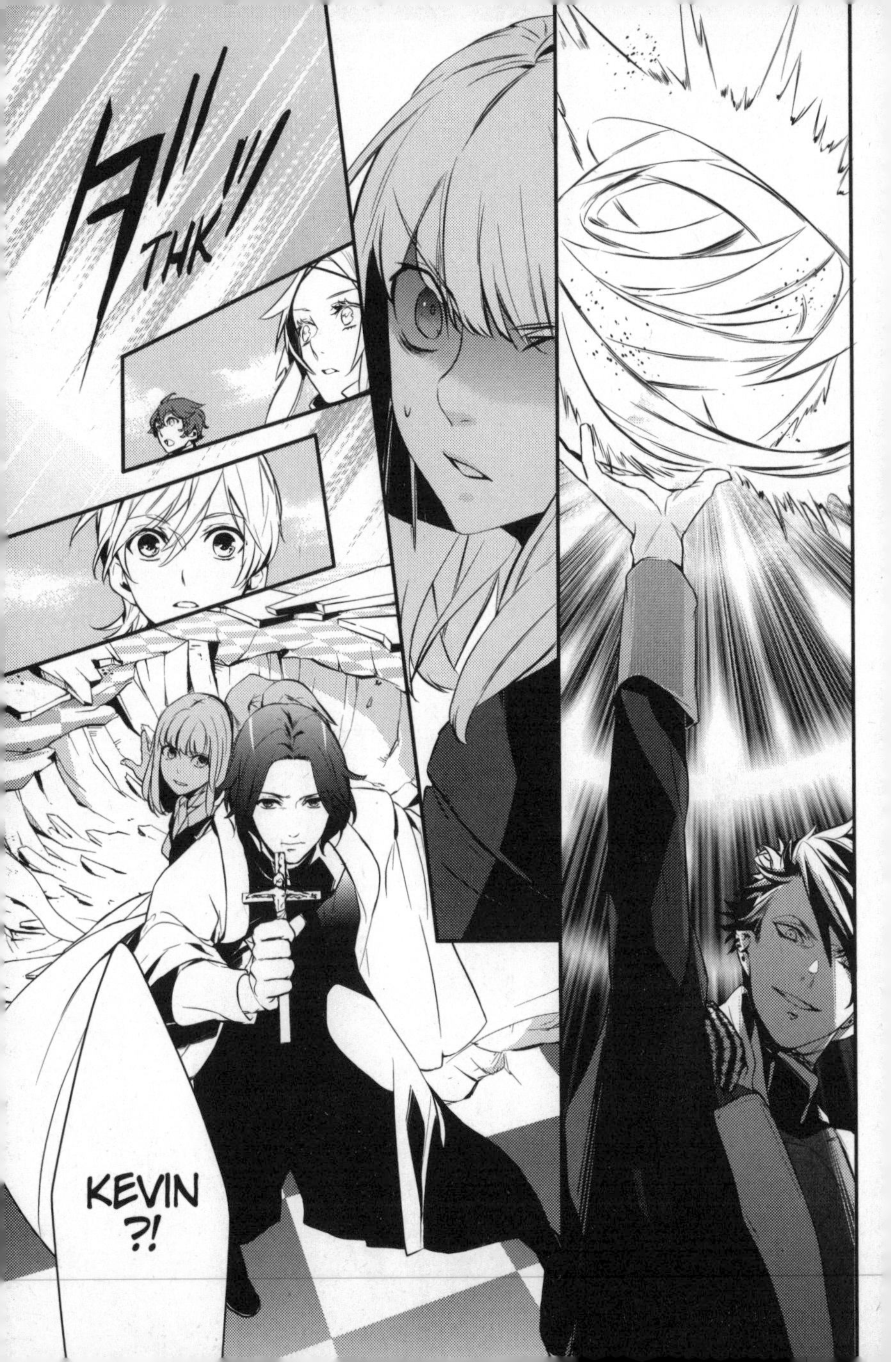

THK
KEVIN ?!

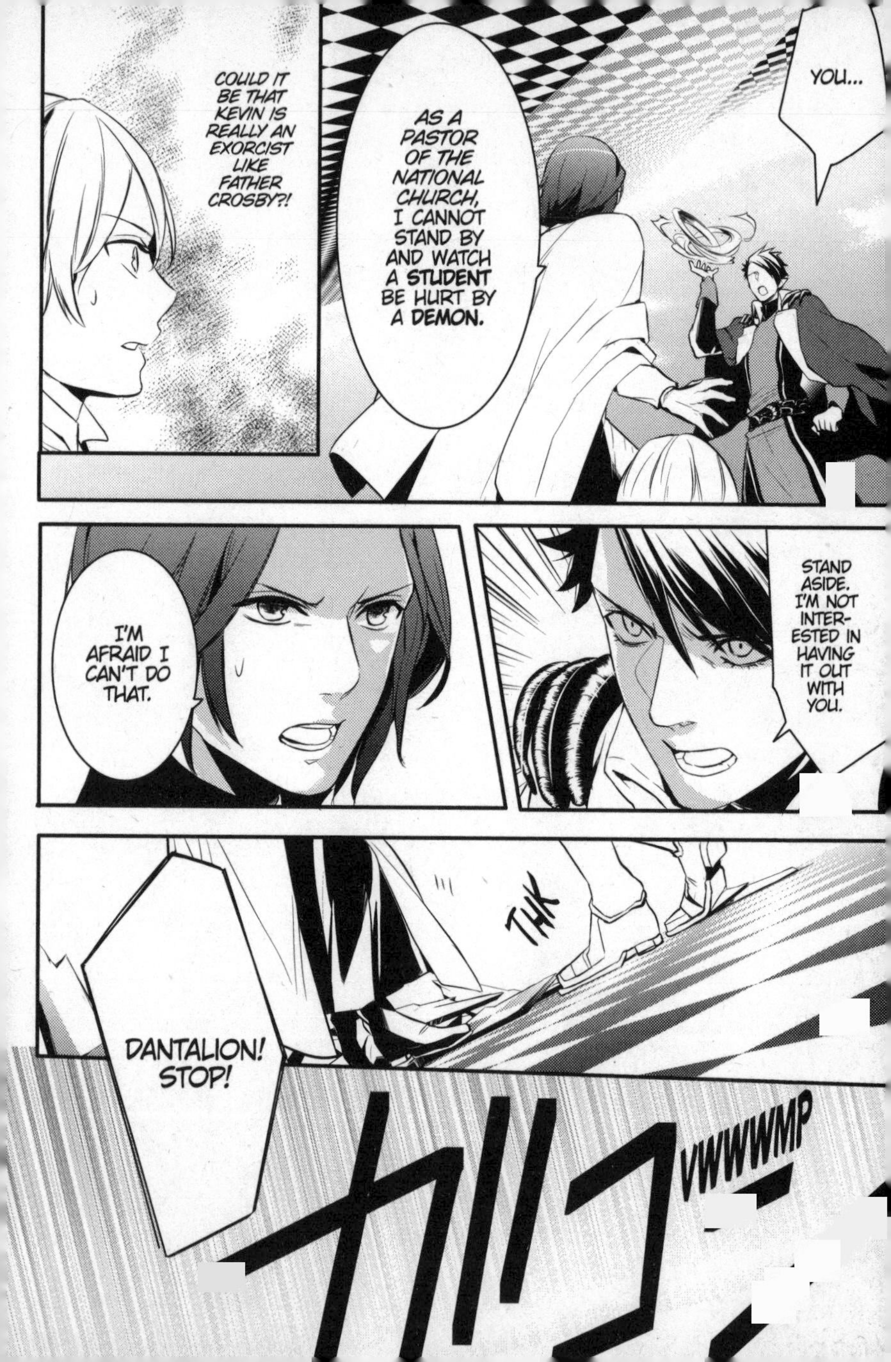
YOU...
AS A PASTOR OF THE NATIONAL CHURCH, I CANNOT STAND BY AND WATCH A **STUDENT** BE HURT BY A **DEMON.**
COULD IT BE THAT KEVIN IS REALLY AN EXORCIST LIKE FATHER CROSBY?!
STAND ASIDE. I'M NOT INTER-ESTED IN HAVING IT OUT WITH YOU.
I'M AFRAID I CAN'T DO THAT.
THK
DANTALION! STOP!
VWWWMP

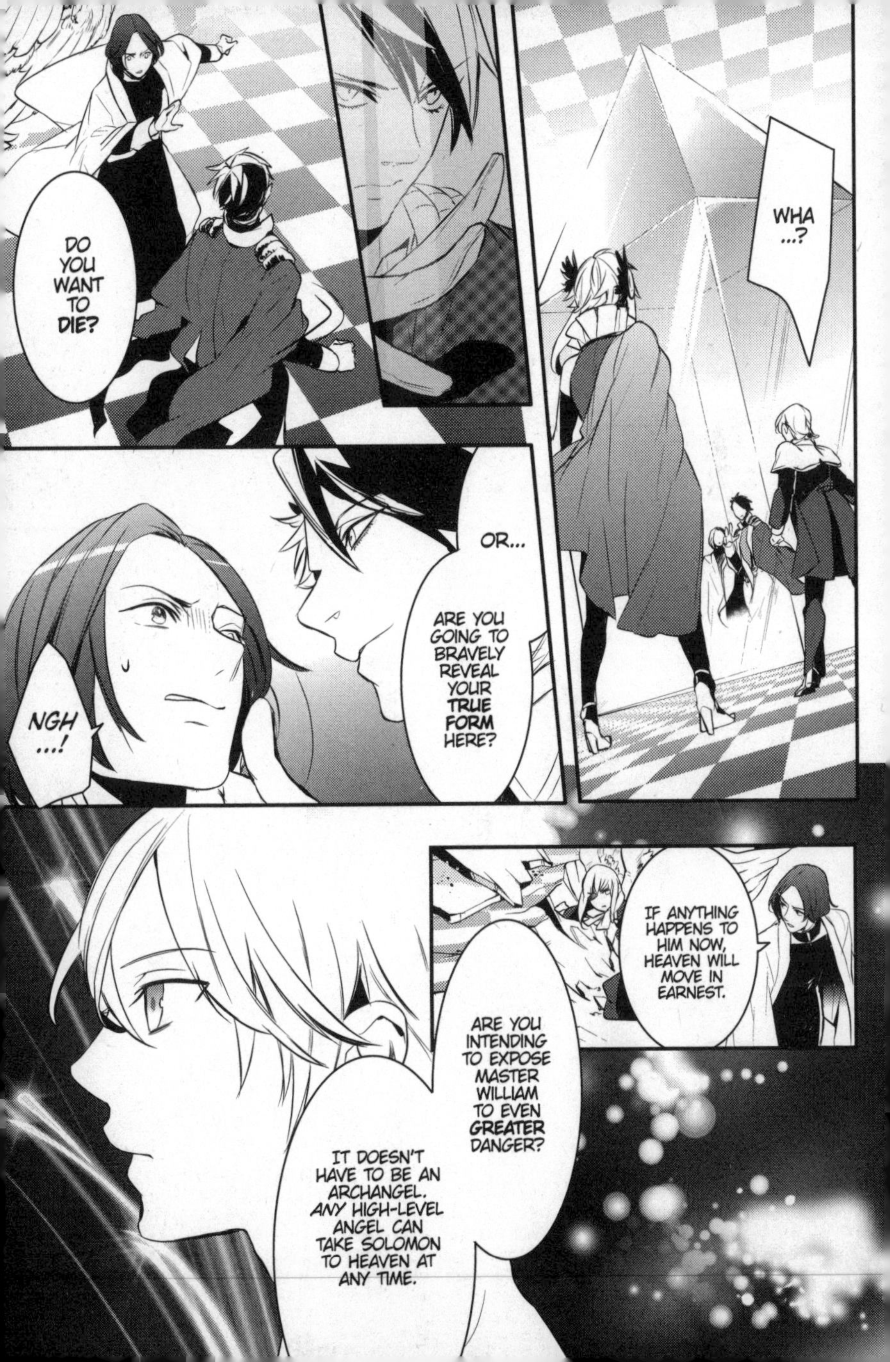
WHA ...?
DO YOU WANT TO DIE?
OR...
ARE YOU GOING TO BRAVELY REVEAL YOUR TRUE FORM HERE?
NGH ...!
IF ANYTHING HAPPENS TO HIM NOW, HEAVEN WILL MOVE IN EARNEST.
ARE YOU INTENDING TO EXPOSE MASTER WILLIAM TO EVEN GREATER DANGER?
IT DOESN'T HAVE TO BE AN ARCHANGEL. ANY HIGH-LEVEL ANGEL CAN TAKE SOLOMON TO HEAVEN AT ANY TIME.

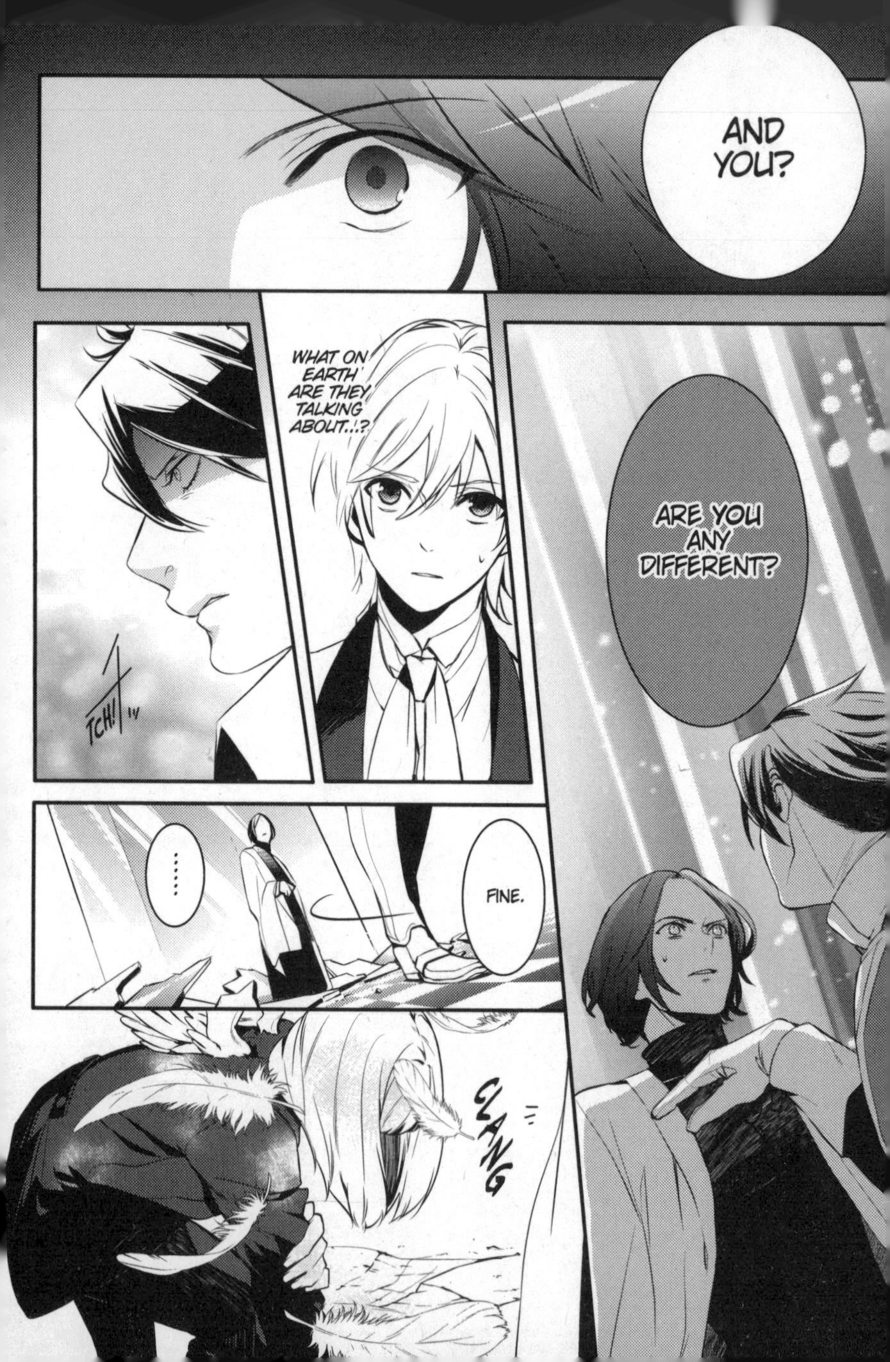
AND YOU?
ARE YOU ANY DIFFERENT?
WHAT ON EARTH ARE THEY TALKING ABOUT...!?
TCH!
FINE.
......
CLANG

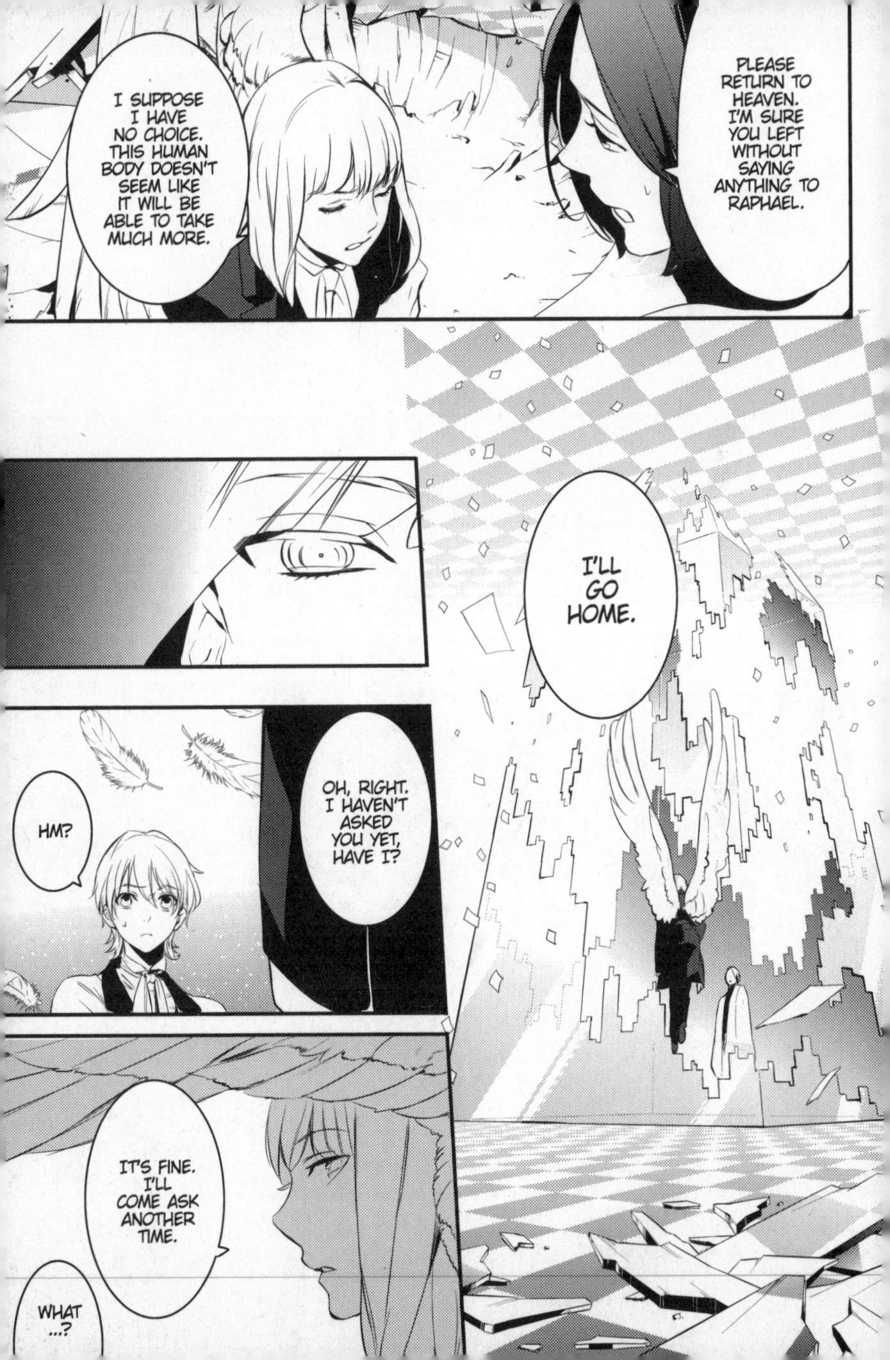

PLEASE RETURN TO HEAVEN. I'M SURE YOU LEFT WITHOUT SAYING ANYTHING TO RAPHAEL.
I SUPPOSE I HAVE NO CHOICE. THIS HUMAN BODY DOESN'T SEEM LIKE IT WILL BE ABLE TO TAKE MUCH MORE.
I'LL GO HOME.
OH, RIGHT. I HAVEN'T ASKED YOU YET, HAVE I?
HM?
IT'S FINE. I'LL COME ASK ANOTHER TIME.
WHAT ...?

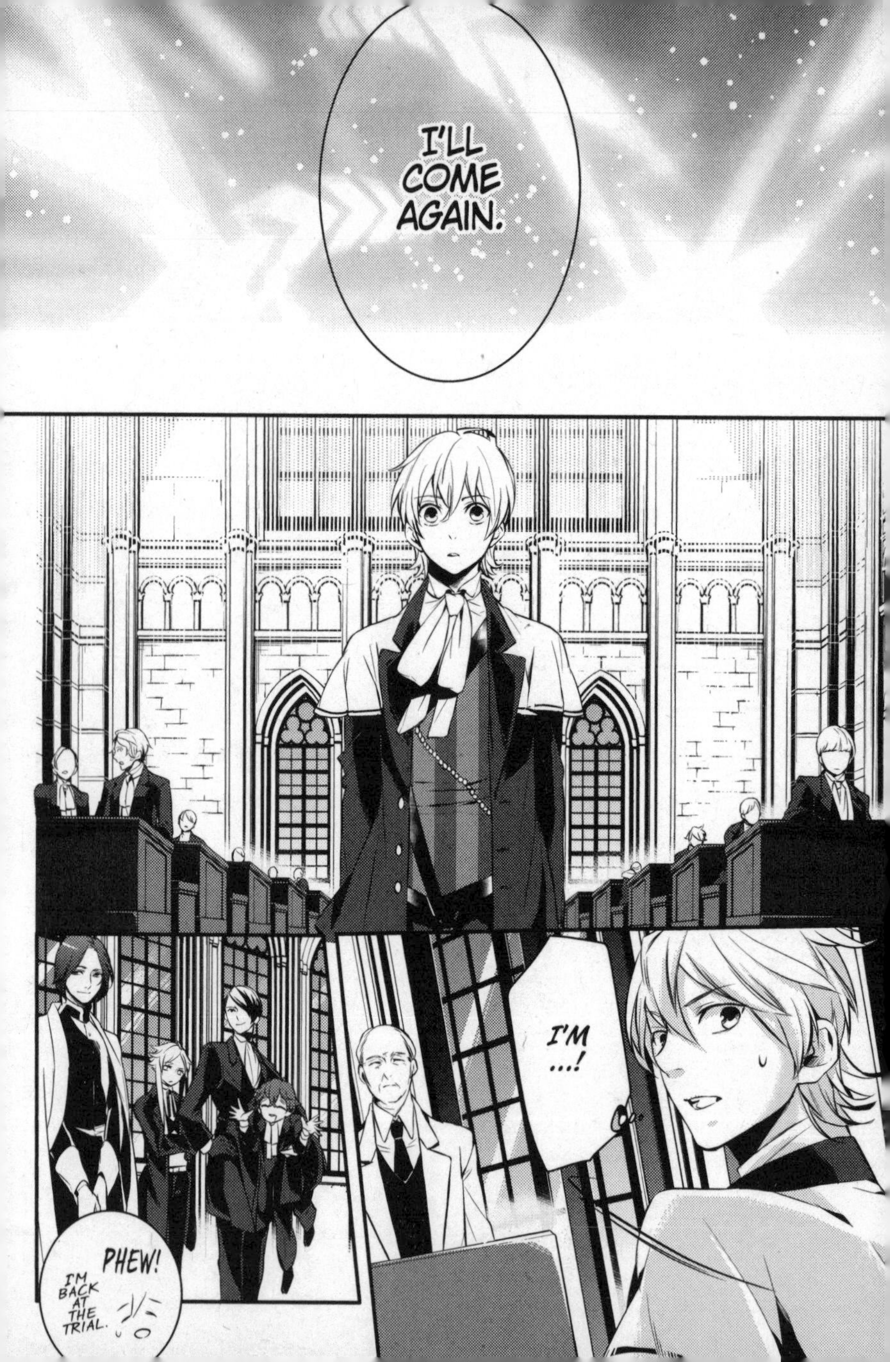
I'LL COME AGAIN.
I'M ...!
PHEW!
I'M BACK AT THE TRIAL.

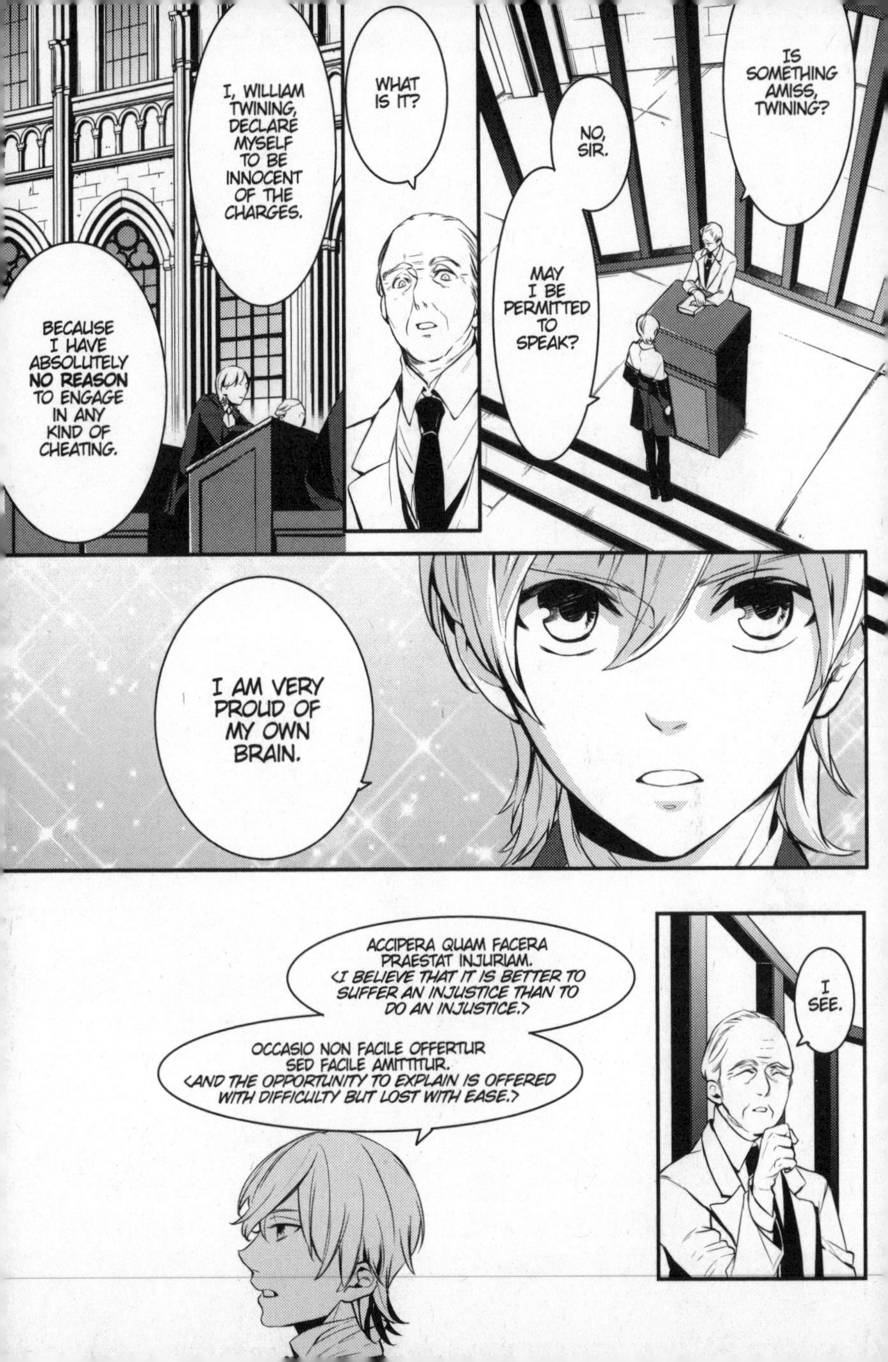
IS SOMETHING AMISS, TWINING?
NO, SIR.
MAY I BE PERMITTED TO SPEAK?
WHAT IS IT?
I, WILLIAM TWINING, DECLARE MYSELF TO BE INNOCENT OF THE CHARGES.
BECAUSE I HAVE ABSOLUTELY NO REASON TO ENGAGE IN ANY KIND OF CHEATING.
I AM VERY PROUD OF MY OWN BRAIN.
I SEE.
ACCIPERA QUAM FACERA PRAESTAT INJURIAM. <I BELIEVE THAT IT IS BETTER TO SUFFER AN INJUSTICE THAN TO DO AN INJUSTICE.>
OCCASIO NON FACILE OFFERTUR SED FACILE AMITTITUR. <AND THE OPPORTUNITY TO EXPLAIN IS OFFERED WITH DIFFICULTY BUT LOST WITH EASE.>

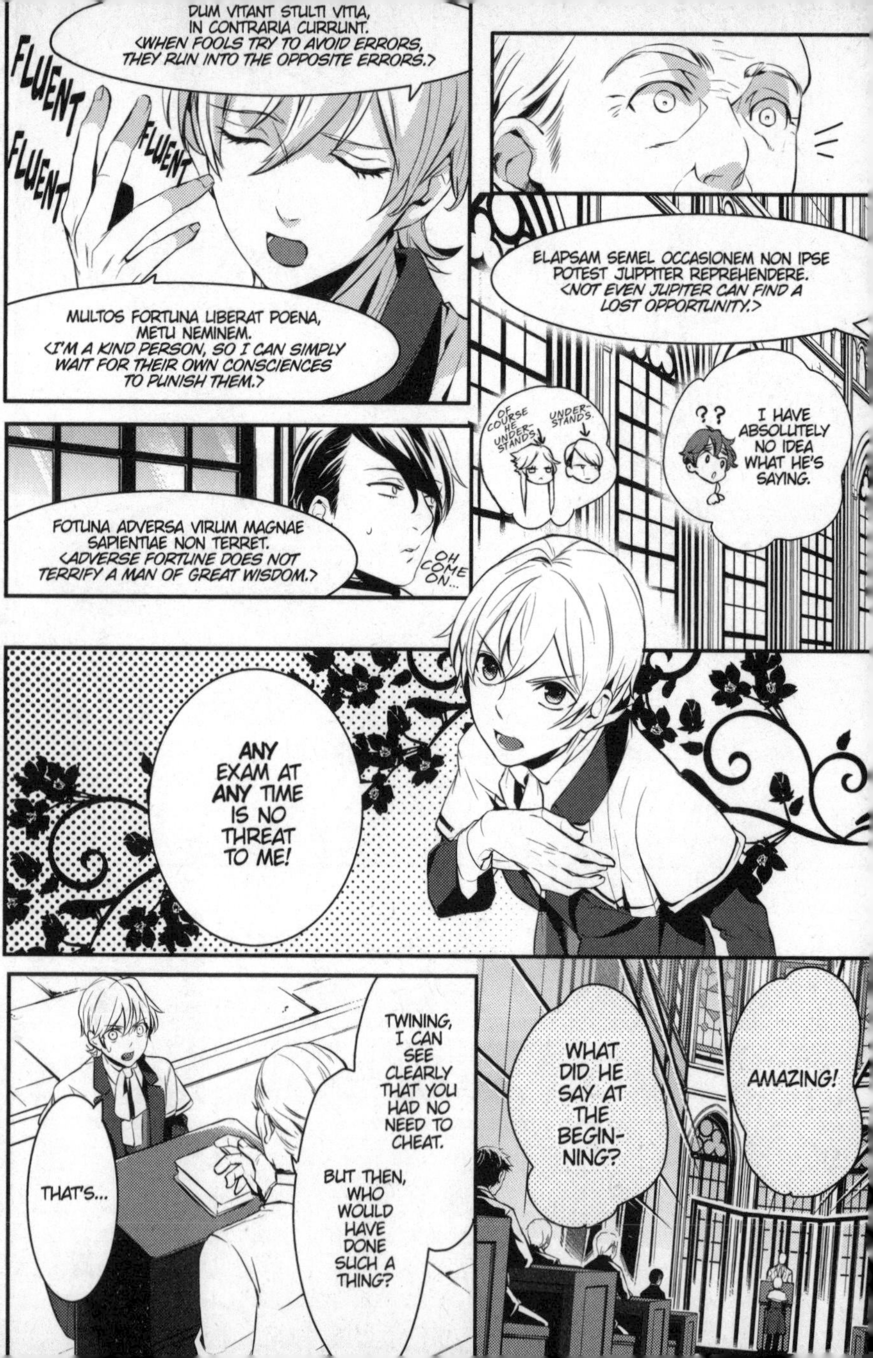
DUM VITANT STULTI VITIA, IN CONTRARIA CURRUNT. <WHEN FOOLS TRY TO AVOID ERRORS, THEY RUN INTO THE OPPOSITE ERRORS.>
FLUENT FLUENT FLUENT FLUENT
MULTOS FORTUNA LIBERAT POENA, METU NEMINEM. <I'M A KIND PERSON, SO I CAN SIMPLY WAIT FOR THEIR OWN CONSCIENCES TO PUNISH THEM.>
ELAPSAM SEMEL OCCASIONEM NON IPSE POTEST JUPPITER REPREHENDERE. <NOT EVEN JUPITER CAN FIND A LOST OPPORTUNITY.>
I HAVE ABSOLUTELY NO IDEA WHAT HE'S SAYING.
??
UNDER-STANDS.
OF COURSE HE UNDER-STANDS.
FOTUNA ADVERSA VIRUM MAGNAE SAPIENTIAE NON TERRET. <ADVERSE FORTUNE DOES NOT TERRIFY A MAN OF GREAT WISDOM.>
OH COME ON...
ANY EXAM AT ANY TIME IS NO THREAT TO ME!
AMAZING!
WHAT DID HE SAY AT THE BEGIN-NING?
TWINING, I CAN SEE CLEARLY THAT YOU HAD NO NEED TO CHEAT.
BUT THEN, WHO WOULD HAVE DONE SUCH A THING?
THAT'S...

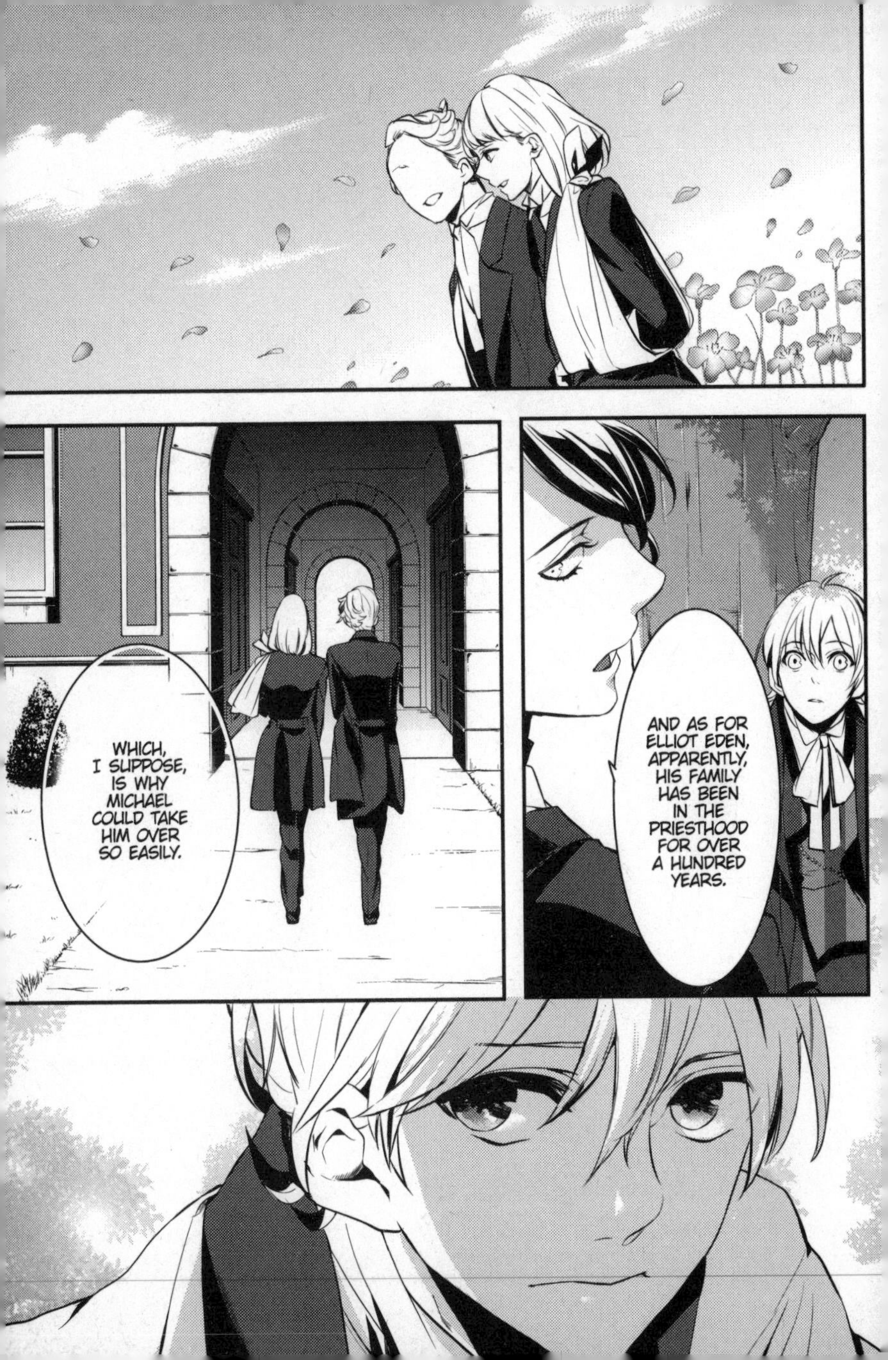
AND AS FOR ELLIOT EDEN, APPARENTLY, HIS FAMILY HAS BEEN IN THE PRIESTHOOD FOR OVER A HUNDRED YEARS.
WHICH, I SUPPOSE, IS WHY MICHAEL COULD TAKE HIM OVER SO EASILY.

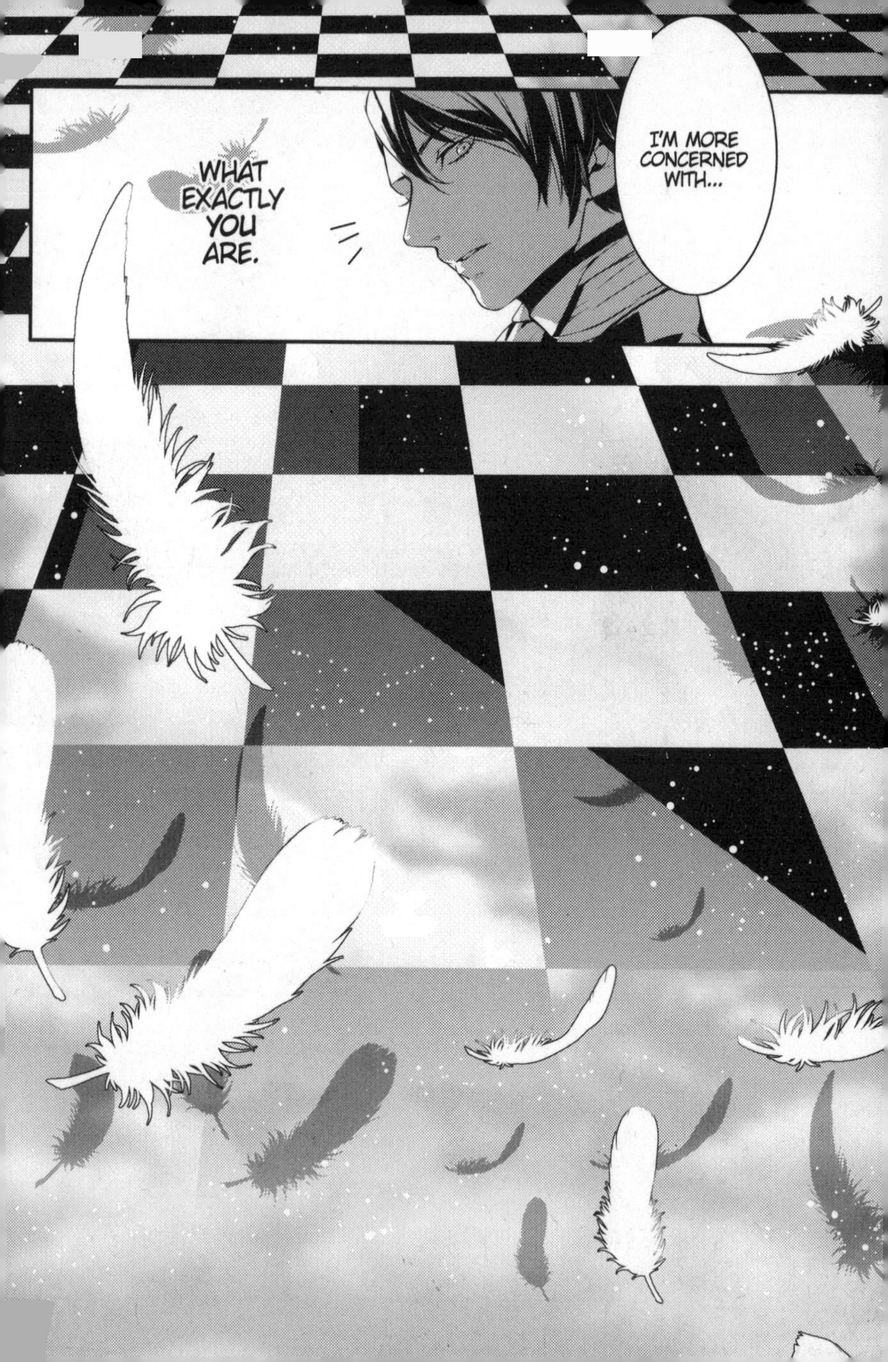
I'M MORE CONCERNED WITH...
WHAT EXACTLY YOU ARE.

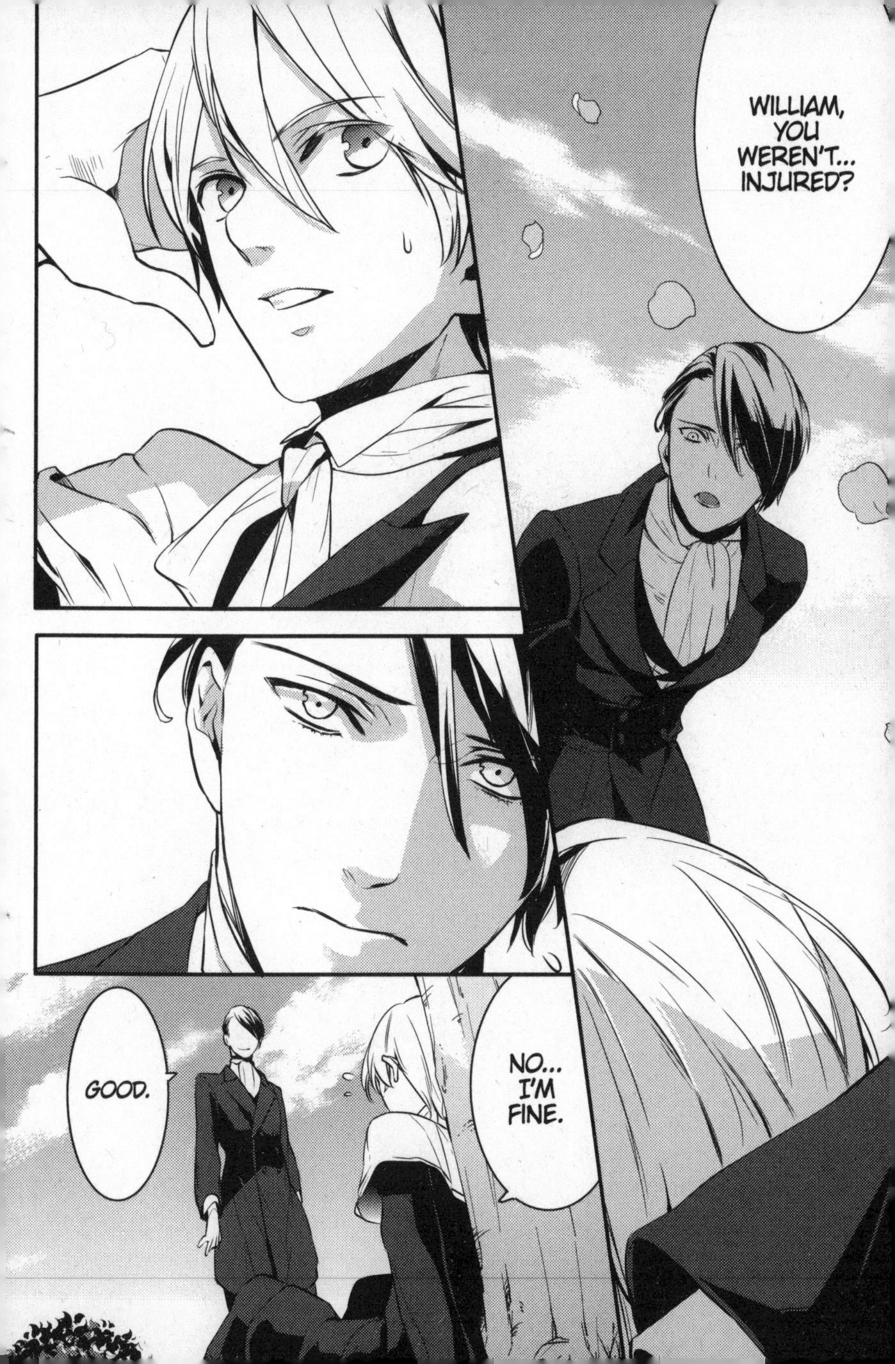
WILLIAM, YOU WEREN'T... INJURED?
NO... I'M FINE.
GOOD.

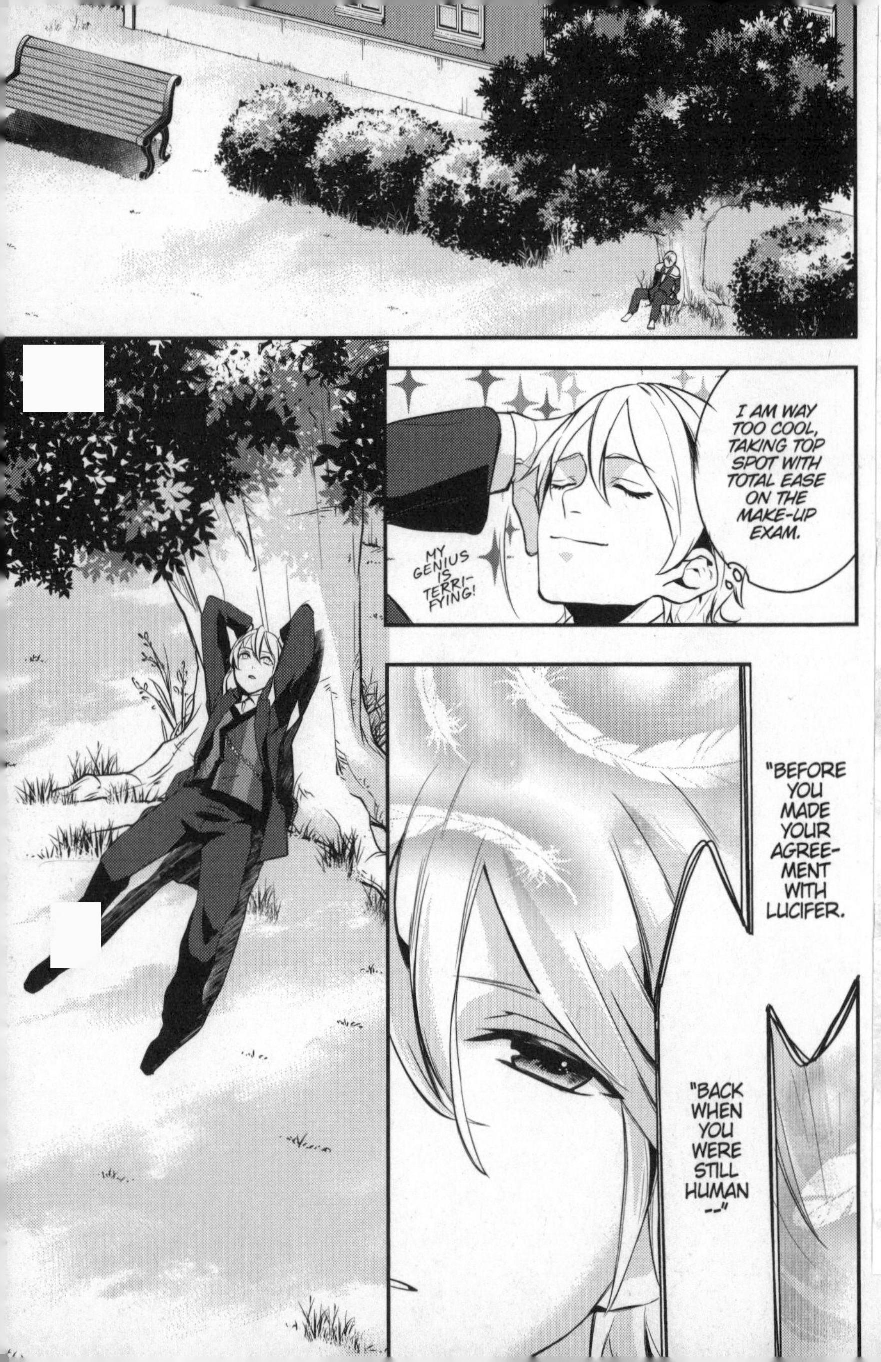
I AM WAY TOO COOL, TAKING TOP SPOT WITH TOTAL EASE ON THE MAKE-UP EXAM.
MY GENIUS IS TERRIFYING!
"BEFORE YOU MADE YOUR AGREEMENT WITH LUCIFER.
"BACK WHEN YOU WERE STILL HUMAN--"

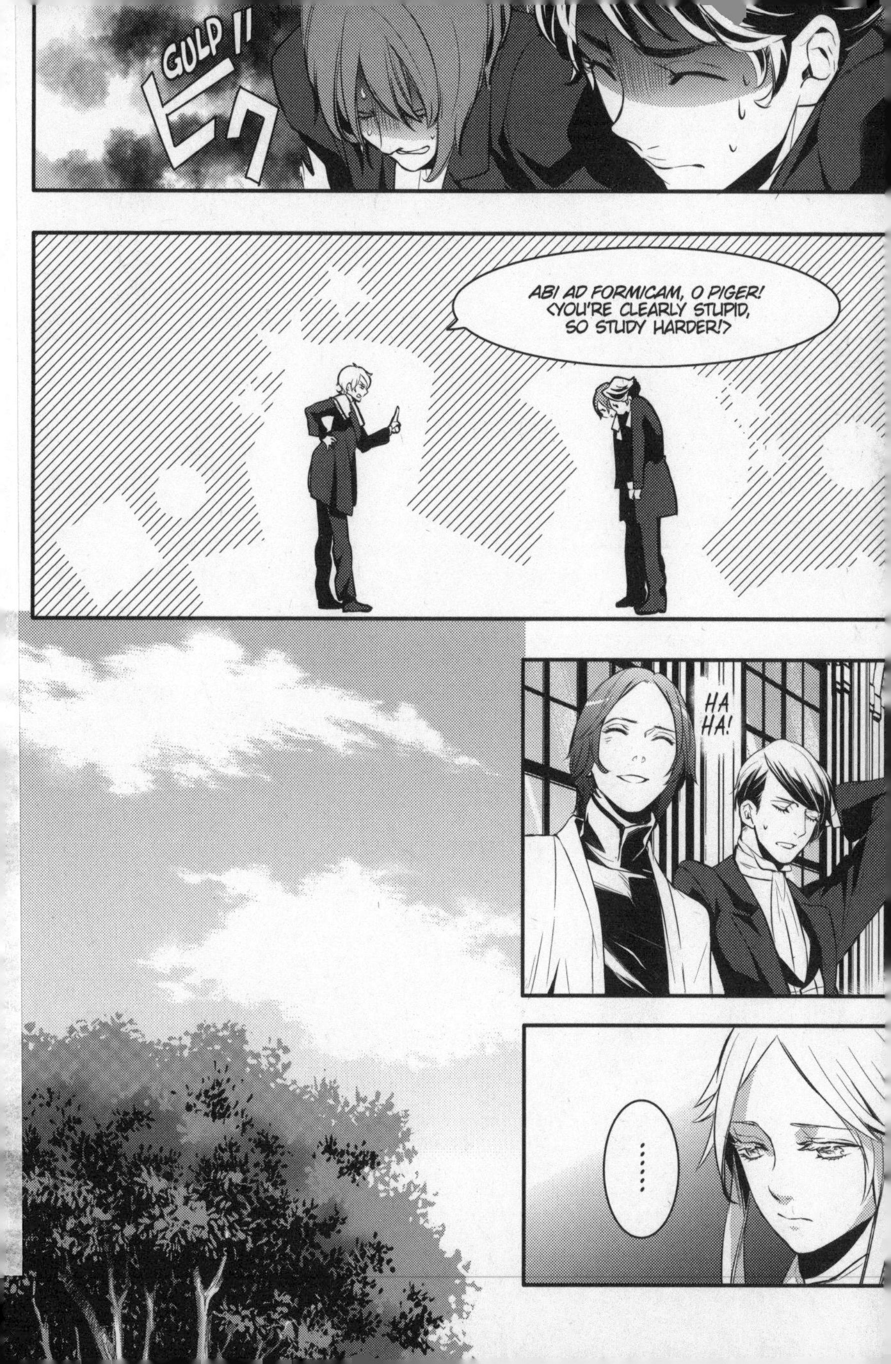
GULP !!
ヒク
ABI AD FORMICAM, O PIGER!
<YOU'RE CLEARLY STUPID, SO STUDY HARDER!>
HA HA!
......

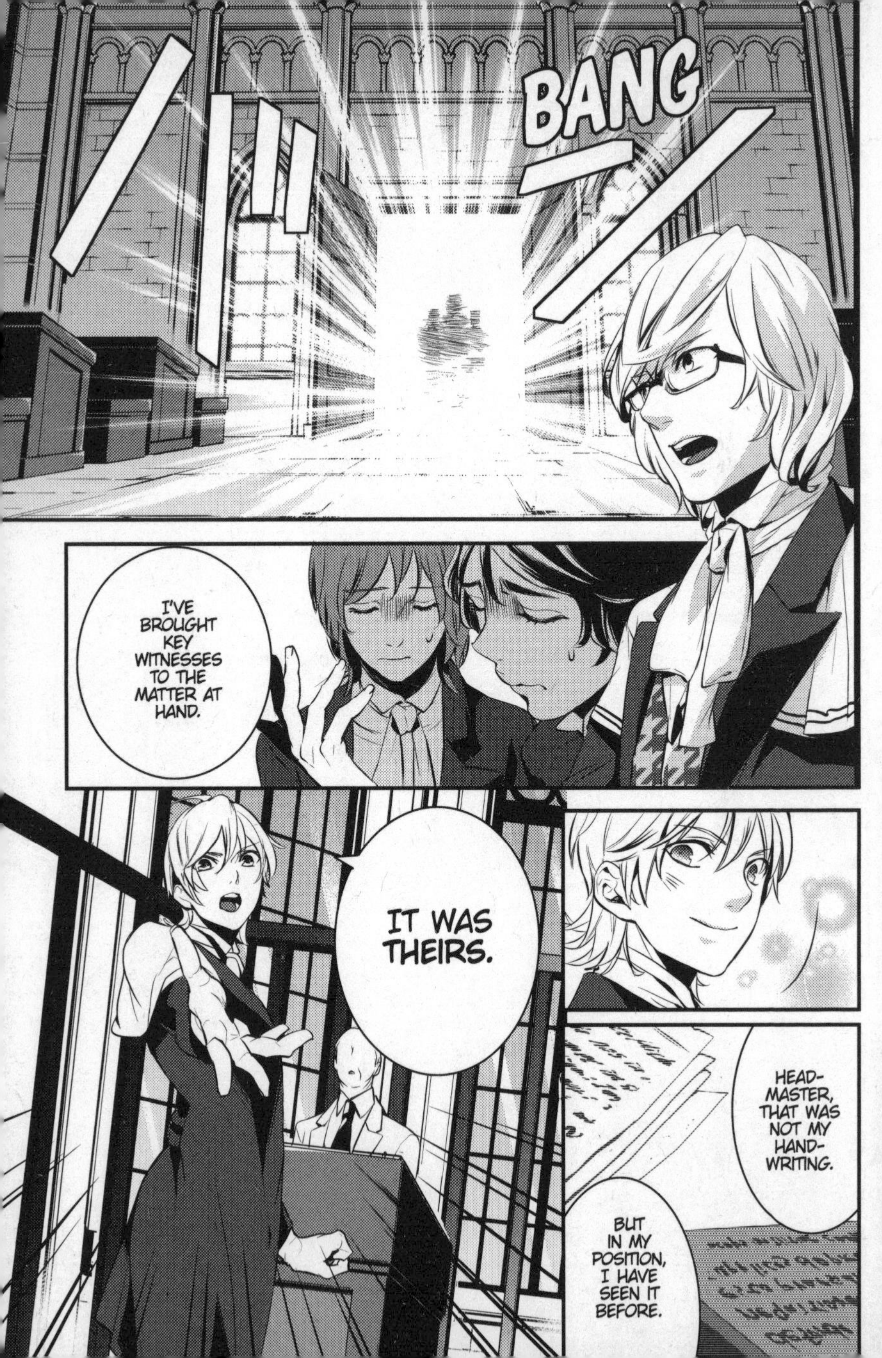
BANG
I'VE BROUGHT KEY WITNESSES TO THE MATTER AT HAND.
IT WAS THEIRS.
HEAD-MASTER, THAT WAS NOT MY HAND-WRITING.
BUT IN MY POSITION, I HAVE SEEN IT BEFORE.

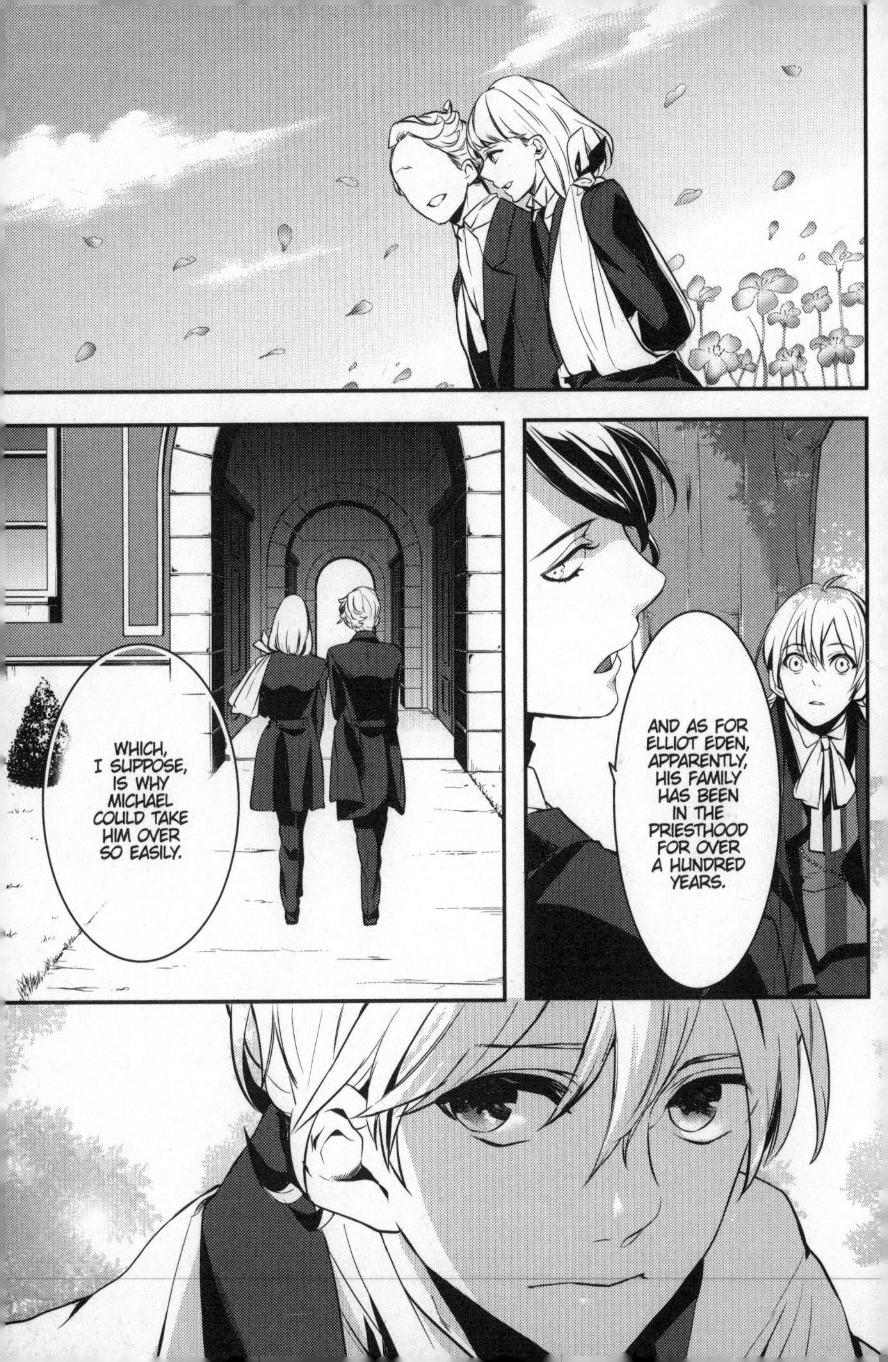
AND AS FOR ELLIOT EDEN, APPARENTLY, HIS FAMILY HAS BEEN IN THE PRIESTHOOD FOR OVER A HUNDRED YEARS.
WHICH, I SUPPOSE, IS WHY MICHAEL COULD TAKE HIM OVER SO EASILY.

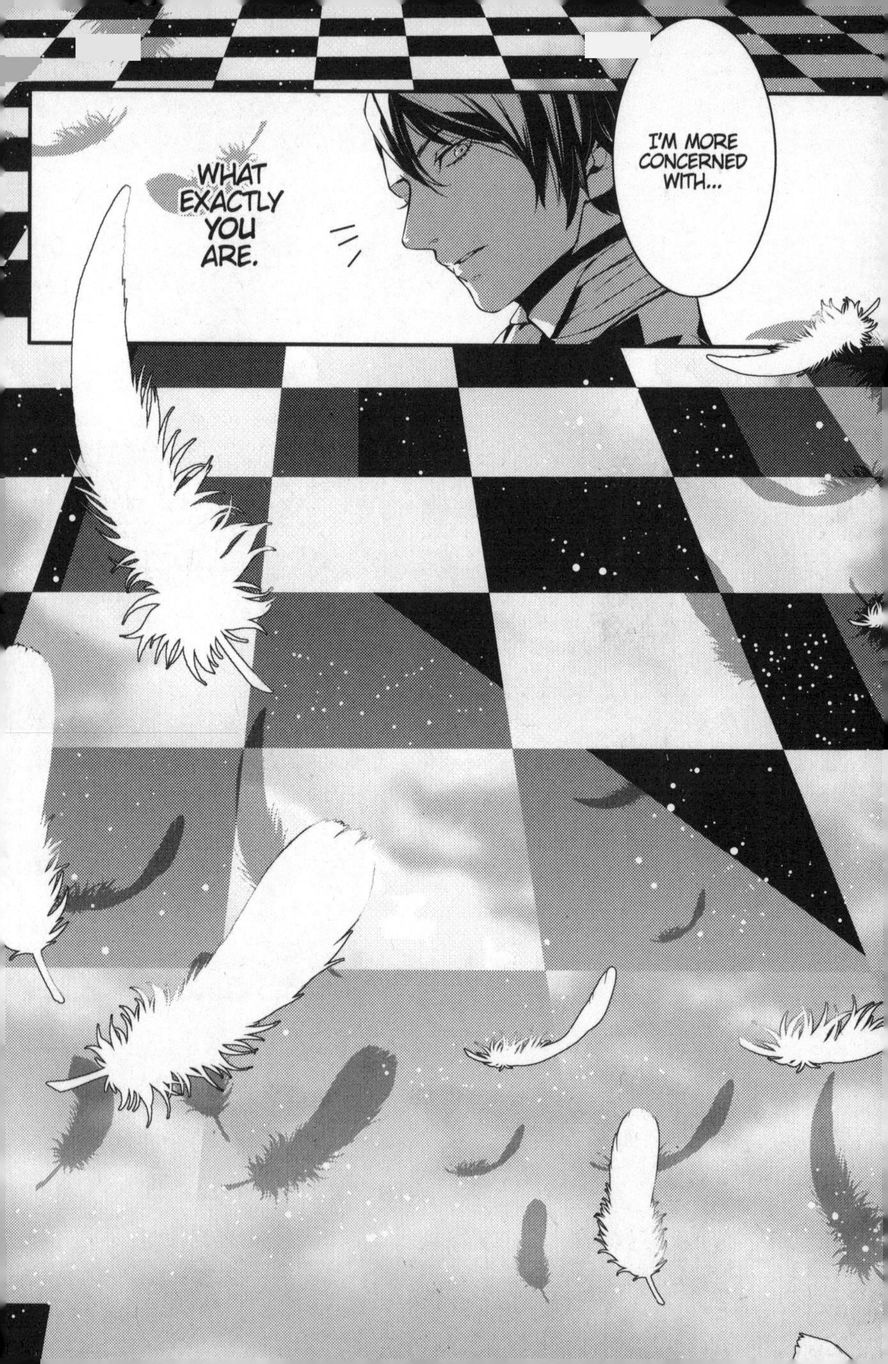
I'M MORE CONCERNED WITH...
WHAT EXACTLY YOU ARE.

Pillar 24

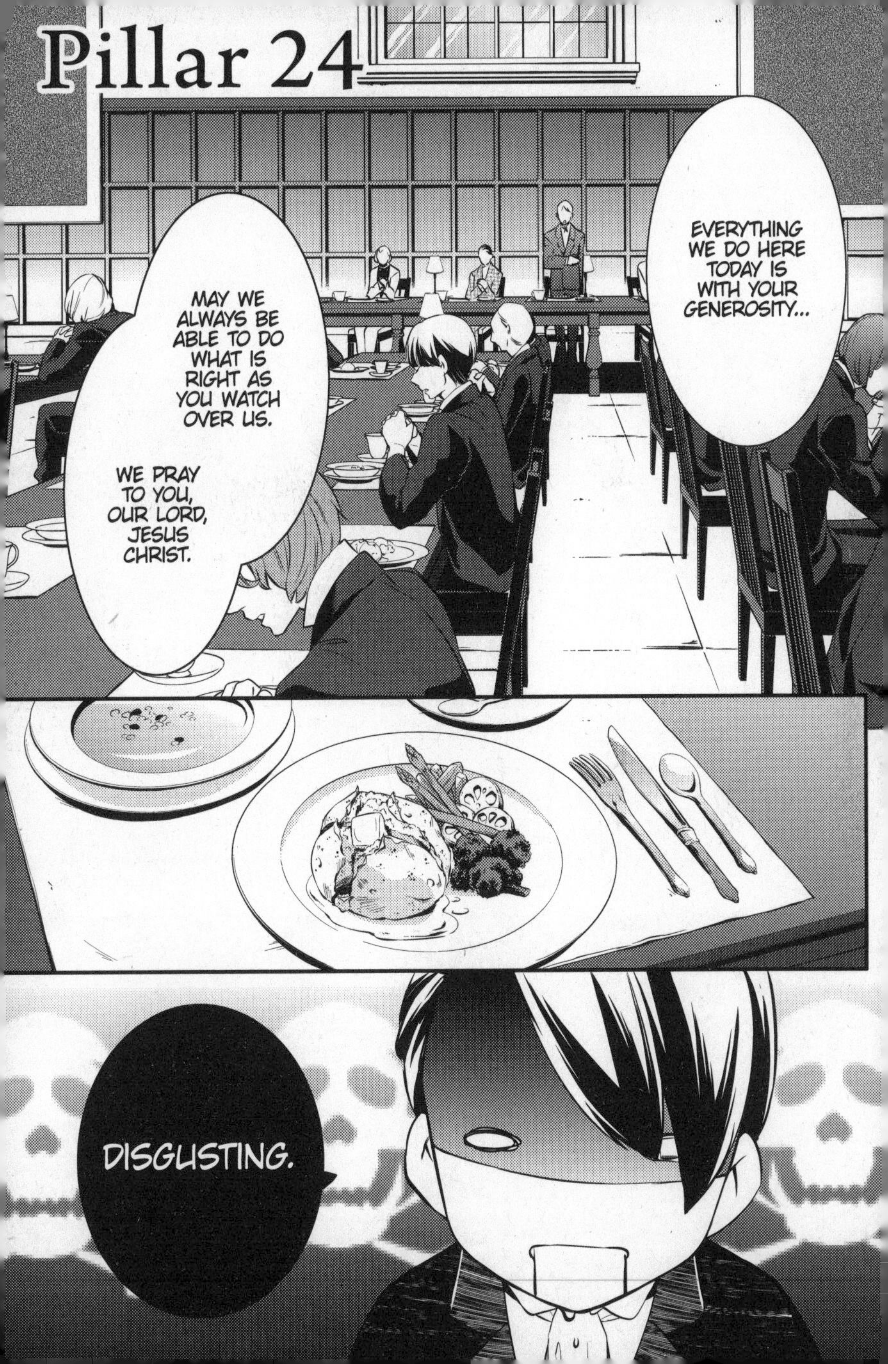
EVERYTHING WE DO HERE TODAY IS WITH YOUR GENEROSITY...
MAY WE ALWAYS BE ABLE TO DO WHAT IS RIGHT AS YOU WATCH OVER US.
WE PRAY TO YOU, OUR LORD, JESUS CHRIST.
DISGUSTING.

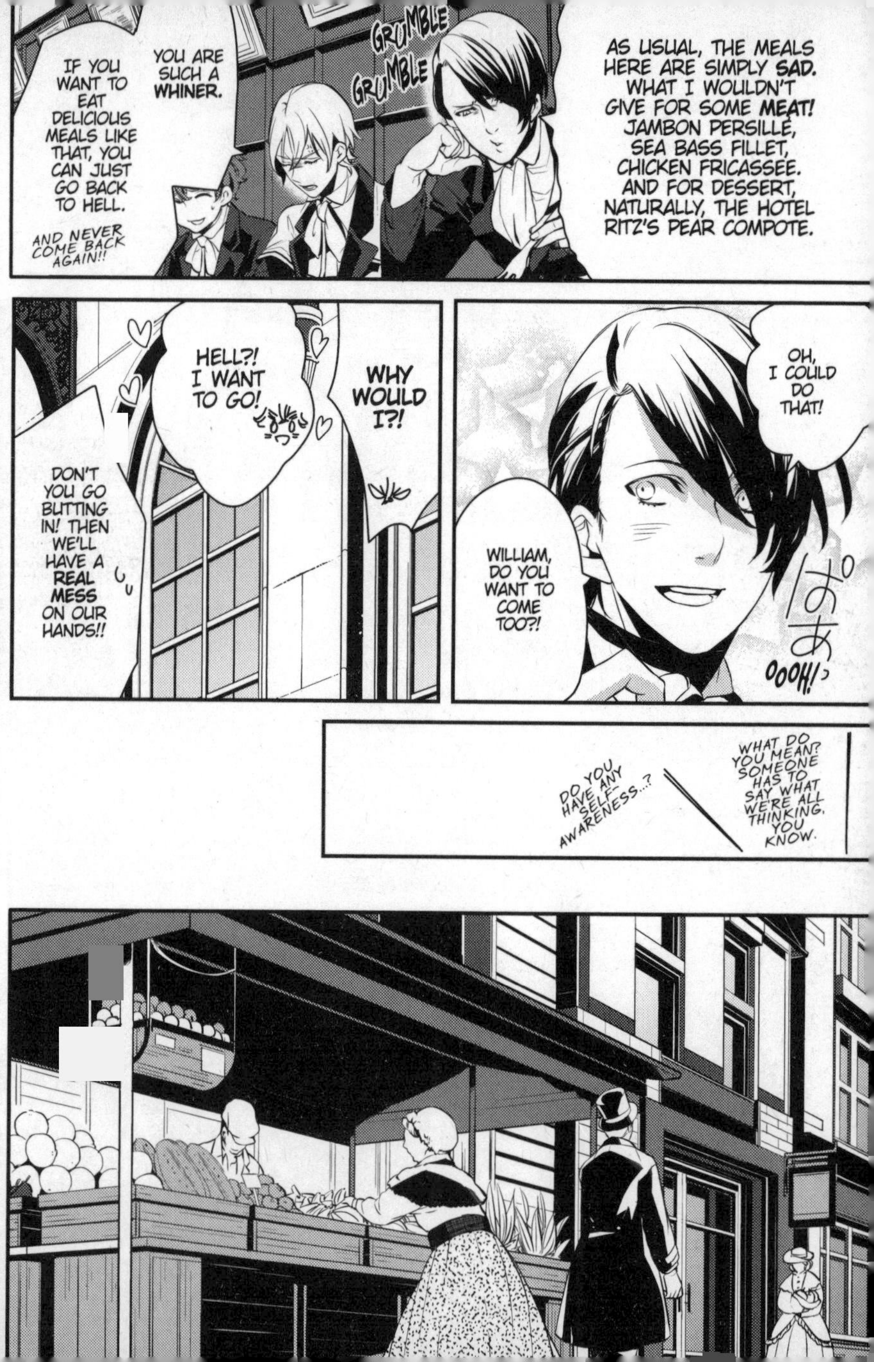
AS USUAL, THE MEALS HERE ARE SIMPLY **SAD.** WHAT I WOULDN'T GIVE FOR SOME **MEAT!** JAMBON PERSILLÉ, SEA BASS FILLET, CHICKEN FRICASSEE. AND FOR DESSERT, NATURALLY, THE HOTEL RITZ'S PEAR COMPOTE.
GRUMBLE GRUMBLE
YOU ARE SUCH A **WHINER.**
IF YOU WANT TO EAT DELICIOUS MEALS LIKE THAT, YOU CAN JUST GO BACK TO HELL.
AND NEVER COME BACK AGAIN!!
OH, I COULD DO THAT!
WILLIAM, DO YOU WANT TO COME TOO?!
ぱあ
OOOH!
WHY WOULD I?!
HELL?! I WANT TO GO!
DON'T YOU GO BUTTING IN! THEN WE'LL HAVE A **REAL MESS** ON OUR HANDS!!
WHAT DO YOU MEAN? SOMEONE HAS TO SAY WHAT WE'RE ALL THINKING, YOU KNOW.
DO YOU HAVE ANY SELF-AWARENESS...?

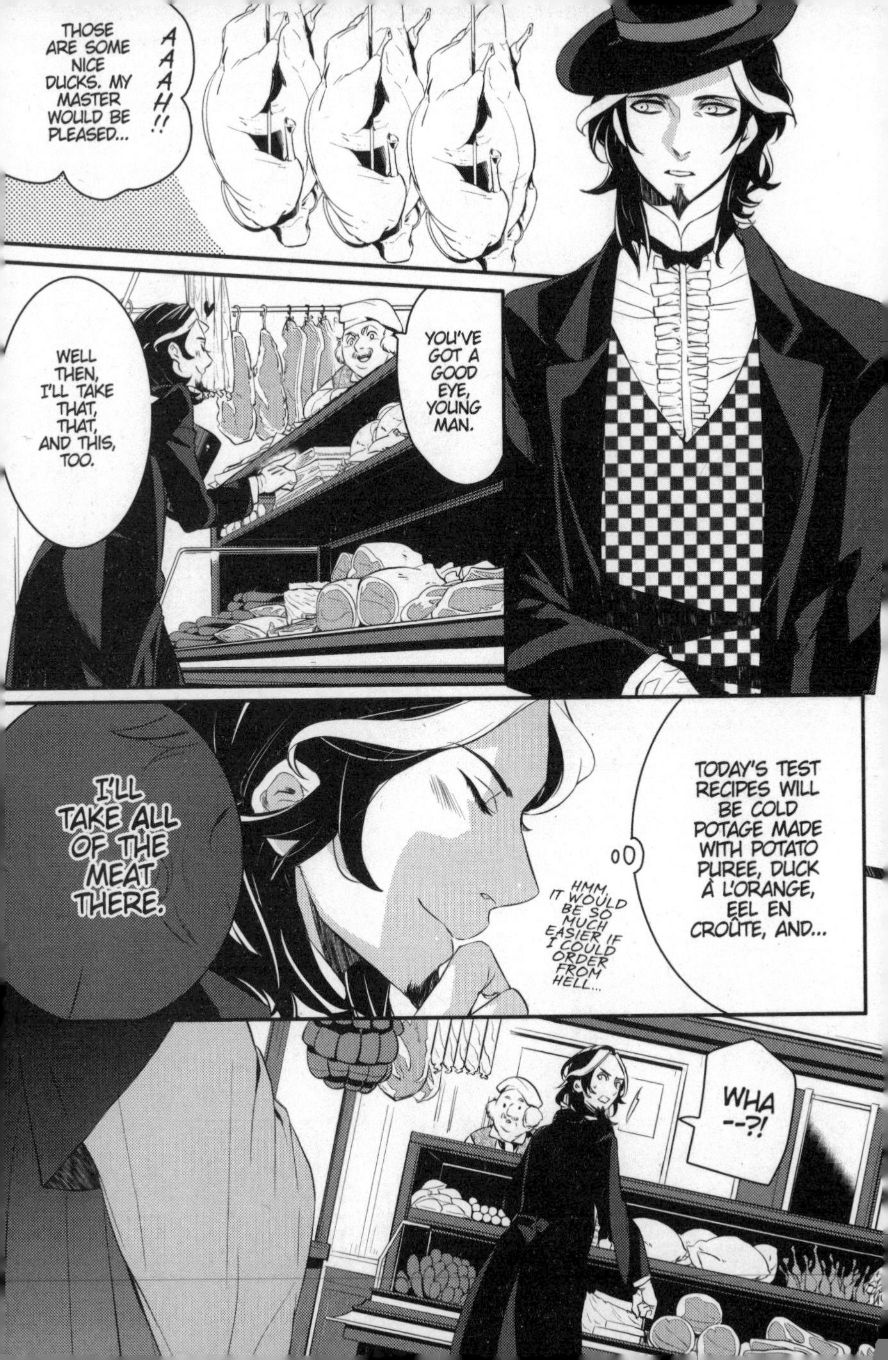
THOSE ARE SOME NICE DUCKS. MY MASTER WOULD BE PLEASED...
AAAH!!
WELL THEN, I'LL TAKE THAT, THAT, AND THIS, TOO.
YOU'VE GOT A GOOD EYE, YOUNG MAN.
I'LL TAKE ALL OF THE MEAT THERE.
TODAY'S TEST RECIPES WILL BE COLD POTAGE MADE WITH POTATO PUREE, DUCK À L'ORANGE, EEL EN CROÛTE, AND...
HMM, IT WOULD BE SO MUCH EASIER IF I COULD ORDER FROM HELL...
WHA--?!

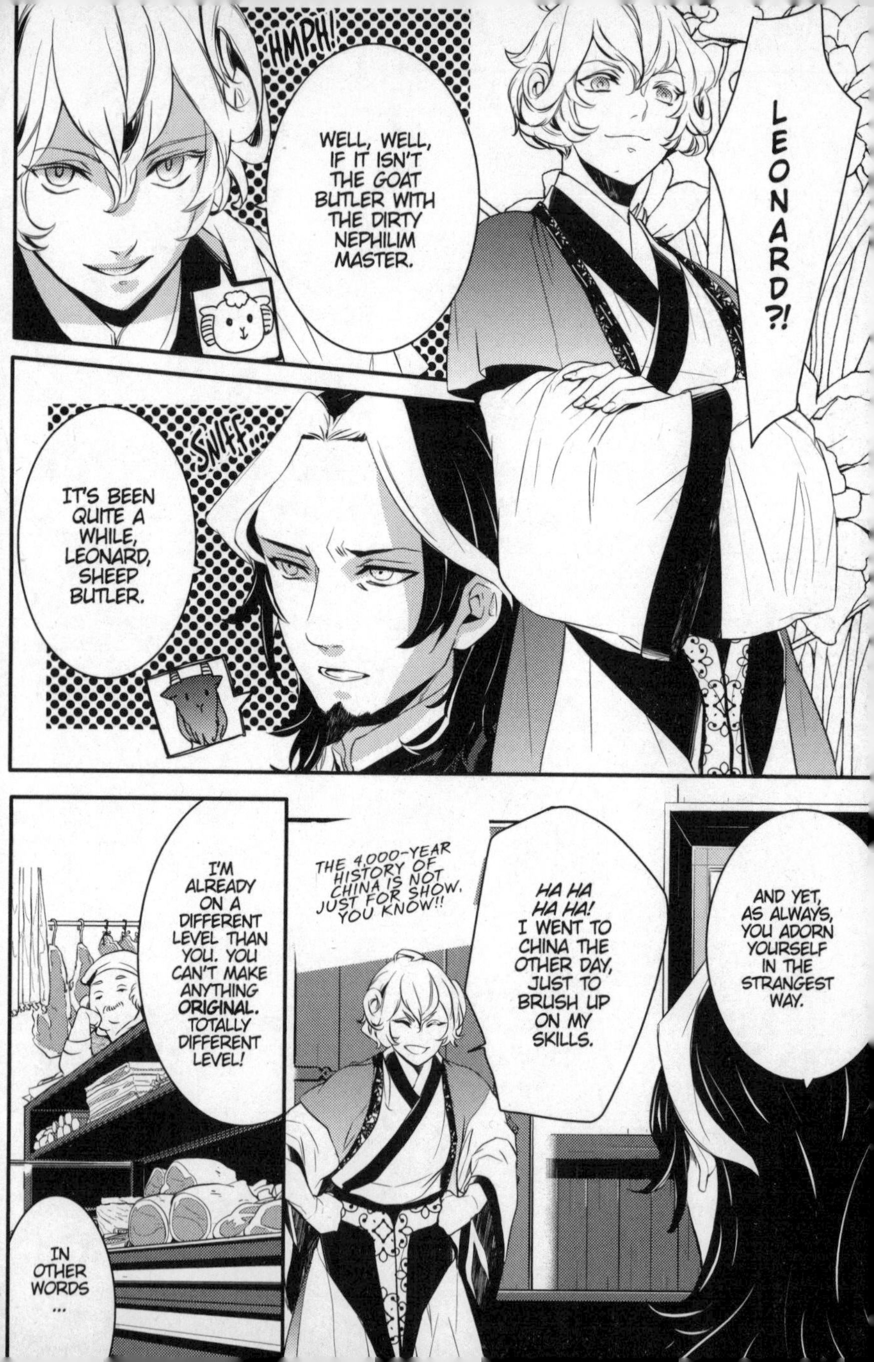
LEONARD?!
HMPH!
WELL, WELL, IF IT ISN'T THE GOAT BUTLER WITH THE DIRTY NEPHILIM MASTER.
SNIFF...
IT'S BEEN QUITE A WHILE, LEONARD, SHEEP BUTLER.
AND YET, AS ALWAYS, YOU ADORN YOURSELF IN THE STRANGEST WAY.
HA HA HA HA! I WENT TO CHINA THE OTHER DAY, JUST TO BRUSH UP ON MY SKILLS.
THE 4,000-YEAR HISTORY OF CHINA IS NOT JUST FOR SHOW, YOU KNOW!!
I'M ALREADY ON A DIFFERENT LEVEL THAN YOU. YOU CAN'T MAKE ANYTHING ORIGINAL. TOTALLY DIFFERENT LEVEL!
IN OTHER WORDS ...

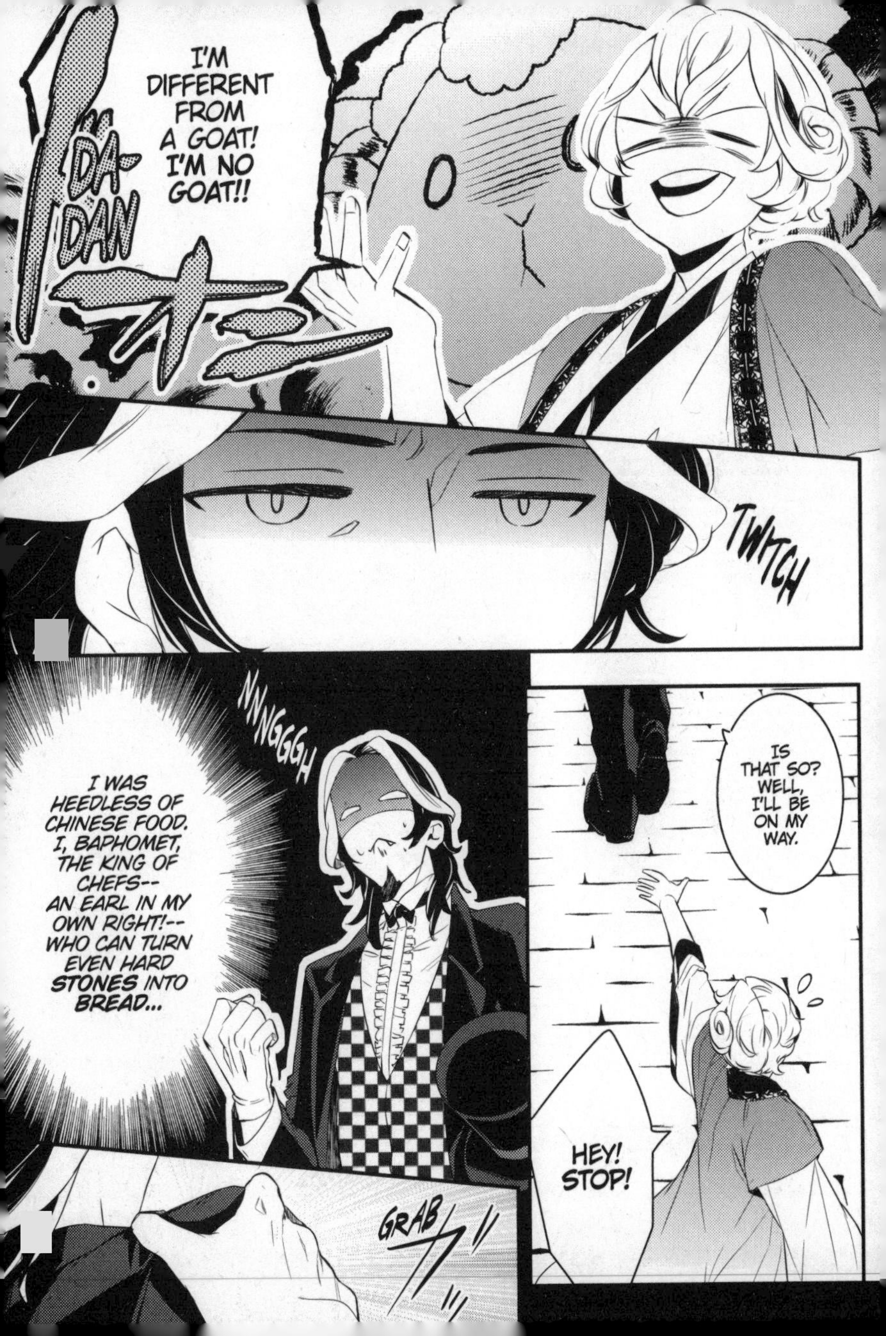
I'M DIFFERENT FROM A GOAT! I'M NO GOAT!!
DA-DAN
TWITCH
IS THAT SO? WELL, I'LL BE ON MY WAY.
NNNGGGGH
I WAS HEEDLESS OF CHINESE FOOD. I, BAPHOMET, THE KING OF CHEFS-- AN EARL IN MY OWN RIGHT!-- WHO CAN TURN EVEN HARD STONES INTO BREAD...
HEY! STOP!
GRAB

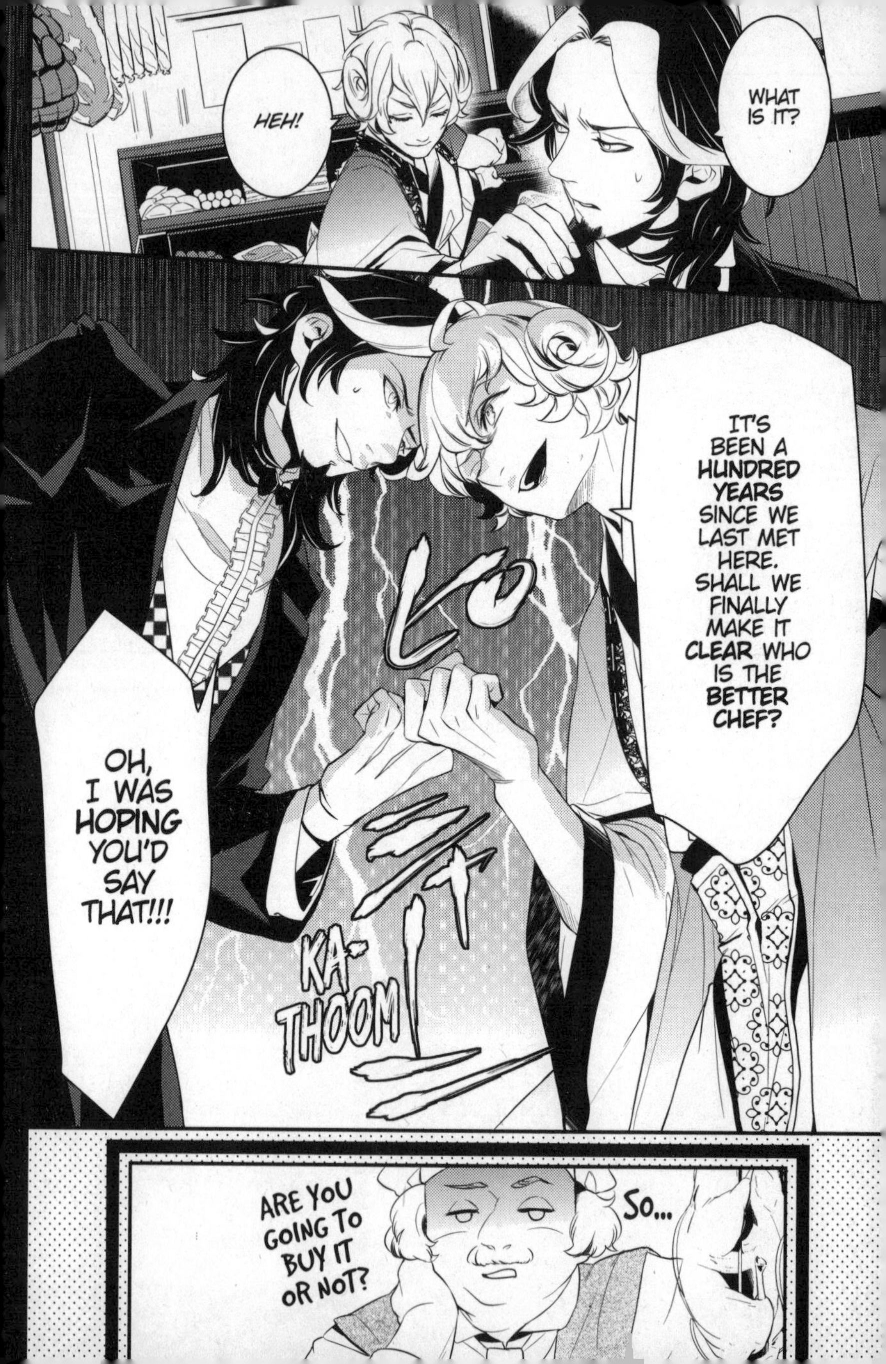
WHAT IS IT?
HEH!
IT'S BEEN A HUNDRED YEARS SINCE WE LAST MET HERE. SHALL WE FINALLY MAKE IT CLEAR WHO IS THE BETTER CHEF?
OH, I WAS HOPING YOU'D SAY THAT!!!
KA-THOOM
So...
ARE YOU GOING TO BUY IT OR NOT?

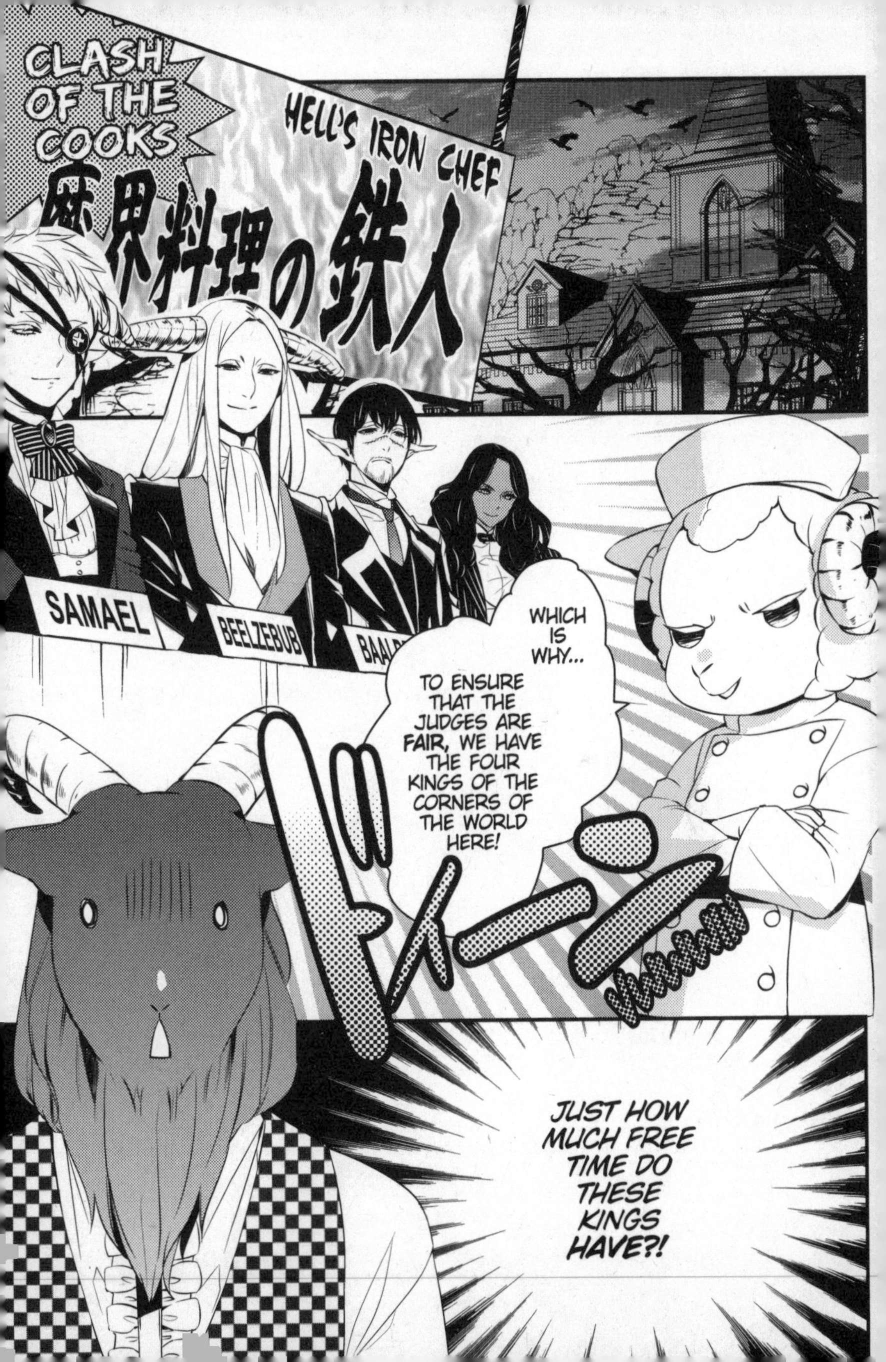
HELL'S IRON CHEF
CLASH OF THE COOKS
魔界料理の鉄人
SAMAEL
BEELZEBUB
BAAL
WHICH IS WHY...
TO ENSURE THAT THE JUDGES ARE FAIR, WE HAVE THE FOUR KINGS OF THE CORNERS OF THE WORLD HERE!
JUST HOW MUCH FREE TIME DO THESE KINGS HAVE?!

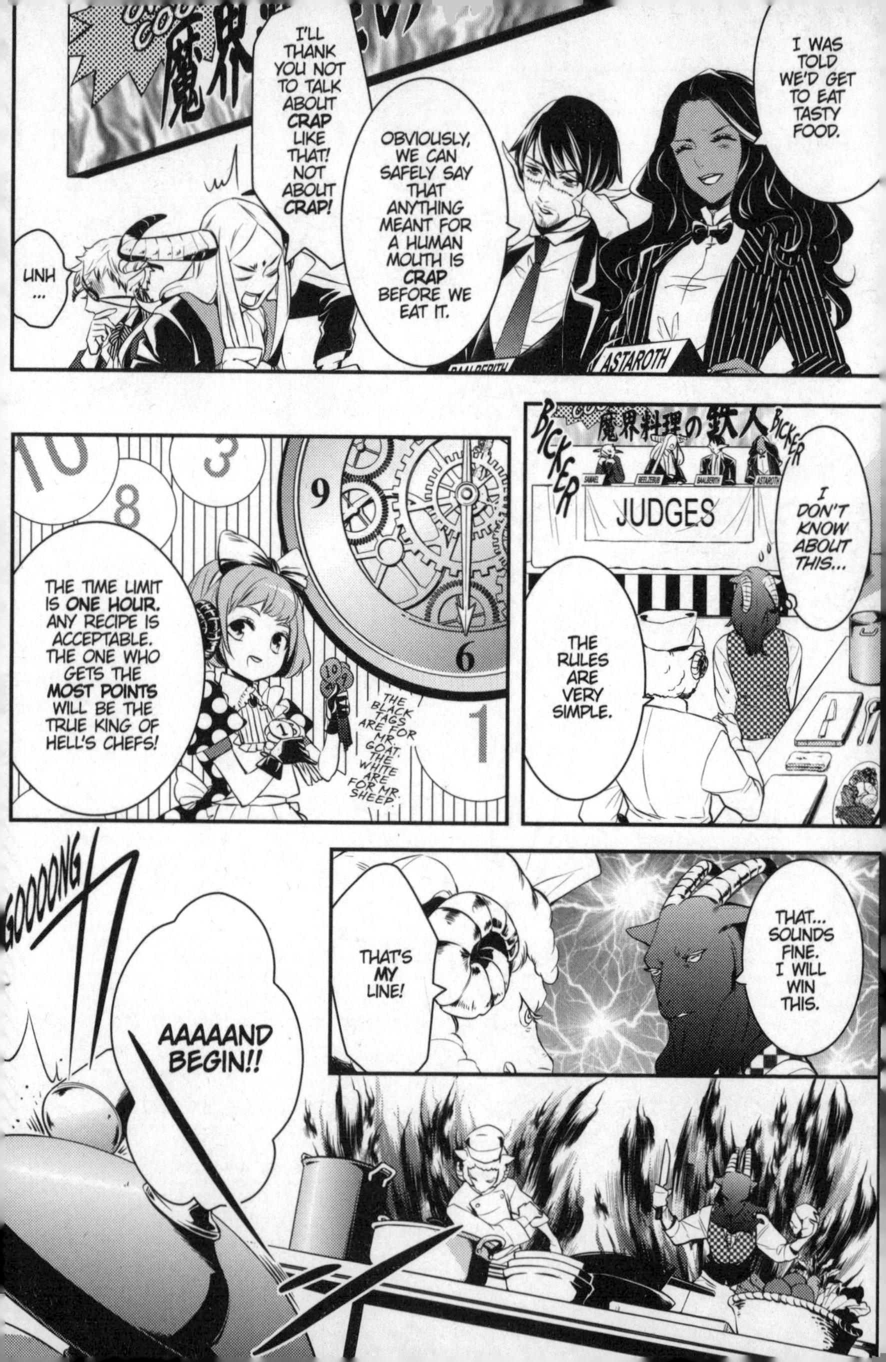
魔界
I WAS TOLD WE'D GET TO EAT TASTY FOOD.
OBVIOUSLY, WE CAN SAFELY SAY THAT ANYTHING MEANT FOR A HUMAN MOUTH IS CRAP BEFORE WE EAT IT.
I'LL THANK YOU NOT TO TALK ABOUT CRAP LIKE THAT! NOT ABOUT CRAP!
UNH ...
ASTAROTH
魔界料理の鉄人
BICKER
BICKER
SAMAEL
BEELZEBUB
BAALBERITH
ASTAROTH
JUDGES
I DON'T KNOW ABOUT THIS...
THE RULES ARE VERY SIMPLE.
THE TIME LIMIT IS ONE HOUR. ANY RECIPE IS ACCEPTABLE. THE ONE WHO GETS THE MOST POINTS WILL BE THE TRUE KING OF HELL'S CHEFS!
THE BLACK TAGS ARE FOR MR. GOAT. THE WHITE ARE FOR MR. SHEEP.
THAT... SOUNDS FINE. I WILL WIN THIS.
THAT'S MY LINE!
AAAAAND BEGIN!!
GOOOONG

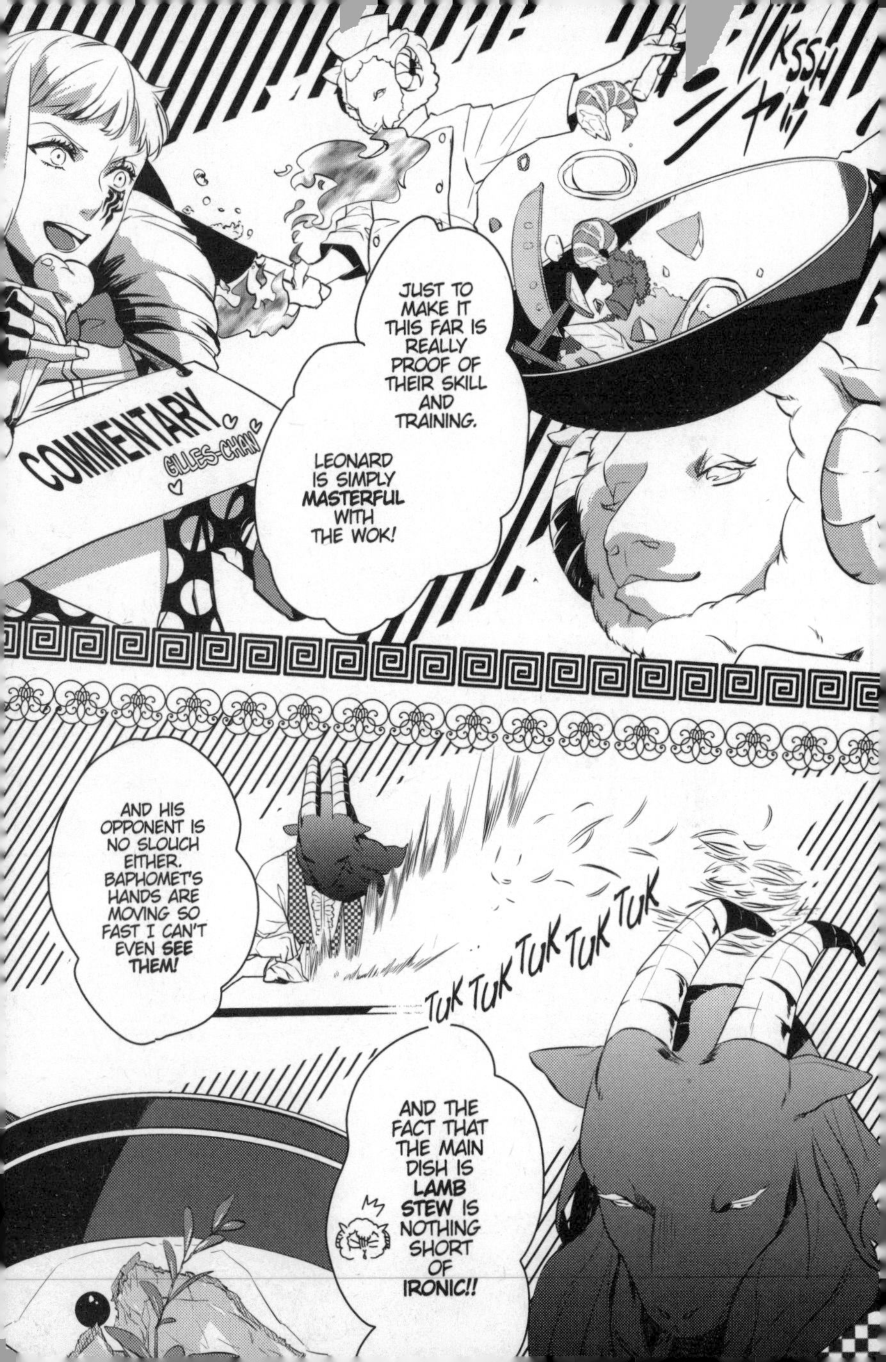

KSSH
シャッ
COMMENTARY
GILLES-CHAN
JUST TO MAKE IT THIS FAR IS REALLY PROOF OF THEIR SKILL AND TRAINING.
LEONARD IS SIMPLY **MASTERFUL** WITH THE WOK!
AND HIS OPPONENT IS NO SLOUCH EITHER. BAPHOMET'S HANDS ARE MOVING SO FAST I CAN'T EVEN **SEE THEM!**
TUK TUK TUK TUK TUK
AND THE FACT THAT THE MAIN DISH IS **LAMB STEW** IS NOTHING SHORT OF **IRONIC!!**

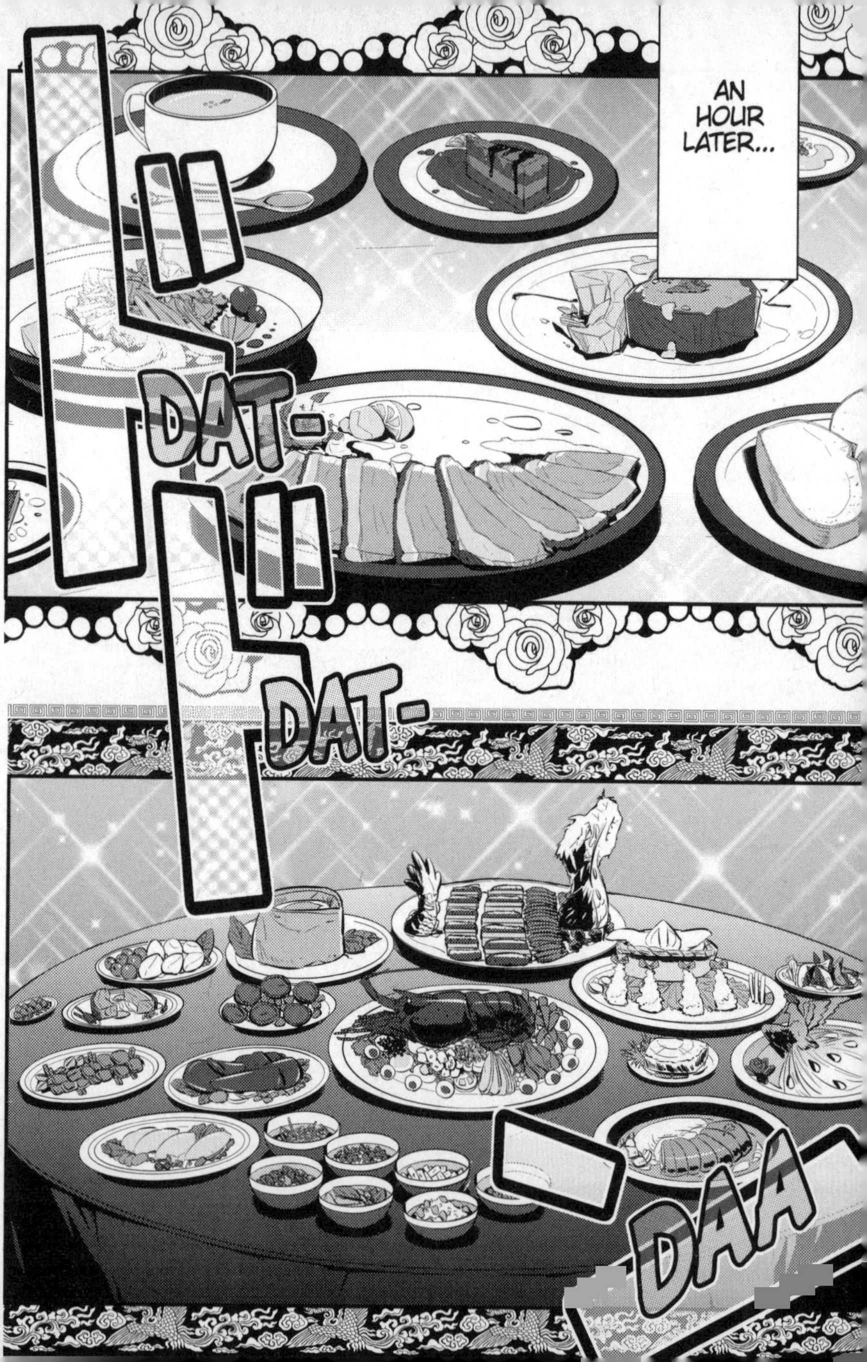
AN HOUR LATER...
DAT-
DAT-
DAA

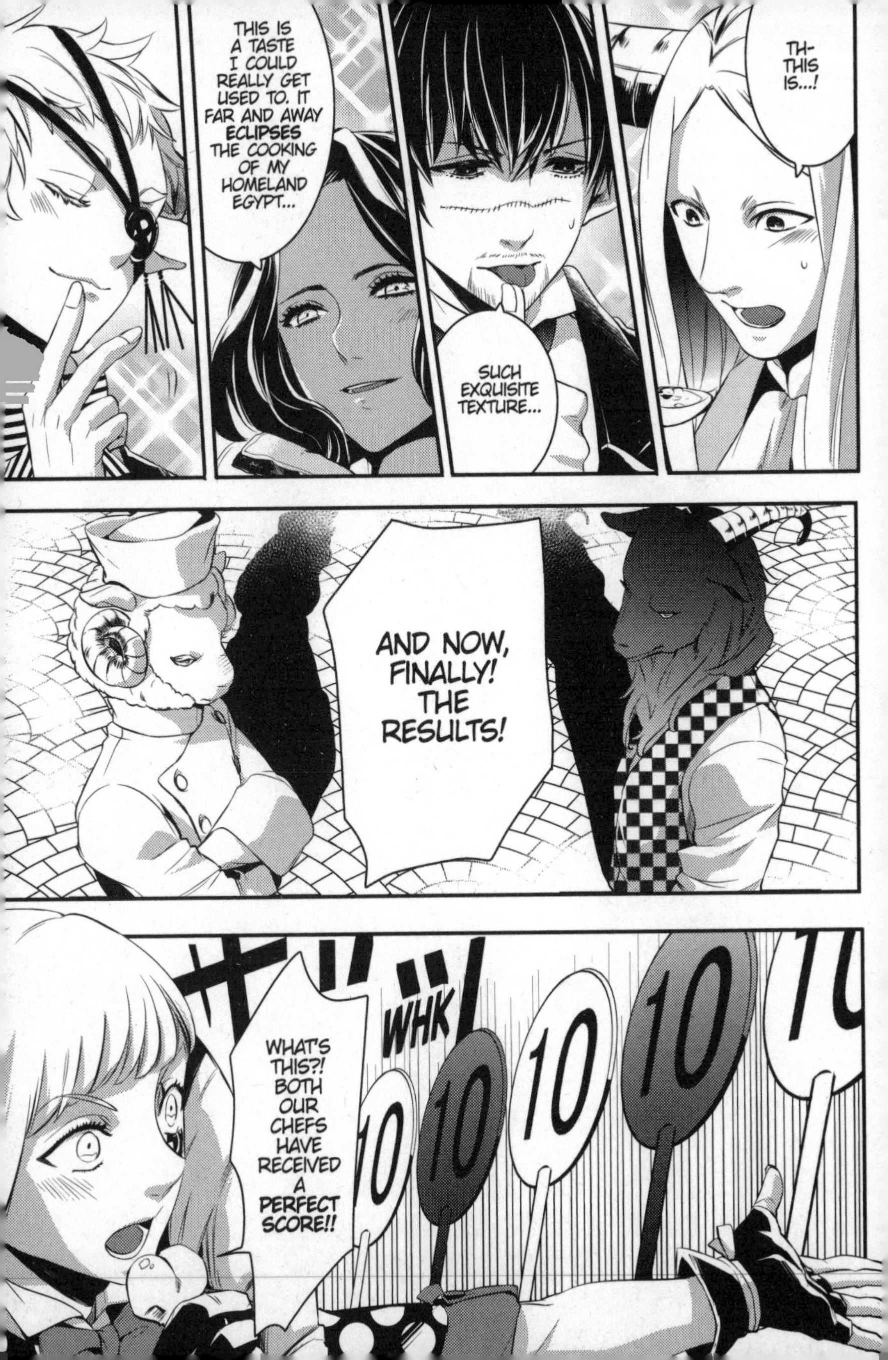
TH-THIS IS...!
SUCH EXQUISITE TEXTURE...
THIS IS A TASTE I COULD REALLY GET USED TO. IT FAR AND AWAY ECLIPSES THE COOKING OF MY HOMELAND EGYPT...
AND NOW, FINALLY! THE RESULTS!
WHK
10
10
10
10
10
WHAT'S THIS?! BOTH OUR CHEFS HAVE RECEIVED A PERFECT SCORE!!

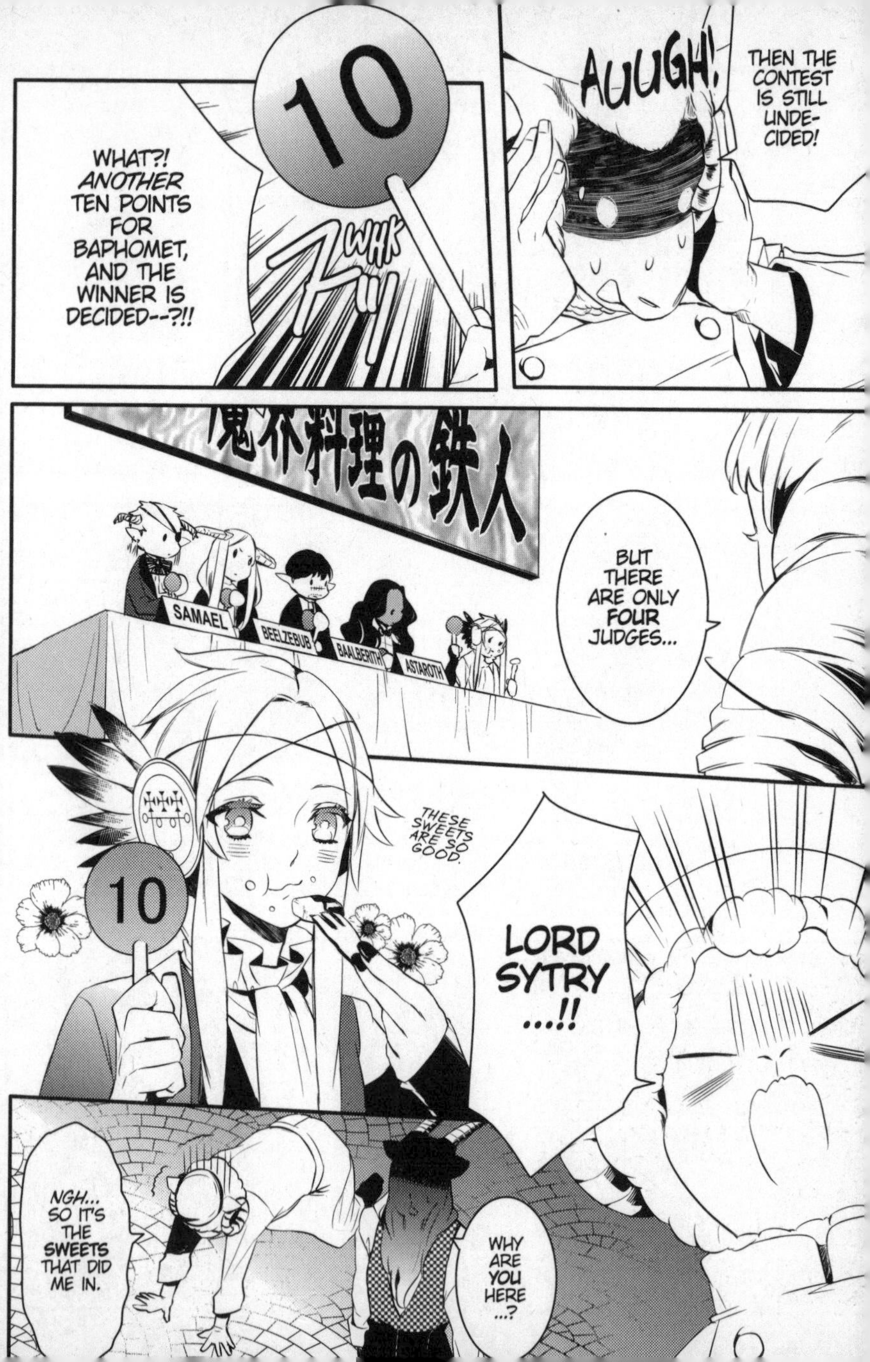
AUUGH!
THEN THE CONTEST IS STILL UNDE-CIDED!
WHAT?! ANOTHER TEN POINTS FOR BAPHOMET, AND THE WINNER IS DECIDED--?!!
10
ZWHK
BUT THERE ARE ONLY FOUR JUDGES...
魔界料理の鉄人
SAMAEL
BEELZEBUB
BAALBERITH
ASTAROTH
LORD SYTRY ...!!
THESE SWEETS ARE SO GOOD.
10
WHY ARE YOU HERE ...?
NGH... SO IT'S THE SWEETS THAT DID ME IN.

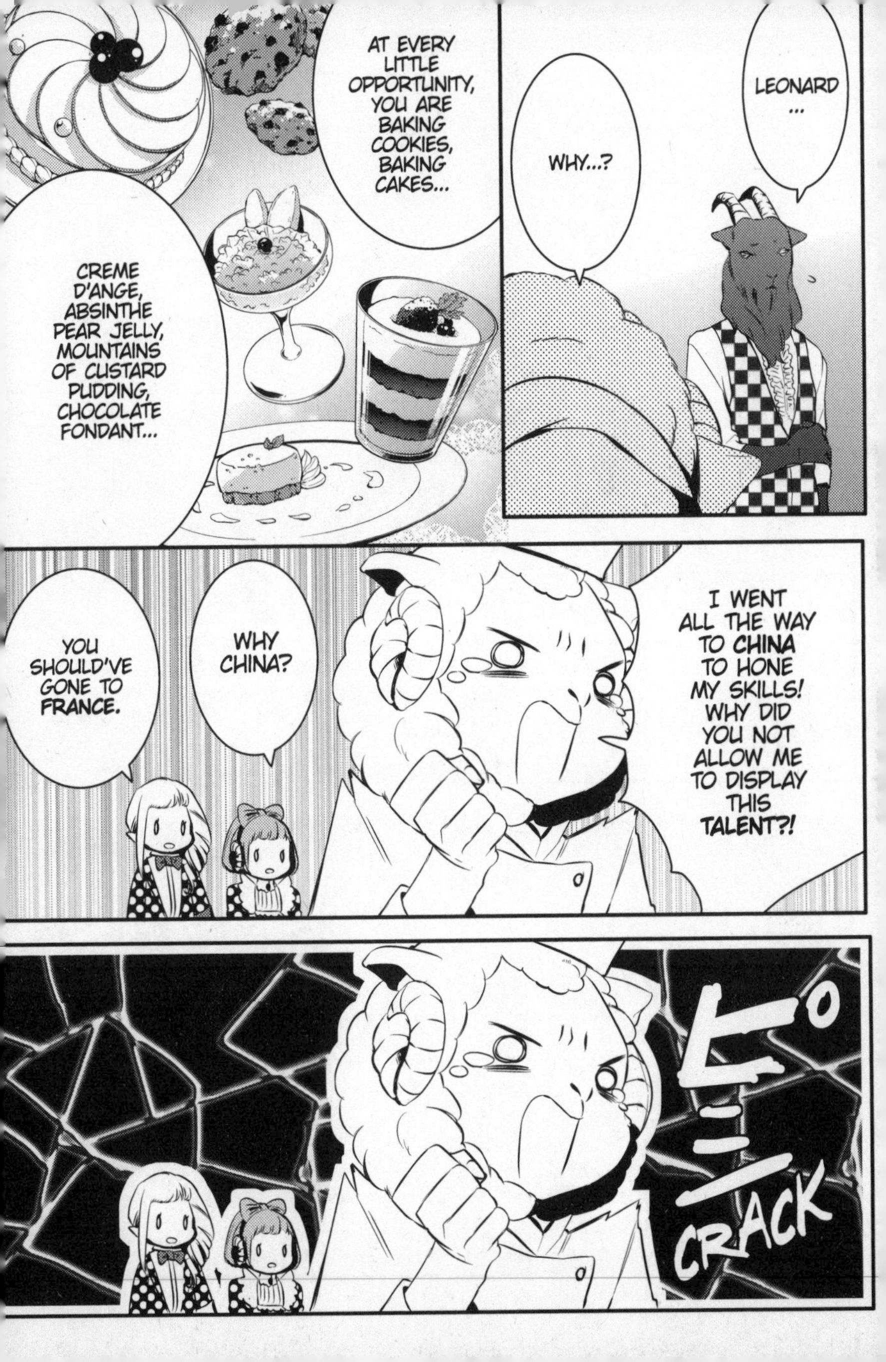
LEONARD ...
WHY...?
AT EVERY LITTLE OPPORTUNITY, YOU ARE BAKING COOKIES, BAKING CAKES...
CREME D'ANGE, ABSINTHE PEAR JELLY, MOUNTAINS OF CUSTARD PUDDING, CHOCOLATE FONDANT...
I WENT ALL THE WAY TO CHINA TO HONE MY SKILLS! WHY DID YOU NOT ALLOW ME TO DISPLAY THIS TALENT?!
WHY CHINA?
YOU SHOULD'VE GONE TO FRANCE.
CRACK

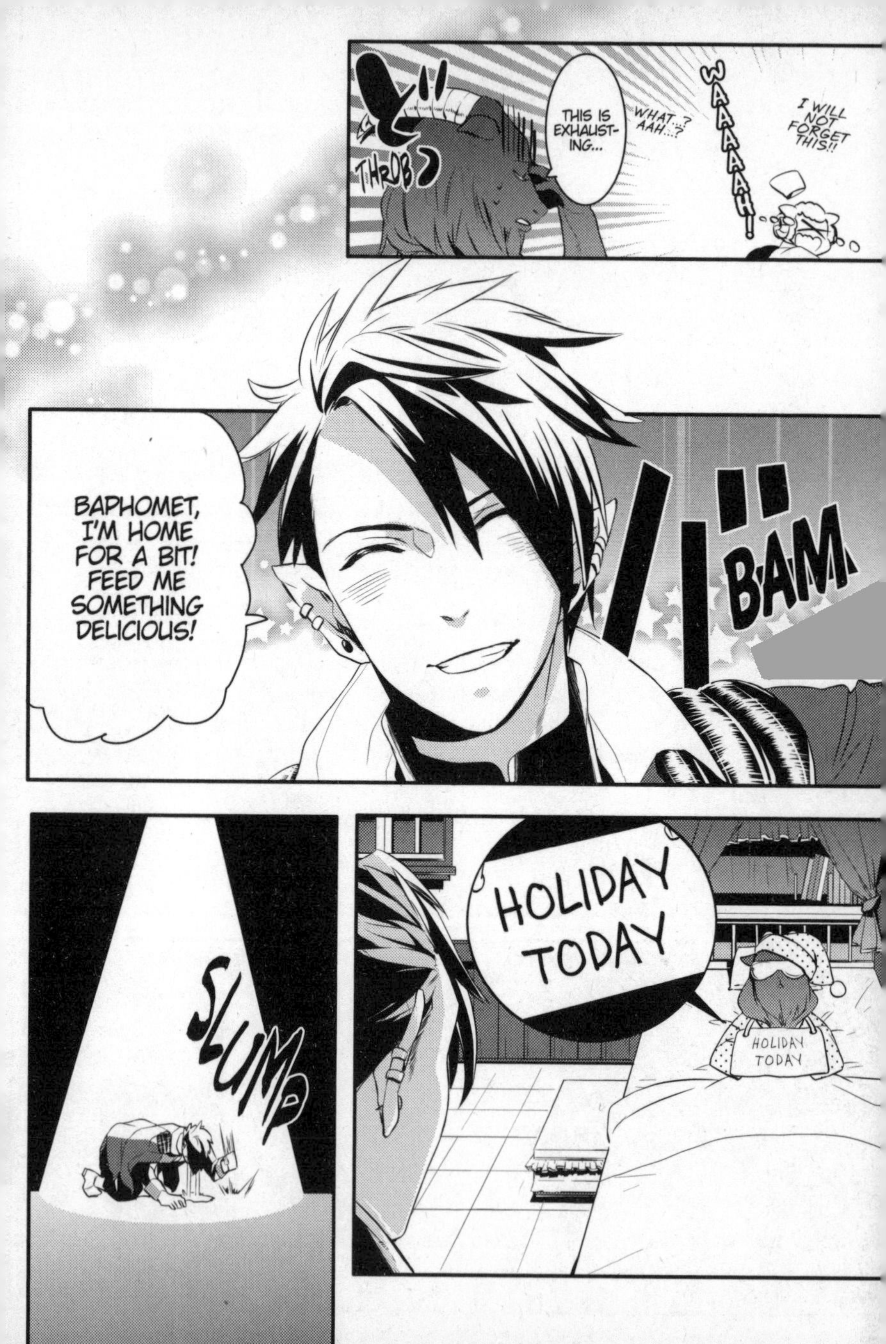
I WILL NOT FORGET THIS!!
WAAAAAAAH!
WHAT...? AAH...?
THIS IS EXHAUST-ING...
THROB
BAM
BAPHOMET, I'M HOME FOR A BIT! FEED ME SOMETHING DELICIOUS!
HOLIDAY TODAY
HOLIDAY TODAY
SLUMP

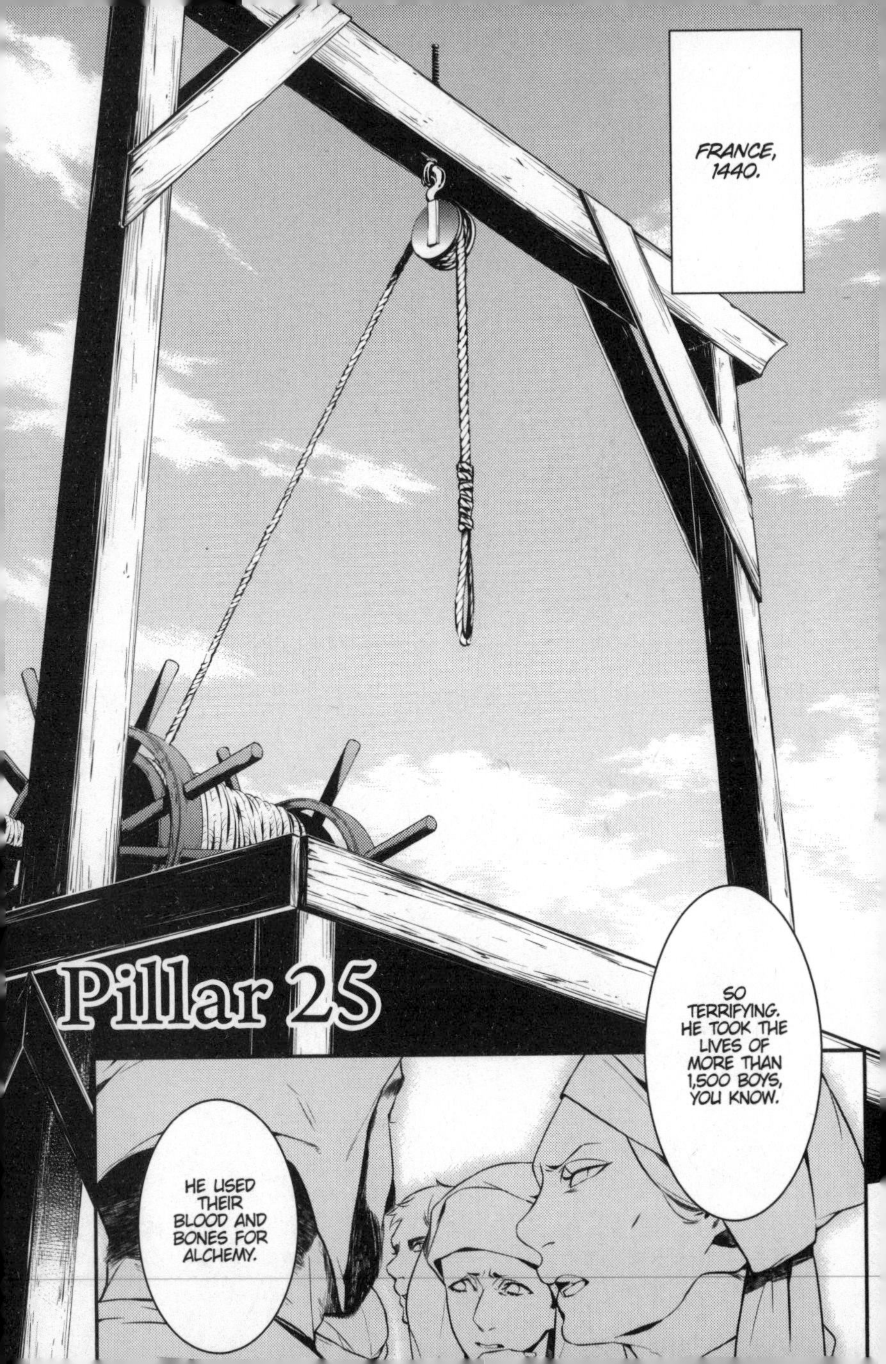
FRANCE, 1440.
Pillar 25
SO TERRIFYING. HE TOOK THE LIVES OF MORE THAN 1,500 BOYS, YOU KNOW.
HE USED THEIR BLOOD AND BONES FOR ALCHEMY.

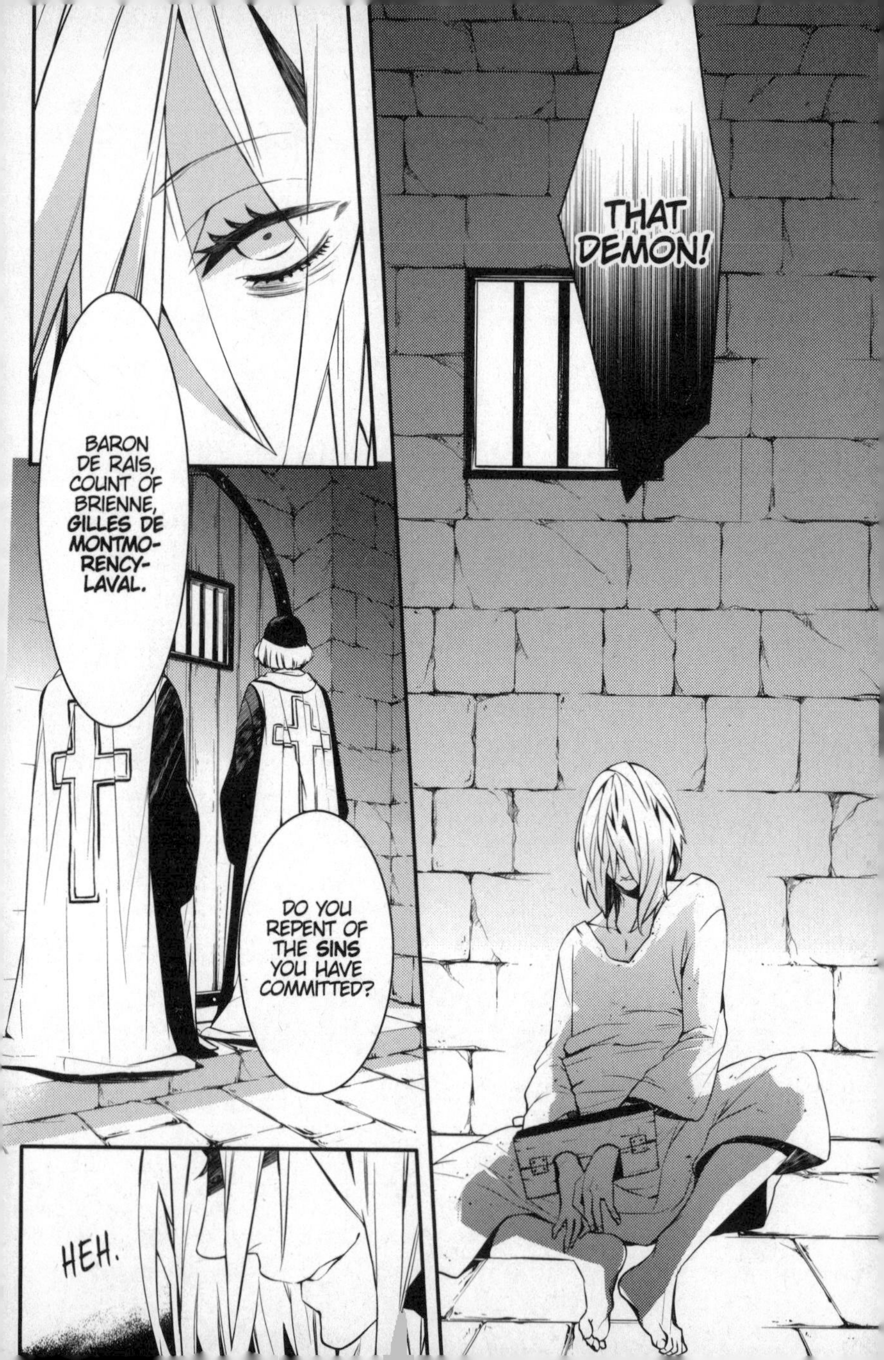
THAT DEMON!
BARON DE RAIS, COUNT OF BRIENNE, GILLES DE MONTMO-RENCY-LAVAL.
DO YOU REPENT OF THE SINS YOU HAVE COMMITTED?
HEH.

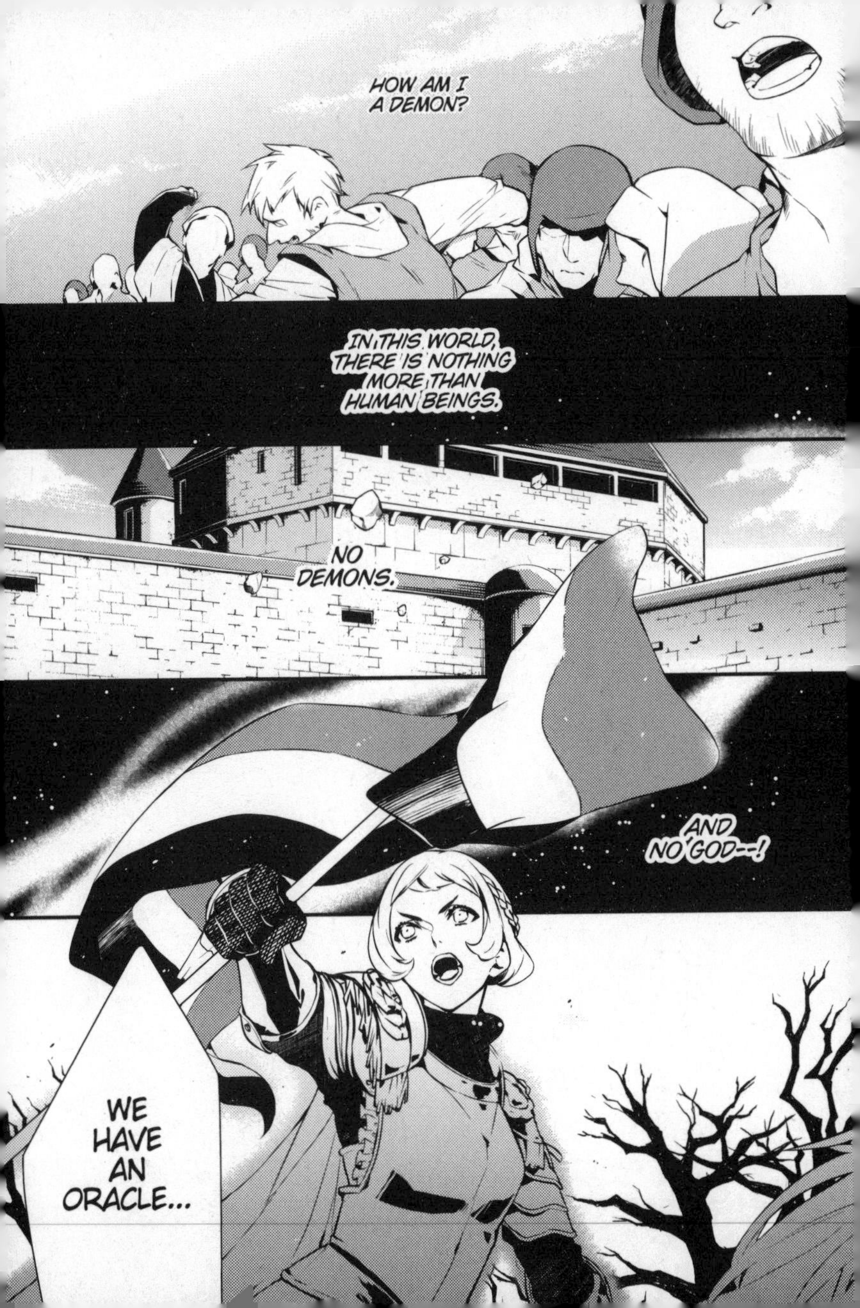
HOW AM I A DEMON?
IN THIS WORLD, THERE IS NOTHING MORE THAN HUMAN BEINGS.
NO DEMONS.
AND NO GOD--!
WE HAVE AN ORACLE...

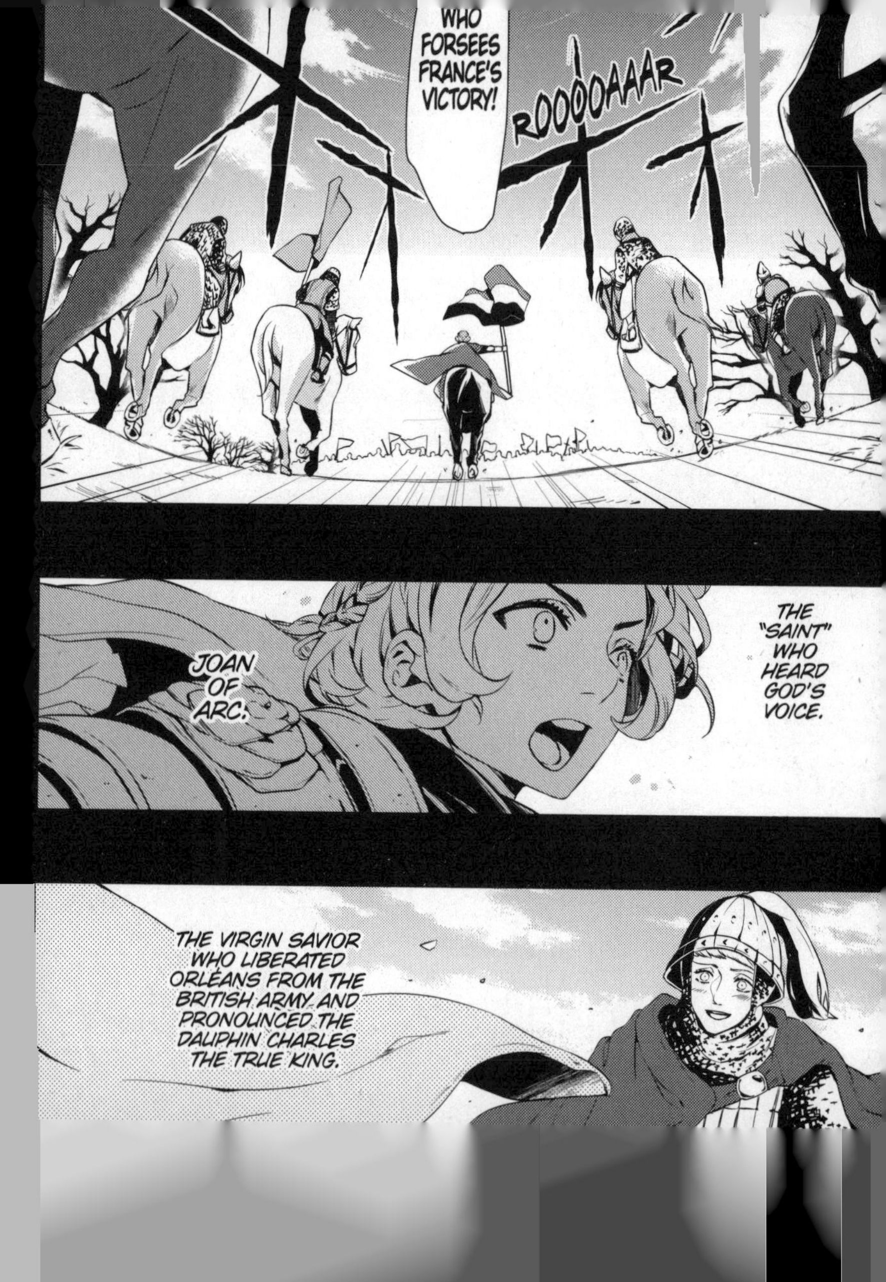
WHO FORSEES FRANCE'S VICTORY!
ROOOOAAAR
THE "SAINT" WHO HEARD GOD'S VOICE.
JOAN OF ARC.
THE VIRGIN SAVIOR WHO LIBERATED ORLÉANS FROM THE BRITISH ARMY AND PRONOUNCED THE DAUPHIN CHARLES THE TRUE KING.

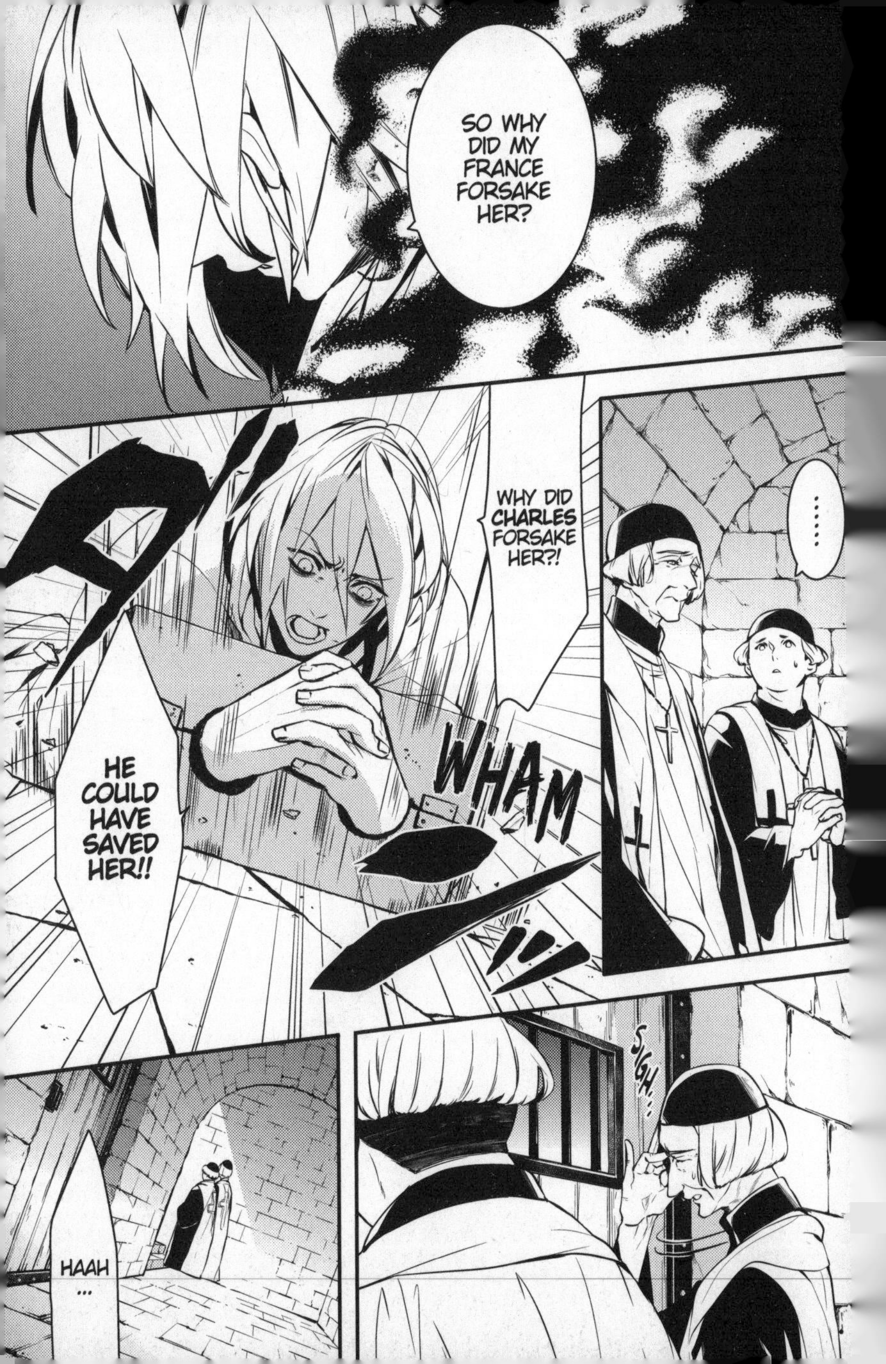
SO WHY DID MY FRANCE FORSAKE HER?
......
WHY DID CHARLES FORSAKE HER?!
HE COULD HAVE SAVED HER!!
WHAM
SIGH...
HAAH ...

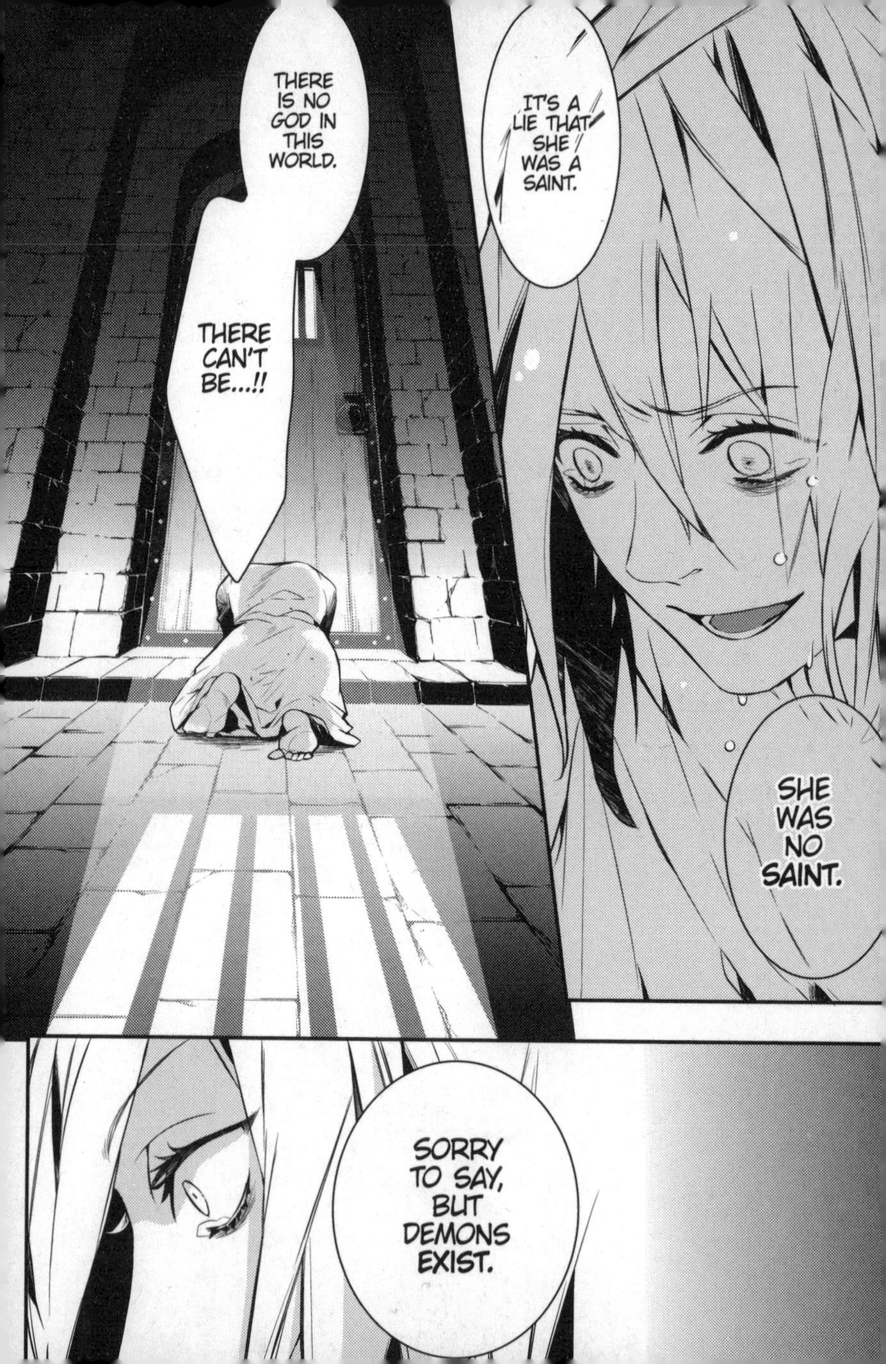
IT'S A LIE THAT SHE WAS A SAINT.
THERE IS NO GOD IN THIS WORLD.
THERE CAN'T BE...!!
SHE WAS NO SAINT.
SORRY TO SAY, BUT DEMONS EXIST.

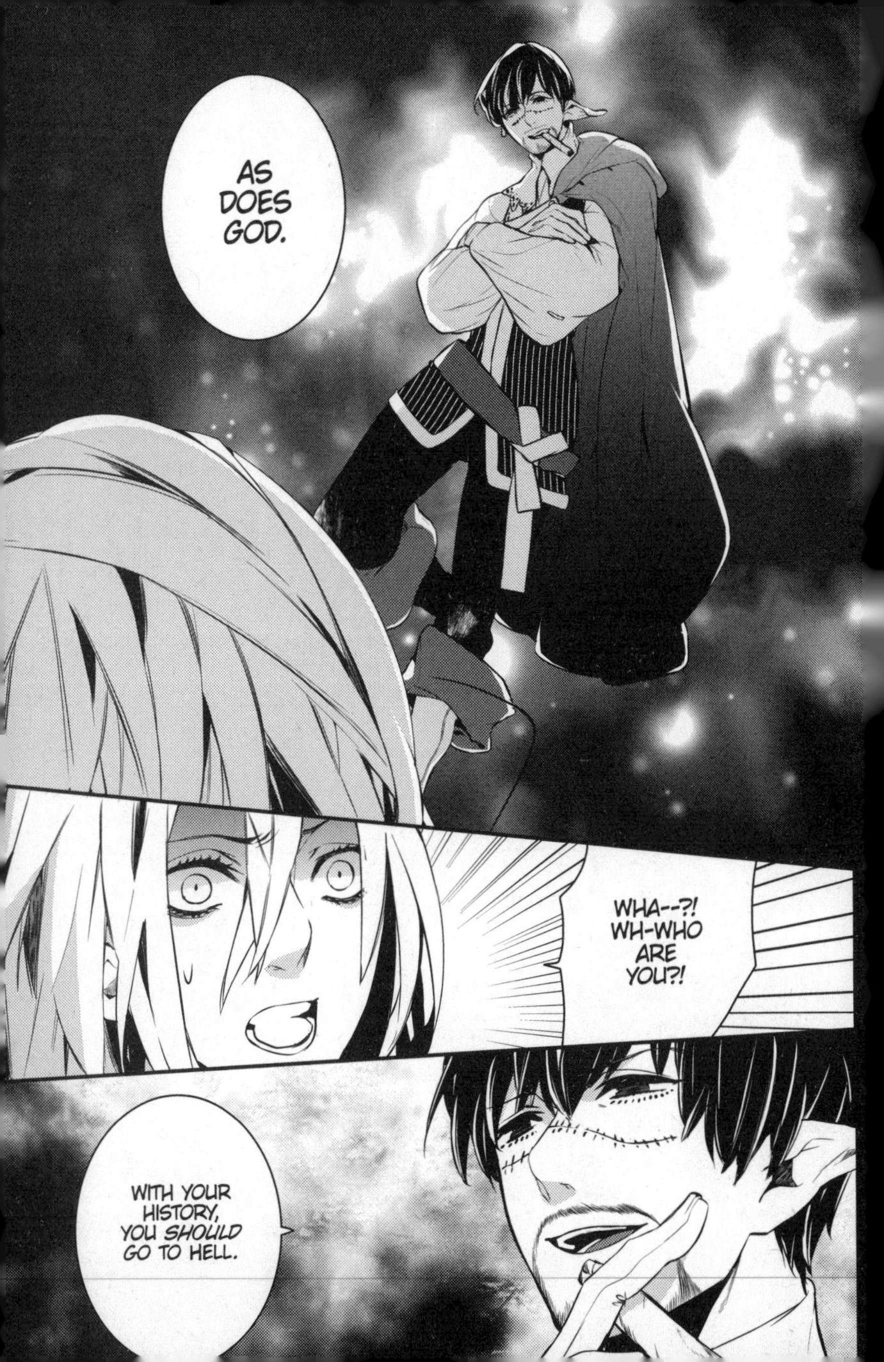
AS DOES GOD.
WHA--?! WH-WHO ARE YOU?!
WITH YOUR HISTORY, YOU SHOULD GO TO HELL.

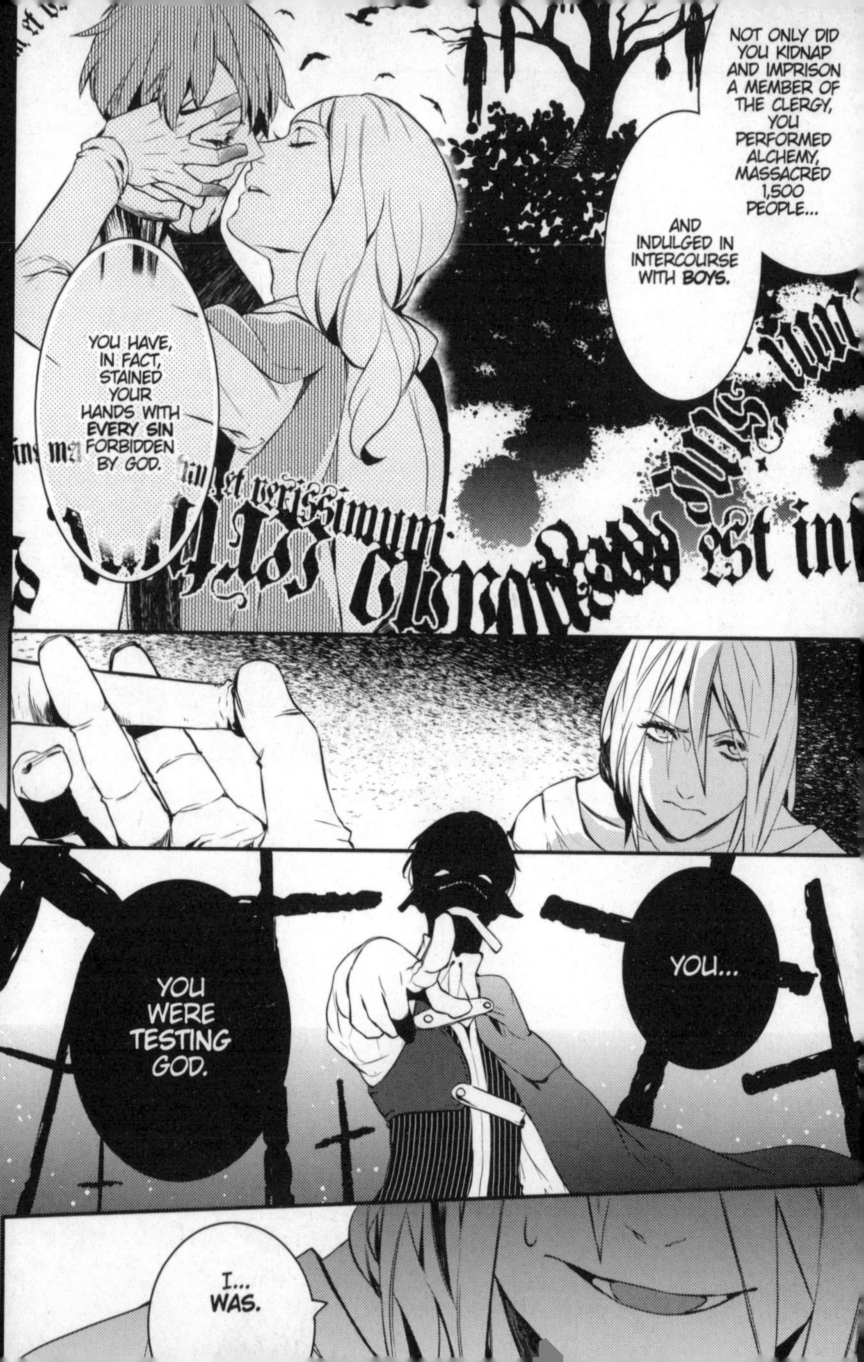
NOT ONLY DID YOU KIDNAP AND IMPRISON A MEMBER OF THE CLERGY, YOU PERFORMED ALCHEMY, MASSACRED 1,500 PEOPLE...
AND INDULGED IN INTERCOURSE WITH BOYS.
YOU HAVE, IN FACT, STAINED YOUR HANDS WITH EVERY SIN FORBIDDEN BY GOD.
YOU...
YOU WERE TESTING GOD.
I... WAS.

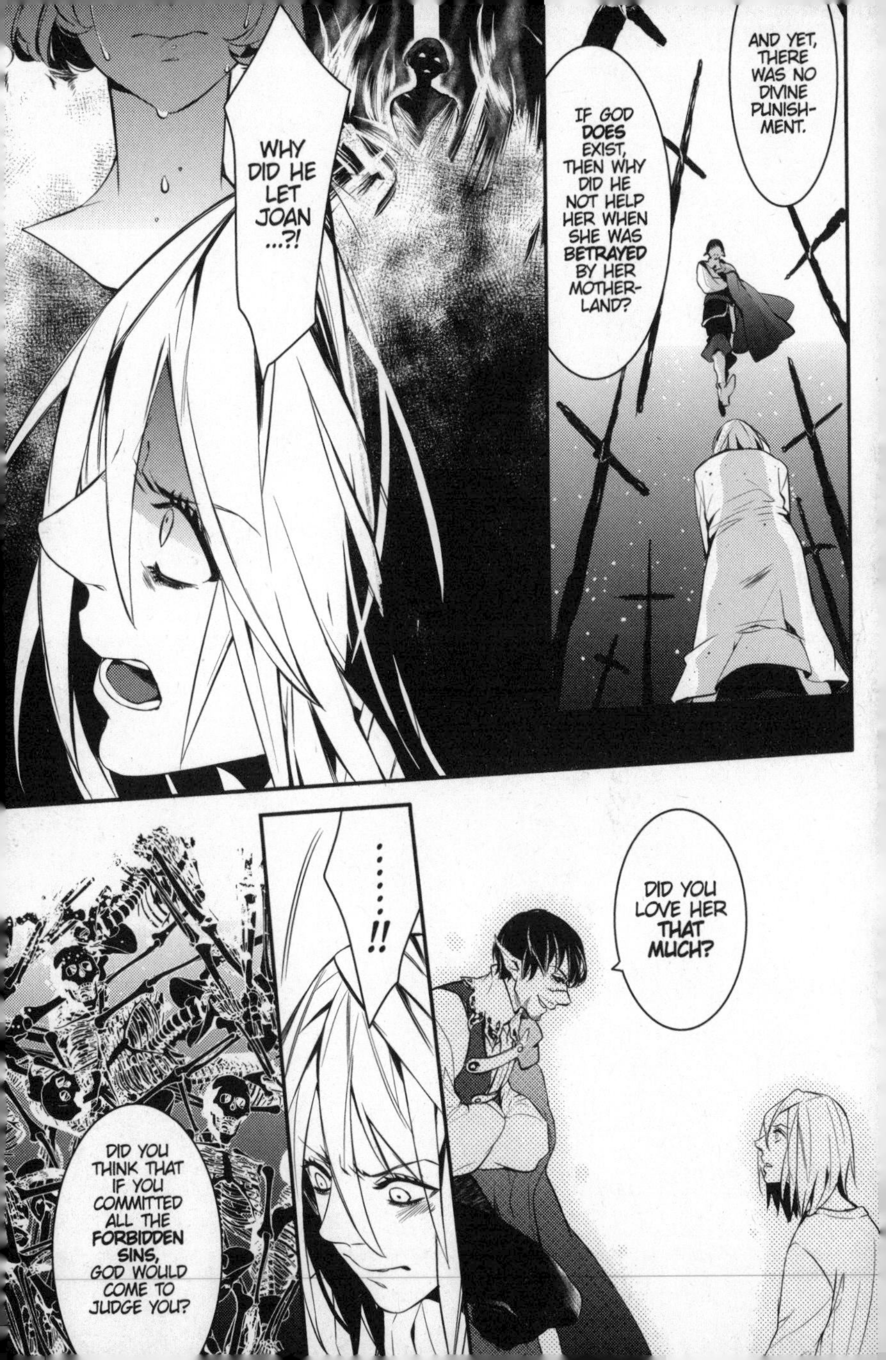
AND YET, THERE WAS NO DIVINE PUNISHMENT.
IF GOD DOES EXIST, THEN WHY DID HE NOT HELP HER WHEN SHE WAS BETRAYED BY HER MOTHERLAND?
WHY DID HE LET JOAN ...?!
DID YOU LOVE HER THAT MUCH?
......!!
DID YOU THINK THAT IF YOU COMMITTED ALL THE FORBIDDEN SINS, GOD WOULD COME TO JUDGE YOU?

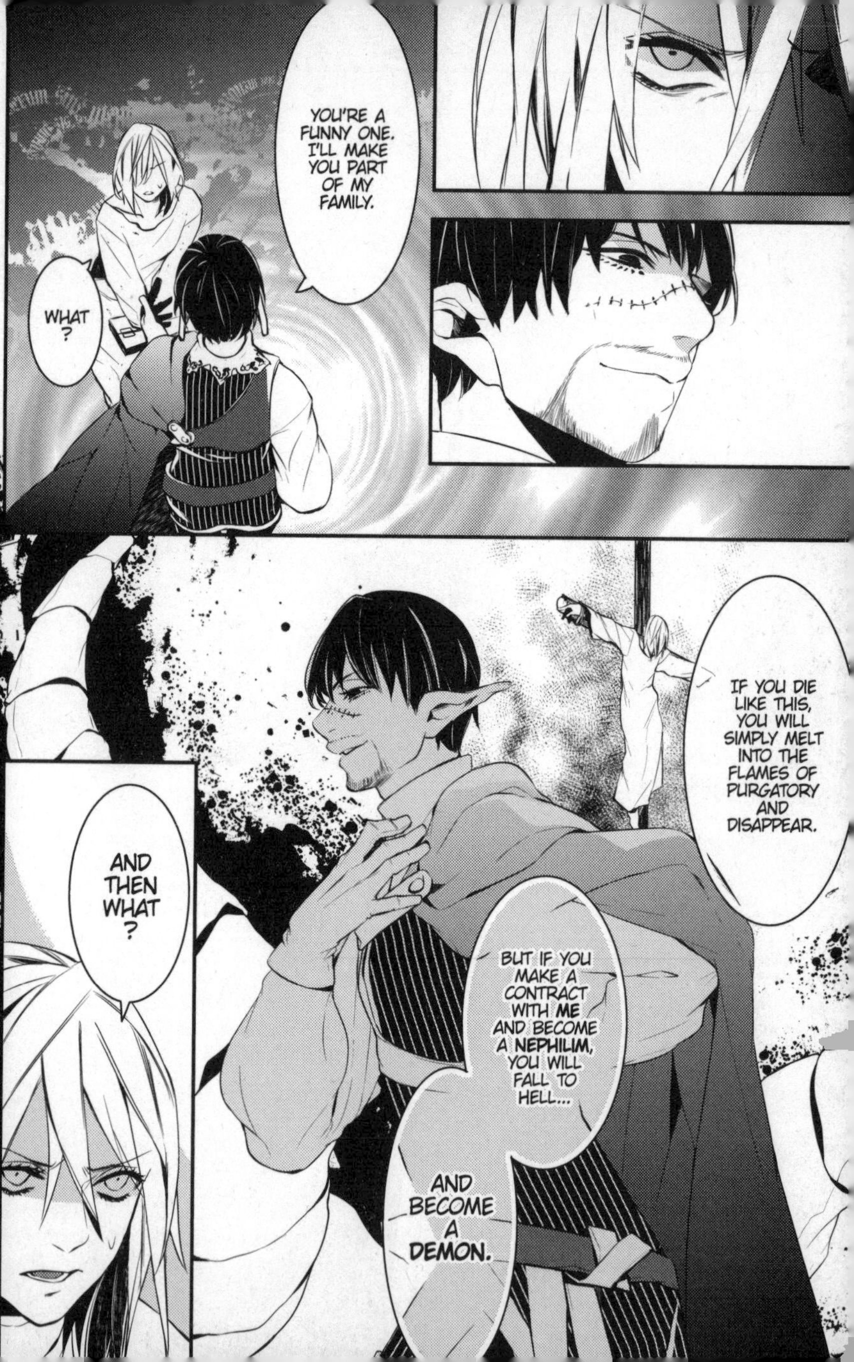
YOU'RE A FUNNY ONE. I'LL MAKE YOU PART OF MY FAMILY.
WHAT?
IF YOU DIE LIKE THIS, YOU WILL SIMPLY MELT INTO THE FLAMES OF PURGATORY AND DISAPPEAR.
AND THEN WHAT?
BUT IF YOU MAKE A CONTRACT WITH ME AND BECOME A NEPHILIM, YOU WILL FALL TO HELL...
AND BECOME A DEMON.

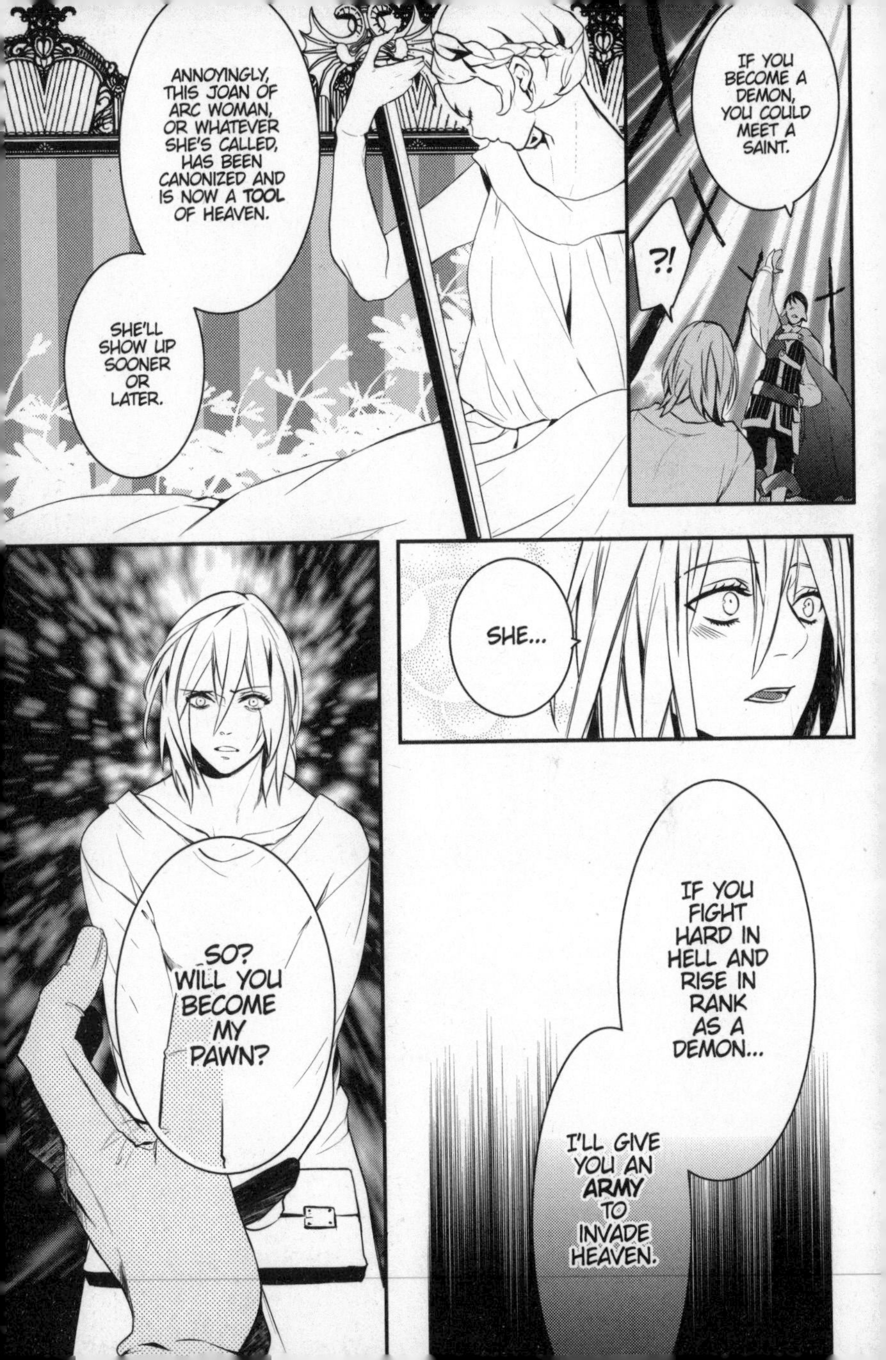
IF YOU BECOME A DEMON, YOU COULD MEET A SAINT.
?!
ANNOYINGLY, THIS JOAN OF ARC WOMAN, OR WHATEVER SHE'S CALLED, HAS BEEN CANONIZED AND IS NOW A TOOL OF HEAVEN.
SHE'LL SHOW UP SOONER OR LATER.
SHE...
IF YOU FIGHT HARD IN HELL AND RISE IN RANK AS A DEMON...
I'LL GIVE YOU AN ARMY TO INVADE HEAVEN.
SO? WILL YOU BECOME MY PAWN?

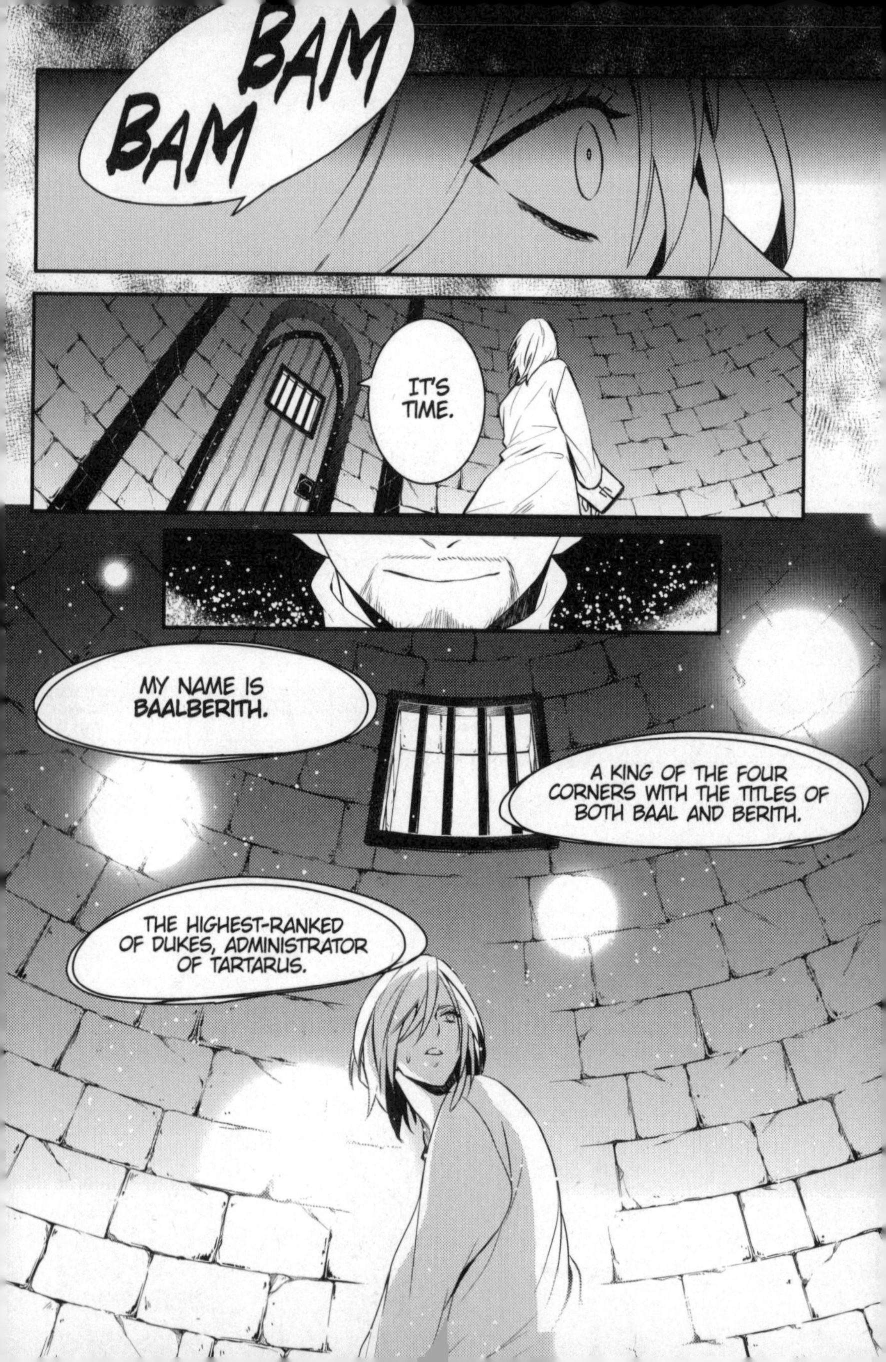
BAM BAM
IT'S TIME.
MY NAME IS BAALBERITH.
A KING OF THE FOUR CORNERS WITH THE TITLES OF BOTH BAAL AND BERITH.
THE HIGHEST-RANKED OF DUKES, ADMINISTRATOR OF TARTARUS.

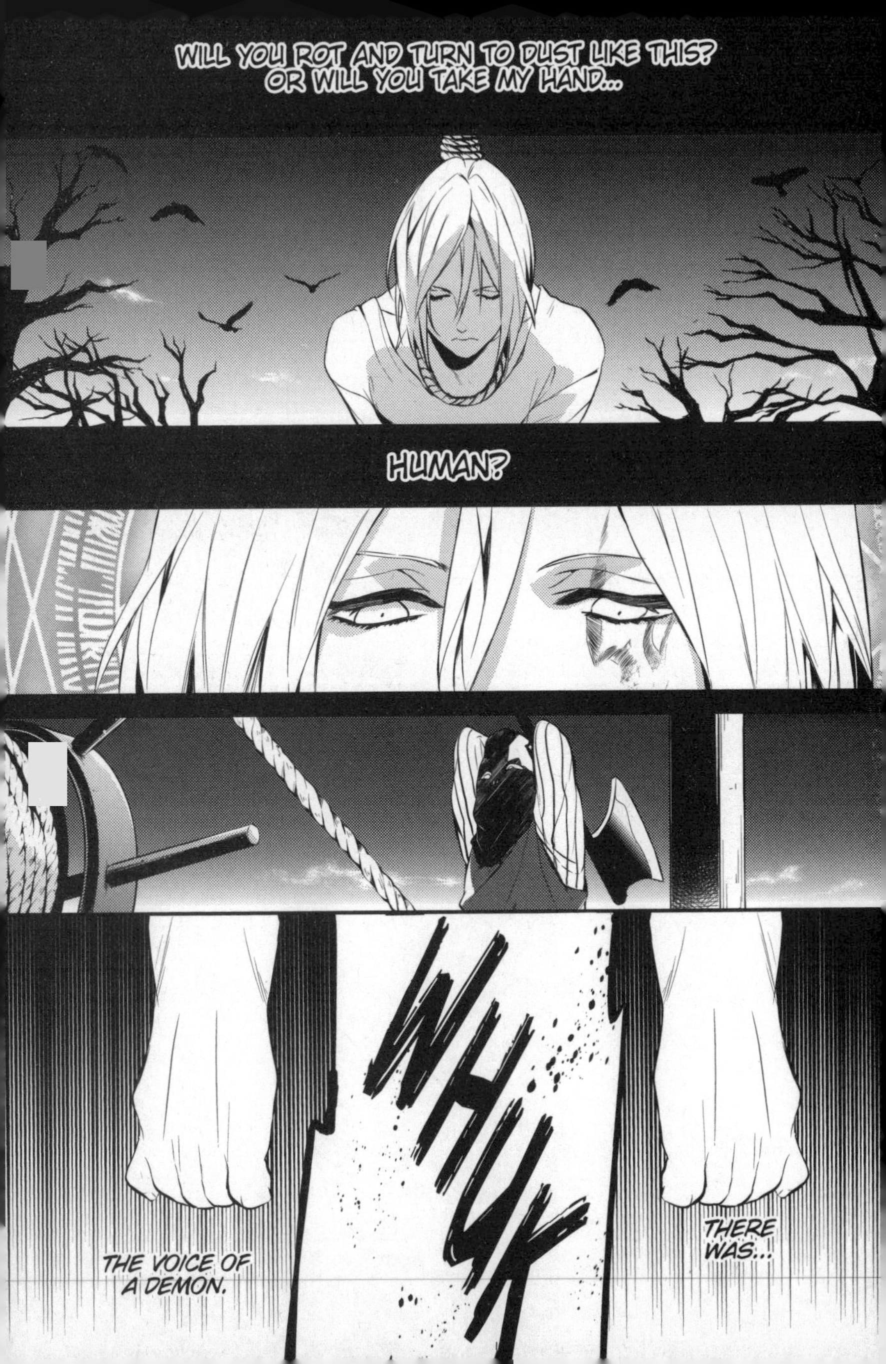
WILL YOU ROT AND TURN TO DUST LIKE THIS?
OR WILL YOU TAKE MY HAND...
HUMAN?
WHUK
THERE WAS...
THE VOICE OF A DEMON.

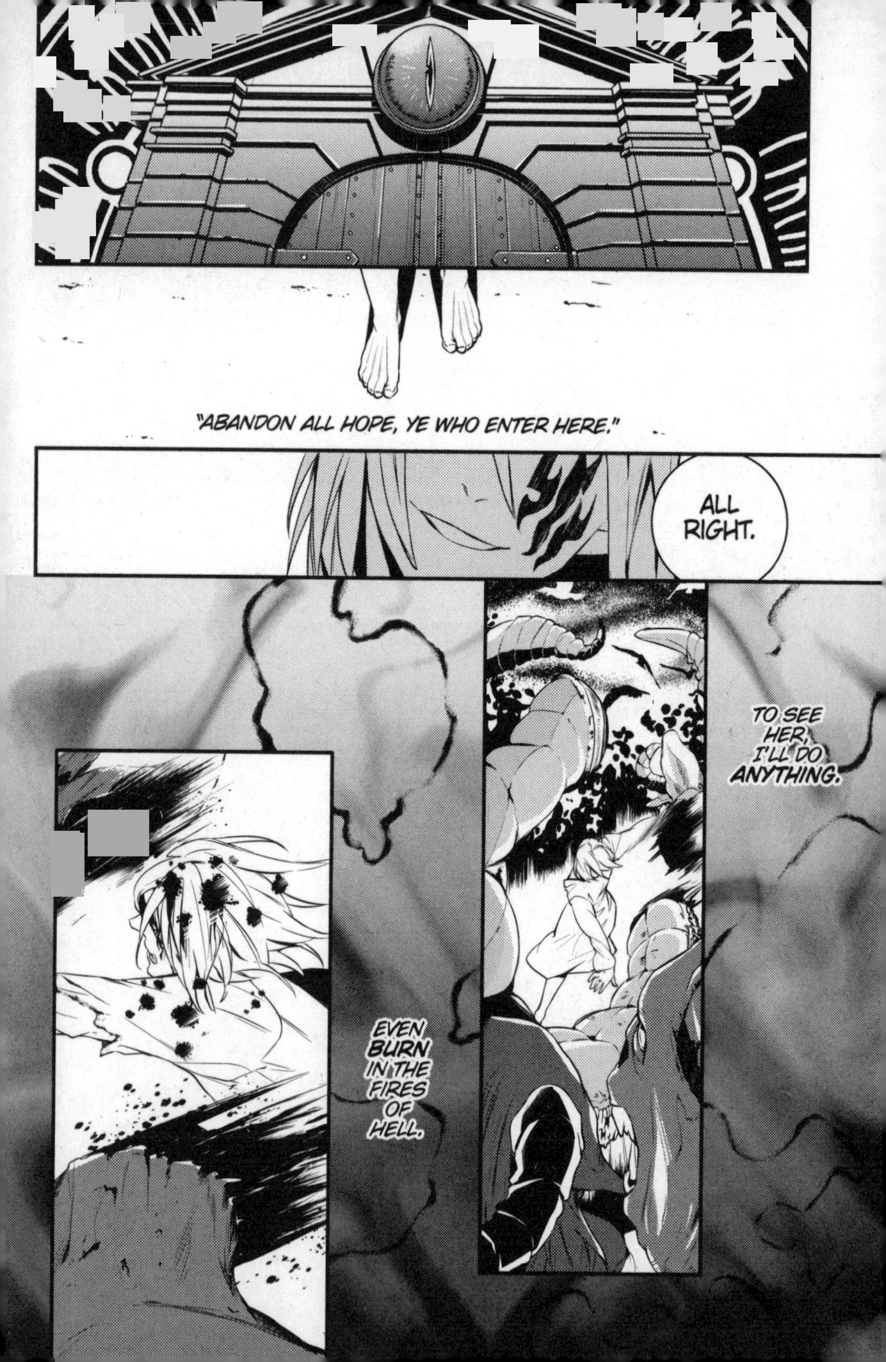
"ABANDON ALL HOPE, YE WHO ENTER HERE."
ALL RIGHT.
TO SEE HER, I'LL DO ANYTHING.
EVEN BURN IN THE FIRES OF HELL.

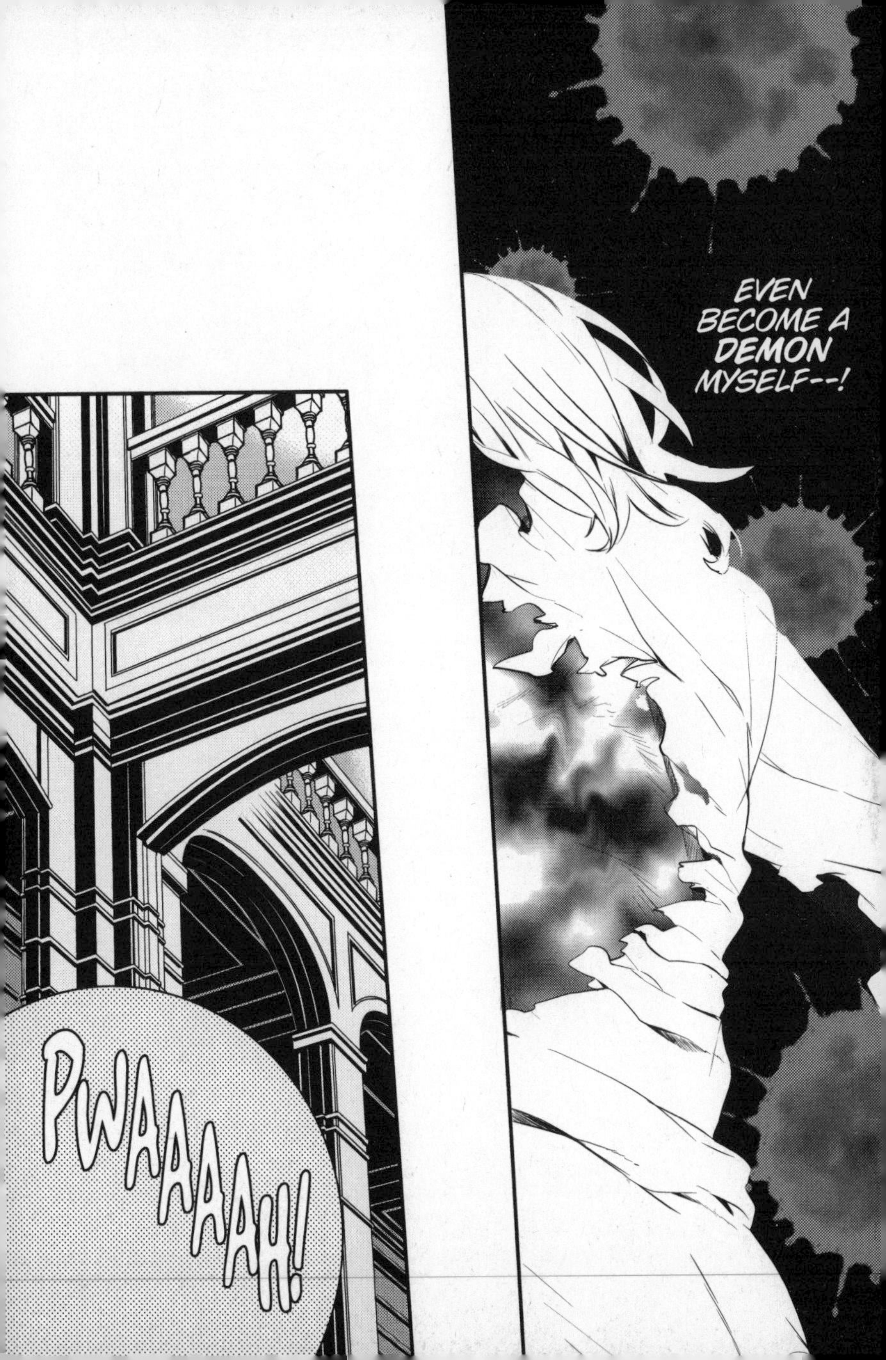
EVEN BECOME A DEMON MYSELF--!
PWAAAAAH!

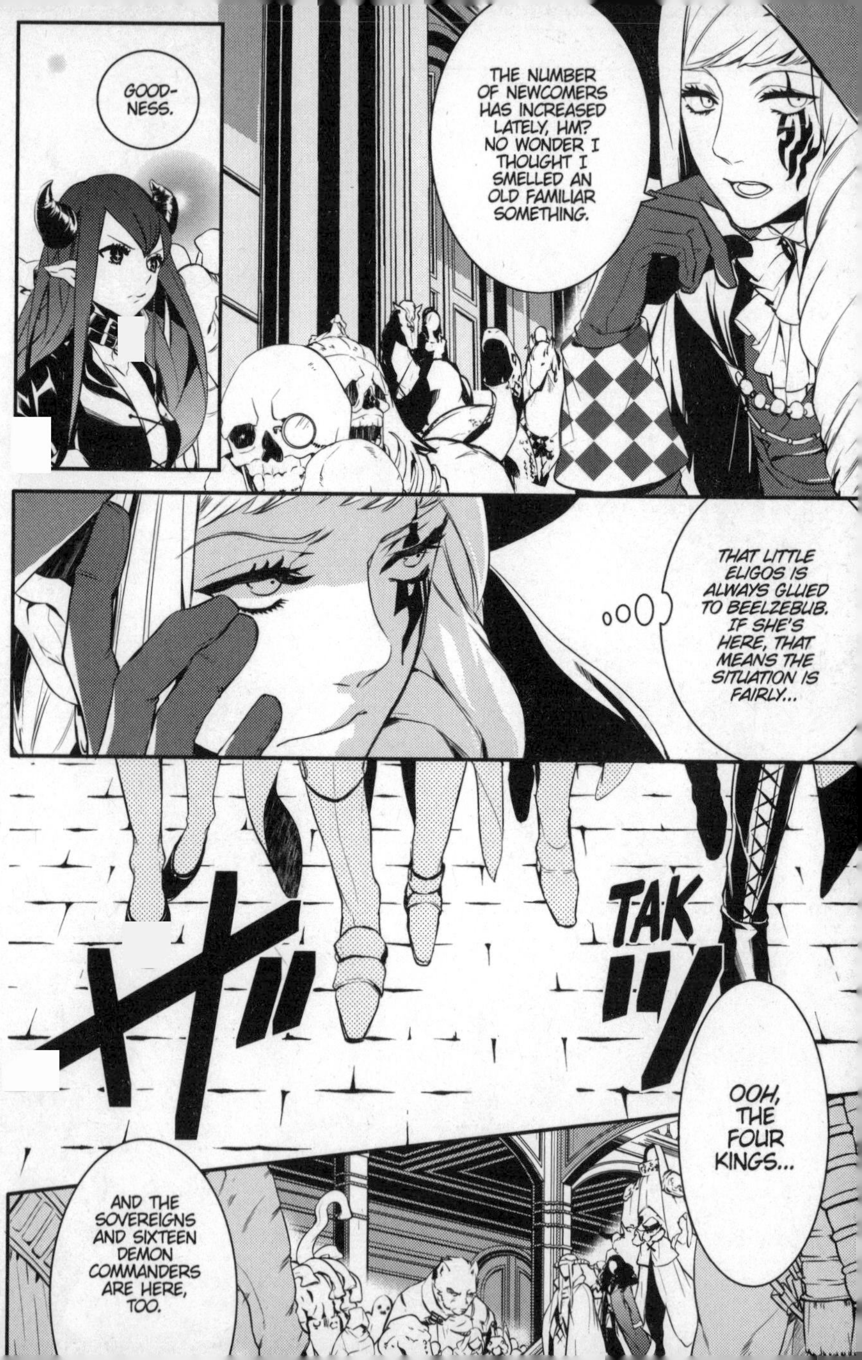
THE NUMBER OF NEWCOMERS HAS INCREASED LATELY, HM? NO WONDER I THOUGHT I SMELLED AN OLD FAMILIAR SOMETHING.
GOOD-NESS.
THAT LITTLE ELIGOS IS ALWAYS GLUED TO BEELZEBUB. IF SHE'S HERE, THAT MEANS THE SITUATION IS FAIRLY...
TAK
OOH, THE FOUR KINGS...
AND THE SOVEREIGNS AND SIXTEEN DEMON COMMANDERS ARE HERE, TOO.

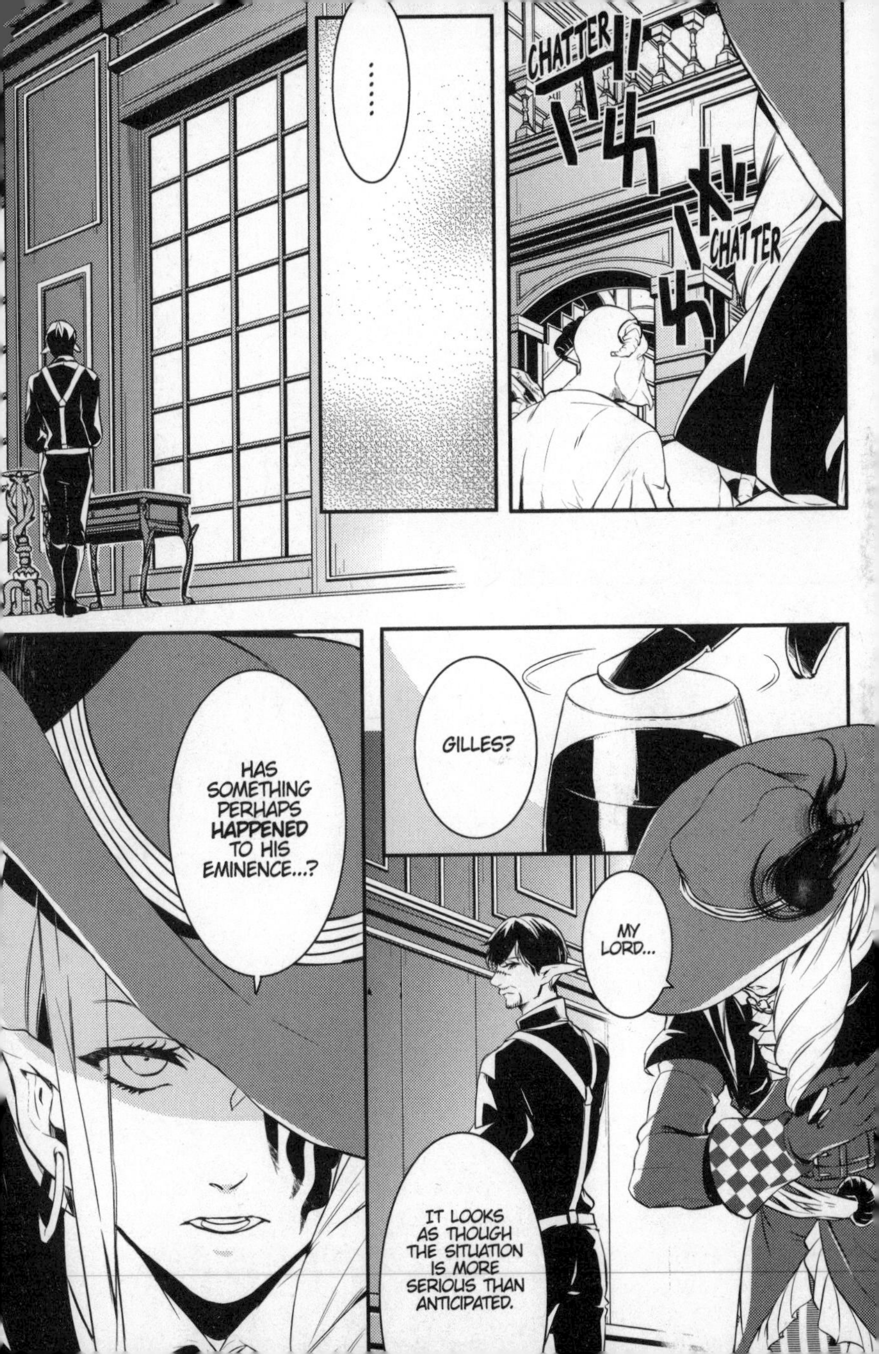
CHATTER
CHATTER
......
GILLES?
MY LORD...
IT LOOKS AS THOUGH THE SITUATION IS MORE SERIOUS THAN ANTICIPATED.
HAS SOMETHING PERHAPS HAPPENED TO HIS EMINENCE...?

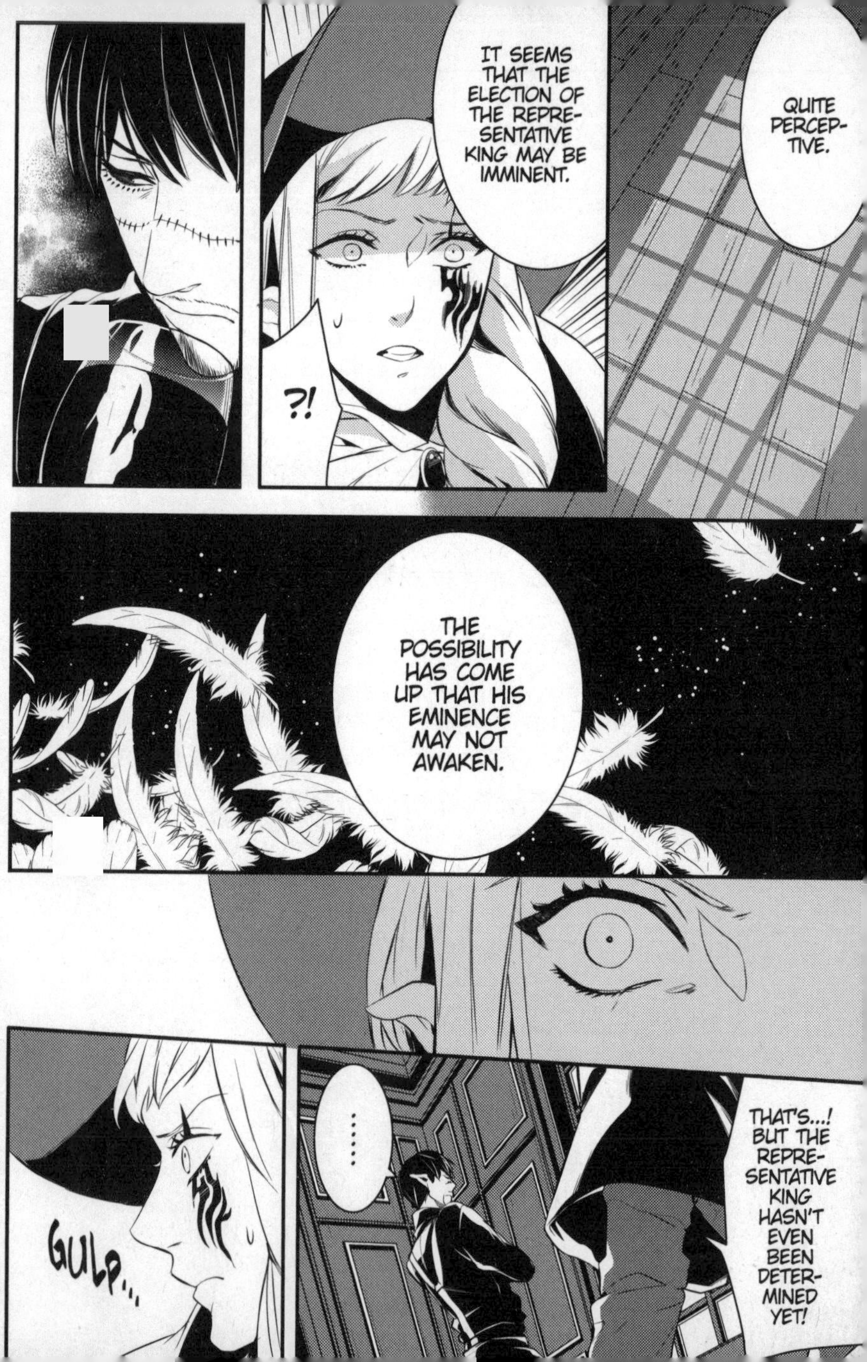
QUITE PERCEPTIVE.
IT SEEMS THAT THE ELECTION OF THE REPRESENTATIVE KING MAY BE IMMINENT.
?!
THE POSSIBILITY HAS COME UP THAT HIS EMINENCE MAY NOT AWAKEN.
THAT'S...! BUT THE REPRESENTATIVE KING HASN'T EVEN BEEN DETERMINED YET!
......
GULP...

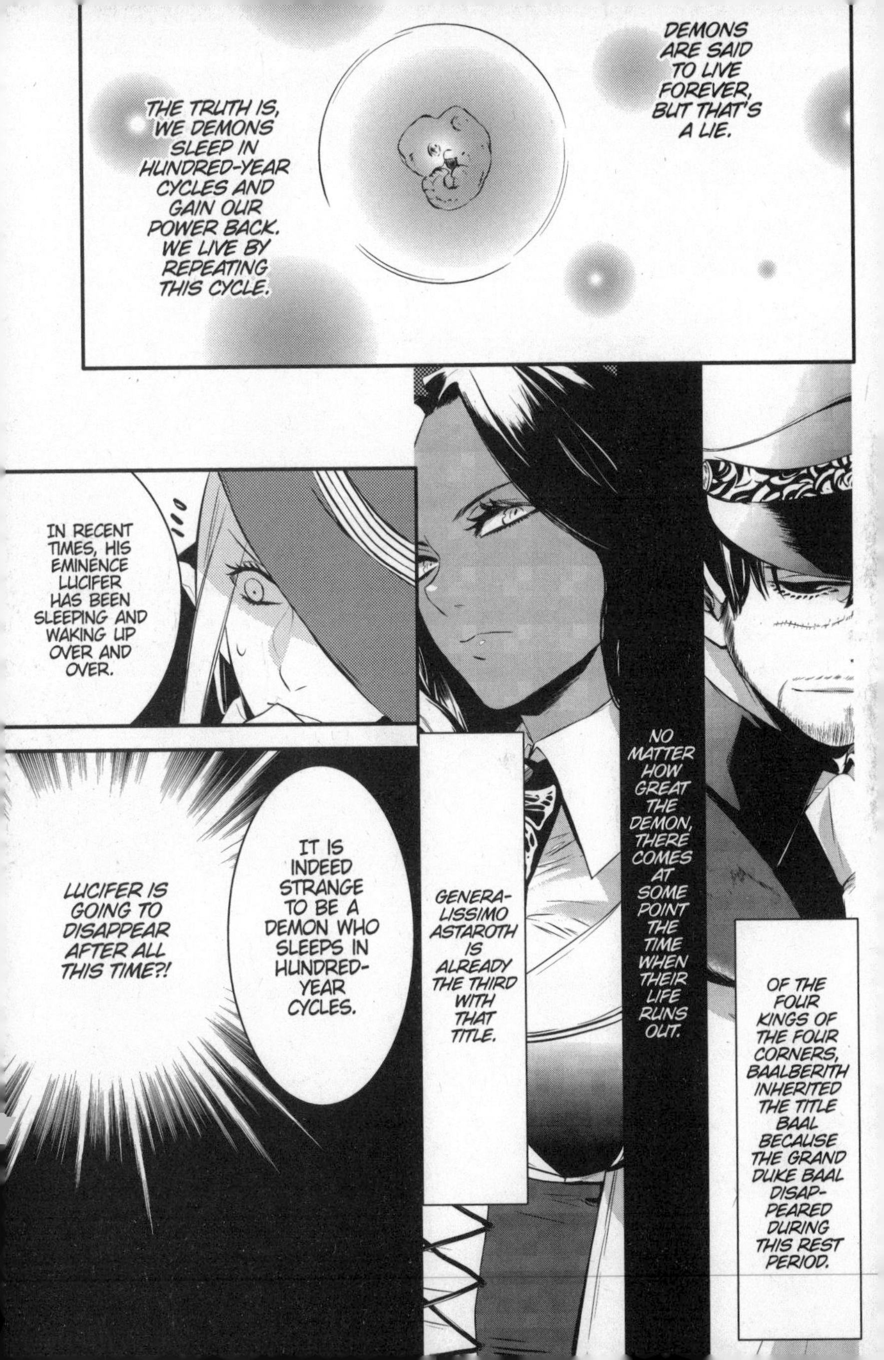
DEMONS ARE SAID TO LIVE FOREVER, BUT THAT'S A LIE.
THE TRUTH IS, WE DEMONS SLEEP IN HUNDRED-YEAR CYCLES AND GAIN OUR POWER BACK. WE LIVE BY REPEATING THIS CYCLE.
NO MATTER HOW GREAT THE DEMON, THERE COMES AT SOME POINT THE TIME WHEN THEIR LIFE RUNS OUT.
OF THE FOUR KINGS OF THE FOUR CORNERS, BAALBERITH INHERITED THE TITLE BAAL BECAUSE THE GRAND DUKE BAAL DISAP-PEARED DURING THIS REST PERIOD.
GENERA-LISSIMO ASTAROTH IS ALREADY THE THIRD WITH THAT TITLE.
IN RECENT TIMES, HIS EMINENCE LUCIFER HAS BEEN SLEEPING AND WAKING UP OVER AND OVER.
IT IS INDEED STRANGE TO BE A DEMON WHO SLEEPS IN HUNDRED-YEAR CYCLES.
LUCIFER IS GOING TO DISAPPEAR AFTER ALL THIS TIME?!

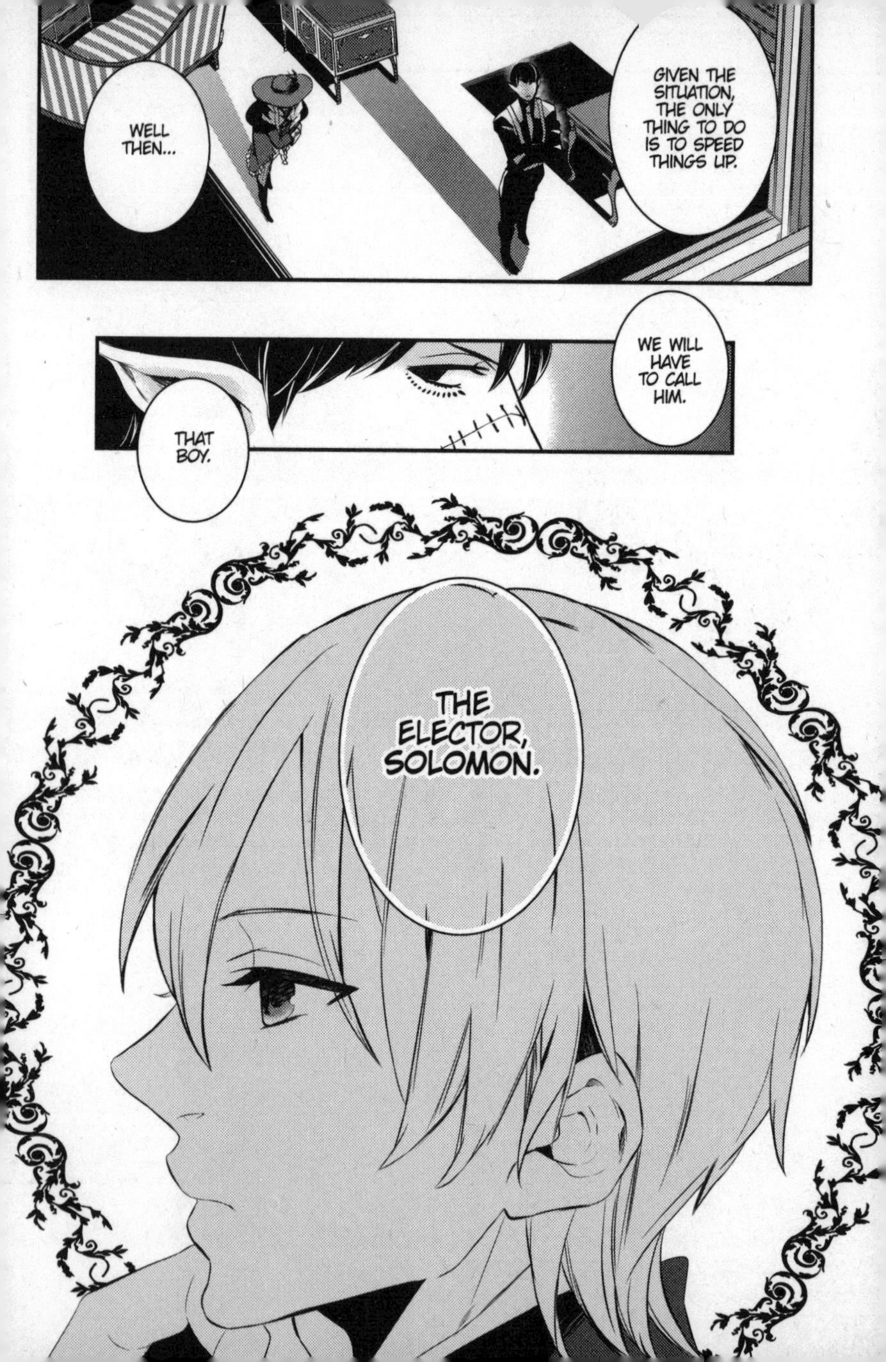
GIVEN THE SITUATION, THE ONLY THING TO DO IS TO SPEED THINGS UP.
WELL THEN...
WE WILL HAVE TO CALL HIM.
THAT BOY.
THE ELECTOR, SOLOMON.

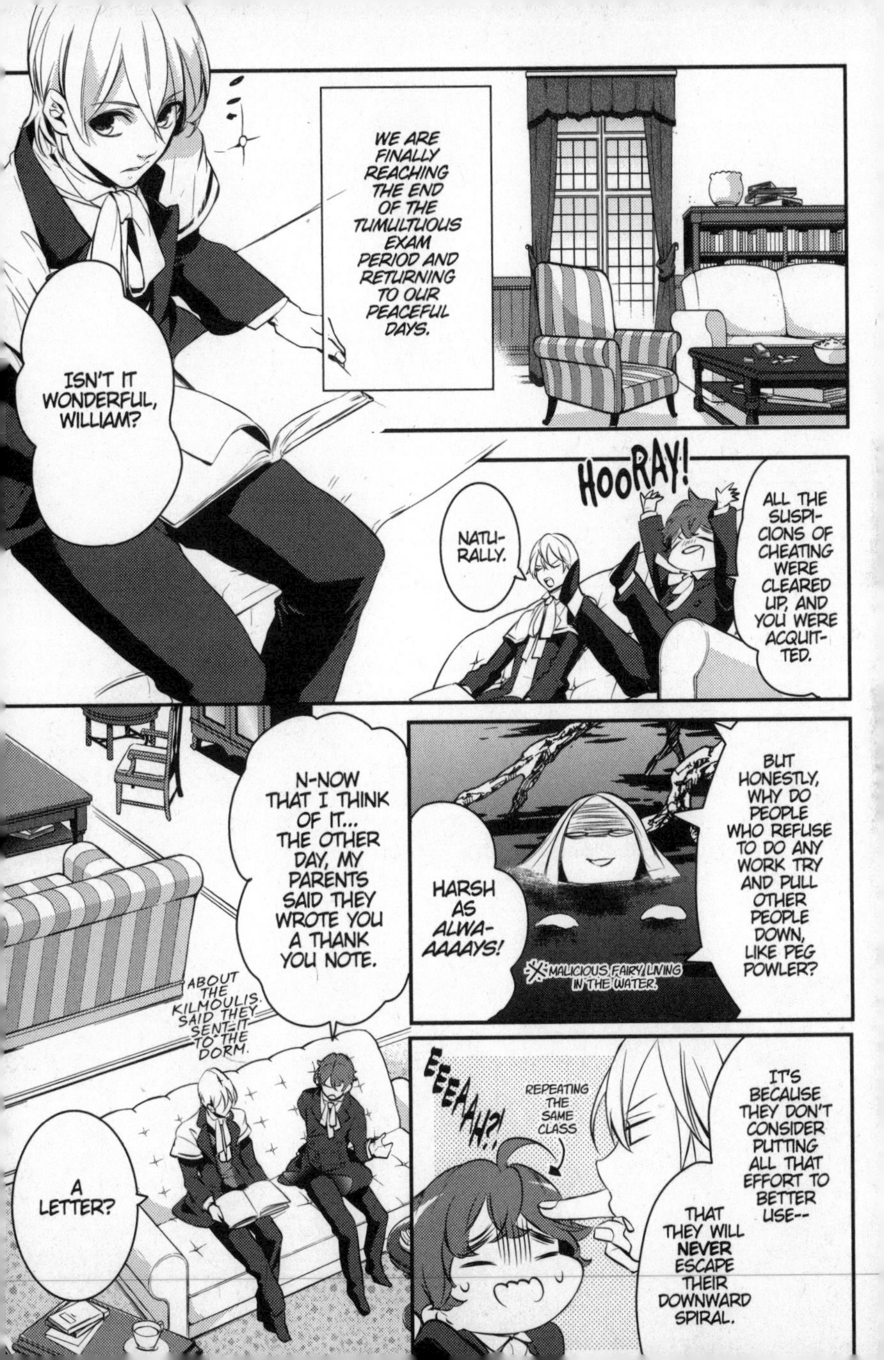
WE ARE FINALLY REACHING THE END OF THE TUMULTUOUS EXAM PERIOD AND RETURNING TO OUR PEACEFUL DAYS.
ISN'T IT WONDERFUL, WILLIAM?
ALL THE SUSPICIONS OF CHEATING WERE CLEARED UP, AND YOU WERE ACQUITTED.
HOORAY!
NATURALLY.
BUT HONESTLY, WHY DO PEOPLE WHO REFUSE TO DO ANY WORK TRY AND PULL OTHER PEOPLE DOWN, LIKE PEG POWLER?
HARSH AS ALWAAAAYS!
※MALICIOUS FAIRY LIVING IN THE WATER.
IT'S BECAUSE THEY DON'T CONSIDER PUTTING ALL THAT EFFORT TO BETTER USE--
THAT THEY WILL NEVER ESCAPE THEIR DOWNWARD SPIRAL.
EEEAAH?!
REPEATING THE SAME CLASS
N-NOW THAT I THINK OF IT... THE OTHER DAY, MY PARENTS SAID THEY WROTE YOU A THANK YOU NOTE.
ABOUT THE KILMOULIS. SAID THEY SENT IT TO THE DORM.
A LETTER?

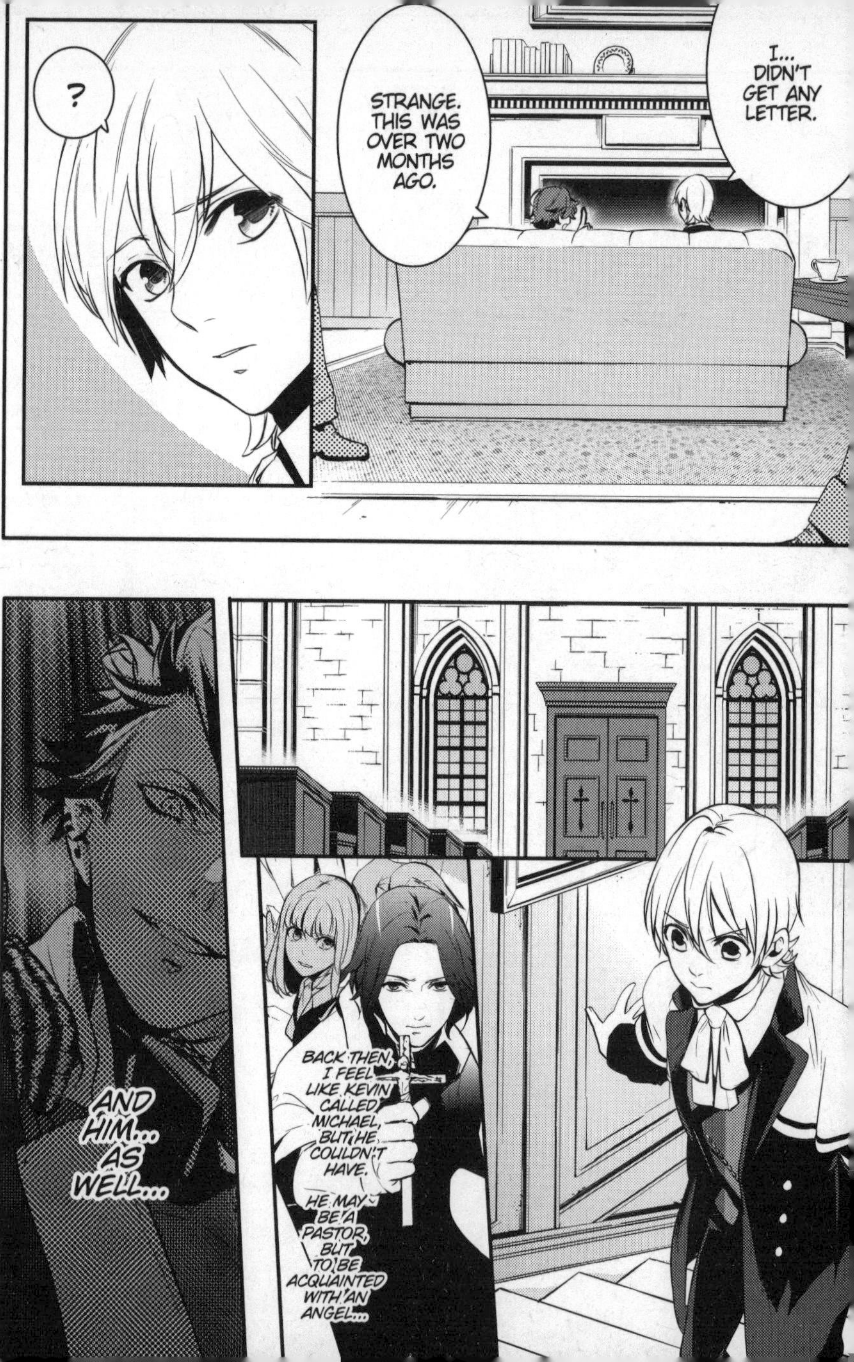
I... DIDN'T GET ANY LETTER.
STRANGE. THIS WAS OVER TWO MONTHS AGO.
?
BACK THEN, I FEEL LIKE KEVIN CALLED MICHAEL, BUT HE COULDN'T HAVE.
HE MAY BE A PASTOR, BUT TO BE ACQUAINTED WITH AN ANGEL...
AND HIM... AS WELL...

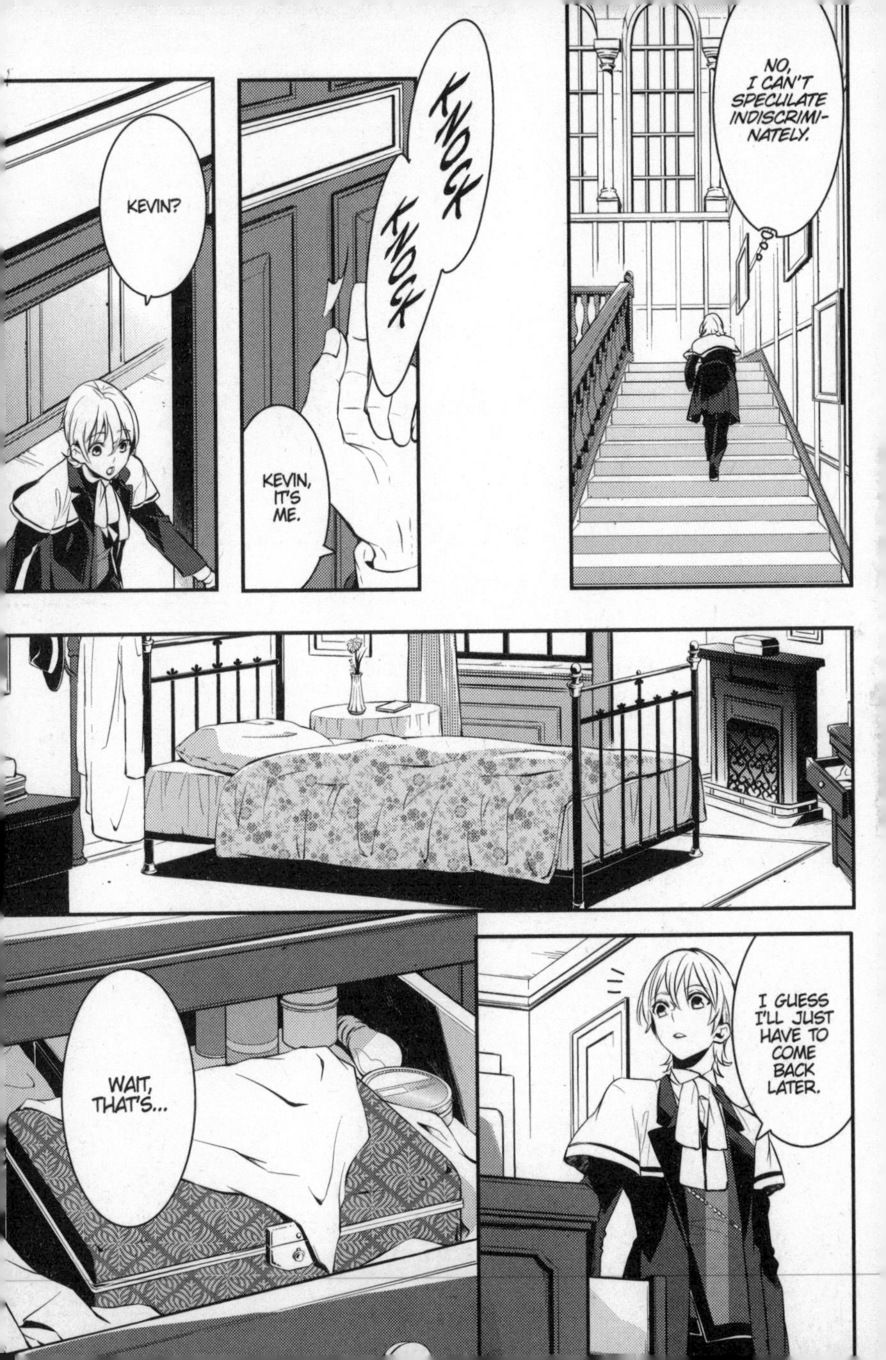
NO, I CAN'T SPECULATE INDISCRIMI-NATELY.
KNOCK KNOCK
KEVIN, IT'S ME.
KEVIN?
I GUESS I'LL JUST HAVE TO COME BACK LATER.
WAIT, THAT'S...

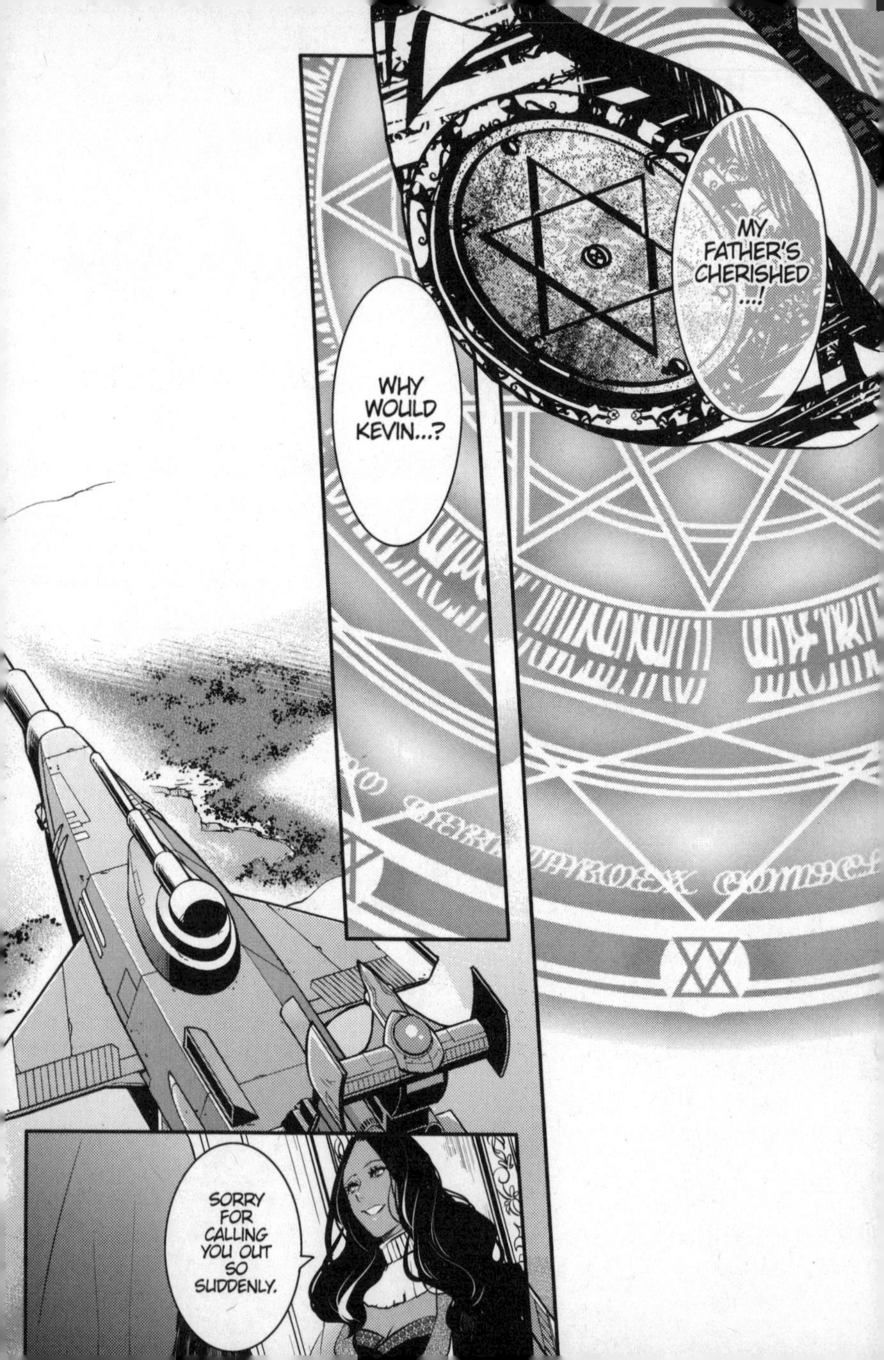
MY FATHER'S CHERISHED ...!
WHY WOULD KEVIN...?
SORRY FOR CALLING YOU OUT SO SUDDENLY.

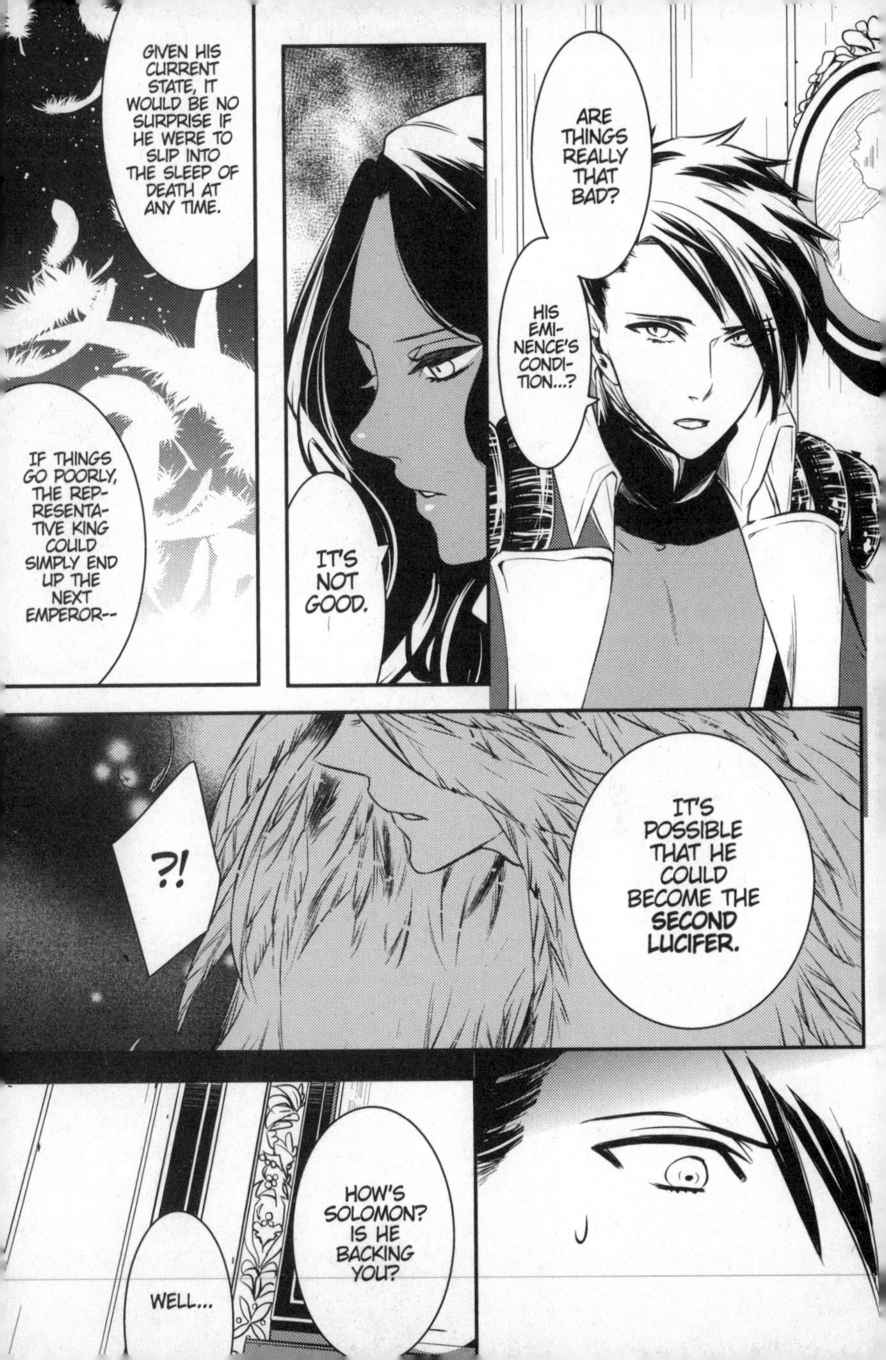
ARE THINGS REALLY THAT BAD?
HIS EMINENCE'S CONDITION...?
IT'S NOT GOOD.
GIVEN HIS CURRENT STATE, IT WOULD BE NO SURPRISE IF HE WERE TO SLIP INTO THE SLEEP OF DEATH AT ANY TIME.
IF THINGS GO POORLY, THE REPRESENTATIVE KING COULD SIMPLY END UP THE NEXT EMPEROR--
IT'S POSSIBLE THAT HE COULD BECOME THE SECOND LUCIFER.
?!
HOW'S SOLOMON? IS HE BACKING YOU?
WELL...

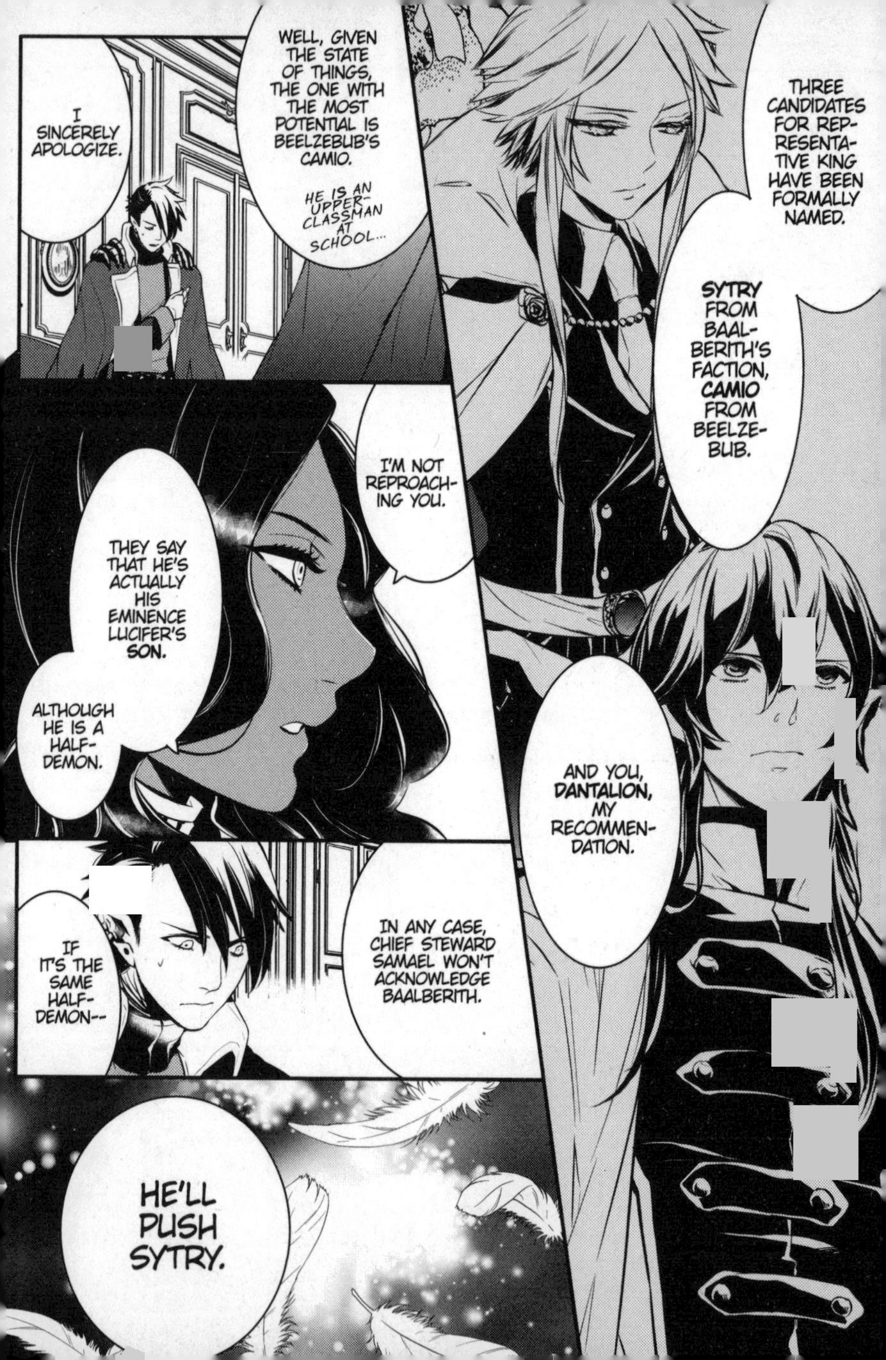
THREE CANDIDATES FOR REPRESENTATIVE KING HAVE BEEN FORMALLY NAMED.
SYTRY FROM BAALBERITH'S FACTION, CAMIO FROM BEELZEBUB.
AND YOU, DANTALION, MY RECOMMENDATION.
WELL, GIVEN THE STATE OF THINGS, THE ONE WITH THE MOST POTENTIAL IS BEELZEBUB'S CAMIO.
HE IS AN UPPERCLASSMAN AT SCHOOL...
I SINCERELY APOLOGIZE.
I'M NOT REPROACHING YOU.
THEY SAY THAT HE'S ACTUALLY HIS EMINENCE LUCIFER'S SON.
ALTHOUGH HE IS A HALF-DEMON.
IN ANY CASE, CHIEF STEWARD SAMAEL WON'T ACKNOWLEDGE BAALBERITH.
IF IT'S THE SAME HALF-DEMON--
HE'LL PUSH SYTRY.

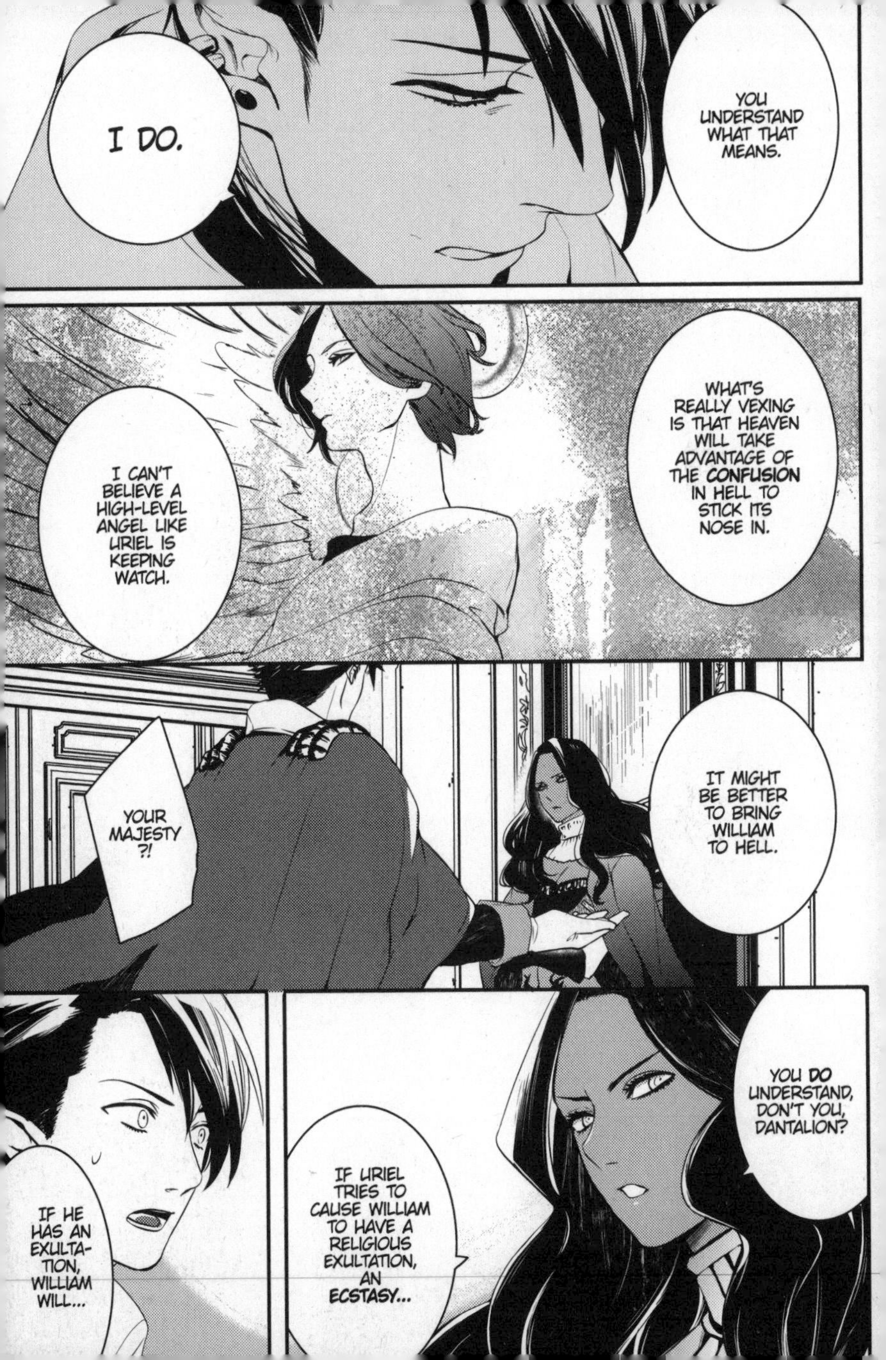
YOU UNDERSTAND WHAT THAT MEANS.
I DO.
WHAT'S REALLY VEXING IS THAT HEAVEN WILL TAKE ADVANTAGE OF THE CONFUSION IN HELL TO STICK ITS NOSE IN.
I CAN'T BELIEVE A HIGH-LEVEL ANGEL LIKE URIEL IS KEEPING WATCH.
IT MIGHT BE BETTER TO BRING WILLIAM TO HELL.
YOUR MAJESTY ?!
YOU DO UNDERSTAND, DON'T YOU, DANTALION?
IF URIEL TRIES TO CAUSE WILLIAM TO HAVE A RELIGIOUS EXULTATION, AN ECSTASY...
IF HE HAS AN EXULTA-TION, WILLIAM WILL...

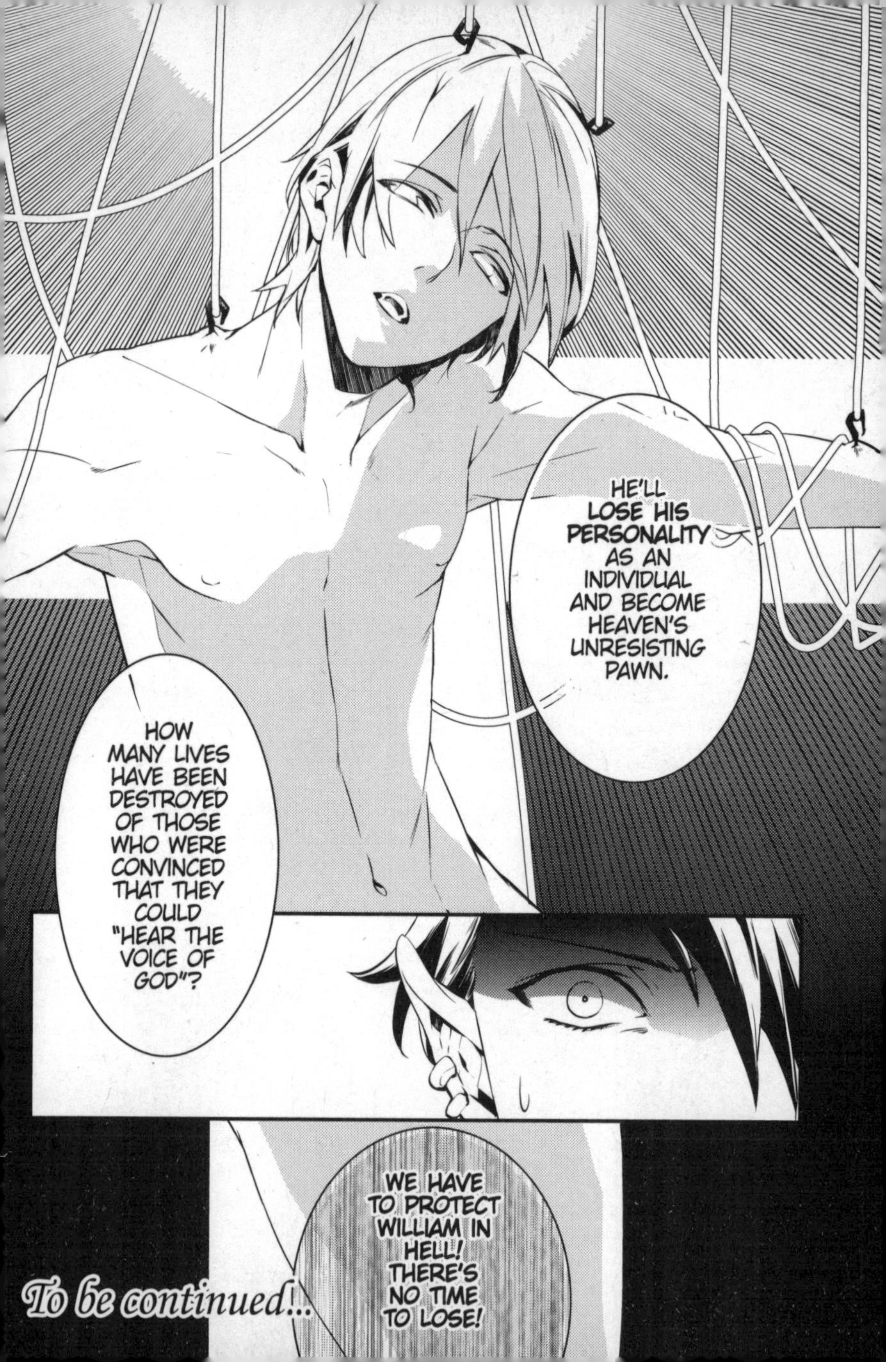
HE'LL LOSE HIS PERSONALITY AS AN INDIVIDUAL AND BECOME HEAVEN'S UNRESISTING PAWN.
HOW MANY LIVES HAVE BEEN DESTROYED OF THOSE WHO WERE CONVINCED THAT THEY COULD "HEAR THE VOICE OF GOD"?
WE HAVE TO PROTECT WILLIAM IN HELL! THERE'S NO TIME TO LOSE!
To be continued!...

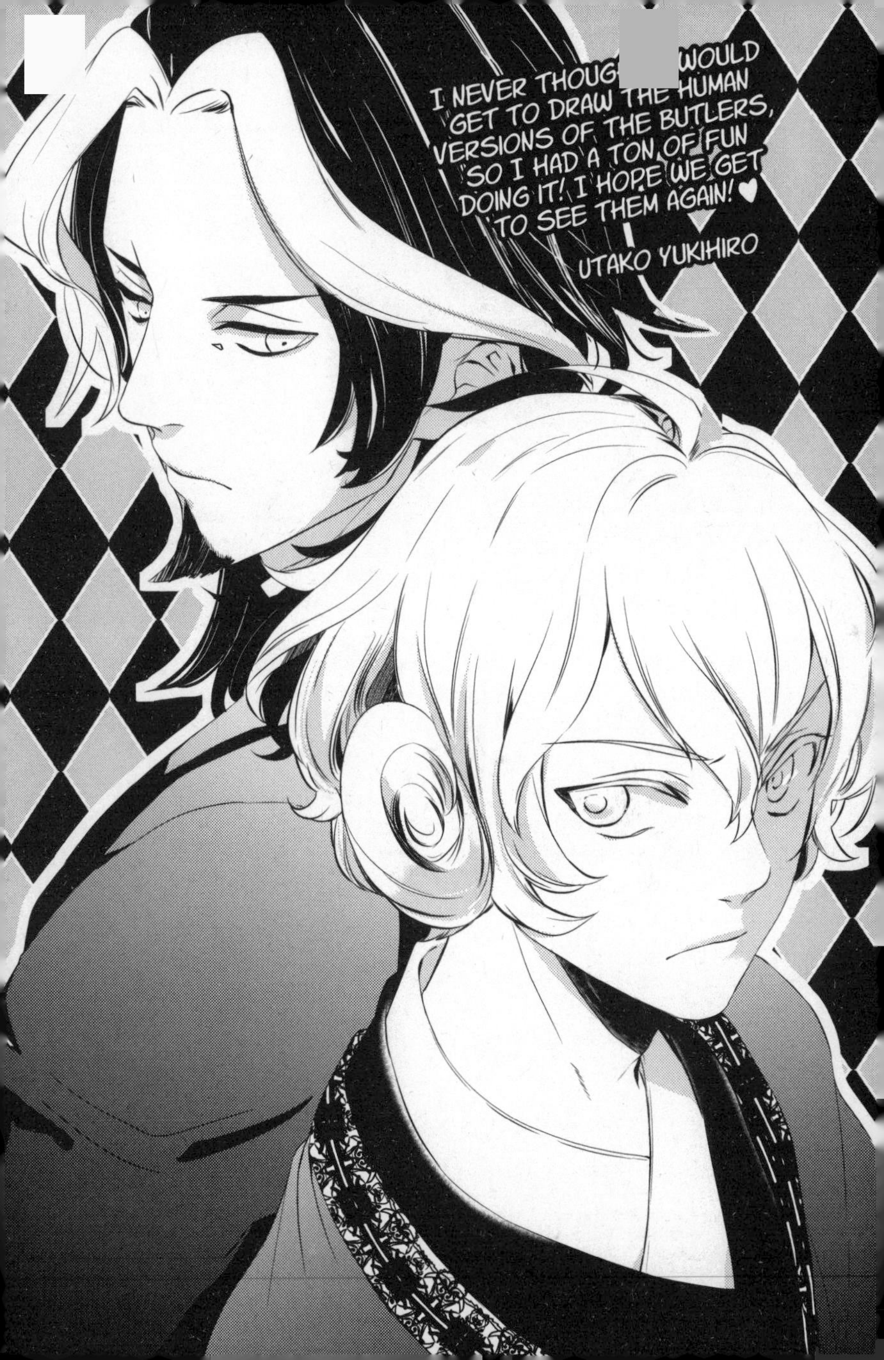
I NEVER THOUG WOULD
GET TO DRAW THE HUMAN
VERSIONS OF THE BUTLERS,
SO I HAD A TON OF FUN
DOING IT! I HOPE WE GET
TO SEE THEM AGAIN! ♥
UTAKO YUKIHIRO

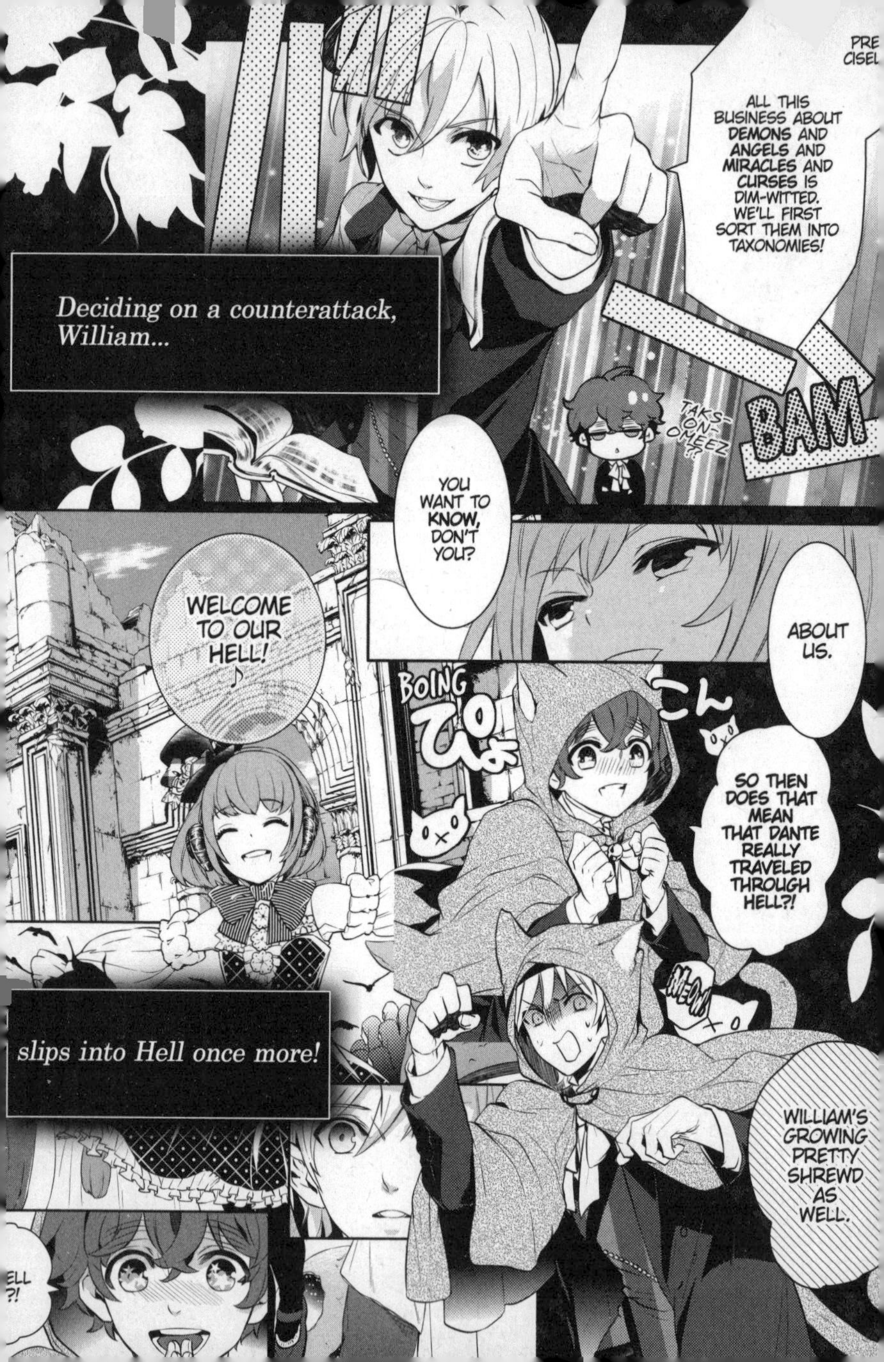
PRECISEL
ALL THIS BUSINESS ABOUT DEMONS AND ANGELS AND MIRACLES AND CURSES IS DIM-WITTED. WE'LL FIRST SORT THEM INTO TAXONOMIES!
Deciding on a counterattack, William...
BAM
TAKS-ON-OMEEZ ?!
YOU WANT TO KNOW, DON'T YOU?
ABOUT US.
WELCOME TO OUR HELL! ♪
こん
BOING
ぴょ
SO THEN DOES THAT MEAN THAT DANTE REALLY TRAVELED THROUGH HELL?!
MEOW
slips into Hell once more!
WILLIAM'S GROWING PRETTY SHREWD AS WELL.
ELL ?!